THE LIFE OF
BENJAMIN
BANNEKER

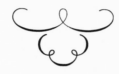

SILVIO A. BEDINI

THE LIFE OF BENJAMIN BANNEKER

Charles Scribner's Sons · New York

C γ

To
LEANDRA AND *PETER*

I have been the more careful to investigate those particulars, and to ascertain their reality, as they form an interesting fact in the history of Man.

—Senator James McHenry (letter quoted in *Banneker's Almanac for 1792*)

CONTENTS

ILLUSTRATIONS

(Following page 102)

PREFACE

◆❀◆❀◆❀◆❀◆❀◆❀◆❀◆❀◆

MY ATTENTION was first directed to Benjamin Banneker more
than thirteen years ago while collecting information about early
American clockmakers and makers of mathematical instruments.
The story of an unschooled tobacco planter who had constructed
a successfully operating striking clock, supposedly without ever
having seen one, was intriguing. I soon discovered that the home-
made clock was only one, and perhaps the least, of Banneker's
accomplishments. Late in life, this son and grandson of slaves
had undertaken to teach himself mathematics and astronomy sufficiently to calculate ephemerides published in almanacs, and had
taken part in the historic survey of the Federal Territory (now
the District of Columbia). Obviously, this man was not just another of the many surveyors, navigators, science teachers, philomaths, or makers of instruments but one whose work merited
closer study. And thus began the search for the full story of
Banneker the man of science, which led to the exercise of all the
possible resources available to the historical detective.

The most interesting aspect was the sleuthing work required to disclose the facts, one by one, and the exhausting hunt
for those rare surviving documents relating to his life and work.
Never had the tangible memorabilia of a man's life vanished so
completely as had Banneker's. The first step seemed to be to collect copies of all known published references. Eventually this
compilation included more than a hundred items, ranging from
brief notices to substantial biographical sketches in periodicals or
as chapters in works on Afro-American history, as well as one
book-length fictionalized biography for children.

Curiously enough, Banneker was brought into prominence

from time to time as a reflection of the popular interest in the cause of antislavery and the role of the Negro in American society, rather than for the substance of his achievements. For the most part, these accounts drew on material that had already appeared in print without further study or evaluation of his work. Banneker's accomplishments developed from modest to outstanding and finally to unique proportions. In due time he was credited with attainments that were not in fact realized. Today the same erroneous exaggerations are perpetuated. Instead of emerging as a source of inspiration, Banneker's name has become clouded with doubt, due to outright misstatements. Actually, he was a man of modest ability and performance, who, by means of his efforts, contributed a tangible bit to the fabric of science in America.

The life of Banneker might have been like that of many other men of his time who found inspiration in the sciences and seized the opportunities at hand to pursue them. It is a little more, however, because Banneker was a free Negro in an era when the Negro was held in subjugation and the world was just beginning to realize that the color black was an accident of nature and not a sign of inferiority. At any other time in history, his work would have merited a far more accurate appraisal.

Originally a full-length biography of Banneker was not intended. Primarily this book was meant to present his attainments in proper focus and to evaluate their importance in comparison with those of other early American men of science. A few years ago, a brief account of early American scientific instruments and their makers brought requests for further information about Banneker from many scholars and students. Inevitably the awakened interest led me to review the materials collected for a more substantial presentation, with the realization that surely there was never a less promising subject for an exhaustive study.

The research which followed, and on which this biography is based, was divided into several major segments. There was, for instance, the story of Banneker's family and early life. The investigation of civil records and the search for personal papers began in the Maryland Historical Society, then moved to the State of Maryland Hall of Records, and eventually into many other county and community archives in Maryland. The enthusiastic participation and dedicated cooperation of librarians, archivists, and officials were important factors in the completion of this work.

The dramatic story of how Banneker's precious astronomical notes and borrowed texts had escaped destruction at the time of his death raised the question of whether they still existed and where they could be found. Such materials might help to adjust and bring into focus the image of the man and the value of his work. Presumably these materials had been left to a descendant of the neighbor who had encouraged Banneker and to whom they had been returned. The search for descendants assumed forbidding proportions. Time and again the pressure of other research projects made it necessary to set this undertaking aside because of repeated frustrations. As the years went by, the recurring expressions of interest from others encouraged renewed attempts to locate Banneker's missing journal of notes, his commonplace book, and other memorabilia. The logical repositories failed to yield these treasures, and I was faced with the conclusion that they no longer existed. It was not until the manuscript was well in progress that a stroke of unbelievable luck led to the discovery of all the known memorabilia and more.

Another segment of the research was the careful investigation and analysis of Banneker's calculations for ephemerides. Neither in manuscript nor in published form was there any explanation of how the eighteenth-century almanac-makers arrived at their calculations, forecast the weather, or gathered other elements of the published almanacs. I had to begin from the beginning, using copies of the same texts that Banneker had borrowed, and teach myself the equivalent in mathematics and astronomy so as to duplicate Banneker's calculations. In this arduous task I was fortunate in being able to call upon the expertise and faithful assistance of other specialists.

A third aspect of the research dealt with the manner in

which Banneker's almanacs reached publication—a significant achievement in itself for a black man in his time and region. The trail led from Baltimore to Philadelphia and to the records of the Pennsylvania Society for the Abolition of Slavery. The Historical Society of Pennsylvania proved to be a treasure trove of manuscripts concerned with Negro history which had not been studied. The lack of a systematic index or catalogue of these papers made it particularly difficult, so that they had to be searched by means of time periods and names of persons known to have been associated with Banneker.

Finally, there was the problem of evaluating whatever had been written about Banneker since his death. An extensive study of the known published works (see the Bibliography) revealed that only four of these accounts were based on contemporary sources. The earliest was the sketch by Senator James McHenry, then the memoir by John H. B. Latrobe published forty years after Banneker's death, and finally, two useful sketches by Martha E. Tyson derived from information obtained from surviving acquaintances who had known the self-taught astronomer during his lifetime.

Except for these four references, the numerous other biographical pieces contributed no new information. The reported magnitude of his achievements reflected the climate in which the issue was debated. No new research was conducted, and earlier errors were not only perpetuated but frequently exaggerated. This practice has continued to the present time, so that the modern reader has had no accurate resource readily available. It matters little that the writers have erred in the number of pounds of tobacco paid by Banneker's father for his farm, for instance, or that the year of his death is incorrectly given. Far more important is that Banneker's attainments, which were impressive and substantial, should be truthfully reported and evaluated, and most of all, that his philosophy of life should be understood so that it may serve as an example to others. Better than any other lesson to be derived from Banneker's life and work is the one he so admirably exemplified: that the thirst for knowledge is not limited to youth, and that the process of learning recognizes no barriers of race or creed.

In an effort to make this volume as useful as possible, supplementary materials have been added for readers with special interest in science. Many of the manuscripts described or quoted are privately owned or form part of large public collections which are not fully indexed or catalogued. Certain texts have accordingly been selected so that reference can be made to the important manuscripts related to Banneker; these are included in the section called Documents. The collection of published works has required years of search. A complete list will be timesaving and of practical use for others interested in the subject. Because the sequence of their publication reveals how the world remembered Banneker, and when and why, this compilation is presented chronologically instead of alphabetically.

Some assumptions could not be avoided in the present work, to explain how the daily course of Banneker's life was lived. Every effort has been made to subdue such assumptions to the documented facts as well as they could be recovered. It has been occasionally necessary also to dwell on apparently unimportant minutiae and details of Banneker's daily existence. Yet, in reviewing his life, the tedium is important to an understanding of the simple pleasures he found in the world of nature around him and in his studies. These were important to his existence, the savor of which can be preserved in a general narrative only with the greatest difficulty.

In the course of fitting together the fragments of fact as they were recovered, Banneker emerges in the mind's eye as an impressive being of flesh and blood. Here I have told, as truly as it was possible to re-create, what Banneker thought and believed, what he attempted and what he achieved.

THE LIFE OF
BENJAMIN
BANNEKER

I

THE HERITAGE AND THE LAND

There is nothing that is less in our power, and less our own than our birth, and therefore of all pretences a man takes hold of to value and prefer himself to others, that of his birth appears the most groundless; and the truth is, a man does seldom insist upon it, but for want of another merit.

Banneker's Almanac for 1794

BENJAMIN BANNEKER LIVED his entire life, which spanned three quarters of a century, almost to the day, in Baltimore County in tidewater Maryland. During his lifetime he witnessed major changes in the development of Maryland, from an English province to a state in the new republic. He and the members of his family were at the same time victims and beneficiaries of many of the colony's problems and their resolutions during this period, so that the story of Banneker's life becomes, in many ways, the story of eighteenth-century Maryland.

At the end of the seventeenth century, much of that part of southeastern Maryland known as the tidewater was still a wilderness. It was a rich, wild region divided by a waterway which created the eastern and western shores. In contrast to the lower horizon of the opposite side of the bay, the western shore was more elevated and undulating, presenting vistas of open fields in green valleys against a dark background of dense forest that studded the sturdy, low hills.

Separating the shores was the great Chesapeake Bay, which extended 170 miles to the head of the bay from the capes at its ocean entrance and ranged in width from three to eight miles. Feeding into this great body of water were forty-eight tributaries varying from two to one hundred miles in length. Many of these rivers were navigable and sufficiently wide and deep to permit seagoing vessels to penetrate them for considerable distances.

The bay's tides moved inland to the western shore for a distance of approximately thirty miles to seek the openings of the major waterways, such as the Severn, South, Rhodes, and West rivers, and finally the broad mouth of the Patapsco River. The tides extended fully twenty miles up the Patapsco from its entrance between Rock Point and North Point, until the river narrowed considerably as it turned westward. It began to lose its tides at the mouth of a great gorge at the river town of Elkridge Landing. The larger vessels that came to trade with the surrounding countryside could not go up the Patapsco, and lay at anchor off North Point, where they received their cargoes by river transportation.

Patapsco was an Indian name which appeared in at least nineteen variations in the colonial records. It derived from the word *pota* in the Algonquin language, meaning "to jut out," *psk* meaning "a ledge of rock," and the locative *ut* meaning "at," so that the original form was *Pota-psk-ut* or "at the jutting ledge of rock" or "at the rocky corner." Originally this was applied not to the river itself, but to a locality on the river which has been identified as "White Rocks." This was a formation of limestone ledge which projected over the river opposite the point where Rock Creek joins the Patapsco River. Still prominent today and well known to fishermen, they originally rose much higher out of the water and displayed a more extensive surface when white men first came into the region. Captain John Smith did not use the name Patapsco, and when he explored the Chesapeake region in 1608, he named the river Bolus. Patapsco first appeared on a map in 1660, and in the land records only several years before that date with the first grants made in that region.[1]

Scattered along the river were occasional towns or seaports, now extinct, which were established in thinly settled sections of the tidewater region after the mid-seventeenth century. Created by Act of Assembly, the towns were directed to be self-supporting, and the inhabitants of neighboring regions were required to bring their products to the towns to be sold in the warehouses established for that purpose. By the same token, ships coming into the rivers were required to anchor at these ports and unload their cargoes there in exchange for local products. The towns were thus enabled to support themselves from warehouse fees. The warehouses were supplemented with stores maintained by agents of merchants in Glasgow, Bristol, and London. In these were sold clothing, hardware, stationery, agricultural tools, and other imported goods which provided comfort and luxury to the primitive community.

Each town had its own "husting," or court, with jurisdiction over ordinary offenses and civil suits. The first buildings to be erected in each new river town were a church, a guildhall or courthouse, and warehouses. A town council was formed to govern the community. Market days were established several days a week, during which an active business was carried on. Autumn fairs of four and five days' duration attracted inhabitants throughout the region. Products of the farms and plantations were displayed, and buyers and sellers were brought to-

gether. Entertainment was furnished by minstrels and mounte-
banks, and the common games of chance competed with a
variety of outdoor sports. Slaves and tracts of land were frequently raffled during these gatherings, and horse races were
sometimes featured. Many of these towns contained a slave
market where slaves in numbers were unloaded from the ships
and sold, to be distributed among the plantations. Londontown,
for instance, was designated in 1706 as a port for the unloading
of Negroes in addition to wares and commodities, and cabins
of unusual construction existed east of the town and survived
until recent times.[2]

Several such river towns sprang up along the Patapsco
River at the end of the seventeenth century, but none existed
very close to the area in which the story takes place until the
first quarter of the eighteenth century. Probably the most important community in the area was the first county seat of
Baltimore County. It was a small community, also called Baltimore, established on the Bush River in what is presently Harford
County. The old Baltimore was originally intended to become
the capital city of the province of Maryland. In 1674 an act of
Assembly authorized the erection of a courthouse, and two years
later an ordinance was passed designating sites where inns could
be kept. Old Baltimore was the county seat for twenty-five or
thirty years, after which it was removed to Gunpowder, where
it remained until 1712. Few records were maintained during this
early period because of the sparseness of the settlements, thus
creating particular difficulties for the historian.

The tobacco plantations on both sides of the Patapsco were
farmed by slave labor. Each of them formed an individual community because of the limitations of communication, and maintained its independence from the outside world. Large numbers
of artisans were required to supply the plantations' needs, ranging from blacksmiths, coopers, housewrights, cobblers, and
millers. Although the major crop was tobacco, many of the
plantations harvested a substantial amount of grains for their
own use, and some of them operated their own gristmills. In

such cases, millers were brought from England, either as free men or as indentured servants. For those larger plantations situated at a distance from the river towns, it was necessary to make their own importations. The planters sold their tobacco through English or Scottish agents and as part of their return they imported goods which were delivered to their plantation wharves by the English vessels calling for the tobacco. Depending on the favorability of the market in London, the planters frequently ordered more goods than they required for the plantation's needs. The surplus was kept in a storehouse from which it was later distributed to non-importing planters and farmers in the region. Sale of such items was announced by the plantation cannon.

Large plantations summoned all workers to begin each work day by firing a cannon at sunrise. When a planter had selected those items which he needed from the shipment and was ready to dispose of the balance, he fired his cannon at sunset. This was a signal recognized by other planters and farmers throughout the area, and during the next several days they would find time to call at that plantation to purchase or trade for their needs. Included in such sales was a wide range of agricultural implements, a variety of cloth, from the most common sort to fine brocades and silks; china and glassware; books, wines, shoes, and many other goods which were not produced in the province.

Planters and farmers arrived on horseback, sometimes with one or more pack horses in tow if they anticipated making substantial purchases. The plantations were connected with each other and with the river towns by horse trails and by the "rolling roads" in a network that branched out in all directions, like the strands of a cobweb. The "rolling roads" were an unusual form of thoroughfare created for the transportation of hogsheads of tobacco by hand from the plantations to the docks. The method employed was quite ingenious. Each hogshead served as its own means of transportation by having a pin or gudgeon fastened into each end; hoop shafts were attached to these, and fastened to the collars of horses, which thus rolled the load to the docks. Often a similar device was used for hauling the hogsheads by laborers. Another simple means was to have hogsheads merely rolled by manpower. These "rolling roads" survived to become the basis of the highway system through the region.

At the beginning of the eighteenth century, the law required that all public and main roads be cleared and grubbed fit for travel twenty feet wide. The roads that led to the county courthouse were to be marked with two notches on the trees on both sides of the road, and another notch at a distance above the other two. Any road leading to a place of public worship was marked with a slip cut down the face of the tree near the ground.

Another important means of travel was provided by the river and its tributaries. The province maintained ferries over the rivers and other large streams, which provided a means of transporting the hogsheads of tobacco by water when it was more convenient.

Tobacco was the dominant subject in the life of the majority of the people in the province of Maryland since the earliest period of its colonial existence. This crop was grown upon at least one half of Maryland's arable land and provided the chief product and support of its people as well as the foundation of its trade and commerce. Tobacco growing excluded the cultivation of grain almost entirely, and furthermore prevented the introduction of manufactures. The currency of the colony was in tobacco, and even the county payment was made in this tender.

The emphasis of an entire province on a single commodity had unfortunate results. Tobacco production was increased beyond its true value, and its price was consequently diminished, until the new code regulated its production and retarded its depreciation.

It was not until 1763 that the colony passed the "tobacco code" "to amend the staple of tobacco, for preventing frauds in His Majesty's customs and for limiting the fees of officers." This act provided for the most minute details of inspection, warehousing, and shipment of tobacco, as well as punishment for opening hogsheads, burning, and stealing. Every provincial officer as well as every laborer in the province was to be paid in tobacco, all debts could be discharged in tobacco, and all duties were to be paid with it. Because of the importance of the product, stringent laws for its purity and for its inspection were strictly observed.[3]

The production of tobacco did not, however, totally obscure other needs. From time to time the Assembly passed laws to encourage industry and manufactures. Efforts were made to promote tillage and the raising of provisions, and the erection of water mills in order to encourage the production of flour for export. However, it was not until the eve of the War for Independence that these efforts achieved some success.

Few communities existed on the Patapsco River in the late seventeenth century. Occasional large plantations flourished on both sides of the river in the mountainous regions. The upper reaches of the Patapsco with its great falls provided a wealth of water power which was harnessed to operate small mills, but large sections remained virtually unexplored and uninhabited. Farther up the gorge from the site of Elkridge Landing steep hills rose on both sides of the river, with rocky ledges overhanging the impressive mountain torrent. A low valley which extended just below the great falls was locally known as "The Hollow." It was enclosed on all sides by sloping hills densely covered with trees and undergrowth. Wild turkeys were plentiful, and herds of deer found shelter there. Among the major threats to travelers were wildcats that lived there unhindered from the time of the Indian settlements, in rocky ledges and caverns near small streams. Before the land became thickly settled, wolves roamed the region, sometimes in packs of as many as forty or fifty. Bears also were sometimes encountered, and added to these dangers of the wilderness were snakes, including the black snake, red-bellied water snake, corn snake, and rattlesnake.

It was in this region that our story begins, with the arrival of an Englishwoman named Molly Welsh, around the turn of the century.*

Young Molly, a servant or milkmaid on a cattle farm, said to be in Wessex County, England, was doing her chores at milking time, when a cow knocked over a pail of milk. Her employer accused her of stealing the milk, and for this offense Molly was arrested. According to the criminal code in England at that time, stealing was one of more than three hundred felonies for which the penalty was death on the gallows. Conviction as a felon during this period was not necessarily evidence of crime, however; the least excuses were used to gather involuntary convicts for shipment to the American colonies to supply labor for the plantations. Cruel as the system was, it was mitigated by two means, the pleading of clergy and royal pardon.

When a person was convicted of a felony, he had the privilege of "calling for the book." If the prisoner could read the book, sentence of death was reduced to branding of the thumb. The other method was the judges' submission, after each session, of a list of persons considered worthy of mercy. A pardon under the Great Seal could then be issued for those listed. It was the ability to read that saved Molly from death on the gallows.

Although it was not legal to penalize a felon to transportation or exile, it was possible to pardon him on the condition that he or she leave the country. Soon after the beginning of the seventeenth century, Parliament modified the common law to enable certain classes of offenders in clergy to be sentenced to transportation. By the middle of the seventeenth century a system of conditional pardons had been refined and continued in use for a century to come. The new system required that after each major assize the justices submit to the secretary of state a pardon signed by two justices for those convicts believed

* There is no certainty about the correct spelling of Molly's last name inasmuch as no documents relating to her have survived. Both "Welsh" and "Walsh" have been used, but it seems likely that the former is the correct version.

worthy of reprieve from the gallows. When the document was signed by the king, countersigned by the secretary of state, and passed to the chancery, it was issued. The prisoners then appeared in open court to plead their pardons; if successful, they then became available for shipment overseas, for a period of exile fixed at seven years. The sheriffs made arrangements for transportation with merchants trading in the plantations, and the latter realized their profit from selling the convicts as indentured servants overseas.[4]

No organized system for transportation of convicts existed, and they frequently underwent great hardships before they arrived in the colonies. They were often made to await the next jail delivery in the care of sheriffs without provision for their support. The sheriffs were not permitted to deliver felons to the transporters without a license. Despite requests to the Parliament to enact legislation to improve the situation, many years passed before any action was taken.

The selection of the ship on which the felons were to be transported was left to the discretion of the sheriffs, who consigned the prisoners to one of the ship captains who had petitioned to transport convicts. Payment of a bond was required from the merchants to give security to the sheriffs for the safe conveyance of their charges.[5]

There is much confusion about the dates of the major events in Molly Welsh's life. According to a date provided in Tyson's work, Molly arrived in the province of Maryland around 1683.[6]

Although the laws of the province excluded the importation of convicts at the time Molly was presumed to have arrived, it is probable that transported convicts were nevertheless permitted to land, possibly under the title of indentured servants, when they came within the right of clergy.

The voyage from England to the New World was a terrible experience, particularly for the transported convicts. Judged by modern standards, the vessels were extremely small, few being over two hundred tons. The number of passengers varied from one hundred fifty to two hundred, including as many as twenty-five under twelve years of age. The ordinary price for passage from England to Virginia and Maryland was six pounds, although it was sometimes reduced for large parties. The length of the voyage varied from 47 to 138 days. Often after the ship's departure from London, it could be delayed by storms which detained it in another English port for several weeks before getting under way. The great uncertainty about the length of the voyage invariably caused problems in providing sufficient food and water for passengers and crew. Since the food consisted chiefly of bread or ship biscuit, salt meat, peas, and cheese, the difficulty arose primarily from lack of space for storage. The passengers generally received the same rations as the sailors, including a weekly allowance of seven pounds of bread, cheese and butter, and a weekly allotment of one half pound of pork, with peas on five days.

After arrival in Chesapeake Bay, a vessel might take as long as three or four months delivering English goods and collecting tobacco for the cargo on the return voyage up the bay and along the rivers.[7]

Disposition of the felons and indentured servants was made by the shipmasters as their vessels moved up the Chesapeake Bay to some of the river landings, and duly announced in the local newspapers. As an example, a notice in *The Maryland Gazette* announced the arrival on June 29, 1767, of the ship *Blessing's Success* from London with "a parcel of healthy country servants, for seven years; amongst which are many valuable Tradesmen . . . to be disposed of on board the said Vessel laying in the North West Branch of Patapsco River on Friday the Third Instant." [8] A similar announcement which appeared several years later read:

> Just imported from Bristol, in the Ship Randolph, Capt. John Weber Price, One Hundred and Fifteen Convicts, men, women, and lads: Among whom are several Tradesmen, who are to be sold on board the said Ship, now in Annapolis Dock, this Day, Tomorrow, and Saturday next, by Smyth & Sudler.[9]

The transported convicts were popularly called "Seven Years Passengers" or "Kings Passengers," and many advertisements in newspapers of the regions announced their arrival from time to time.[10] The announcements varied, and occasionally a writer with a wry sense of humor reported the arrival of "Eighty passengers, sent in for the term of Seven Years on account of their Ingenuity," or the arrival of "Sixty-eight of His Majesty's Seven Years Passengers, who had too much Ingenuity to be suffer'd to live in England."

Molly arrived in the province of Maryland around 1683 on an English vessel that docked at one of the major ports of entry, which may have been Providence (later Annapolis) or else Londontown. There she was sold, in accordance with the custom, to defray the cost of her passage. Purchased by a tobacco planter with a plantation on the Patapsco River, Molly was required to work seven years as an indentured servant to pay for the voyage.

The role of the servant in the colonies requires definition. A servant was in fact any person brought into the colonies for hire, and great numbers in this category arrived who indentured themselves for varying periods of time to work off the costs of transportation and board of the overseas voyage. There was great need for workers on the plantations and in the cities of the New World, and English shipmasters searched out and assembled persons in all conditions of poverty from the cities and the countryside of England. They transported them at their own expense, well aware that they would recover their investments and with profit on the colonial shores. These dregs of humanity included not only farm laborers and house servants, but also tradesmen and craftsmen, such as carpenters, masons, mechanics, shipwrights, and members of that educated but frequently impoverished class—teachers and clerks who were eagerly sought as tutors or as clerks on the plantations. The period of indenture ranged from five to seven years, and was a form of voluntary slavery. During the period of service the employer was required to provide clothing, food, shelter, and washing, and in return the servant was required to be obedient at all times, to serve his master well, and particularly not to steal. A master could not punish a servant with more than ten lashes for a single offense. No servant was permitted to travel a distance of more than ten miles beyond his master's premises without a written pass.

Upon completion of the period of servitude, a reasonable provision was made to enable the servant to establish himself in gainful employment. In the province of Maryland, the freed servant was entitled to receive fifty acres of land, an ox, two hoes, a gun, and clothing. Clothes, in the case of a man, included a new suit of kersey, stockings, a hat, and shoes. Each woman was provided with a skirt and waistcoat of penistone (a coarse woolen cloth), a linen smock and a blue apron, two linen caps, stockings, shoes, and three barrels of Indian corn. Although the new landholder received the land without cost, he was thereafter required to pay an annual quit rent in order to keep the land for himself and his heirs. Shortly after the first landings in the province, however, the land allotments were reduced to one half of the acreage, and the system was abandoned altogether in 1683. Thereafter land was available only by purchase.

Molly worked out the period of her indenture faithfully and without incident. She was reasonably well treated by her master, and she made use of her time by learning as much as she could about this new country, so different from her own. Whether she was a house servant or a plantation hand is not known, but the latter seems more likely, since she was later able to develop a farm of her own. Finally, around 1690, Molly won her freedom. There was little that a single woman could do in the wilderness by herself, with the few items she acquired with her freedom rights; and it must have been a bewildering prospect. Molly was a courageous and strong-willed woman, however, and after considering all possibilities, she decided to establish a farm of her own. She had neither money nor other forms of legal tender with which to purchase land, and had received none as part of her freedom fees. She probably rented a small farm for a modest fee, to be paid annually in tobacco, located on a suitable and inexpensive tract of land in the undeveloped region not far from the edge of the Patapsco and adjoining a tributary called Cooper's Branch. It was situated conveniently near the rolling road, approximately twelve miles north of the mouth of the Patapsco.

Her new home was in the midst of wilderness, but it held few terrors for a woman who had already survived such experiences as Molly had undergone. At first she worked alone, clearing a small section of the land that was relatively free of trees, and planting her bushels of Indian corn as well as some tobacco. She concentrated on the care of her crops, and she had rewarding harvests. She had no friends, and there were in fact very few people living in that region. There may have been one or two Indian families[11] living in cabins some distance away, but there was no Indian settlement of any size at that time.*

Although Molly worked alone, it is possible that she received assistance in the beginning from friendly neighboring planters or their employees. She was evidently very industrious, and was a successful farmer. From time to time she put aside a little money until at last she was able to purchase land of her own, perhaps the very piece of ground she had been farming. This was an impressive achievement, and her new status as a landowner gave Molly new impetus to carry on. After several years had passed she had put aside enough tobacco, besides what she sold to fill her needs, to purchase some assistance for managing the farm.

Molly had deliberated over this action for many months. She could not afford the highest quality of slaves, because they brought good prices and were quickly sold after arrival at the major ports of entry. She had taken the time to visit the nearby river towns when English or New England ships moved north-

* Occasional references occur in the Baltimore County court proceedings to Indian residents of the county, and reports of the Baltimore County Garrison noted the existence of Indian cabins from time to time. Indians were attached to the fort built in the county in 1692 and paid in "green matchcoats" (a kind of garment), instead of money.

ward up the bay to sell their slaves. She had also given thought to buying one or two male slaves from one of the "soul drivers" or "soul agents" who came along the rolling roads several times each year, driving gangs of slaves that had remained unsold on shipboard. Too frequently these were ill or otherwise in poor physical condition. The system prevailed into the nineteenth century, and Sutclife, for one, reported having encountered such gangs several times during his travels between Baltimore and Georgetown between 1804 and 1806.[12]

Molly was opposed to slavery on general principle, particularly after her own experience. When she evaluated the alternatives, however, she found herself without choice in the matter if she meant to survive and prosper in this strange New World. Once her decision had been made, she planned to carry it out when she next delivered her tobacco crop to the landing.

Tradition handed down in the family reported that in 1692 Molly purchased her two slaves "from a ship anchored in the Bay." This would have been one of the larger English or New England slave ships that could not navigate the Patapsco and anchored outside North Point. It would have been necessary for Molly to make her way down the river, which she may have done with her tobacco crop at the end of the summer.[13]

Slaves were purchased by the traders at a prime cost of £4 to £6 per head and sold in Virginia and Maryland at prices ranging between £16 and £20 at the end of the seventeenth century. The prices rose to £40 per head by the mid-eighteenth century. Prices fluctuated according to age, sex, physical condition, and accomplishments of the slaves, and also with the season. Higher prices for slaves were realized in the Chesapeake during the spring and early summer, due to the need for extra labor on the plantation during the working months. The prices dropped sharply after the crops were harvested near the end of the year.

Molly was able to pay only modest prices, and then in tobacco credit. She finally selected two young male Negroes from those offered. One of them looked particularly healthy and strong, and she quickly visualized his usefulness on the farm. The other lacked these characteristics, but there were qualities about him that she could not identify and which appealed to her. Furthermore, his price was particularly reasonable and she was certain he would be a good investment.

Molly's hopes were quickly realized in her first choice, and her fears were confirmed with the second. The strong slave, whose name has not survived, proved to be extremely energetic and willing, and he soon adapted himself to the climate and the work. He seemed to enjoy felling the great trees to clear another section of the farm, and he assisted her in erecting the new tobacco building she needed, as well as with other chores.

The other slave had a different disposition. He was neither as strong nor as adaptable as the first, and Molly gave him the lighter tasks of the farm. He was not inclined to work willingly. Molly gradually managed to communicate with him and learned a little of his background. His name was Bannka or Bannaka, and he claimed to be the son of an African chieftain. Molly spoke of him later as an African prince, the son of the king of his country. He had been captured by slave traders, sold to a slave ship, and brought to the American colonies. Despite his royal blood, or probably because of it, Bannka was disinclined to work, and Molly had great difficulty in utilizing him on the farm. All that is known about Molly and Bannka consists of descriptions and anecdotes handed down by the Banneker family from one generation to another, and afterward collected in interviews with survivors and contemporaries conducted by Martha E. Tyson many decades later.[14] According to one description, he was "a man of bright intelligence, fine temper, with a very agreeable presence, dignified manners, and contemplative habits."

Several years later, Molly gave her two slaves their freedom. In general, manumissions were infrequently given in the province of Maryland, and then only usually because of blood relationships or in recognition of good and faithful service.

The manumission of slaves was accomplished by one of three methods during the early history of Maryland. A slave could be manumitted by word of mouth, by last will and testament, or by means of a deed. A formal statute of 1752 abolished the first two methods. Although manumission by deed was rarely employed prior to this date, it became a standard practice by the time of the Revolutionary War.[15]

The unnamed diligent slave had joined the Christian faith, but Bannka held to the beliefs of his African ancestors, as well as his name, which eventually was changed by popular usage to "Banneky."

Soon after Molly had given the two slaves their freedom, she married Banneky, probably in about 1696. She did so at considerable risk to her own freedom, for the laws governing miscegenation were stringent at that time. The intermarriage of white and black had become a serious problem in several of the British colonies in America after the middle of the seventeenth century, and legislation regarding its control became increasingly strict and was rigidly enforced. The status of the two classes of servants, the white servant and the Negro slave, varied greatly because the former became free upon the expiration of his term of service, whereas the slave generally remained in servitude all his life.

By 1661 Maryland was forced to enact a law which specified:

And forasmuch as divers freeborn *English* women, forgetful of their free condition, and to the disgrace of our nation, do intermarry with negro slaves, by which also divers suits may arise, touching the issue of such women, and a great damage doth befall the master of such negroes, for preservation whereof for deterring such free-born women from such shameful matches, be it enacted, That whatsoever free-born woman shall intermarry with any slave, and after the last day of the present assembly, shall serve the master of such slave during the life of her husband; and that all the issues of such free-born women, so married, shall be slaves as

their fathers were . . . And be it further enacted,
That all the issues of *English*, or other free-born
women, that have already married negroes, shall serve
the master of their parents, till they be thirty years of
age and no longer.[16]

The law was further enforced by a revision in 1681, but
miscegenation continued, and new later laws enacted to prevent
it only produced a greater problem, with the need to provide
for the care of illegitimate children resulting from such marriages. By 1681 it had become illegal in Maryland for any minister to join in marriage any Negro and "a white woman servant
freeborn." As of 1684 any such woman who married a Negro
or bore his child forfeited her freedom and became a servant
"to the use of the Minister of the Poor of the same Parish." Laws
even more stringent were enacted in 1715 and 1717 in Maryland,
providing severe punishment for any white man or woman who
cohabited with a Negro, free or slave.[17]

Molly Welsh considered the hazards carefully before she
undertook marriage, and once her decision was made, she proceeded without further hesitation. Perhaps she concluded that
her little farm in the wilderness was too remote to warrant the
attention of the law. She changed her name to that of her husband, adopted his people, and thereafter withdrew completely
from her white neighbors.

In due time four daughters were born to the Bannekys.
The oldest was named Mary, followed by Katherine, Esther,
and another daughter whose name has not survived. The young
family led a peaceful existence in the wilderness, and eventually
they prospered.

Not for one moment, however, did Molly relax her watch-
fulness and awareness of the dangers that might threaten her and
hers. The unusual circumstances of her family, because of mixed
blood, was a subject of unrelenting concern. Official records in
that period left much to be desired, and documentary evidence
of freedom achieved was essential, but may not have existed for

her, her husband, or, later, her son-in-law. Frequently it was not possible to obtain tangible evidence, and the unsuccessful search for documentation tends to support the possibility that none existed originally, and that her family security remained in jeopardy.

Meanwhile the region along the Patapsco River was becoming increasingly populated. Several river towns had sprung up within a day's ride from Molly's farm, and more and more of the land of that part of the country was being developed into tobacco farms, as a result of the new outlets for the tobacco crops. Prominent among the new settlements was Joppa, which was established in 1707 on the tract of land called Taylor's Choice, northwest of Foster's Neck. It developed into a confluence of the several rolling roads that passed through Baltimore and Harford counties. It became the county seat in 1712 and developed rapidly as a center for the tobacco trade as a result of an Act of Assembly of 1724 which specified:

> There shall be allowed to all debtors whatsoever, owing any tobacco to any person or persons whatsoever, such debtor bringing his tobacco to the town aforesaid, and there paying the same to his creditor or creditors, or his or their receivers, the sum of ten pounds of tobacco, per cent for every hundred pounds of tobacco so brought to the place aforesaid, and there paid as aforesaid; to be deducted out of such debtor's said debt, or allowed of in bar or discount of any action to be brought against any debtor or debtors, by any creditor or creditors, in any court within this province.

This method of paying old debts not only proved to be popular but also had a beneficial effect on the commercial growth of Joppa. Soon after its establishment as a county seat, Joppa had not only a courthouse, prison and pillory, and tobacco warehouses, but many town houses of imposing size and construction built by affluent officials and merchants. These homes, which formed a social center for the community, were at some distance from the teeming wharves that were dotted with numerous warehouses and taverns, and where English vessels frequently docked to collect the tobacco and to deliver imported goods. Joppa grew quickly in size and importance, but its fate was already predetermined by the competition that was soon to develop from Baltimore Town, a new community on the Patapsco River which was first settled in 1730.

Another river town of growing importance was called Patapsco, and was later renamed Elkridge Landing. It was established in 1725 by the second Caleb Dorsey of Hockley. He added to the lands his father had owned in the region and opened iron mines, built forges and mills, and developed a port of entry from which he shipped his mining products to England. He became known as "the rich iron merchant of Elkridge Landing," and in 1738 he built Belmont, an imposing family mansion which still survives.* Elkridge Landing was a port of entry developed from the Ridge of Elks, which extended between the points now defined by the towns of Laurel, Ellicott City, and Clarksville. Prior to the establishment of the port, the Ridge had served as a summer resort for the families of wealthy planters of Anne Arundel County.

The first sadness that came to Molly's family was the death of Banneky, at a relatively early age. Perhaps his constitution had been undermined by the severe winters to which he was unaccustomed, or he may have been a victim of one of several epidemics of yellow fever that raged through the region at the time. Molly once more found herself alone, with the additional burden of four young children to raise. When the children were old enough, they assisted her with the chores. The time passed quickly, and suddenly Molly realized that her children were grown and soon, one by one, they would marry and leave her. By this time, she had secured her future and her land, and she began to think about the future of her children.

* Belmont today is a conference center owned and maintained by the Smithsonian Institution in Washington, D.C.

II

HOME AND
FAMILY

THE FIRST OF MOLLY'S BROOD to leave the family was her oldest
daughter, Mary, born about 1700. She had grown into a handsome young woman. Her complexion combined the fairness of
her mother with her father's dark color, and she was tall and well
proportioned. Mary was described as

. . . (her opportunities considered) a woman of un-
common intelligence. She had a knowledge of the

properties and uses of herbs, which was often of advantage to her neighbors. Her appearance was imposing, her complexion a pale copper color, similar to that of the fairest Indian tribes, and she had an ample growth of long black hair, which never became gray. Her grandsons, the children of one of her daughters, used to speak with admiration of her many good qualities and her remarkable activity. They loved to relate that when she wished to prepare a basket of chickens for market, "she would run them down and catch them without assistance." This continued her practice when she was over seventy years of age.[1]

In 1730, when Mary was a mature young woman, she married a Negro named Robert, a native African from Guinea who had been captured and sold into slavery. He was transported to the tidewater from a slave ship that had docked along the bay ports and purchased by a tobacco planter who lived near Molly. Robert was a willing worker and religiously inclined. He learned about the Christian faith and eventually was converted and became a member of the Church of England. When he was baptized he was given the name of Robert, and at the same time he received his freedom. It was sometime thereafter that he and Mary Banneky were married. Having no surname of his own, he took that of his wife and proudly became Robert Banneky.[2]

At first Robert moved in with the Banneky family and assisted Molly on her farm, putting aside the share of profits that he and Mary earned so that they could eventually purchase their own land. Molly welcomed another pair of strong hands to supplement those of her family, and several years passed in peaceful content. Each autumn Robert and Mary totaled their share of the tobacco receipts, and each year brought their dream closer to realization.

Five years passed before another of Molly's family was ready to leave the brood. On May 22, 1735, her daughter

Katherine was married to James Boston, a young Negro from the same region.[3]

It was not until nine years later, on September 22, 1744, that Esther, the third daughter, married William Black in St. Paul's Parish.[4]

The fourth daughter married a man named Henden, and may have died at an early age. Her son, John Henden, had been, according to his own account, "raised from a little child" by his grandmother, Molly Welsh. He was still living in 1836, although of an advanced age; Martha Tyson described him as having ". . . always been considered a man of strict integrity, and was for a number of years employed by Ellicott & Co., and had charge of their stables."

Records relating to the Banneker families are to be found in the registers of St. Paul's Church of Baltimore, which is the oldest parish on the Patapsco River. Originally known as Patapsco Parish, its name was changed to St. Paul's Parish in 1692, under the official act of the General Assembly that gave a church establishment to the province of Maryland and christianized the names of the churches. In 1694 the tax list for the support of the parish numbered 231 persons. In 1702, the original church building was replaced with a brick building on the same site. With the settlement of the city of Baltimore in 1728, the center of the community was moved and the church was abandoned and fell into decay. A new church was constructed in 1756 at the corner of the present Lexington Street, and the graves were moved to the new burial ground at that time. The burial ground was moved several times thereafter, but no graves of principals relating to Banneker's life have survived.

While Mary and her young husband continued to live and work with Molly, they had a family of their own. Their first child was a son, Benjamin, born on November 9, 1731. The second child was a daughter whose name has not been preserved. In the years that followed two more daughters were born to them, Minta and Molly, the latter named after the grandmother.

Molly's farm continued to be the scene of active family life, for no sooner were her own young children grown than a second generation replaced it. These were happy times for all of them, and when Molly looked around her at the faces of the several generations of her family, she must have given thought to the strange ways of fate. According to the testimony of one of her grandsons, she was not only a white woman, but of very fair complexion and probably with blond hair.[5] Yet every member of her family, including children and grandchildren, were black, some of the darkest hue. Theirs was an unusual heritage, combining the traditions of English country life which Molly imparted to them in stories about her girlhood in England, the mystic lore of the African continent, conveyed in the accounts of Bannka and of Robert, intermingled with the customs and conditions of the province they lived in.

The one feature of their lives that each of them recognized, from personal experience or from hearsay, was the gift of freedom, which they cherished above all other aspects of their life together.

Molly took particular pleasure in the family of her eldest child. Robert had proved to be not only an excellent farmer and a good provider but for her also a veritable pillar of strength. He was becoming impatient, however, because as his own family developed he was eager to establish himself independently. He and Mary carefully saved a part of their share of the crop receipts each year, until finally Robert was able to buy a small tract of land of his own. This consisted of twenty-five acres, situated in that region called Ragland, east of the Patapsco Falls and near Molly's farm. It was densely wooded and appropriately named Timber Poynt. Originally called Timber Spot, it was situated in Baltimore County. The land had been acquired by John Howard by a warrant granted by His Lordship's Land Office and surveyed for him on February 23, 1729, by Philip Jones, Jr., who changed its name on the certificate to "Timber Poynt." It is not known just when Robert Banneky purchased the land, but it was surveyed for him at the time of its acquisition by J. Gardner.[6]

Robert spent the winter months clearing sections of his land and planting it in tobacco, corn, and some wheat. He added a small vegetable garden and a few fruit trees as time was available. Little by little he was able to develop some security for himself and his family. He probably continued to assist Molly on her farm, and he and Mary continued to put aside as much as they could of their tobacco receipts each year. Robert was not satisfied with Timber Poynt; he visualized it only as a step to a dream. He wanted a larger farm so as to fulfill all the family needs and hopes for their future. He had a specific tract in mind, a piece of land consisting of 100 acres which had formerly been part of a larger plantation called Stout. It was situated near Molly's farm, with the advantages of high ground as well as a useful stream. Finally came the day that Robert and Mary had saved enough to pay the price asked for the property. Robert arranged a meeting with its owner, Richard Gist.

Gist was a man of prominence in Baltimore County. He was the son of Christopher Gist, who had settled on the southern side of the Patapsco River as early as 1682. Richard Gist was one of the commissioners responsible for the founding of Baltimore, and was appointed by an Act of the Assembly dated July 14, 1729. These commissioners were appointed for life and were all regarded as men of consequence. In addition to serving as a justice of the peace, Gist was at this time deputy surveyor of the western shore of the province.[7]

An agreement was reached; Robert tendered his receipts for seven thousand pounds of tobacco in exchange for the land. On March 10, 1737, an indenture was drawn for the conveyance of the one hundred acres jointly to Robert Banneky and Benjamin, his son.[8] This deed is an impressive document, even today. It was elaborately written in the decorative hand of the county clerk, J. Wells Stokes, and contained the traditional resounding legal phraseology.

This indenture made this tenth day of March in the
year of our Lord one thousand seven hundred and thirty
seven between Richard Gist of Baltimore County in the
province of Maryland Government: of the one part and
Robert Bannaky and Benjamin Bannaky his son of the
county and province aforesaid of the other part, Wit-
nesseth that the said Richard Gist for and in consideration of seven thousand pounds of tobacco in hand paid
to the said Richard Gist the receipt whereof he doth
hereby acknowledge and doeth by these presents acquit
and discharge them the said Robert Bannaky and Benjamin Bannaky his son their heirs and assigns for ever
from every part and parcel thereof hath given granted
bargained and sold placed in escrow and confirmed
unto them the said Robert Bannaky and Benjamin
Bannaky his son their heirs and assigns forever one
hundred acres of land lying in the said county. . . .

One can imagine the thoughts that must have coursed
through the minds of Mary and Robert Banneky when the deed
was signed. With the purchase of the land they ensured freedom
and security for their children, regardless of any accidents of fate
that might yet befall their family. That a former Negro slave
and the daughter of another Negro slave could become land-
holders at a time when slavery flourished around them must have
seemed a most impressive achievement, not only in their own
eyes but in those of their friends and neighbors.

The manner in which the indenture was recorded is highly
significant. Robert purchased the land not only in his own name
but also in that of his son, jointly. When he died, the farm would
become the sole property of Benjamin without question and
without need of legal involvement. Robert's future was vested
in his son, and he attempted to make every provision at his command for ensuring Benjamin's independence after he was gone.

The Banneky farm had an interesting history, which could

be traced back to a land grant made in the seventeenth century by the Lord Proprietor to a certain Captain Thomas Bale. The original tract was named "Stout" and consisted of 529 acres. In 1701 it was surveyed for Captain Bale, at which time he sold 200 acres to John Whipps and described in the rent roll as being ". . . on ye N. Side ye falls of Patapsco Begin^g above Bales Branch now so called. Poss.^r 200 ac. John Whipps part of this Tract . . ." [9]

The Maryland rent rolls were records of annual quitrents and alienation fees imposed on the transfer of land in the province by the lord proprietor in England. In addition to the record copy maintained in Maryland, a duplicate copy was sent to him in England.

Separate rolls were drawn up for each county and there was a further subdivision of each county into hundreds. Each entry included the name of the tract of land as given in the patent, the acreage, the date of survey, the name of the original grantee, the location of the tract, the amount of annual rent, and the name of the "possessor" of the tract at the time that the rent roll was compiled. Lessees were not included under "possessor," however. During the seventeenth and eighteenth centuries Baltimore County consisted of what has since been divided into Harford County, a part of Carroll County, and that section of Anne Arundel County on the south side of the Patapsco River from the bay westward to the highlands beyond Elkridge, in addition to the present Baltimore County. The county at that time was divided into three "hundreds," namely, Spesutia Hundred, Gunpowder Hundred, and Patapsco Hundred. The last named was again subdivided into Patapsco Upper Hundred and Patapsco Lower Hundred. That region now encompassing Ellicott City and Oella was included in Patapsco Upper Hundred.

On January 19, 1733, Whipps divided his part of Stout, retaining 100 acres of his land and selling the remainder to the surveyor, Richard Gist. It was his moiety of Stout which Gist sold to Robert and Benjamin Banneky four years later.[10] The remainder of the original grant called Stout formed part of a larger plantation which had been conveyed by deed on November 5, 1717, by Anthony Bale to Christopher Randall, and part of which was purchased from Roger Randall in 1754 by an iron-monger named William Williams. The Williams land was re-surveyed on April 29, 1761, and renamed Mount Gilboa.*

Robert had now become a landowner of some consequence. He retained possession of Timber Poynt at the same time that he owned Stout. The Tax List for Upper Patapsco Hundred for the year 1737 listed "James Bannacar [sic] and his wife . . . 2 taxables." The error in the name was inadvertent; the record undoubtedly related to Robert, because the Baltimore County Debt Book contains the following entry.[11]

Robert Banniker, D^r.
Pt. Stout   —   100 [acres] —   0.4.0.
Timber Point   —   25 [acres] —   0.1.0.
                                                        ———
                                                        0.5.0.

The annual tax was one shilling for each twenty-five acres owned.

The Bannekys had a struggle at first, for the purchase of the land required all that they had been able to save at considerable sacrifice during the seven years of their marriage. They may have continued to live on Molly's farm at first, or it is possible that by this time Robert had been able to construct a small cabin on Timber Poynt for his family. Whichever may have been the case, he now had his work cut out for him. The first task was to clear an area of the new farm suitable for planting in tobacco and another on which to build their permanent home. He was fortunate in that the land had been acquired early enough in the year to give him time to do the preliminary clearing before the

* On April 24, 1771, a part of this tract was sold by Williams to Joseph, Andrew, Nathaniel, and John Ellicott, and on the same date the Ellicott brothers purchased an adjoining tract called Teal's Search from Emmanuel Teal. These two parcels were subsequently developed by the Ellicott brothers into Ellicott's Lower Mills (now Ellicott City).

spring planting. He worked long hours each day so as to make as much progress as possible.

Robert first removed the underbrush from a large area, and then grubbed out the larger roots. He planted a hasty crop of corn and another of tobacco in the midst of the standing timber, so that no time would be lost. Once that had been done, he went on to clear another portion of the property, following the removal of the underbrush by cutting down the trees. After they had thoroughly dried, he started a great fire on a windy day, which destroyed most of the branches and even some of the trunks. He was careful to fell the trees in one direction, so that he could plow the land with the furrows in the same direction as the felled trees. There was no time to spend on removing the stumps; these were left in the ground to decay.

During the following spring and summer months, Robert took whatever time he could spare from Molly's farm to continue work on his own. He had lost no time in planting a crop in the first year. After the initial planting, he started building a house to accommodate his growing young family. He selected the best trunks of the trees he had felled, trimming them so that he could take them to the sawmill up the river and have them sawn into boards and trimmed into logs, for the construction of the house. It was a hectic spring and summer, but everyone joined in the spirit of the new enterprise, and even Benjamin had to do his share of the work. Finally, after the crop had been harvested and brought to market, Robert and Mary were free to devote all their energies to finishing their home before the winter set in.

Robert did not share the privilege of white planters in the region who got together from time to time in mutual endeavors such as house raisings, corn huskings, and crop gathering. As free Negroes, his family were outcasts from such community life as existed at that time. During the eighteenth century there was a rising tide of sentiment directed against free Negroes, and he found himself in constant fear of violating statutes or offending an influential white neighbor.

The house was not elaborate but it was sturdy. Robert constructed a one-room log cabin with a loft. It was roofed with clapboards, and the great logs in the walls were chinked with clay on both sides against the cold and the heat. Openings were cut for windows, but since he could not afford glass, he fashioned heavy wooden shutters that could be closed against the cold and provide protection from the outside. The floor was a rough puncheon floor—split logs with the faces smoothed—and the fireplace, which occupied most of one side of the room, was constructed with stones dug out from the fields and assembled with sticks, moss, and clay.

The furniture was sparse, made by Robert himself with the use of such simple tools as his ax, an adze, and an auger. The most important piece was the table, on which many of the family tasks were performed. It consisted of a rough-hewn slab with legs inserted into holes on the underside drilled with an auger. He made stools for each member of the family in the same manner. The beds consisted of wooden slabs laid across poles supported on forked posts. After sundown the cabin was lighted by burning pine knots. Later, as the farm prospered, he was enabled to acquire a few items of furniture of slightly better quality in exchange for tobacco. The utensils that Mary had for her home were few. An iron pot was essential and greatly treasured. An iron fork and a tin cup probably completed her kitchen equipment, supplemented with pots and utensils made from gourds grown on the farm.

Food for the family consisted largely of small game which Robert hunted and trapped in the woods about him, and fish which he caught in the river not far from his home. These were supplemented with corn bread and porridge, eggs, milk, and poultry from the farm. Corn bread made from home-grown corn was constant fare.

In addition to mush and milk, the poor people in the tidewater area lived mostly on hominy. In addition to molasses hominy, there was a less frequent kind called "great hominy," which was made with meat or fowl. Hominy was made by beating the ears of dried maize in a mortar to remove the hull. It was then boiled with a piece of beef or salt pork with some kidney beans. It served as the constant basic food, and was supplemented with vegetables such as parsnips, turnips, carrots, potatoes, simmel [cymling?] squashes, and cabbage, as well as beef, bacon, and mutton as available.[12]

Accompanied by his young son, Robert also went fishing in Cooper's Branch, where they found as many as four types of perch, rockfish, catfish, drum, sheepshead, and eels, as well as shad in the month of May. Cockles and oysters were available in abundance and supplemented the family's daily fare.

Game also abounded, including partridges, wild geese and ducks, hares, fox squirrels, flying squirrels and ground squirrels, wild turkeys, opossums, and raccoons. Robert carefully skinned the hares and other small animals he caught for food, for the skins could be tanned and used for outer winter clothing. He also discovered that there was a market for good pelts; he traded them at the landings for needed commodities.

Mary Banneky had a great interest in herbs. During her years on the farm she sought out woodland plants that had medicinal value, and she collected information about herbs and remedies from her neighbors. She raised sassafras, ginseng, and snakeroot. She also sought out the bayberry bushes and carefully collected the berries, useful for making candles. She may have raised some flax and hemp and a little cotton, which she could spin and weave for cloth to be used in the home as well as for clothing. She made her own brooms from reeds collected from the banks of the Patapsco. Mary may even have applied her knowledge of herbs to the brewing of persimmon beer, a great favorite in that part of the country. It was flavored with the leaves of a plant called "cassona," which may have been wintergreen.

As time went on, Robert continued to improve his home. Although he had no nails, or at least only a few, he learned to fasten his furniture together with pegs in the traditional manner. In due time, as Mary saved the soft downy feathers from the chickens and other fowl used for the family menu, she was able to make feather mattresses.

In the spring Robert set out young fruit trees, and after several years he had an impressive orchard of apples, pears, plums, and other fruits. After a winter or two, he learned to fence in his trees to keep the young deer from scraping the trunks with their antlers in the winter. Eventually he added a few hives of bees, and the children had honey as an unbelievable luxury.

The immediate need for a blacksmith and other trades took Robert to the nearest community, such as Elkridge Landing. From time to time a traveling journeyman stopped at the farm on his way through the countryside, enabling the Bannekys to take care of other farm needs.

Tobacco culture required constant work which occupied their lives from dawn until dusk seven days a week without intermission until the coming of the winter. Benjamin accepted it as his lot and shared to some degree his parents' pride in ownership of the land, exulting with them when the season had been a good one. Despite all their efforts, the annual yield was not great. History is silent on the subject, but it is likely that, due to their status as free Negroes and relatively small planters, they were unable to hire labor to work with them on the farm. It is just as doubtful that they could have or would have owned slaves, as some other free Negroes did, and consequently they operated the farm entirely by themselves. At first there were only Robert and Mary, assisted to an increasing degree by their children as each of them grew up to participate in the chores.

Robert had learned the culture of tobacco from his former master, and had the experience of his years working on Molly's farm as well. Early in the spring, in March or April, depending on the lateness of the frosts each season, he took the tobacco seed he had saved from the previous year's crop and carefully planted it in seedbeds. The seedbeds were laid in the woods in an area of virgin mold which had been cleared of the trees which had then been burned on the site for enrichment of the soil. The

tiny seeds were imbedded in the layer of ash over the virgin mold
—a difficult task because the seeds were so tiny. The tobacco
plants made their first appearance about a month later and by
June had become strong enough to handle for replanting. Robert
and his family watched over them anxiously until, as tradition
required, the new plants "be grown to the Breadth of a Shilling." [13] They were then carefully removed and planted in newly
cleared woodland in parallel rows of little hillocks about three
feet apart. The transplanting could be accomplished only in wet
weather when the ground was soft.

Then followed a period of anxious watching and waiting.
Robert and Mary and even Ben spent their time weeding around
the hills to ensure that the young plants grew strong without
obstruction, and picking off the insects from the tender shoots.
The soil of their farm was a light sandy loam, not very rich, so
that the plants did not support as many leaves as they would have
in soil of a richer quality. When the shoot had put out about ten
to fifteen leaves the top of the plant was broken or cut off to ensure that the plant grew no higher and that the leaves would
receive all of its strength. Meanwhile the plant put out suckers
between the leaves, and each week Robert and his family surveyed the rows of hills and plucked off the suckers.

The topping operation required considerable skill and was
usually done by Benjamin's father. The plant was topped by
pressing it between the thumb and forefinger, with the thumb-
nail as the cutting instrument. Topping was done just before
the plants came to flower. Robert first went through the fields
row by row to select the plants that seemed to be the finest and
strongest, to be reserved for seed for the next year's crop. Since
the tobacco flower tended to be self-fertilized, it was important
to prevent the seed plants from being crossed with those of inferior quality. He covered the flower heads with small cloth bags
which he secured to the stems with string after removing the
small leaves and branches just below each flower head. This was
another of the chores for the children, for as the flower developed, it was necessary to adjust the bags from time to time to

leave room for development. When the seeds were mature, the seed pods turned brown and the flower head became partially dried. Then the seed head was cut off and hung in a cool, dry place to air-dry. Eventually it was shelled out and the seed preserved for the coming year in a safe place protected from rats and mice.[14]

Meanwhile, he fought a constant battle with the pests to which the tobacco plants were heir. He had to be alert against the small flies and flea beetles that could soon destroy all the seedlings if they were not removed. Robert made an infusion of sassafras bark and kept it always on hand to spray the seedlings to keep them free of the flies.

During the first weeks after transplanting, he again had to watch out for cutworms and hornworms that developed in the soil and would come out and cut off the shoots. Equally destructive were the aphids and slugs; and finally, when the young plants had grown to full size and strength, he was faced with the problem of tobacco caterpillars. These often arrived in great numbers and covered the tobacco planting. It seemed to young Benjamin that there could be no other plant that required as much time and attention as did tobacco, for it was usually his lot to watch for the insects and to get rid of them as they appeared. When he was old enough, he joined his parents with their farmwork in the spring, and again at various times of the year in grubbing the soil to prepare for the transplantation of the seedlings. There was little pleasure in wielding a mattock or grubbing hoe; each night he went to bed exhausted. He preferred the hilling hoe rather than the mattock, because that phase of the work was somewhat more interesting although just as exhausting. To prepare the hills he had to stand with his foot advanced, whereas with the hilling hoe he had to throw the soil from all sides around his leg, then withdraw his foot and flatten the top of the hill. Later, when the young shoots started to come up, he used yet another hoe to chop out the weeds that grew profusely, particularly during the hot spells.

The most active time in the summer was August, when the

tobacco plants had come to perfection, about six weeks or so after topping. Robert waited for a period of dry weather, when there was a minimum of wind, before cutting the plants. He and his family worked quickly, letting the leaves lie on the ground for not more than half a day until they drooped down on the stalks. Then they collected the stalks and brought them to their tobacco house on their shoulders. There they split the ends of the stalks, and as fast as they had been prepared they were hung on tobacco sticks as closely together as possible without touching. Here they were allowed to remain for five or six weeks. The crop was ready for the next operation when the stalk in the middle of the leaf would snap by bending it. Then when the air had sufficiently moistened the leaves so that they could be handled without breaking, they were struck down and stripped from the stalks. Finally they were bound up into bundles and packed into hogsheads for use.

After the first year or two that he had been working on his farm, Robert was able to estimate the crop yield per acre and per year. One thousand pounds of tobacco yield per acre was considered good in his time, and he strove to achieve it. Each acre required from four hundred to five hundred man-hours of work, and he probably was able to produce a maximum of two thousand pounds of tobacco in a year, with an equal amount totaled from the efforts of Mary and young Benjamin. This yield was in addition to a few barrels of corn.

There is great range in the estimates of tobacco production per hand in the seventeenth and eighteenth centuries in the colonies of Virginia and Maryland. In 1619, 1,143 pounds per worker was claimed by John Pory in Virginia, while one Richard Brewster claimed to have produced an average of 700 pounds per man in addition to a crop of corn. Estimates of the normal production per man at the beginning of the eighteenth century ranged from 1,000 to 2,700 pounds per man, so that it would be reasonable to consider that Robert Banneky, with his limited facilities, probably produced an average somewhere between those two amounts.[15]

The tobacco was prepared for shipment in hogsheads, which Robert purchased from the cooper at Elkridge Landing or at another river town. The size and details of construction were regulated by law to ensure that the volume of each hogshead was always the same and measurable. In Maryland the hogshead was required to be forty-eight inches high by thirty-two inches in diameter at the head with "a bulge proportionable." [16]

Robert delivered the tobacco in hogsheads to tobacco brokers at the landings. He was paid for it in tobacco notes, and the broker in turn shipped it to the English market on the seagoing vessels which came into the bay and up to the landings. The tobacco notes of the merchants specified the net weight received, the name of the warehouse, and the type of tobacco, whether it was Oronoko, or sweet-scented, stemmed, or leaf. These notes were readily negotiable within the same county or in adjacent counties and could be used as legal tender. They were widely used for the payment of taxes, fees, and other similar purposes.

The cultivation of tobacco was not particularly hard work, but it required continuous attention from seeding time in the early spring until the next seeding, except for that interval during the late autumn and winter when the frost prevented any work on the crop. Tobacco growing held many hazards which could reduce a planter to poverty in one or two seasons. The threat of crop failure due to the weather was ever present, and it was also possible to ruin an entire crop by improper curing or by inadequate prizing into the hogsheads. A depression in the market due to overproduction might seriously affect the value of a crop, and the quality of the cooperage available also could have an important influence on the sale.

Although the crops of the large plantation owners were generally handled by a London or outport merchant in all details of marketing and transportation, small planters such as Banneky generally sold their crops outright to a factor or agent at one of the landings to which they transported their hogsheads.

The planter received a lower price for his tobacco, but he avoided most of the risks and delays. These factors were agents of large English merchants and resided permanently in the port or landing, working for a salary or on a percentage basis. Frequently they combined a store with their warehouse, in which they kept European and English goods imported from England and the West Indies. They retailed these goods to the planters in exchange for farm products.

Young Benjamin shared the burdens of the farm with his parents. He did not resist the never-ending chores and found much in the daily work to interest him. He calculated, for instance, that the entire process of tobacco cultivation included not less than thirty-six separate operations. Even as a small boy he had a great interest in statistics and in any form of mathematical endeavor, which he developed as he grew older.

The tobacco crop was not the only work that had to be done on the Banneky farm. There was the crop of corn that had to be planted, weeded, hilled, and nurtured until the fall, for this was the crop that fed the family to a large degree. There was also a little wheat grown, but probably not enough to bring to market but merely to satisfy the family needs.

Among Benjamin's chores was "cowpenning," which meant moving their several head of stock from one planting area to another and setting up portable fences around them. The purpose of this task was to accumulate manure to enrich the soil. Whenever time permitted, Benjamin and his father took the farm wagon down to the marshes along Cooper Branch or the Patapsco and shoveled out marsh soil, which consisted of dark, rich loam. This they would bring up to the upper meadows and spread on the ground to dry. Later they cleared it of roots and rocks and used it to build the hills for the planting of a new crop of tobacco.

Judging from studies made of inventories of eighteenth-century Maryland planters, Robert Banneky probably belonged to that class of small planters having an estate worth £100 or less.[17] This would have provided no more than a "country living." In addition to his acreage, his property consisted of not more than half a dozen cows, two saddle horses, a few swine, and a limited assortment of household and farming utensils and tools. It was unlikely that his productivity of tobacco exceeded six hogsheads a year. He probably occasionally sold a heifer, a pig, and some bushels of corn to local traders to supplement his income.

The winter months were almost as active as those of spring and summer, but there was some variety in the tasks which the planter performed during this period. The farm animals had to be cleaned and fed daily, and there were other daily requirements. Robert would spend some of his time felling trees to clear additional acreage, and after the branches had dried, he would burn the brush. The usable wood was sawn into boards, cut into logs, and brought back to the barns and stored for future use. Some of it would be utilized for riving staves or shingles. The planter's wife and daughters would spend their time spinning and weaving and making clothes for the family. Winter was a good time for trapping and hunting, and the pelts acquired would be dried and tanned and used for outer clothing. Fine pelts of desirable animals could be sold to local traders or exchanged for other goods. It was also the time for making farm repairs. On days of good weather the planter would inspect and repair the walls and fences around the farm, prune his orchards of fruit trees, and cultivate his stand of wild grapes.

Much of Benjamin's free time as a small boy was spent at his grandmother's farm, where she taught him to read and write. She was particularly concerned that he should become a religious man. Partly to practice his reading and partly to learn its contents, on every Sabbath day she had Benjamin read to her from her copy of the Bible. She had sent to England for it, and it was described by her grandchildren as being a volume of large size. It was one of Molly's few treasures, which she enjoyed sharing with her young grandson. He soon outstripped her in information and became especially interested in the history of the province and its early settlers. She was impressed with the agility of his mind, ability to learn quickly, and his remarkable memory even as a child. The hours she spent with him were filled with pleasure, and she looked forward eagerly to his visits.

Molly taught young Benjamin all she knew, and the ability to read and write delighted him immeasurably, opening great new worlds for him. His father and mother were very proud of his achievement and hopeful for his future. Molly arranged to send Benjamin to a small country school that had recently been established in the neighborhood. The one-room school was kept open only during the winter months and was taught by one schoolmaster. It was attended by several white children and two or three black children who received instruction together. Jacob Hall, a classmate, later recalled Benjamin's consuming interest in study even then, saying that as a boy Benjamin was not particularly fond of play or light amusements, and that "all his delight was to dive into his books." [18]

Little is known about Benjamin's associates as a boy or as a man, but their numbers were necessarily limited by the remoteness of his home and the needs of the farm. Attendance at the country school became a major event in the boy's life, leaving a profound impression on him later. Jacob Hall, who remained his life-long friend, was, like Benjamin, a free Negro, whose father had been a slave belonging to Walter Hall, a wealthy planter in Anne Arundel County. The elder Hall had been given his freedom and a bonus of thirteen acres of land in Baltimore County in reward for his faithful service. Benjamin and Jacob maintained a friendship from childhood for the remainder of their lives. When Jacob was older, he was employed for more than forty years as the keeper of the graveyard of the Society of Friends of Elkridge Landing. He and his family continued to hold the land given to his father until late in the nineteenth century.

Because of the short session, Banneker's schooling was limited. When he was old enough to work with his father full time, it was no longer possible to attend classes. He especially enjoyed arithmetic and all similar mathematical exercises.

Although unable to continue his schooling, Benjamin nevertheless pursued his reading, and he continued his education in this manner for the rest of his life. He had no books of his own, other than the use of his grandmother's Bible, but it is possible that his former schoolmaster may have lent him texts to use at home. He later commented that he had "advanced in arithmetic as far as Double Position" by his own efforts.[19] It seems fairly certain that Benjamin was not taught Double Position in the country school but learned it by himself later. Double Position is no longer a familiar term, but it was included in school texts as late as the mid-nineteenth century. In Eaton's *Treatise* "the Method of Double Position" is given for the purpose of obtaining an answer that would now be handled with an equation by any high school freshman algebra student. In Double Position a value is assumed for the number to be derived, which is inserted into given conditions, computed, and then it can be seen how far wrong the result may be. One then repeats, and since by this time the number sought has been bracketed, the correct solution is achieved.*

The years passed quickly for young Benjamin on his father's farm, and with each season he explored more and more of the natural wonders around him. He spent his spare time roaming through the cleared fields and in the neighboring forests. He soon learned to appreciate the wild beauty of his surroundings, which were most unusual and unmatched elsewhere in the county.

Not more than a mile from his house the mighty Patapsco River flowed over its rocky bed enclosed on both sides by chains of uncultivated hills. The water ran its course with a mighty sound along its bed laden with broken rocks not yet worn

---

* The rule or method of Double Position has been known from antiquity, sometimes by other names. In Europe, for instance, it was also known as the Rule of Double False.

smooth. Some of them projected above the surface and the river dashed angrily against them, creating an unceasing, sepulchral roar. Along the looming hills on either side, the trees were stunted because of the poor soil, and they bent almost horizontally in an effort to survive, with their sparse foliage barely shading the ground. A scrubby undergrowth with large patches of yellow sandy soil covered the unwooded areas, surrounded by great stands of tall trees along the water's edge and covering the hilltops. Within a short distance from the river was a spring of cool, soft water protected by a grove of tall trees which was traditionally claimed to have been a camp ground used by Indians when they came down from the northern region to fish. Shad and herring were taken in great numbers high up in the Patapsco before the mills were built and the new mill dams provided obstruction.

During his boyhood and into his manhood, Banneker was very much alone. Limited in his travel and association with others by the rigorous requirements of the farm, he saw few people other than his parents, his sisters, and some relatives. His family did not share his literary and educational interests although they were impressed with his enthusiasm and evident capabilities. Consequently, he became more and more withdrawn into himself, and his senses became all the more alert to the world around him. He developed a keen awareness of nature and became deeply observant of the habits of all living things in the wild life of the region.

Throughout his youth Banneker's unusual ability with matters of mathematics was apparent. He was equally interested and skilled in mechanics, and there were many opportunities for him to apply them in running his farm. Almost to the advent of the Revolutionary War, tidewater Maryland had no established shops of public craftsmen such as blacksmiths, tinkers, cobblers, or tailors. Men with such skills did exist, but they were few and itinerant, traveling about the province from one plantation or community to another. It was necessary for the farmer or plantation owner to have his own skilled artisans if he could afford them, or to buy tools with which to perform the most necessary functions himself.

It was while he was still a very young man that Banneker achieved a piece of work that made him famous in his community and in literature. This first scientific achievement was associated with a theme that preoccupied him during the major part of his life. This was the theme of Time. In all of his young life he had seen but two timepieces. One was a sundial; the other was a pocket watch. When or how he saw these timepieces is not known, and the fact that a borrowed watch served as a model for the clock he subsequently constructed is based on Banneker's own statement which he made to neighbors. There is no evidence that he tried to copy the sundial, which was probably a pewter dial cast in a soapstone mold, a type then in common use. Soapstone was available in the region of Ellicott's Lower Mills and was mined commercially in certain parts of Maryland during the nineteenth and twentieth centuries.

Interestingly enough, such a dial, made by or for George Ellicott in 1779 for the latitude of 40°, has survived.*

It is not known whose watch he borrowed. It may have belonged to a merchant at one of the landings where he brought his tobacco for sale, or to a traveling man who came through the region. The watch aroused his latent mechanical skill. Its intricate mechanism captured his mind completely. There is every evidence that he was a most acute observer, that he noted everything in detail, and that he remembered accurately what he had seen. There is no greater evidence of this ability than in the construction of his clock.

Banneker conveyed his memories of the wheelwork of the

---

* The soapstone mold for this sundial was owned by the late Colonel Henry D. Paxson of Philadelphia, who had acquired it in Bucks County, Pennsylvania. Several castings were made from it, and one of these was deposited in the Smithsonian Institution in 1900. The dial bears the date "1779" and the initials "G. E.," which are believed to be those of George Ellicott. The mold would have been made about seven years after George Ellicott arrived with his relatives to found Ellicott's Lower Mills. He would then have been about nineteen years old.

watch into drawings, then applied his natural mathematical skill
into calculating the relative size and number of teeth of the
wheels. First he drew a diagram of the wheels and gears, balance
regulator, and spring barrel, then converted these into three-
dimensional parts. He labored long over the project, carving the
wheels and pinions from selected pieces of hard-grained wood
that he had collected and seasoned for the purpose, fashioning
each part with a knife, carefully laying out the teeth of the
wheels and pinions, and modifying the parts one by one as required to fit them together. At last the movement was finished,
and it was a successful striking clock made entirely of wood,
except for occasional parts of iron and brass wherever necessary.
Banneker then went on to make an appropriate dial and casing
for it, and this miracle of untutored craftsmanship actually
worked. Banneker's own pleasure in it was equaled only by the
wonder and astonishment of people who visited the farmhouse
and saw it. His fame spread rapidly through the valley. Those
who had known nothing about Benjamin Banneker the farmer
learned about him as the maker of a fascinating timepiece. He
was only twenty-two years old at the time, and his achievement
was looked upon as remarkable.

It will be useful here to discuss clocks and watches in tidewater Maryland during the first half of the eighteenth century.
Timepieces were well known on the American continent from
the very first English settlements. Clockmakers flourished in the
larger cities soon after the colonies were established in the seventeenth century. Often they were craftsmen who combined the
making of clocks and watches with other skills such as silver-
smithing or pewtering; generally they had been trained in England.

Clocks and watches were frequently called for by Chesapeake planters. When consigning tobacco being shipped to their
factors in London, planters customarily asked the latter to purchase needed articles such as clothing, tools, and furnishings.
Records have survived of such orders made by Edward Lloyd,
the seventh member of his family bearing the name, of Wye

House. In correspondence with his London factors, Messrs. Oxley, Hancock & Co., he requested the latter to provide him with ". . . an elegant Watch Clock, proper to fix on a Chimney Piece; also a Sett of fashionable Decorations to set off a Dining or Supper Table that will accomodate 20 People . . ." [20]

It is doubtful that Banneker had ever seen a book about clockmaking; such volumes were rare even in large communities. The literature of the region consisted primarily of imported English periodicals such as *The Spectator, The Tattler* and *The Gentleman's Magazine,* and the regional newspapers. Books on religion and the works of the poets were popular, especially Addison, Pope, Shakespeare, Milton, and Dryden. Other books were undoubtedly available from time to time, including school texts and handbooks on building trades, surveying, navigation, and related subjects. The source of Banneker's technical knowledge about striking clocks remains a mystery. Completed in 1753, his clock continued to operate until his death, more than fifty years later.

During a visit to his home by Mrs. George Ellicott and some friends in 1790, her daughter noted that

> . . . his clock struck the hour, and at their request he gave them an account of its construction. With his inferior tools, with no other model than a borrowed watch, it had cost him long and patient labor to perfect it. It required much study to produce a concert of correct action between the hour, minute and second machinery, and to cause it to strike the hours. He acknowledged himself amply repaid for all his cares in its construction by the precision with which it marked the passing time. . . .[21]

A number of watch- and clockmakers were already established in Maryland prior to the time that Banneker made his clock. In Annapolis alone there were at least four such craftsmen prior to 1750. Among these may be mentioned John Batterson, a watchmaker who moved to Annapolis in 1723; James Newberry, a watch- and clockmaker who advertised in the *Maryland Gazette* on July 20, 1748; John Powell, a watch- and clockmaker believed to have been indentured and to have been working in 1745; and Powell's master, William Roberts.

On July 10, 1759, when Banneker was twenty-eight years old, Robert Banneky died. Burdened now with the entire responsibility for the farm and the care of his mother and sisters, Banneker had little time for his studies and pleasures. According to the terms of the original deed, the entire farm became his own, without shares for his mother and sisters. "Timber Poynt," the first tract of land which Robert had acquired, was probably divided at Robert's death among his three daughters.

By this time Banneker's sisters had married and had left the family roof. Very little information concerning them is available, but it is known that each of them was married and settled in the vicinity. Banneker's second sister, Minta, married a young man named Black, while Molly, the youngest sister, married a man named Morten. Her son, Greenbury Morten, was well known in the region and was later employed at Ellicott's Lower Mills. Whether Minta's husband was a relative of the William Black who had married her Aunt Esther cannot be determined.

Meanwhile, Molly Banneky had died. No record of the death can be found in any of the surviving documents, nor is the disposition of her farm recorded. Presumably the land was inherited by her other daughters.

Following in the direction established by his father, Banneker was a competent farmer. His contemporaries reported that he owned two horses and several cows, besides a number of beehives from which the honey was collected and sold. He cultivated a large garden in which he grew vegetables and other staples for his own use and for sale at market. He raised grain, including wheat and corn for his immediate use, but the main effort of the farm was in the growing of tobacco for the market.

According to the Tax List for Patapsco Upper Hundred for the year 1773, Banneker was taxed as the only adult member of his household.* This implied that his mother was no longer living, yet other records indicate that she was alive at least until the middle of 1775. Banneker's name has otherwise been found in civil records only in connection with property transfers, with one exception. He registered a stray animal before Justice Gay at Joppa on October 31, 1761.†

A memorable event in Banneker's life was the acquisition of his first book. At the age of thirty-two, he bought a quarto edition of the Holy Bible, on the flyleaf of which he proudly inscribed:

> I bought this book of Honora Buchanan the 4th day of January 1763. B. B.

Two other entries relating to events in his life were made in the Bible at approximately the same time:

> Benjamin Banneker was born November the 9th, in the year of the Lord God, 1731.

> Robert Banneker departed this life July the 10th, 1759.[22]

In many of his lonely hours, Banneker turned to music. He owned a flute and a violin, and had learned to play both reasonably well. He never mentioned later in life what had led to his interest in music, where he had acquired the instruments, or how he had learned to play them. After the day's work was over, he enjoyed sitting outside his house and softly playing one or the other. Sometimes the members of his family would join him in the twilight, often singing the words when he played a familiar

---

* The Baltimore County Tax List for Patapsco Upper Hundred listed "Benjamin Banneker,—1 taxable." This document is preserved in the Department of Legislative Reference, City Hall, Baltimore, Maryland.

† Noted in the *Court Proceedings* for Joppa, Maryland, for the year 1761.

song. Banneker found utmost satisfaction in the sounds he produced. He undoubtedly had purchased the flute and one or two music books from the stocks imported by one of the larger planters in the area, and he may have traded or purchased the violin from a neighbor at some time in his youth. The pleasure he derived from music, supplemented by the few books he owned, together with his enjoyment of mathematical puzzles, helped to while away the few hours of leisure in the solitude of his farm.

During the decade or more after his father's death, Banneker lived alone with his mother. He was acquainted with the planters in the valley and with the itinerant tradesmen who occasionally passed through the area, but he had no real friends, nor did he seek them. The fact that he was a free man of color restricted his activities in the community. He had learned as a small boy that although the industriousness of his family was respected, there were barriers that could not be hurdled. Banneker was relatively contented with his lot, and he sought to avoid conflicts dealing with the limitations of his station.

As the years went on, however, he became known in the region as a man of some learning. Reading and writing were skills rarely found except among the wealthy plantation owners and their families. His neighbors came to him for assistance in making calculations for one purpose or another, for composing the few letters needed, and for help in other simple matters. As a result, he became a well-known figure, much admired for his dignity, reticence, and gentlemanly qualities. Many came just to see his striking clock, which gradually had become something of a legend in the valley, and for each visitor Banneker left his work to display his achievement with modesty and pride.

III

⟨꙰⟩

FRIENDS AND NEIGHBORS

✦❖✦❖✦❖✦❖✦❖✦❖✦❖✦❖✦

We must think well of that man, who uses his best endeavours to associate with none but virtuous friends.
Banneker's Almanac for 1794

THE MOST IMPORTANT INFLUENCES in Benjamin's life were derived from those individuals who increased his learning. The first
of these had been his grandmother, Molly Welsh. The second
was the unknown Quaker schoolteacher from whom he received
the rudiments of an elementary education. The third was George
Ellicott, who became his neighbor as a young boy and who be-
friended him as a young man. Although twenty-nine years his
junior, George was to become Banneker's friend and the one
who brought about the major fulfillment in his life.

The history of the Ellicott family in America began with
the migration of Andrew Ellicott [I], a wool manufacturer in

England. During a period of business reverses, he came to America with his eldest son, Andrew [II], for a visit to the community of Buckingham in Bucks County, Pennsylvania. During this brief sojourn, the younger Andrew fell in love with a local girl named Ann Bye, whom he later married. He and his father remained in Pennsylvania permanently and never returned to England. In the course of time Andrew [II] and Ann Ellicott became the parents of five sons, Joseph, Andrew [III], Nathaniel, Thomas, and John. When Andrew [II] died in 1741, he left little property, and his family found itself in dire circumstances. A local business associate, Samuel Armitage, undertook the guardianship of the children and found trades for them as they grew older.

Joseph Ellicott, the eldest of the sons, was placed with the family of a man who wove and combed worsted, Andrew [III] went to live with a house carpenter, and Nathaniel made his home with a blacksmith. Thomas and John were still too young to leave their mother.

Armitage noticed that young Joseph had become a good weaver and that he was extremely alert and active. Furthermore, Joseph displayed a preoccupation with mechanics, which led him to seek employment with a millwright named Samuel Bleaker, where he soon developed experience in repairing gristmills. He later married Judith Bleaker, his employer's daughter, and their infant son was named Andrew [IV]. Shortly after his marriage he moved back to his mother's farm, having become unwilling to continue with the weaving craft. With the reluctant support of Armitage, and utilizing the skills of his four brothers, Joseph built a gristmill before he had reached the age of twenty-one. The mill was successful, and the Ellicott brothers became known throughout Bucks County for their mechanical ability.

In 1766 Joseph learned that he had come into a large legacy of property from his late great-grandfather in Cork, Ireland. He journeyed to Great Britain to claim his inheritance and there met several important men of science who influenced his later career. He sold the estate for a substantial amount, then returned to Pennsylvania. He was elected high sheriff and remained in that office in 1768 and 1769, serving also as a member of the provincial assembly.

Meanwhile the Ellicott brothers, having achieved success in Pennsylvania, sought new fields to conquer and new areas in which to expand with the construction of new modern grist-mills of their own design. They became interested in the nearby province of Maryland. Their successful gristmill was owned by Armitage, and the brothers became impatient to establish themselves independently. Joseph in particular was restless. He was forty-four years old and wished to strike out on his own. The brothers took time and care in making their decision. They traveled on horseback through a great part of the middle counties of Maryland, seeking a region in which cereals and wheat could be grown for which their mills would be utilized.

They finally selected two tracts of land lying between the Patapsco River and the Blue Ridge Mountains. They established a mill site near the falls of the Patapsco about ten miles west of Baltimore. The Ellicott brothers acquired approximately seven hundred acres, the major part of which they purchased, reputedly at a cost of about three dollars per acre, from William Williams, a wealthy English merchant and iron founder. He owned considerable tracts of land throughout the region, some of which adjoined the Banneker farm.

When the Ellicotts first visited the area, Williams was operating a large store which he had established many years before. It was situated on a lofty hill in what is now Oella, overlooking the span of the river where the Union Manufacturing Company Works was later established. It was the largest store for many miles around; every spring and fall he imported from England large stocks of goods for every purpose, which were brought in by the vessels plying the tobacco trade. When the new goods arrived Williams announced the occasion by a cannon installed on a high point of the Patapsco hills and which when fired sent its roar reverberating through the region. The residents came from many miles around to buy their needs, on foot along the old Indian paths, and on horseback along the trails and tobacco roads, and along the river on barges. The planters found in his store tools, cloth, books, and the many other commodities so necessary to their way of living.

The Ellicotts acquired the balance of their land from Emmanuel Teal, who owned considerable property in the area. The Ellicott holdings embraced both sides of the river for a distance of four miles and included all the water rights within that span. This was of particular value because a Maryland law of 1669 permitted any man who constructed a water mill to take up twenty acres of land on either side of the stream ". . . and hold the same at the valuation of jurors for eighty years." It was on this land that the brothers began the construction of their new community, which was called Ellicott's Lower Mills.

At the time the Ellicotts arrived, no roads worthy of the name approached "The Hollow." The road from Elkridge Landing ended abruptly within a mile of the site of the future mills at the foot of a great barrier of huge rocks and precipices. The plantations were connected by horseback trails or old Indian trails in addition to the several rolling roads. The only road worthy of the name was the old Frederick Road, built by German settlers of Frederick about 1760. Communication with the outer world was even less frequent. In 1695 the provincial Assembly had established the post rider as a public official to carry the mail from Potomack (now Georgetown, D.C.) to Philadelphia eight times a year, for an annual salary of fifty pounds. John Larkin was the first such officer appointed. One of his regular stops was Elkridge Landing.

Another important factor in the selection of the site was its position in relation to the several major river towns or seaports in that region, which would be a major consideration in marketing the mill's products.

Besides being near Elkridge Landing and Joppa on the Patapsco, The Hollow was within ten miles of the new Baltimore Town, which was a growing modern community, in a region that was still virtually a wilderness. It was in 1727 that the Maryland legislature had authorized the layout of the town on the site of what was then the farm of John Flemming, and by 1740 Baltimore was still little more than a fort, with a wooden board fence around it to protect the inhabitants from the Indians. As late as 1754 Baltimore consisted of not more than twenty houses constructed on the right side of Jones' Falls.

By 1768 Baltimore had grown to such proportions that it demanded and obtained the county seat from Joppa. With the removal of its legislative functions, Joppa slowly lost its position as a commercial center, gradually dwindled in importance, until today its existence is remembered only by a solitary gravestone. The same fate awaited Elkridge Landing and from the same cause. The growing commercial importance of Baltimore, with its greater accessibility and dependable water front closer to the bay, caused the cargoes to go left along the Patapsco. Equally critical was the receding of the waters of the Patapsco at the Landing, which no longer made it possible to receive the ships that formerly came to its wharves. Although Baltimore County was not directly exposed to any major Indian war, nor to the Indian invasions from which other parts of the province suffered between 1749 and 1759, Baltimore City found it necessary to erect defenses. Braddock's defeat, and the advance of the French and Indians, created great fear and consternation in Maryland. Many inhabitants of western settlements fled to Baltimore because it had a great wooden stockade built around it in an earlier period. Rumors of forthcoming invasion of interior settlements by the French and Indians periodically led to the mustering of several companies of volunteers recruited from Baltimore and vicinity and marched out without delay. In the winter and spring of 1756 raiding parties of Indians occasionally came to within thirty miles of Baltimore, spreading terror throughout the region. These hostilities, which lasted more than a decade, prevented the establishment of new settlements by the great number of German "Palatines" and other emigrants who came into the area, and they were compelled to take refuge in the larger towns. The population of Baltimore consequently increased, and it developed into an important young city.

The Ellicott brothers considered the proximity of Ellicott's Lower Mills to Baltimore to be of particular advantage in that the town would provide them with a point of export for their flour. The new mill was a cooperative project, with each of the brothers undertaking a part of the enterprise. Joseph Ellicott was the general superintendent of the project; he spent much time at first commuting between Bucks County and the new installation. John moved to Maryland to live on the premises full time, while Andrew designed the mill buildings that were to be erected. Nathaniel preferred to remain in Pennsylvania, and he subsequently sold his share of the Maryland property to Joseph in exchange for his Buckingham farm.[1]

In January 1771 John and Andrew Ellicott began work on the establishment of their new mills along the Patapsco River. Accompanied by some laborers and two strong teams, they arrived at Croft's Tavern on the old Frederick Road five miles outside Baltimore. It was their project to hew a path through the heavy wilderness from the road to the river. They made slow progress, but managed to cut a way through the wilderness within sight of the water, which was approximately near the present location of the ninth milestone on the Frederick Turnpike. The next stretch was extremely difficult, because the most direct route to the river's shore required cutting their way along the side of a hill for a distance of about a mile, along the strip later known as the "Devil's Elbow." The descent would be very steep and impossible for the horses to go with the wagons. It was not until the end of February that they accomplished this seemingly impossible task, but finally they had forged a way through the forest to The Hollow, the bottom land where the mills were eventually constructed. It was not a pleasant experience, for throughout this rigorous enterprise, each night they heard the wolves howling a short distance from their camp, and wildcats were around them in profusion.

The advent of these tall strangers and their determined although painful conquest of their terrain did not go unnoticed by the inhabitants of the region. Word of the sale of the land, and then of these energetic men as they cut their way into The Hollow flew from one farm and plantation to another. Banneker and his mother were undoubtedly among those to be informed and to keep a constant vigil as the adventurers progressed. Why had they come and what did they plan to do with all the equipment they were transporting? Rumors circulated wildly as the neighbors watched and speculated and waited.

Upon their arrival at the site selected, their first concern was for shelter. They hastily built a shanty and a stable. The next project was the construction of a sawmill, and at the same time they undertook the building of a dam and mill race which was to supply the power for the machinery of both mills. The sawmill was operated up the stream near the present site of the Oella factory and the hewn lumber was floated down the river to the site they had selected for their gristmill.

After these preliminary structures had been completed, the Ellicott brothers were ready to make the great move, which they had planned in considerable detail. They decided to make the journey by water from Philadelphia to New Castle. They assembled their wagons, carts, wheelbarrows, draft horses, household goods of the several families, and their mechanical and agricultural implements, including materials and equipment for the new mill, on board a vessel in the port of Philadelphia.

When the vessel landed at New Castle, the wagons and carts were loaded with the other articles, and the long, slow journey overland across the peninsula began. The brothers and their families moved first across to the Head of Elk (now Elkton). There they loaded their materials once again on another vessel which took them along the Chesapeake Bay to the head of the Patapsco River, and then up the river to Elkridge

Landing (then still known as Patapsco), where they disembarked and unloaded for the last time. From this shipping center, the wagons and carts were loaded once more for an overland journey. They moved along a narrow country road from the Landing until they were within only a mile of their final destination. Here they were forced by the character of the land to change their method of transportation once more. The site of their prospective homes and mills, The Hollow, was a wild valley encompassed on all sides by precipices and great rocks that made wagon travel impossible. The wagons and carts had to be unloaded and the contents carried by parties of men by means of hand barrows until the final destination was reached. Last of all, the wagons were dismantled and carried in detached parts through the rocks, and the horses led separately.

This was an arduous prelude to the beginning of the work itself. Extensive sections of land had to be cleared so that construction could proceed. More temporary shelters had to be provided as more workmen were brought on the scene, and more dams had to be built along the river. Finally, the brothers were ready to begin the construction of the first gristmill, at a point on the river that had been carefully selected for its advantages. The mill was an impressive structure, with its gable end toward the river, and stretched across what later became the turnpike road. The structure was 100 feet long and 36 feet wide, one and a half stories high, and built entirely of stone. It contained five pairs of millstones, each five feet in diameter. The mill was designed with a wide arch underneath the center for the passage of horses with wagons to unload their wheat, corn and rye, which was then hoisted up through the opening in the arch to the top of the mill, where it was processed and cleaned and then brought to the millstones below. At first the Ellicotts did not construct an elevator, nor a conveying screw or a hopper box. These were added later. The flour when ground was carried up manually to the bolting cloths, then passed to the flour chest and packed in sacks and barrels, after which it was lowered through another opening to the mill boys and placed in the carts and wagons waiting below. The mill was completed in 1774, having required two years' labor.

While the mills were being built, the Ellicott brothers did not neglect the problem of transportation. It was essential that they have good means of transportation between their operation and Baltimore Town, and they accordingly improved the rough road they had cut to Croft's Tavern for the use of their flour wagons.

During the first several years that Ellicott's Lower Mills was being constructed, there was no bridge over the Patapsco River, and a ford was used for crossing. Although this sufficed for times of good weather, the river became impassable immediately after heavy rains. The Ellicotts accordingly built the first bridge at a point where the present bridge is now found.

Among the more interested of the local spectators who came to watch the work in progress was Banneker, who had always been fascinated by construction and the use of tools of any kind. As each new project started, he would observe and contribute to the discussion with others who watched. The story that was circulated by the newcomers was that they had come to build a series of great gristmills, but Banneker and the other inhabitants were convinced that the story was in error. Why would these bearded men come such a distance, spending so much money on land and labor to build gristmills, when no grain was being grown anywhere in the region?

Meanwhile, a number of small houses had been built to accommodate the Ellicott brothers and their families. All these smaller buildings were made of stone taken from the several granite quarries which they developed on the site of their new community. The first of the dwellings was a large log house erected on the eastern side of the river, in which were housed the mechanics and laborers whom the Ellicotts had brought from Pennsylvania. It was built as a boardinghouse, with a separate apartment for each family and designed to serve until individual houses could be constructed.

The valley was rich in a variety of trees: oak, hickory,

maple, ash, chestnut, gum, as well as other common varieties. The Ellicott brothers cleared the valley with deliberation, leaving stands of trees for decorative purposes where it was not essential to remove them.[2]

By the time Ellicott's Lower Mills was ready for occupation and production, it had grown into a busy young community. At the last moment, the families of the proprietors were somewhat reluctant to leave Bucks County. The first of the families to come was that of John Ellicott, in 1774, while that of Andrew Ellicott did not make the move until 1797. Joseph Ellicott moved his family in December 1775. In addition to his wife and his own children, he brought also the children of a deceased friend and former neighbor named William Evans. With the advent of the families of the Ellicott brothers, production in the mills was ready to begin. Although the purpose of the mills was to produce flour, no wheat had been grown in the region except for family use. The Ellicotts had anticipated the situation, however, and shortly after their arrival they had cleared fields and planted them in wheat. As soon as the mills were ready for operation, the brothers utilized their own harvest to produce the first flour, which they then took to Baltimore and sold for exporting. In a short time, the neighboring planters realized the potential of the new market and began growing wheat which they provided to Ellicott's mills in abundance.

The arrival of the Ellicotts and their industrious activity were the subject of considerable interest to their established neighbors for many miles around. They came frequently to observe the construction of the buildings as they rose magically one after another where before only a wilderness had existed. The Ellicotts received advice from all sides about their project, and many were those who questioned the wisdom of starting a milling industry in a region where only tobacco was grown. The Ellicotts, who were members of the Society of Friends, were polite to everyone, listened to dire predictions and friendly cautions, and proceeded confidently with their work.

The activity in The Hollow continued to hold Banneker's

keen interest. After a lifetime of peaceful existence it was strange to hear the muffled sounds of unceasing industrial endeavor less than a mile away from his farm. His curiosity frequently brought him to the scene, where he observed the organized activity and cacophony of working noises at close hand. He was intrigued by what he observed, and he visited the scene as often as he could to see what was going on from the seclusion of the hillside. Occasionally he ventured as far as the mills themselves to watch them in operation. He was enthralled by what he saw. The mechanical integrity of the milling operation filled him with admiration. The mills were totally automated; the bags of grain brought to be ground into flour were taken by machinery from the wagons and raised by means of hidden mechanism to the highest part of the mill structure, from which the grain was emptied onto the millstones. After the grain was ground, the meal fell into a bin below from which it was conducted by more machinery to a loading platform where it was poured into barrels standing in a production line. The same machinery loaded the barrels into wagons, which were then driven off to market in Baltimore.

Little by little Banneker became familiar with some of the workmen; eventually he was able to distinguish the proprietors. They were a fascinating breed of men, who seemed to have the same irresistible attraction to mechanics as he did. He kept his distance, however, but it was a very short time after their arrival that he was discovered and sought out by his new neighbors.

The mills built by the Ellicotts were not the first that Banneker had seen. In the past he had occasionally visited two similar installations which existed on the river within three or four miles from his home. These were of the simplest kind, however, where grain was ground for family use for those who did not have handmills. Hood's mill ground only Indian corn while the Dismal Mill, located in what is now Ilchester, ground rye, wheat, and corn.

The Ellicotts were faced with the necessity of obtaining food and other provisions for their workmen until such a time as they could grow their own. Baltimore was too far away for practical purposes, so that a source nearby had to be found. The Banneker farm was conveniently close by, and there they found Banneker and his mother living in comfortable circumstances and capable of providing most of their needs. Mary Banneker agreed to manage the marketing, and almost every day she brought great quantities of poultry, vegetables, fruit, and honey as well as other farm products to the boardinghouse where the laborers were quartered. She was then past seventy, yet she was surprisingly energetic. Mary and Benjamin became well-known figures in the developing new community and Benjamin in particular found great fascination and pleasure in the new people who became his neighbors.

After the boardinghouse, sawmill, flour mill, and a few of the houses had been completed, the Ellicotts undertook to build a store which would serve the many and varied needs of their community. In fact, such a store had already been established on a small scale in one of the apartments of the boardinghouse. There the laborers and Ellicott families, as well as their established neighbors, could purchase the staples, hardware, and other goods they required, and within a very short time a post office was added. The Ellicotts succeeded in establishing a regular mail service, and the small boardinghouse store became the center for the neighboring planters, where they forwarded and collected their mail, where they brought commodities for exchange, and where they purchased what they needed for their own plantations. There they paused to pass the time of day with their neighbors and the "Mill" people, and exchanged the latest news and gossip.

It was at this makeshift country store that Banneker occasionally met the new proprietors. Although his mother was the one who customarily delivered the farm commodities to the boardinghouse, Banneker also found opportunity to call at the store, where he enjoyed listening to the bits of conversations going on around him. He was reticent and quiet, and made himself as unobtrusive as possible. It was his first real opportunity to enjoy the company of a number of people, and eventually he made it a habit to spend his leisure time there. The conversation varied extremely, from the usual comments exchanged between neighbors to discussions of politics and world events. He was especially interested in the men of the Ellicott family, and greatly impressed with their achievements and their goals. Particularly, he found in these leisure hours much food for his unquenchable thirst for knowledge. Little by little he was drawn out into discussions. His conversational powers were described as being of the first order, and he was encouraged to visit the store frequently.[3] The proprietors enjoyed his company and introduced him to many strangers. His natural modest reserve, particularly with individuals with whom he was not well acquainted, gave him an air of great dignity and remoteness. However, when he could be prevailed upon to set this reserve aside, he would join in conversation that was enjoyable to all who listened. He had a great store of traditional lore which he had gathered from listening to others and particularly from the books he read. He could draw on his memory unendingly, and relate anecdotes which fitted the current subject under discussion. One of his favorite topics was the history of the early settlement of the North American continent and the problems and successes of the settlers as they developed the colonies.

During these sessions in the country store, Banneker rarely alluded to himself or to his family, but on occasion he would mention incidents and situations in his own life, relating to his personal struggle for knowledge.

He was particularly interested in the current issues of the times, and was an avid reader of newspapers when he could get them. The first newspaper in Maryland was the *Maryland Gazette*, established in 1745 by Jonas Green, printer to the province. Shortly after the establishment of the Lower Mills, the first newspaper in Baltimore was started by William Goddard. It made its first appearance in 1773, entitled *The Maryland Journal and Baltimore Advertiser*, and Banneker was able to read it regularly at the Ellicott & Co. store.

Mary and Benjamin Banneker were among the first clients of the new store. In a large ledger for the years 1774-1775, a separate account was maintained for Mary Baniker [sic]. Listed was the purchase of a pair of shoes on October 4, 1774, for 9s. 6d., for which she paid cash the next spring. The purchase of unlisted sundries on April 11, 1775, for £1 10s. 10d. was charged against a balance due her, presumably for food she furnished the boardinghouse, leaving a balance owed of one pound. The account for Benjamin Baniker [sic], as entered in this ledger, was more extensive and included a variety of small purchases made at various times from September 1774 to July 1775. Consistent among the entries was the purchase of rum in quantities of a quart or a half gallon each month during that period. He also bought paper, ink, gunpowder, sugar, molasses, cloth, and other necessities. He made periodic payments, and one of them was made on his behalf by Samuel Morton, who was probably the husband of his sister Molly.

An account with Greenbury Morton, Banneker's nephew, revealed that he was employed at both the Lower and Upper Mills in clearing land, and that his labors were repaid by purchases at the store. He was paid at a rate of two shillings a day and occasionally at the higher rate of three shillings. In December 1774 his account was charged "To deduction on the Clearing for being unfinished . . . 5 s." Curiously, the account showed charges against Greenbury's account for payments made to others. Among these were payments to Banneker, who was paid 2s. 6d. on Greenbury's account to Samuel Morton, presumed to have been his father, and to such others as Henry Hissey, "Yr. brother Joshua," and Betty Matthews.[4]

During the years that followed, the War for Independence touched but lightly on Baltimore County, and on Banneker not at all. Free Negroes were exempted from military service in the Continental Army by the Militia Law of 1777. They were eligible to serve by a revision of the law in 1790 but three years later free Negroes were again exempted from military service by a new law which limited such service to white men.

Baltimore had served as the seat of the Congress in 1776 when the British troops moved toward the Delaware River, after which it moved once more to Philadelphia. During the next several years Baltimore became a way station in the passage of troops from the north to the southern provinces, but Maryland did not at any time serve as the scene of conflict. Many of its prominent citizens became important statesmen and soldiers in the war, and Annapolis, the capital city of the province, became a center of political action, although it was not the scene of military activity.

Several members of the Ellicott family played important military roles in the Revolutionary War, although they were members of the Society of Friends. John, the brother who was chiefly responsible for building Lower Mills, lost his right to membership in the Society of Friends because of his involvement in military affairs, but he was reinstated after the war. Jonathan, a brother of George and a son of Andrew Ellicott [III], became a captain of a militia company stationed at Baltimore in 1777, and afterward manufactured the long swords used by officers of the Maryland line and by the dragoons under General Washington's command.

Andrew [IV], the professional surveyor, was commissioned by the Governor of Maryland in 1778 as captain of the Elkridge battalion of the state militia. Before the end of the year he had risen to the rank of major, but he was not in active combat.

George Wall, Jr., a half-brother of the founding Ellicott brothers, had the title of colonel-lieutenant in the County of Bucks. Nathaniel was so much involved in military action that he forfeited his membership in the Society of Friends.

Between 1776 and 1783 the brothers were barely able to sustain themselves at the Mills, and to their own privations due to the war years were the additional problems wrought by the climate and the elements which from time to time caused much damage to the Mills.

Another local manifestation of the war was the French

troops under Colonel Rochambeau's command that halted and remained in Baltimore in 1781 on their return from Yorktown after the surrender. They remained in Baltimore at Sandy Bottom and on Federal Hill until the conclusion of hostilities.

The officers, who were much addicted to field sports, frequently hunted small game in the wooded precincts of the Patapsco River near Ellicott's Lower Mills. They had a favorite spot where they practiced marksmanship day after day. They frequented the store of Ellicott & Co. to make purchases, and tried to improve their knowledge of the English language by conversing with the clerks and the clients.

The war brought considerable hardship to the Ellicott enterprise, however, primarily because of the need for a suitable circulating medium. The Bank of England had provided the only foundation of currency for half the world, but during the war this was no longer available. The several colonies thereupon issued bills of credit to enable internal commerce, which then flooded the country. In addition to their business difficulties, the Ellicotts suffered from the privations of nature. In the spring of 1780 a great freshet in the Patapsco River caused them much damage and loss. The winter had been extremely severe, the water was frozen several feet at the dams, and large masses of ice built up on both sides of the river. The whole countryside was covered with snow many feet in depth. In mid-March, when heavy rains followed an abrupt thaw, the Patapsco flooded. The Ellicotts suffered tragic losses, and much of their property was carried away in the flood tides. Nothing daunted, however, they immediately set to work to rebuild, and they produced better buildings and facilities than before. They received considerable financial assistance from their neighbors, the first Caleb Dorsey (? –1837) and from Charles Carroll of Carrollton.

Other farms and plantations adjacent to the river's reaches suffered violent damage, but Banneker was among those that were spared. The waters rose in Cooper's Branch, flooding a part of his land, but without causing any major destruction. Some of his new tobacco plants were lost, but he had enough land so that he could start a new planting elsewhere on the farm.

The peace of 1783 brought a great change in the economy, and the Ellicott brothers lost no time in adding new improvements to their original mills and developing a variety of associated enterprises.[5] Soon after the proprietors had begun again the operation of the mills, adding stables that could accommodate eighty horses. They then went on to undertake other projects. Among these was a school for the children of their own community and others in the neighborhood. The Ellicotts hired the best teachers available and paid them well. They maintained a control over the curriculum to ensure that the children received the best advantages, and the school flourished. The enrollment increased year by year, until the school became one of the most useful projects undertaken by the Ellicotts.

Ellicott's Lower Mills was a community of rapidly changing character, for year by year new projects were being developed, each of which added new buildings, until soon there was little resemblance to the first primitive settlement. A single contemporary illustration of Ellicott's Lower Mills has survived in a crude drawing made in 1782 by George Ellicott when he was twenty-two years old.* Prominent in the drawing is the stable for eighty horses which were used to haul flour to market at Baltimore. No other buildings were permitted to be built on that side of the river because of the fear of floods, and on occasion as the river rose to alarming heights, the horses would be quickly led out and up the hill behind the stable to save them.†

The last major construction at the Mills was the large warehouse completed in 1790 and situated directly opposite the mills on the road from Baltimore to Frederick. It was constructed of triangular blocks of stone from the granite quarries on the

---

* The original sketch, and a description of it written in 1902 by Lucy Tyson Fitzhugh, granddaughter of George Ellicott, are owned by Mrs. Henry M. Fitzhugh III and Mrs. Charles E. Wilde III.

† Several of the buildings on the sketch may be identified with original buildings which are still standing, including the homes of Jonathan and John Ellicott.

premises and was built by the Spicers, a family of Maryland masons from Harford County. This building was distinguished in this respect from all of the other Ellicott buildings, which were built by Pennsylvanians.

This store and warehouse was carefully planned in advance so that it could accommodate a great variety of goods, with special sections assigned to each. The goods were purchased by agents hired by the Ellicotts, and these agents visited New York and Philadelphia to select items which could be sold at the store for reasonable prices. The goods were then shipped from the city in which they were purchased to Elkridge Landing. Included in the great array of materials were linens and diapers of both fine and coarse quality, silks, satins, brocades, "India china" dinnerware and tea sets, mirrors, mathematical instruments, iron mongery, foodstuffs, and liquors and wines. Articles of finer quality were stored and displayed on shelves behind sashes of glass and in drawers, so that they were protected from dust while easily visible to the purchaser.

The variety of goods, and the careful attention to their protection and handling, brought increased patronage from a wide area around the valley. Many of the planters who had been accustomed to order these same items from their London agents in exchange for the tobacco they exported to England had gradually been converting from tobacco growing to raising wheat and corn, since they found such a ready market for grain at the mills. There they were enabled to engage in the same sort of exchange by means of the store. Even liquors and wines were sold at the store until the discipline of the Society of Friends made it a disownable offense to deal in liquors. After the end of the Revolutionary War the store extended its activities and imported in even greater quantity than before. The Ellicotts dealt for the most part with an English agent in London named Samuel Godfrey, who later joined the Ellicott firm as a partner.

The new store of Ellicott & Co. provided an improved and larger facility for the post office; here the mail was received and forwarded, and newspapers could be purchased. It became the major center of communication not only for the new community but for the entire region. It also served to bring trade to the new store which therefore achieved even greater importance in the region with the development of the main highway between Baltimore and Frederick. Ladies from Baltimore frequently made the eleven-mile journey to the Mills to shop at the new store, where they found many choice materials and other items for their homes. The store flourished until about 1800 but was abandoned and torn down soon afterward.

Among the frequent visitors to the store were Banneker and his mother. News of the arrival of shipments of merchandise spread quickly and the natives of the region were among the first to come to the store to review the goods as they were placed on display, although less frequently to purchase them. While Mary searched through the selections of fabrics and household materials, Banneker looked over the farm tools, books, and periodicals with equal interest.

The major effort of the Ellicott enterprise was planned to be the export of flour to England from Baltimore, and in anticipation they purchased a water lot in Baltimore upon which they erected a wharf and a warehouse. The Baltimore operation was then assigned to Elias, the young son of Andrew Ellicott, who later became the main liaison at Baltimore for the numerous family industries as they developed.

Meanwhile, soon after the project was well underway, Joseph decided to withdraw from the firm. A division of property was made, and in 1774 he purchased the property and gristmill of James Hood, some three miles above the Lower Mills on the Patapsco River.*

The Hood mill was a small one, originally built in 1768 for grinding Indian corn, and Joseph had it torn down and replaced with another larger mill in which were incorporated all of the

* Transferred by indenture dated December 31, 1774, from Benjamin Hood to Joseph Ellicott, a tract of 157 acres for 1,700 pounds in Maryland currency.

latest inventions and modifications which he and his brothers had developed. He added a storehouse for merchandise, stables, houses for laborers, and finally a fine mansion for his own family.

The residence was a large two-story building built on the north side of the road and west of Patapsco Falls, with a number of extra rooms in a gabled third floor. At the end of the gable facing the highway, Joseph installed a large round clock which would serve to tell passersby the time of day. Surrounding the house was a large garden which incorporated useful as well as decorative elements, and which featured a fish pond and a constantly flowing fountain that threw water ten feet high. From the same source, which was a natural spring on the high land west of the house, Joseph supplied the entire garden and provided a water supply for the first two floors of the house. His home was tastefully furnished and became the conversation piece of the region.

At the time of the establishment of Ellicott's Lower Mills, there were two rolling roads and two "rolling landings" in the vicinity. One was described in old deeds as "the rolling road from the head of Patapsco to Dogwood Branch" and the other as "the Ragland rolling road." Both followed a direction approximately south and southeast to a landing at the head of tidewater at or near Elkridge Landing.

The Baltimore–Frederick Turnpike was at that time a very rough thoroughfare, almost impassable at many points during the winter. The road crossed the Patapsco River about four miles above the level of the Banneker farm, at the point where James Hood erected his mill, and continued to Elkridge Landing, the next large community. Many sections of the road were overhung with precipices and great rocks along its sides as it rose out of The Hollow.

Soon after the Lower Mills had been completed, the founding brothers decided to open a wagon road from the Mills to Baltimore, to be built at the expense of their firm, Ellicott & Co. This was to be followed immediately by another wagon road to connect the Mills with Frederick Town in the other direction. This part of the highway would pass by Carroll's Manor, which was the property of Charles Carroll of Carrollton, then the wealthiest capitalist and the most prominent banker in the province of Maryland. The Ellicotts negotiated with him and mortgaged a part of their land for a loan to finance their enterprise, and at the same time they obtained his support for the proposed road to Frederick Town.

The survey and laying out of both sections of the road were the responsibility of young George Ellicott. He was the fourth son of Andrew, the second of the founding brothers. George was only twelve years old when the families moved to Maryland. He had a natural inclination for the sciences, and was undoubtedly encouraged in these studies by his uncle Joseph. He was taught surveying by George Wall, Jr., who had accompanied his half-brothers in their new enterprise. Wall was well known in his native Bucks County as a professional surveyor, "conveyancer," and as a teacher in a private school. During the first years at the Mills, he trained young George so that the latter was fully competent as a surveyor by the time he was sixteen. Wall returned to Bucks County in 1778 and several years later he presented George with his own copy of Gibson's work on surveying.[6]

George's work on the Turnpike proved to be most satisfactory. The section connecting Baltimore with Ellicott's Lower Mills and reaching as far as Carroll's Manor was constructed entirely at the expense of Ellicott & Co. The cost of the section of road from Carroll's Manor to Frederick Town was paid in part by the planters who owned plantations along its route. Although at first it was only a wagon road, it soon developed into the main thoroughfare between the growing communities which formed its terminals; the new road was three miles shorter than the earlier one. George Ellicott's maps of his road survey, which were executed in his own hand, have survived until recent times.

An interesting feature of this highway construction was

what may have been the first mobile kitchen. The Ellicotts, faced with providing food and lodging for the laborers, all of whom were from Pennsylvania, constructed a mobile house which was drawn by horses. In its interior were beds and bedding, besides cooking facilities for everything but bread. It was moved along the route as the roadbuilding progressed. To eighteenth-century Maryland it was a new concept in organized efficiency and reflected many of the other innovations introduced in the Mills.

The development of Ellicott's Lower Mills and subsequently of Ellicott's Upper Mills took place rapidly over a period of five or six years, during which Banneker had become a familiar figure at the mills, and particularly at the Ellicott & Co. store. Because of his mechanical and scientific interests it is not surprising that he became acquainted with young George. The latter had heard a great deal about the unusual farmer from members of his family and others who had already met him and he was curious about a neighbor with similar concerns. The first meetings may have taken place in the family store, but thereafter George frequently visited Banneker's cabin to talk with him. There he discovered and examined the remarkable striking clock, looked over Banneker's meager library, and found much in common with his own interests. Although Banneker was forty-seven while George was only eighteen, they were drawn together by similarities of mind. Banneker learned much from George Ellicott over the long period of their association, but there can be no doubt that young George also profited. The friendship developed without concern for or apparent awareness of the color barrier, which they bridged as easily as they had the difference of age.

Banneker also developed an association with Joseph Ellicott, as a result of their mutual interest in clockmaking. Joseph had constructed a repeating watch prior to 1766, which he took with him on his visit to England. There he met James Ferguson, the popular lecturer on astronomy, and a relative named John Ellicott, who was one of England's foremost clockmakers.

There seems no doubt that Joseph spent some time with his cousin in England, and possibly even studied with him briefly before his return to Pennsylvania. At any rate, he brought back with him a wide variety of clockmaker's tools, as well as a number of timepieces. Shortly after his return, with the assistance of his son, Andrew IV, who was then fifteen years of age, Joseph constructed a large tall-case clock made in the form of a four-sided pillar almost eight feet high. The clock had four faces. One represented the sun, earth, and moon, as well as the other planets shown revolving in their separate orbits around the sun. One dial marked the hours, minutes, and seconds as well as the days, months, and years, in addition to the moon phases. The third dial marked the names of twenty-four musical tunes which played one each hour, with a pointer that could be set against any named tune and would repeat it. The fourth face was a glass plate through which the wheelwork could be observed. The clock became a great conversation piece, and Joseph brought it with him to Ellicott's Mills. He designed the great hall of his mansion to accommodate the clock so that it could be prominently and proudly displayed to all visitors. The clock was first mentioned in the published account of a French traveler in the United States, M. Ferdinand-M. Bayard, who visited the Mills en route to Virginia in the summer of 1791, eleven years after the death of Joseph Ellicott, and the clock at Joseph's residence was shown to him by Joseph, Jr.[7]

Joseph Ellicott had also brought with him from Buckingham several other tall-case clocks he had made and which subsequently became the property of various members of the family. None of them was as elaborate as the four-faced clock, however.

Joseph Ellicott learned of Banneker's horological achievement and in due course of time invited him to the Upper Mills, where he demonstrated the other horological mechanisms he had devised, as well as the great clock. Banneker was amazed and intrigued by what he saw but there is no evidence that there was a continuing relationship between the two men.

Banneker was forty-one years old when the Ellicott families first arrived in The Hollow, and it was not until approximately seventeen years later that he first undertook his studies of astronomy. Among his early interests in the newcomers must have been the surveying for the turnpike, which Banneker observed with serious attention. Conceivably it was during this early period that young George lent Banneker his texts and his surveying instruments with which the latter experimented on his own farm.

The advent of the Ellicott brothers and the establishment of Lower Mills and later of Upper Mills brought about a great change in the tenor of Banneker's life. No longer was he surrounded by only the quiet solitude of the natural life of the hills and fields around his farm. There was now a teeming new community within a short walk from his home, to which he gravitated more and more. The near presence of young George Ellicott and his resources for study provided Banneker with a new font for his avid thirst for knowledge. George's occasional visits to his home were memorable, for the former was interested not only in the sciences but had a love and knowledge of English literature as well, which they shared. Not the least of the new advantages was the Ellicott & Co. store, where he periodically perused the merchandise imported from overseas and where he occasionally found inexpensive books which he purchased for his own small library.

Although he continued the habits of his solitary existence as before, and shared his home life only with his mother and with visits to and from other members of his family, there was now a difference in Banneker's life. He was no longer completely alone in his interests, and the Mills formed his first major link with the outer world.

Meanwhile, George Ellicott developed interest and competence in other sciences as well. Encouraged by his uncle Joseph and by Wall, and possibly by his cousin, Andrew, as well, he became interested in astronomy. Little by little he acquired texts and instruments which were imported through the London agent of the store of Ellicott & Co. Among these was a pair of globes, one terrestrial and the other celestial, made by one of the popular English makers of mathematical instruments of that period. They were probably the work of George Wright of London. Although the globes have not been located, George Ellicott's copy of a treatise by Wright which describes their use has survived,[8] with a note by his daughter pasted inside the cover:

> This copy of the Use of the Globes was purchased by my father in 1789, to accompany a pair of globes, which he desired to make useful to his friends, and often in fine mild weather, after finding the Planets places on the Celestial Globe, and placing their "signs" upon them, he would have the Globe placed on a table in the front of his house, out of reach of the trees, and deliver a gratuitous lecture on Astronomy. He was the best amateur Astronomer I ever met with, and my remembrance of his kindness in giving gratuitous instruction to enquirers of every class, is still grateful to my memory, now nearly 35 years since he left the earth.
> 3rd mo. 1st 1867.   Martha E. Tyson.

The Wright treatise on the globes was extremely useful, and George supplemented his scientific apparatus with the purchase of several fine telescopes made by English craftsmen, with which he surveyed the night skies during his leisure hours.

It was during this same period that George was courting the attractive young Elizabeth Brooke, daughter of the founder of nearby Sandy Spring. He became concerned not only with convincing her of his own merits but of the pleasures of his hobby as well. In 1786 he presented her with a copy of Ferguson's *Introduction to Astronomy*, a slim volume bound in fine leather and written in a simple style intended for the instruction of young people, particularly young ladies.[9] The text was in the form of a dialogue between a student at Cambridge

University named Leander and his sister Eudosia, to whom he attempted to explain the rudiments of astronomy.

History is silent concerning Elizabeth's progress with the science, but her approval of the earnest young man is unquestionable, for she married him four years later, in 1790. George had built his own home at the Mills next door to his brother Jonathan in 1789, a large but unpretentious two-story house of granite from the Ellicott quarries. In this house, which survives, the young newlyweds began their life together, and George utilized one of the gabled bedrooms on the third floor for his observatory.

From time to time George acquired other books for study, ordered from their agent in England. He owned copies of Leadbetter's two-volume work on astronomy and a copy of the *Tabulae Motuum Solis et Lunae . . .* of Tobias Mayer, edited by Rev. Nevil Maskelyne. George's daughter later wrote of his scientific preoccupations as follows:

> George Ellicott . . . was one of the best mathematicians, and also one of the finest amateur astronomers of the time, and was fond of imparting instruction to every youthful inquirer after knowledge who came to his house. As early as the year 1782, during the fine clear evenings of autumn, he was in the habit of giving gratuitous lessons on astronomy to any of the inhabitants of the village who wished to hear him. To many of these, his celestial globe was an object of great interest and curiosity. He was perfectly at home on a map of the heavens, as far as the telescopes, and writers of his time had given revelations.[10]

It is almost a certainty that among the first of "those inhabitants of the village who wished to hear him" was Banneker, and it is easy to imagine the wonderment with which he first observed the details of the heavens through George's telescope and identified the stars and constellations he had observed in the sky with the latter's celestial globe.

A closer association was inevitable, for they shared many interests which were foreign to others around them. To Ellicott, Banneker demonstrated a natural genius for mathematics and proved to be an eager student who understood and enjoyed his own preoccupations. To Banneker, Ellicott was a man of special learning with the capability and energy of satisfying his constant and consuming curiosity and thirst for greater knowledge. Yet a span of years intervened before Ellicott provided Banneker with the sources for further study. This can be explained partly by George's occasional long absences from home on business and his involvement with the needs of the family industries. At the same time Banneker had to spend most of his daylight hours in the care of his farm, which left little time for leisurely pursuits. In the years since Mary Banneky's death, when he was left alone in the world, he learned to do his own cooking, his own cleaning and mending and washing—chores that must have taken more of his precious leisure. Withal, Banneker had nevertheless found a new direction for his thirst for learning, and he was well on his way to the new avocation which was to change the course of his later years.

IV

WORK AND STUDY

◇❈◇❈◇❈◇❈◇❈◇❈◇❈◇❈◇❈◇

That which we call alternately the morning and the evening star; as in one part of the orbit she rides foremost in the procession of night, in the other ushers in and anticipates the dawn; is a planetary world, which with the four others, that so wonderfully vary their mystic dance, are in themselves dark bodies, and shine only by reflection; have fields, and seas and skies of their own, are furnished with all accommodations for animal subsistence, and are supposed to be the abodes of intellectual life; all which, together with our earthly habitation, are dependent upon that grand dispenser of divine munificence, the sun. . . .

"The Planetary and Terrestrial
Worlds comparatively considered,"
Banneker's Almanac for 1792

Work and Study

BANNEKER'S INTEREST IN ASTRONOMY developed rapidly, spurred by his occasional encounters with George Ellicott and the latter's encouragement. Ellicott in turn found in this dignified man, so much older than himself, a kindred spirit and an eager pupil whose remarkable aptitude for mathematical matters was matched by his consuming desire to learn. Banneker's mind was so agile and his memory so retentive that George found himself unable to keep them fed. At some time in the autumn of 1788 he offered to lend Banneker several of his own books and instruments. With the increasing burden of his work in the prospering Mills, he found himself with no time for his avocation, and he was pleased that someone else could use his materials. He promised Benjamin that as and when he could find the time, he would stop in occasionally to teach him what he knew of the subject and that thereafter Benjamin would be able to progress by himself.

On the very next opportunity George found to ride in that direction, he brought along several of his texts and a few of his instruments to Banneker. The instruments included a pedestal telescope and a set of drafting instruments for making observations of the times of the stars on the meridian, of their southing, and of their rising and setting. He apologized for being unable to stay to give Banneker some preliminary instruction since he was on his way to a business appointment, but he promised to return as soon as he could for a longer visit.*

Before making his departure, however, he paused to take another look at the interior of Banneker's modest abode. The only table was a crude structure which Benjamin's father had constructed many years ago, and it was neither stable nor smooth enough for using a telescope or making calculations. He remembered an old table which was no longer being used in his own home, and he made a mental note to send it along.

* In his letter to Goddard and Angell dated August 20, 1791, which was printed in the first issue of Banneker's Almanac for 1792, James McHenry wrote that "It is about three years since Mr. George Ellicott lent him [Banneker] 'Mayer's Tables,' 'Ferguson's Astronomy,' 'Leadbetter's Lunar Tables,' and some astronomical instruments. . . ."

Banneker could hardly wait for George to be gone. He set the books and the instruments on his table, then caressed the long bright brass tube of the telescope lovingly while he tried to focus it at a point outside the window. He admired the workmanship of the drafting instruments as he removed them from their velvet-lined case and tested them one by one to determine their function. Last of all he examined the books, and his mind reeled as he perused the complicated diagrams and the impressively unintelligible text. Darkness had fallen without his knowledge by the time he could bring himself to put his new treasures aside. Throughout the evening, as he returned to the books on the table, he asked himself again and again whether he was not presuming too much in the undertaking he had set himself.

George kept his promise to furnish Banneker with a table; he looked around his home for a suitable one to lend him. He thought at first of parting with a rather fine modern oval cherry drop-leaf table that might be spared but decided that it would make the farmer uncomfortable and possibly embarrassed. The table was too fine and elegant to fit with the rude furnishings of the cabin, and Banneker might not accept it either as a gift or a loan. George finally selected a heavier table that had served the family for generations in Bucks County and was now seldom used. It had ample surface, was extremely sturdy, and would serve quite well. Several days later George had the table loaded on a wagon and delivered.

Banneker was surprised and touched that George had remembered. The massive oval drop-leaf table was of heavy construction, which he realized as he struggled to help the driver remove it from the wagon and carry it into the house. It had obviously seen hard service throughout several generations of the Ellicott family, as evidenced by the scars on the surfaces and the worn bottoms of the pad feet. Despite its age and weight, however, it seemed to be designed exactly for Banneker's needs. He placed it under his window with one of the leaves unopened against the wall, so that he could open or drop the other leaf as required. The top of the table, which was in a three-board section, and the leaves, which reached the floor, were made of heavy pine; the turned gate-legs and stretchers were of maple. A long drawer traversed the length of the table so that it could be opened at either end. He placed the instruments and the books carefully on its surface, and was delighted with the fresh atmosphere which had been brought into his home with the new acquisitions.*

Young George had also sent along as a gift a saucer-type candleholder of tin, which had a broad base so that it would sit firmly on the table. The old black iron hogscraper candlestick which Banneker had been using was of uncertain stability at best, and the additional light supply made it much easier to work in the evenings. He forgot his chores as he sat long at his table tinkering with the instruments and looking at the impressive diagrams and tables in the volumes.

The first book he chose to read was James Ferguson's *An Easy Introduction to Astronomy*. In fact, this was the same book George had given his wife before they were married, and which he had borrowed from her so that Banneker could use it. There can be no doubt of the high esteem in which he held his friend, nor of the impression of Banneker he must have imparted to Elizabeth that made her willing to lend it.

The style of Ferguson's work was simple; Banneker was able to grasp the principles described with ease. It provided basic instructions, with illustrations for constructing projections of eclipses by means of such basic drafting instruments as a pair of compasses and a ruler. The author suggested that the process would be less tedious if a sector were used, because all the measurements could be derived from it and the trouble of dividing could be avoided. Although Benjamin began his studies with compasses and ruler, he subsequently borrowed a sector from Ellicott, and eventually purchased one of his own.

* Two tables owned by descendants of George Ellicott are traditionally claimed to have been the one lent to Banneker. One is presently owned by Dr. Robert T. Fitzhugh; the other is presently the property of other descendants, who prefer to remain anonymous.

Ellicott included also a more advanced work by Ferguson, although he surmised that Banneker would not be able to use it until he had mastered the easier one.[1]

Another of the volumes was considerably more advanced. It was a copy of *Mayer's Tables*, edited by the Reverend Nevil Maskelyne, and published in England in the original Latin with an English translation all in one.[2]

A fourth work lent by Ellicott, which Banneker found particularly useful, was Charles Leadbetter's *A Compleat System of Astronomy*.[3] It was one of the most comprehensive works on astronomy of its time and provided much of the advanced data not available in Ferguson's book.

Although lack of time prevented George from providing needed guidance in his beginning studies, Banneker was undeterred, and proceeded to work by himself. He read the borrowed books through one by one, then turned to the instruments to test out what he had learned. The opportunity to sight at the stars through a telescope whenever he wished was a source of the greatest pleasure to him, and the night hours passed swiftly as he kept his eye glued to the eyepiece and studied the structure of the firmament. With only his own thoughts for company, he contemplated the miracle of circumstance that offered him such an unusual opportunity, not shared by anyone he knew except George Ellicott. As he sought out and found the stars and identified them in his books, he remembered also the stories he had read about the legendary figures from which their names were derived.

When he had familiarized himself sufficiently with the celestial bodies, Banneker attempted to make a projection of an eclipse of the sun. His books provided all the instruction he required, and he had the simple tools at hand for the drawing. He had already made great progress in the study of logarithms that the calculation required, and the projection was eventually completed. He checked over his work carefully, then impatiently awaited George's next visit so that he could show it to him. George's business activities kept him occupied elsewhere, however, and as time passed, Banneker could wait no longer. He forwarded his sketch with a covering letter to George at the store of Ellicott & Co. and went on with his studies.

He realized with some concern that his preoccupation with his new studies had caused his farm to suffer. During the period that followed, he tried to make up for the lapse. While he worked in the fields during the day his mind was constantly on his studies. Each evening when he returned home, he reached for his instruments and his books and spent long hours with them. The weeks passed quickly. Finally, when Banneker visited the Ellicott store seeking news of George, he discovered that the latter had been away on a prolonged business trip and that it would be some time before he returned. Banneker's life had taken on new meaning and a new direction, and he found himself again and again putting off work that needed to be done so that he could have more leisure for his avocation. He was annoyed with himself for his sloth, as he termed it, but found himself powerless to keep his mind fixed on his regular duties.

When George received the projection and the letter, he was speechless with surprise. He suddenly recalled that he had not returned to see Banneker to explain the books he had lent him or provide him with the beginning lessons he had promised. He was also immediately aware that such instruction was obviously no longer necessary, as demonstrated by the work in hand. Carefully reviewing the drawing, he was greatly impressed with his friend's efforts. True, he had made a trifling error in his calculation, but there was no question that Banneker had an unusual affinity for mathematics and had made remarkable progress in mastering the science. George made the necessary correction on the drawing and returned it with a note apologizing for being unable to visit him at that time but promising to do so as soon as he could.

Banneker was pleased and at the same time chagrined by George's comments. He was angry with himself for making such an error and ashamed because it was so apparent, yet he was aware of George's surprise and evident pleasure over his own accomplishments. He realized the nature of his error and set about to find out why he had made it, in a renewed study of his reference works. The source of his miscalculation, he discovered with some astonishment mixed with satisfaction, was unquestionably a disparity in two of the sources he had been using. Unconvinced at first by his findings, he returned to them again and again until he was certain. When he wrote again to George Ellicott, he was happy to point out the apparent discrepancies in the publications of two of the English leading authorities on astronomy.[4] He assured George that he had not been offended by the latter's comments and corrections, but that he could explain the reason for his error:

I Receiv'd your Letter at the hand of Bell but found nothing Strange to me In the Letter Concerning the Number of Eclipses tho according to authors the Edge of the penumber only touches the Suns Limb in that Eclips that I left out of the Number—which happens April 14th day at 37 minutes past 7 O'Clock in the morning and is the first we shall have, but Since you wrote to me I Drew in the Equations of the Node which will Cause a Small Solar Defet but as I Did not intend to publish, I was not so very peticular as I should have been, but was more intent upon the true method of projecting a Solar Eclips—It is an Easy matter for us when a Diagram is laid down before us to draw one in resemblance of it, but it is a hard matter for young Tyroes in Astronomy when only the Elements for the projection is laid down before him to draw his Diagram to any degree of Certainty——

Says the Learned L e a d b e t t e r the projection that I shall here describe, is that mentioned by W^m. Flamsted—When the Sun is in Cancer, Leo, Virgo, Libra, Scorpio, or Saggittary, the Axes of the Globe must lie to the right hand of the Axes of the Ecliptic, but when the Sun is in Capercorn, Aquarious, pisces, Aries, Taurus or Gemini then to the left——

Says that wise Author F e r g u s o n, when the Sun is in Capercorn, Aquarius, pisces, Aries, Taurus, and Gemini the Northern half of the Earth Axes lies to the right hand of the Axes of the Ecliptic, and to the left hand whilst the Sun is in the other Six Signs——

Now M^r. Ellicott two Such learned Gentlemen as the above mentioned, one in direct opposition to the other, Stagnates young beginners, but I hope the Stagnation will not be of long duration for this I observe that Leadbetter Count the time on the path of Virtex, 1.2.3. &c. from the right to the left hand or from the Consequent to the Antecedent——But Ferguson on the path of the Vertex Count the time 1.2.3. &c. from the left to the right hand according to the order of Numbers, So that that is regular Shall Compensate for irregularity ——Now Sir if I can overcome this difficulty I Doubt not being able to Calculate a Common Almanack—— So no more but remain y^r. faithful friend M^r. George Ellicott. . . ."

Banneker's reference to "young Tyroes" was not his own figure of speech but one borrowed from the preface to Leadbetter's work, in which the latter had stated, "I have given you all the Terms of Art used in Astronomy; by which the young Tyro is taught to speak properly. . . ."

Despite the confusion expressed in his letter to George Ellicott, Banneker had not in fact discovered an error in one or the other of the two authors. The results of the procedures described by Ferguson and Leadbetter were the same. Banneker's confusion arose because he had both of these sources available to him for consultation simultaneously. If he had had either one without the other, the problem would not have arisen. The apparent conflict occurred in the individual statements made by Ferguson and Leadbetter concerning the position of an axis of the earth in relation to the axis of the ecliptic. Ferguson described the geometrical computation of a solar eclipse from a sun-oriented position, and his projection was drawn as viewed by the observer at the sun looking toward the earth. Leadbetter, on the other hand, assumed the opposite position, and viewed the projection as if the observer were behind the earth and looking through it at the sun. Both authors described the procedure in almost exactly the same words, but from entirely different vantage points. The apparent conflict in the two methods can be easily described in projecting a solar eclipse when the sun is in the first zodiacal constellation, Aries. This is known as the first such constellation because it occupies the position where the ecliptic crosses the celestial equator at the vernal equinox, the first day of spring. Ferguson states that when the sun is in Aries, the axis of the earth appears at the right of the axis of the ecliptic, which is the case only if the earth is viewed from the vantage point of the sun. Leadbetter, on the other hand, specifies that the axis of the earth should appear at the left of the axis of the ecliptic, which is the case when the sun is viewed from the earth. Ferguson's method is the one which is commonly used in many texts on astronomy of the present time.[5]

Of the two authorities, Ferguson's work was the easier to use because he wrote as he lectured, in a simple flowing style with numerous illustrations to explain his meaning. Leadbetter's writing, however, had to be read with extreme concentration, word by word and line by line. It is only after the realization is made that he describes the moon moving in a backward direction that his opposite vantage point becomes apparent. When Banneker tried to make one or more of the several projections of solar eclipses used as examples by both authors he became aware of the cause of confusion and realized that there was in fact no error in either of his sources. He did not encounter the same problem in the projection of lunar eclipses, however, since both Ferguson and Leadbetter utilized the same approach and vantage point. He came to a realization of the cause of his confusion soon after his letter was written, and the notes in his manuscript journal made within the next several years indicate that he preferred to work with Ferguson rather than Leadbetter.

It had never occurred to George that Banneker might calculate an ephemeris for an almanac until the latter made a casual reference to it in his letter. After he had thought about it, he could see no reason why Banneker would not be able to produce such a set of calculations. It might even be possible to find a printer for them, and he encouraged his friend to undertake the project. Banneker was at the same time intrigued and fearful of the prospect. The awareness that young Ellicott, who was far more knowledgeable in the subject than he, considered him capable of preparing an almanac was high praise indeed, and an expression of confidence far greater than he had anticipated. Banneker then went on to undertake other more complicated calculations. Before the end of the summer he had not only mastered the projection of eclipses with accuracy, but was able to produce the various other calculations required. By now he had not only exhausted the several works that Ellicott had lent him, but he managed to borrow or purchase several other volumes to assist him in his project. These he mentioned from time to time in the pages of a manuscript journal that he kept, and he occasionally copied out important directions and formulas that would be of future use.

More than ever before, Banneker now applied himself seriously to the preparation of an ephemeris. He hesitated to think that there was even the slightest possibility of selling it and having it published in an almanac, but he realized that it provided the best exercise possible for his new interest. He had probably purchased almanacs each year during his long career as a farmer, and these would have been among his most prized possessions, inasmuch as they provided virtually the only current reading material available to him. Like many farmers throughout the American colonies, he may have inserted pages in the pamphlets on which he had kept a diary of the important events relating to his farm, such as unusual weather, sale of crops, and related entries. Thus he was able to study the format and content of the common almanac of the period, upon which he could model one of his own.

The almanac played an important role in colonial American family life, a role best described by Tyler as follows:

> No one who would penetrate to the core of early American literature, and would read in it the secret history of the people in whose mind it took root and from whose minds it grew, may by any means turn away, in lofty literary scorn, from the almanac—most despised, most prolific, most indispensable of books, which every man uses, and no man praises; the very quack, clown, packhorse, and pariah of modern literature, yet the one universal book of modern literature; the supreme and only literary necessity even in households where the Bible and newspaper are still undesired or unattainable luxuries.[6]

From their first appearance in the colonies in 1639 until Banneker's time, the almanacs were the only secular current publications available. Although at first their content was limited to little more than the ephemeris, they were gradually expanded to include other subjects such as astrology, chronological tables of scientific data, history, and literary items with occasional poetry. In many regions of the continent the almanac was the only printed work other than the Bible that was available to the family. Although weekly newspapers were published, there was no rural circulation until after the middle of the eighteenth century. The daily newspaper was primarily an urban publication but infrequently distributed outside of the specific community. The common household calendar, so familiar today, did not come into general use until about 1870, and until that time it was the almanac that served that purpose.

The almanac was of interest and use to three separate

groups of people. First of all, to the navigators who sailed to or from the American shores, as well as the shipmasters engaged in commerce on the inland and coastal waterways. They consulted it for the times of the rising and setting of the sun, moon, and certain fixed stars, from which they could calculate their true position (or at least within seventy miles of it, which was the best that could be done in that period). Next, it was useful to the householder, who referred to its pages for daily information and for the dates of special events, also to the farmers and others who relied on the almanac for the dates of planting, weather forecasts, and information about the moon's eclipses and phases. Finally, it served all the other members of the family who sought entertainment and learning in its pages for lack of other reading matter.

For the common man, in a period when timepieces ordinarily consisted of sand glasses and sundials, and clocks and watches were rare luxuries, the times of sunrise, noon, and sunset were of considerable importance, as well as the changes of the moon, eclipses, and conjunctions.

Early in the eighteenth century one publisher included a column entitled "Sun fast and slow" which enabled the regulation of clocks and watches at noon by means of sundials. Particularly useful for weather prognostication were the added columns for the positions and declinations of the sun and moon.

Besides such critical data, the pages of the small, cheaply assembled and poorly printed pamphlet were filled with Scriptural quotations, proverbs, allegorical stories and puritanical essays, all of which contributed to the molding of the national character.

The content of the almanac underwent several changes. During the seventeenth century it was published chiefly in the New England colonies and consequently reflected the religious influence. Sermons were often included in the content, and no opportunity was lost to derive moral lessons from astronomical phenomena. Parables, short stories, and essays provided only the slightest sugar-coating for strong exhortations to industriousness, temperance and frugality; models of virtue and piety were offered as guides for daily living.

By the beginning of the eighteenth century, the almanac changed distinctly in tone from its religious bias to a more practical direction, with emphasis on education. Literary and historical content of sorts was the new order. This form of publication achieved its peak with Benjamin Franklin's *Poor Richard's Almanac*. For the first time it attempted to entertain, and Franklin's homilies, along with homely wisdom cast in contemporary language, brought to the almanac a new popularity. An important philomath of the same period was Nathaniel Ames, who added yet another dimension in the form of verse, imaginative and superior to most of the poetry of his time.

The almanac was a popular seller. Each printer sought to publish one of his own because a successful almanac was a virtual assurance of prosperity. Some concept of the market for this type of publication may be derived from the fact that Franklin reported that he sold as many as ten thousand copies of his issues annually at the modest price of fivepence. His chief competitor, Nathaniel Ames, claimed to have sold as many as sixty thousand a year "for five coppers single."

By the beginning of the last decade of the eighteenth century, the almanac had become the most common printed item in the new American republic. Printers in every state vied with each other in developing a new marketable item, and each printer endeavored to hire a competent philomath to calculate an ephemeris for an almanac that would be exclusively his own. There were not enough competent astronomers available, however, and the almanac makers found such a ready market for their calculations that they frequently sold copies of their ephemeris for each year to several printers in neighboring cities, and sometimes to several within their own community.

The almanac makers were a rare breed. Few were scholars in the true sense and most of them were mathematical practitioners who were self-taught in the practical aspects of astronomy.

(88)

An exception to this general rule must be made for the seventeenth century, however. Of forty-four almanacs published in the American colonies before 1687, forty-one were compiled by twenty-six Harvard College postgraduate students during the course of their three years of studies for a degree of Master of Arts.

In general the makers of almanacs were drawn from a wide range of other occupations; they included statesmen, navigators, surveyors, instrument makers, and such others as developed a competence in the study of astronomy, in which they were almost invariably self-taught.

At the time that Banneker undertook the preparation of an ephemeris, the eighteenth century was drawing to a close, and the content of the almanac was once more beginning to change. The new emphasis would be upon local causes and national events; and because of the increased competition, with great numbers of almanacs being published in many of the states, they were to become more specialized, and many were directed at specific professions.

After Banneker had determined the various types of calculations required, he set himself methodically to the task of compiling his results one after the other for each month of the coming year.

A picture of the man at work is provided by Martha E. Tyson in her description of a visit made by her mother, Mrs. George Ellicott, accompanied by some of her young friends, in 1790. This was the first year of Elizabeth's marriage, and she was curious to see the talented farmer about whom her husband had spoken so frequently, and to whom she had lent her own volume on astronomy. She described the incident almost half a century later to her daughter, who reported the scene as her mother had related it to her:

> His door stood wide open, and so closely was his mind engaged that they entered without being seen. Immediately upon observing them he arose and with much

courtesy invited them to be seated. The large oval table at which Banneker sat was strewn with works on astronomy and with scientific appurtenances. He alluded to his love of the study of astronomy and mathematics as quite unsuited to a man of his class, and regretted his slow advancement in them, owing to the laborious nature of his agricultural engagements, which obliged him to spend the greater portion of his time in the fields. . . . His mother had died previous to this, and he was the sole occupant of his dwelling.[7]

Thus with only his clock for company, Banneker found the hours slipping rapidly away as he worked on his project. George Ellicott's visits encouraged him to continue and the winter months passed rapidly for him. By the beginning of autumn the ephemeris was completed at last, and Banneker reviewed his results again and again to ensure their accuracy. He was determined that young George would not find another error in his mathematical work. He copied his results into the customary format of the published almanacs and it is entirely possible that he may have used one of the almanacs calculated by Major Andrew Ellicott, George's cousin, who was a professional surveyor.

The work was done at last, and as Banneker looked proudly at the neatly copied sheets for each of the twelve months of 1791 one more time before assembling them, he felt somewhat in awe of his own achievement. He was convinced that it was publishable, and eager to see if it would be accepted. He decided to send it first to one of the printers in Baltimore.

At this time there were three printers working in Baltimore: William Goddard, who was then operating a print shop in partnership with his brother-in-law, James Angell; the recently established Baltimore branch of the Wilmington firm of Samuel and John Adams; and John Hayes, who was then the publisher of the *Maryland Gazette*.

Banneker's first choice was probably the most prominent

of the Baltimore firms, Goddard and Angell. The printer was not interested, however, and in due course the ephemeris was rejected. Banneker tried again, sending his work to another of the printers but again meeting with failure; he found the ephemeris waiting for him one day in the mail room of the store of Ellicott & Co. He was determined to make a third attempt. This time he selected John Hayes, reputed to be an excellent printer. Hayes was a well-educated Englishman who worked first in a printing firm in Philadelphia before moving to Baltimore in 1783 to revive *The Maryland Gazette or Baltimore General Advertiser* as a weekly paper. He continued his paper until the beginning of 1792 and then briefly undertook another career. He returned to printing, however, and late in 1794 tried to revive his newspaper with the name *Maryland Register and General Advertiser*, but without success. He continued to print stationery forms, occasional books, and related materials during the next decade. He was active in the Maryland Society for Promoting the Abolition of Slavery and other charitable causes.

Hayes was already well known to Banneker as the publisher of the almanacs calculated by Major Andrew Ellicott. Ellicott had sold his ephemerides for the years 1781 through 1785 to Mary Katherine Goddard, but it is likely that they were printed by John Hayes, since she did not have her own press then. Ellicott's almanac for 1786 was published by the newly organized firm of Goddard and Langworthy, but the association was not continued. On January 1, 1787, Goddard's partnership with Langworthy was dissolved, and Goddard took as his new partner his brother-in-law, James Angell. Langworthy became the new headmaster of the Baltimore Academy, where he also taught the classics, and at which Ellicott was the instructor of natural philosophy and mathematics.* For

* The Baltimore Academy was established on Charles Street in Baltimore in 1786 under the patronage of the Reverend Doctors Carroll, West, and Allison, as a school for youth intended for the learned professions. Prior to this time the young men had been sent to schools in Pennsylvania and abroad. The school survived for only a short period.

the next few years Ellicott sold his ephemerides to John Hayes, Goddard's major rival, probably with an improved financial arrangement. Meanwhile, Goddard felt the loss of Ellicott inasmuch as the almanac was an important source of income, and he sought a replacement. He arranged with Benjamin Workman, an instructor at the University of Pennsylvania, to calculate the ephemeris for an almanac for the year 1787, which he published late in 1786, at the same time launching a bitter attack on Hayes. Undoubtedly urged by Hayes, Ellicott compiled an errata list for Goddard's almanac, which was published by Hayes in his newspaper. This led to an attack on Goddard by a writer using the pseudonym "Juvenal," which continued for some time, and was believed to be Goddard's former partner, Langworthy.[8]

Banneker waited anxiously for a reply from Hayes, and when there was no response, he wrote to him again. Hayes informed him that he had sent the calculations along to Major Ellicott in Philadelphia for a review of them, and that he would inform Banneker when he had received the latter's comments.

It was at this point that Banneker decided to communicate directly with Major Ellicott with the purpose of obtaining a decision. His concerns and reservations about his accomplishment were clearly reflected in a revealing and touching letter to the surveyor,[9] sent in the spring of 1790:

Maryland Baltimore County near Ellicotts
Lower Mill May the 6th: 1790

S[r]// I have at the request of Several Gentlemen Calculated an Ephemeris for the year 1791 which I presented unto M[r]. Hayes printer in Baltimore, and he received it in a very polite manner and told me that he would gladly print the Same provided the Calculations Came any ways near the truth, but to Satisfy himself in that he would Send it to philadelphia to be inspected by you and at the reception of an answer from you he Should know how to proceed and now S[r]. I beg that you will not be too Severe upon me but favourable in giving your approbation as the nature of the Case will permit, knowing well the difficulty that attends long Calculations and especially with young beginners in Astronomy, but this I know that the greater and most useful part of my Ephemeris is so near the truth that it needs but little Correction, and as to that part that may be Somewhat deficient, I hope that you will be kind enough to view with any eye of pitty as the Calculations was made more for the Sake of gratifying the Curiosity of the public, than for any view of profit, as I suppose it to be the first attempt of the kind that ever was made in America by a person of my Complection——

I find by my Calculation there will be four Eclipses for the ensuing year but I have not yet Settled their appearance, But am waiting for an answer from Your HONOUR to Mᵣ. Hayes in Baltimore——

So no more at present, but am Sᵣ. your very humble and most obedient Serᵛ.

B Banneker

Andrew Ellicott's reply to Banneker has not survived, nor is there a record of any report he may have made to Hayes. Ellicott did not find the calculations complete but they were reasonably accurate. He may have concluded that too much work would be required to make the calculations acceptable for publication. Meanwhile Hayes delayed a reply for the next few months and finally decided not to publish Banneker's almanac after all, despite his earlier indication of interest. He had delayed so long, however, that it was not possible for Banneker to submit it to another printer in time for its publication for distribution in the following year.[10] Hayes used as his excuse the fact that he had been printing the almanacs with the calculations prepared by Andrew Ellicott and he did not wish to make a change at this time inasmuch ". . . as he was publically known for the name of Ellicott."

This was a great disappointment to Banneker. He turned for assistance once more to his friends at Ellicott's Lower Mills. By one of the greatest possible coincidences of time and place, Banneker's almanac fitted into the scheme of things far beyond his anticipations and served a much greater purpose than he had ever visualized.

The fates had been working on Banneker's behalf without his awareness, through the antislavery movement which had been developing not only in Philadelphia but throughout the world. At the first Continental Congress in 1774 a committee had been appointed to develop a plan for effecting non-importation, non-consumption, and non-exportation of foreign goods, and upon their recommendation a proposal was passed which included the resolution that there would be no importation or purchase of slaves that had been imported after December 1, 1774. After that date the slave trade was to be completely discontinued. Despite the intent of the legislation, at least thirteen years passed before the resolution could be wholly effected. The onslaught of war helped to break up the trade in slaves, but the economic forces of the country had suffered from the war by the reduction of labor, particularly in the South. These forces sought to recover by reviving the slave trade. The English slave trade was resumed after the end of hostilities and in this country the trade was reopened in parts of the South. A sharp division of opinion on the subject was growing throughout the United States, however. The Congress of the Confederation did not succeed in resolving the problem, although peripheral aspects of the trade were considered.

Meanwhile an antislavery movement was growing on both sides of the Atlantic with increasing impetus, fed by the co-operative efforts of the Society of Friends in the New England and the Middle Colonies. Not only did the members of the Society disown fellow sectarians who persisted in holding slaves, but they maintained a large and steady correspondence with Quakers in England over a period of many years. The Friends even managed to convert members of other religious groups to their cause, and a strong sentiment against slavery began to develop even in the states of North Carolina and Virginia.

Correspondence on the slavery question between Quakers in England and the American colonies had continued even during the War of Independence, and the movement grew proportionately after the close of hostilities. In London, Benjamin Franklin provided assistance to the cause by publishing an extract of Anthony Benezet's tracts attacking the slave trade in *The London Chronicle*. Later he cooperated in Granville Sharp's campaign to eradicate the trade in England. Newspapers and periodicals in London and Edinburgh took up the cause and published strong attacks on the slave trade, spurred by tracts being furnished in large numbers by Quakers in Philadelphia and elsewhere. Members of the British Parliament were being propagandized with copies of these tracts mailed to them from America, and by the decade following 1783 the agitation against the trade became even more impressive. Late in 1783 a deputation from the yearly meeting of the Society of Friends in Philadelphia presented a resolution to the Congress, but it had little noticeable effect. Nor did slavery occupy an important place in the resolutions of the Federal Convention of 1787, although there was considerable debate over the question. Concessions were made and a bargain was finally achieved in which the Congress resolved that the slave trade would be ended prior to 1808. The clause led to great discussion and protest throughout the nation, and in many of the state conventions there was opposition to its inclusion.[11]

In Philadelphia, meanwhile, an organization consisting mostly of Friends had been formed in 1775 and taken the name, Society for the Relief of Free Negroes unlawfully held in Bondage. Benjamin Franklin was elected its first president, and the founding membership included such other prominent figures as James Pemberton and Benjamin Rush. In 1787 the Society was reorganized under a new name, The Pennsylvania Society for Promoting the Abolition of Slavery, the Relief of Free Negroes unlawfully held in bondage and for Improving the

Condition of the African Race, and it became even more active than before. In 1789 the Society was incorporated and individuals from other states were permitted to join. Elias Ellicott and Joseph Townsend of Baltimore were elected to membership on June 5, 1790.[12]

One of the programs of the Pennsylvania Society was the development of the antislavery movement in other states, and with its assistance similar satellite societies were formed in New York, New Jersey, Rhode Island, Delaware, Virginia, and Maryland. The first antislavery society formed in Maryland is of particular interest because it played an important role in the publication of Banneker's almanacs. It was modeled closely after the parent Pennsylvania Society, even to its name, the Maryland Society for Promoting the Abolition of Slavery, and the Relief of Free Negroes and others unlawfully held in Bondage. The Society was founded on September 8, 1789, and one of its chief instigators was Joseph Townsend, a Baltimore businessman, who served as its first secretary. In his dual capacity as a member of the Pennsylvania Society and secretary of the Maryland organization, Townsend was to play an important role in Banneker's future. He was born in East Bradford Township in Chester County, Pennsylvania, and remained on his father's farm until the age of twenty-two. He witnessed the Battle of Brandywine and the passage of the British Army under General Howe. In June 1782 he moved to Harford County, Maryland, and settled at the Little Falls of Gunpowder. After teaching school for a year, he moved to Baltimore and became deeply involved in civic responsibilities of that growing community.

Shortly after his arrival in Baltimore, he made several attempts to establish himself in trade. In 1792 he advertised that he had for sale eight-day tall-case clocks, and in 1797 he advertised the sale, at his shop at 18 Baltimore-Street in Baltimore, of *A New Introduction to Reading—Or; A Collection of Easy Lessons, Arranged on an Improved Plan.* . . . This was a fourth edition of an English text which he advertised as having published himself.

Townsend served on the Board of Health during the three epidemics of yellow fever in 1794, 1798, and 1800, and was involved in the development of Maryland Hospital. In 1794 he was sent as one of the representatives of the Maryland Society to the first convention of abolitionist societies held in Philadelphia, and he represented the Maryland Society also at the second convention held in 1795.[13]

The Society had the support of significant figures in Baltimore business and political circles. It dedicated itself to an ambitious program, as described in its constitution:

> . . . The human race, however varied in color or intellects, are all justly entitled to liberty, and it is the duty and interest of nations and individuals, enjoying the blessings of freedom, to remove this dishonor of the Christian character from among them.
>
> From the fullest impression of the truth of these principles; from an earnest wish to bear our testimony against slavery, in all its forms; to spread it abroad, as far as the sphere of our influence may extend, and to afford our friendly assistance to those who may be engaged in the same undertaking, and in the humble hope of support from that Being, who takes an offering to himself what we do for each other.
>
> We the subscribers, have formed ourselves into the Maryland Society for promoting the abolition of slavery, and for the relief of free negroes and others unlawfully held in bondage.[14]

The first president of the new Society was Philip Rogers, and James Carey was elected the first vice-president. Other prominent citizens of the community who were members included General Joseph Sterett, William Winchester, Judge

James Winchester, Adam Fonerden, William Pinkney, Judge Chase and Archibald Robinson. The English philanthropist, Granville Sharp, asked to become a member and was duly elected, and served the Society as its English correspondent. Gerard Hopkins served on the Electing Committee, and among the members of the Acting Committee were Elisha Tyson and Elias Ellicott. It was the duty of the Acting Committee to seek out cases which required the Society's interference, to file petitions for freedom on behalf of individuals held in bondage illegally, and to arrest kidnapers of free Negroes and to bring them to punishment. The Committee was responsible also for submitting to the grand jury of the county cases of outrageous misconduct of masters in the handling of slaves. In the pursuit of this mission, Elisha Tyson distinguished himself by his dedication to the cause to such a degree that his name became associated with the defense of human rights. The dramatic accounts of his bravery in personally freeing captured Negroes from prison and slave ships have become a part of Baltimore history.

One of the first endeavors of the Society was the petitioning of a repeal of the law of 1753 prohibiting manumission by last will and testament, and its replacement with more practical legislation. A special committee appointed for the purpose succeeded in having introduced in the House of Delegates a bill which led to great controversy throughout the state. The repeal was supported on the floor by William Pinkney, one of the youngest members of the legislative body as well as a founding member of the Society. His impassioned speech had a strong effect on the proposal, which nevertheless lost by a small margin of the vote. The Society then circulated copies of Pinkney's speech and it was published in newspapers throughout the state.

The Society kept the proposal for the repeal alive, but it was not until 1796 that they achieved the results they desired. In that year, when the bill came to a vote a second time, it was passed.

The Maryland Society was more successful in some of its

efforts than in others. By the end of 1795 they had effected the release of 138 free Negroes, but their efforts to establish a school for Negro children were unsuccessful.[15]

The Maryland group had the strong support of its sister Society in Philadelphia, and there was constant communication between the members. Evidence of this is found in a letter from Joseph Townsend to James Pemberton.[16] In this communication he reported that the liberation of approximately fifty slaves was contingent upon the rendering of a court decision then pending.*

Pemberton was the first vice-president of the Pennsylvania Society and succeeded Franklin as president in 1790. He remained in that office for thirteen years, during which the Society flourished and expanded. Pemberton held many public offices, including membership on the Board of Overseers of the Philadelphia public schools, and was on the first board of managers of the Pennsylvania Hospital. He was elected to membership in the American Philosophical Society in 1768 and served also in many capacities with the Society of Friends in Philadelphia. He was the author of numerous religious documents and tracts. During the war he had opposed armed resistance to Great Britain and was consequently arrested, imprisoned, and deported to Virginia. After his return he gave up all interest in politics.

The friends of the Negro throughout the country, and in particular the organized antislavery groups, were making every effort during this particular period to collect evidence and examples to disprove the common claim that the Negro was an inferior being. The most active group was the Pennsylvania Society for the Promotion of the Abolition of Slavery, which in addition to its own positive efforts provided inspiration to such similar organizations as the Maryland Society and its English counterpart. Anthony Benezet in Philadelphia collected whatever materials he could find which he sent to the English

* See Document 1.

abolitionists. One of his American-born former pupils, William Dillwyn, organized a small group in London which became a center for propaganda. The students at a school for Negroes which had been established in Philadelphia were described to English sympathizers as examples of Negro capacity for learning when given the opportunity. English periodicals sympathetic to the cause sought to publish Negro contributions in any field, but with little success. Consequently, the discovery of a free Negro in Baltimore County who had become a self-taught amateur astronomer, and who had calculated an ephemeris for an almanac, was an important event.

It was James Pemberton who first associated this unusual achievement with its value as propaganda. Banneker's letter to Major Andrew Ellicott arrived in late spring, at a time when Ellicott was involved with the survey of the lands ceded by the State of New York at Lake Erie. The rest of the summer and autumn he spent in the field at Presque Isle, from which he returned in mid-October. Upon his return to his home in Philadelphia he turned over to James Pemberton the letter from Banneker that he had received earlier in the year as a subject of possible interest to the Pennsylvania Abolition Society. Pemberton realized the potential immediately, and he made several copies of the letter. One of these he returned to Ellicott for his letter file on or about October 30, with the inscription at the bottom:

> Literal Copy from the Original
> James Pemberton
> Philad^a. 30. 10 mo. 1790.[17]

At the same time he forwarded another copy to Joseph Townsend at Baltimore asking him to provide him with any further information that he could find about this man of unusual talent, Banneker. Townsend replied in mid-November, advising Pemberton that "I have not as yet procured the necessary information respecting the Black man's Calculations of the Almanack but shall attend to it & comply with thy request accordingly——" [18]

Townsend grasped the significance of the assignment at once, and he lost no time in conferring with his associates in the Maryland Society. He was fortunate in discovering that several of his fellow members were acquainted with Banneker, including Elias Ellicott, George's brother, and the printer, John Hayes. By the time that he received his next communication from Pemberton[19] he was in a position to provide some new data,[20] namely:

> I have made inquiry respecting the Negro Man mentioned in my two last—Elias Ellicott informs that the Calculation of the Almanack was nearly brought to perfection but is refer'd to next season—John Hayes says that the author presented it to him in due time for publication, but as he had for years past been in the practice of printing Ellicotts he did not like to Change as his was publickly known by the name of Ellicotts, on which account he objected, not as he had any reason to doubt its exactness—If I can discover anything further respecting him or his performance I shall convey it accordingly——*

Pemberton readily foresaw the popular appeal of an almanac with an ephemeris calculated by a free Negro, and he visualized that it could in fact be used as an illustration of the mental capability of the Negro when given sufficient opportunity. Under his leadership, other members of the antislavery movements in Philadelphia and in Baltimore directed their efforts in a cooperative endeavor to publish Banneker's almanac.

* The remainder of this long letter was devoted to discussion of a Negro woman in Montgomery County who had applied for freedom, and the Society's efforts on her behalf and the presentation of a Memorial by the Society before the General Assembly and Townsend's own involvement in this endeavor. Pemberton noted that he had received the letter on December 2 and replied on December 10, 1790.

It was already too late to undertake the printing in time for distribution for the year the almanac was calculated, and the project had to be postponed. Townsend and Pemberton and others had done all they could and felt greatly frustrated, but there was no alternative. They would attempt to issue an almanac in the following year. Meanwhile, Banneker was about to be offered another unique opportunity, which was to take him away from his farm for the first and only time in his life.

1. *Portrait reproduced on the title page of Benjamin Banneker's almanac for 1795, printed for John Fisher*

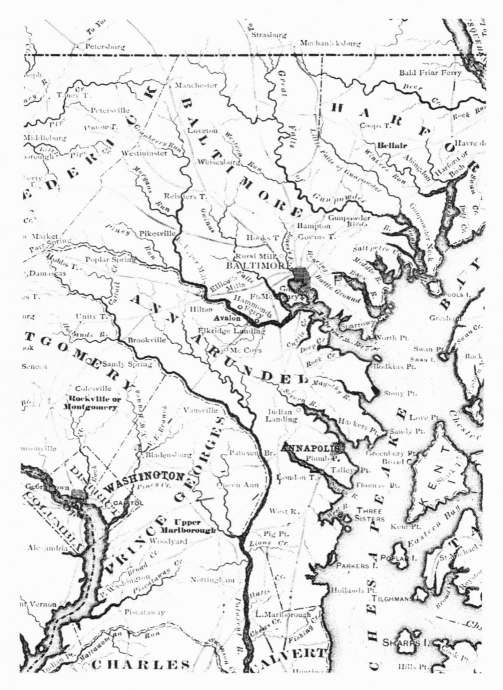

2. Map showing Baltimore County, Maryland, in which Banneker lived

3. Baltimore Town in 1752. Drawn on stone by J. Bachmann

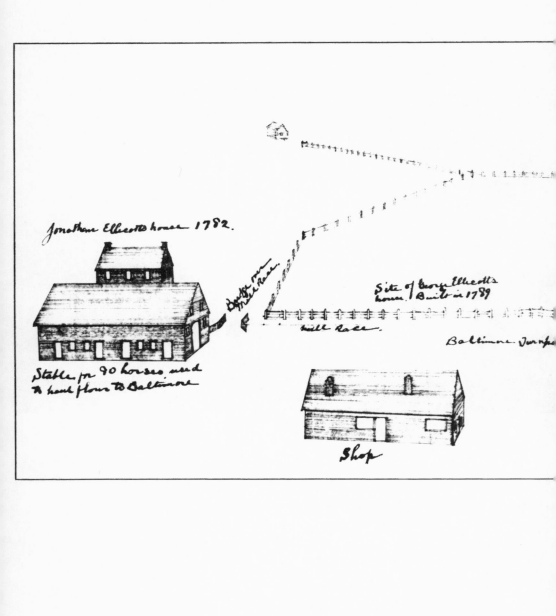

Jonathan Ellicott house 1782.

Stable for 90 horses used
to haul flour to Baltimore

Site of George Ellicott's
house. Built in 1789

Mill Race.

Baltimore Turnpike

Shop

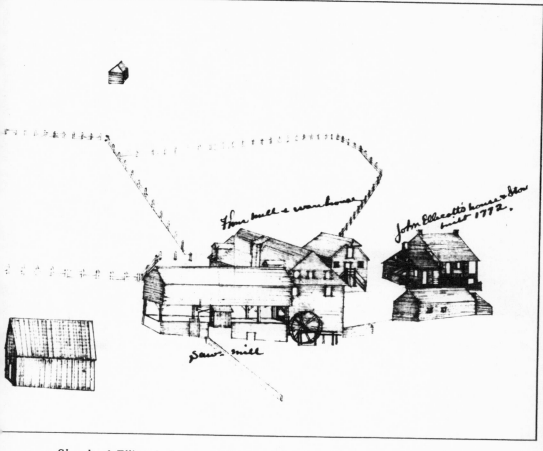

Flour mill & warehouse

John Ellicott's house & store
built 1772.

Saw-mill

4. Sketch of Ellicott's Lower Mills drawn by George Ellicott in 1782, ten years after the original settlement

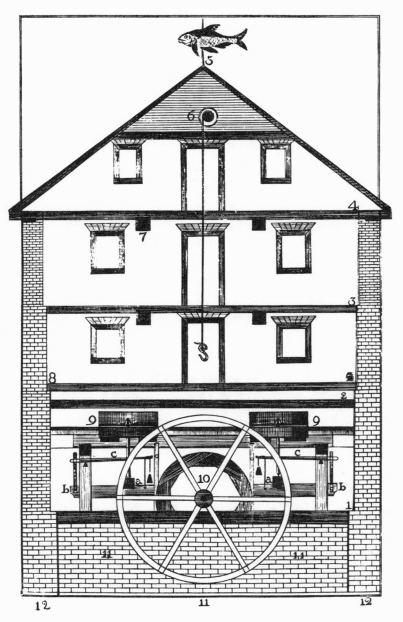

5. Exterior view of a mill house of one of the Ellicott automated mills

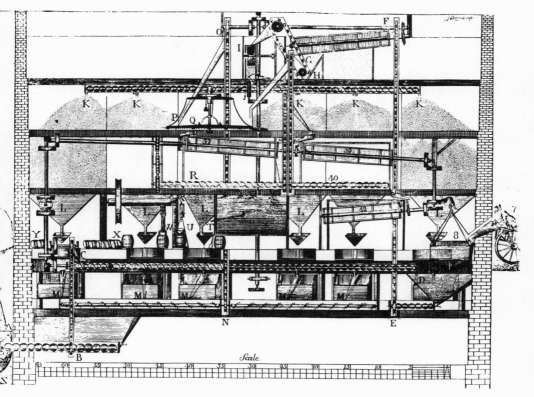

6. *Automated mill of the type constructed by the Ellicott brothers, showing delivery of grain, grinding into flour, and packaging of flour in barrels for shipment*

7. *The store of Ellicott & Co. (second from left, with second-story porch), home of John Ellicott (next right), and that of Jonathan Ellicott (far right) (From a lithograph by E. Sachse & Co., Baltimore, 1854)*

8. *The Friends Meeting House at Ellicott Lower Mills, which Banneker sometimes attended; at right is the Ellicott family graveyard (From a lithograph by E. Sachse & Co., Baltimore, 1854)*

9. *Movement of a wooden striking clock made by Benjamin Cheney, c.1760, which is similar to the clock constructed by Banneker*

10. *Candlesticks and candle mold believed to have been used by Banneker*

11. Maple and pine dropleaf table believed to be the one loaned to Banneker by George Ellicott in 1789

Maryland Baltimore County near Ellicotts

Sr } Lower Mills May the 6th: 1790

I have at the request of Several Gentlemen, Calculated an Ephemeris for the year 1791 which I presented unto Mr. Hayes printer in Baltimore; and he received it in a very polite manner and told me that he would gladly print the Same provided the Calculations Came any ways near the truth, but to Satisfy himself in that he would Send it to philadelphia to be inspected by you and at the reception of an answer ~~from you~~ he Should know how to proceed and now Sr I beg that you will not be too Severe upon me but as favourable in giving your approbation as the nature of the Case will permit, knowing well the difficulty that attends long Calculations and especially with young beginners in Astronomy, but this I know that the greater and most useful part of my Ephemeris is so near the truth that it needs but little Correction, and as to that part that may ~~in Some~~ be Somewhat deficient, I hope that you will be kind enough to view with an eye of pitty as the Calculations was made more for the Sake of gratifying the Curiosity of the public, than for any view of profit, as I Suppose it to be the first attempt of the kind that ever was made in America by a person of my Complection ————

I find by my Calculation there will be four Eclipses for the ensuing year but I have not yet Settled their appearances, But am waiting for an answer from Your Honour to Mr. Hayes in Baltimore —

So no more at present, but am Sr Your very humble and most

obedient Servt

B. Banneker

12. Letter from Banneker to Major Andrew Ellicott, concerning his calculations for an almanac for 1791 (see pages 92–93)

13. Major Andrew Ellicott (Photographed from a miniature "done by a Spanish lady" in New Orleans in 1799)

14. Transit and equal altitude instrument made by Andrew Ellicott and used in his boundary surveys, including that of the Federal Territory

15. *Plain surveying compass made by Benjamin Rittenhouse for Andrew Ellicott and used in the latter's surveys; it is signed with both names*

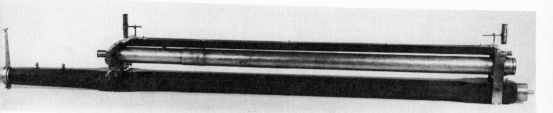

16. *Large zenith sector made by David Rittenhouse, modified by Andrew Ellicott and used in making astronomical observations in the survey of the Federal Territory and other surveys*

Sir   Philadelphia Aug. 30. 1791.

I thank you sincerely for your letter of the 19th. instant
and for the Almanac it contained. no body wishes more than
I do to see such proofs as you exhibit. that nature has given
to our black brethren, talents equal to those of the other colours
of men, & that the appearance of a want of them is owing
merely to the degraded condition of their existence both in
Africa & America. I can add with truth that nobody wishes
more ardently to see a good system commenced for raising the
condition both of their body & mind to what it ought to be, as
fast as the imbecillity of their present existence, and other cir
-cumstances which cannot be neglected, will admit.   I have
taken the liberty of sending your almanac to Monsieur de C
-dorcet, Secretary of the Academy of sciences at Paris, and mem
-ber of the Philanthropic society, because I considered it as a
document to which your whole colour had a right for their
justification against the doubts which have been entertained
of them. I am with great esteem, Sir

                    Your most obedt. humble servt.

                              Th: Jefferson

Mr. Benjamin Banneker
    near Ellicott's, lower mills. Baltimore county.

17. Draft copy of Thomas Jefferson's reply to the letter written to him by Ban-
    neker August 19, 1791 (see pages 157–158)

Benjamin Banneker's
PENNSYLVANIA, DELAWARE,
MARYLAND and VIRGINIA

Almanack,

AND
EPHEMERIS,
FOR THE YEAR OF OUR LORD,
1792;

Being BISSEXTILE, or LEAP-YEAR, and the SIX-
TEENTH YEAR of AMERICAN INDEPENDENCE,
which commenced *July* 4, 1776.

CONTAINING, the Motions of the Sun and Moon, the true
Places and Aspects of the Planets, the Rising and Setting of
the Sun, and the Rising, Setting and Southing, Place and Age
of the Moon, &c.—The Lunations, Conjunctions, Eclipses,
Judgment of the Weather, Festivals, and other remarkable
Days; Days for holding the Supreme and Circuit Courts of the
United States, as also the usual Courts in *Pennsylvania, Delaware, Maryland,* and *Virginia.*—ALSO, several useful Tables,
and valuable Receipts.—Various Selections from the Commonplace-Book of the *Kentucky Philosopher,* an *American Sage;*
with interesting and entertaining Essays, in Prose and Verse—
the whole comprising a greater, more pleasing, and useful Variety, than any Work of the *Kind* and *Price* in *North-America.*

BALTIMORE: Printed and Sold, Wholesale and Retail, by
WILLIAM GODDARD and JAMES ANGELL, at their Print-
ing-Office, in *Market-Street.*—Sold, also, by Mr. JOSEPH
CRUKSHANK, Printer, in *Market-Street,* and Mr. DANIEL
HUMPHREYS, Printer, in *South-Front-Street, Philadelphia,*
and by Messrs. HANSON and BOND, Printers, in *Alexandria.*

18. *Title page of Banneker's almanac for 1792, published in Baltimore by Goddard
& Angell*

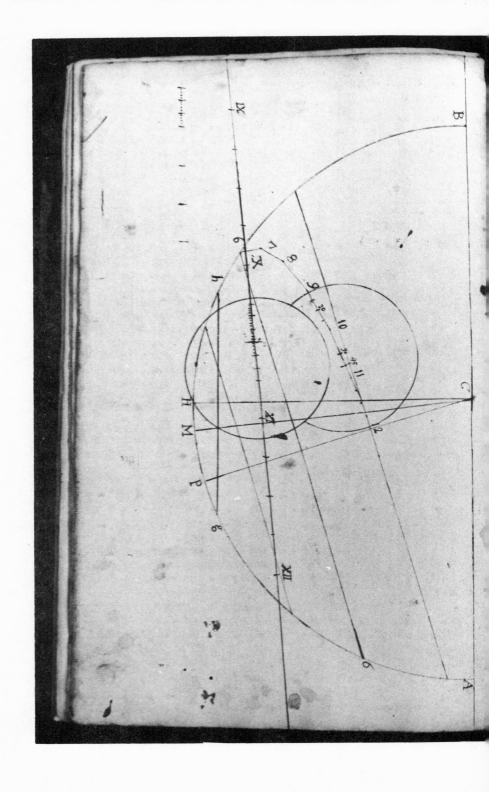

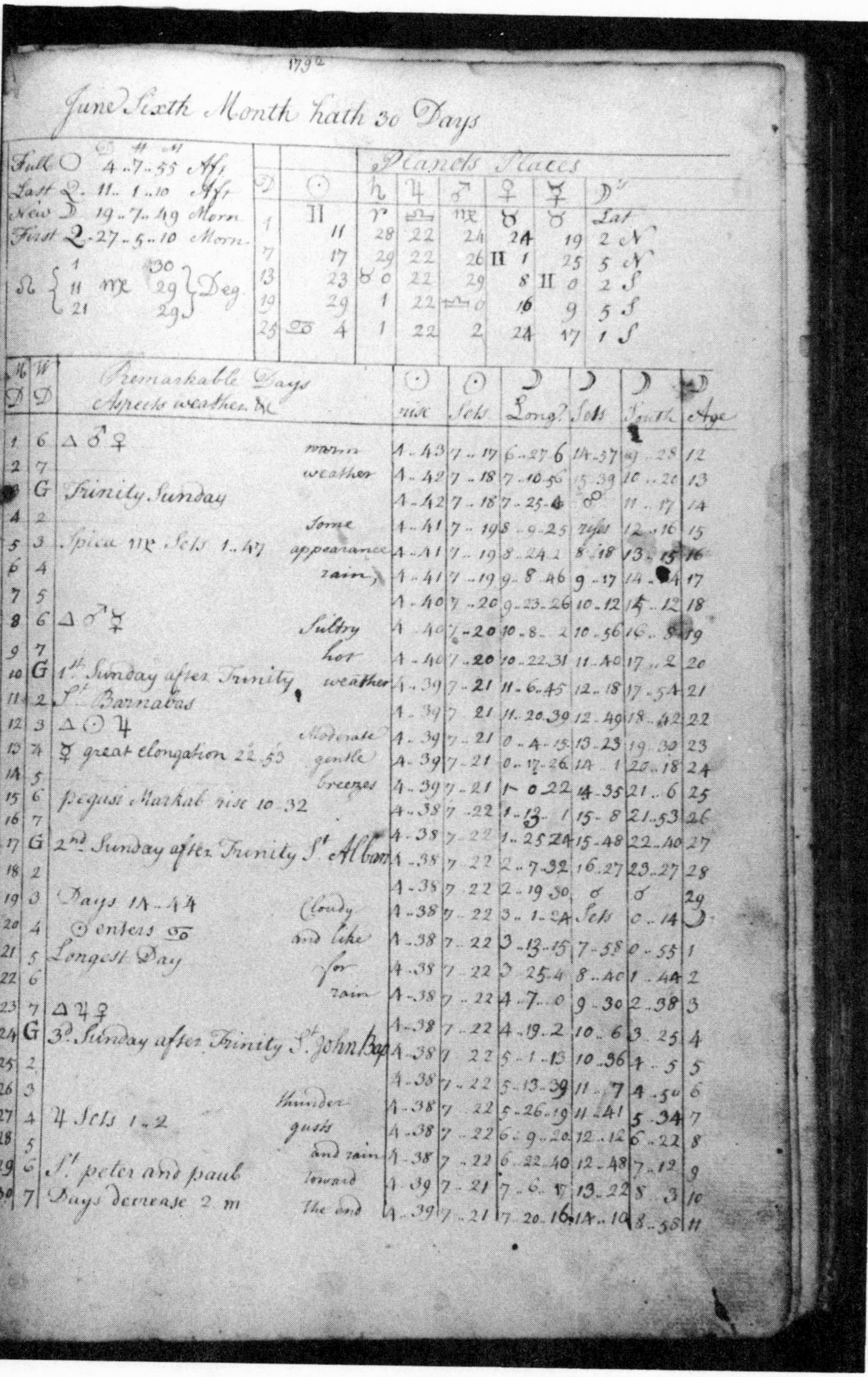

1792

June Sixth Month hath 30 Days

	D	H	M	
Full ☉	4	7	55	Aft
Last ☾	11	1	10	Aft
New ☽	19	7	49	Morn
First ☾	27	5	10	Morn

☊ { 1 ♍ 30; 11 29; 21 29 } Deg.

D	☉	♄	♃	♂	♀	☿	☽'s Lat
	♊	♈	♎	♍	♉	♉	
1	11	28	22	24	24	19	2 N
7	17	29	22	26	♊ 1	25	5 N
13	23	♉ 0	22	29	8	♊ 0	2 S
19	29	1	22	♎ 0	16	9	5 S
25	♋ 4	1	22	2	24	17	1 S

M D	W D	Remarkable Days Aspects weather &c		☉ rise	☉ Sets	☽ Long?	☽ Sets	☽ South	☽ Age
1	6	△ ♂ ♀	warm	4..43	7..17	6..27 6	14..37	9..28	12
2	7		weather	4..42	7..18	7..10.56	15..39	10..20	13
3	G	Trinity Sunday		4..42	7..18	7..25..4	☍	11..17	14
4	2		Some	4..41	7..19	8..9..25	rises	12..16	15
5	3	Spica ♍ Sets 1..47	appearance	4..41	7..19	8..24..2	8..18	13..15	16
6	4		rain	4..41	7..19	9..8..46	9..17	14..[illegible]4	17
7	5			4..40	7..20	9..23..26	10..12	15..12	18
8	6	△ ♂ ☿	Sultry	4..40	7..20	10..8..2	10..56	16..8	19
9	7		hot	4..40	7..20	10..22..31	11..40	17..2	20
10	G	1th Sunday after Trinity	weather	4..39	7..21	11..6..45	12..18	17..54	21
11	2	St Barnabas		4..39	7..21	11..20..39	12..49	18..42	22
12	3	△ ☉ ♃	Moderate	4..39	7..21	0..4..15	13..23	19..30	23
13	4	☿ great elongation 22..53	gentle	4..39	7..21	0..17..26	14..1	20..18	24
14	5		breezes	4..39	7..21	1..0..22	14..35	21..6	25
15	6	Pegusi Markab rise 10..32		4..38	7..22	1..13..1	15..8	21..53	26
16	7			4..38	7..22	1..25..24	15..48	22..40	27
17	G	2nd Sunday after Trinity St Albon		4..38	7..22	2..7..32	16..27	23..27	28
18	2			4..38	7..22	2..19..30	☌	☌	29
19	3	Days 14..44	Cloudy	4..38	7..22	3..1..24	Sets	0..14	☽
20	4	☉ enters ♋	and like	4..38	7..22	3..13..15	7..58	0..55	1
21	5	Longest Day	for	4..38	7..22	3..25..4	8..40	1..44	2
22	6		rain	4..38	7..22	4..7..0	9..30	2..38	3
23	7	△ ♃ ♀		4..38	7..22	4..19..2	10..6	3..25	4
24	G	3d Sunday after Trinity St John Bap		4..38	7..22	5..1..13	10..36	4..5	5
25	2			4..38	7..22	5..13..39	11..7	4..50	6
26	3		thunder	4..38	7..22	5..26..19	11..41	5..34	7
27	4	♃ Sets 1..2	gusts	4..38	7..22	6..9..20	12..12	6..22	8
28	5		and rain	4..38	7..22	6..22..40	12..48	7..12	9
29	6	St peter and paul	toward	4..39	7..21	7..6..5	13..22	8..3	10
30	7	Days decrease 2 m	the end	4..39	7..21	7..20..16	14..10	8..55	11

19. A projection of a lunar eclipse, from Banneker's Manuscript Journal; calculations for the month of June, 1792, on the facing page of the Journal

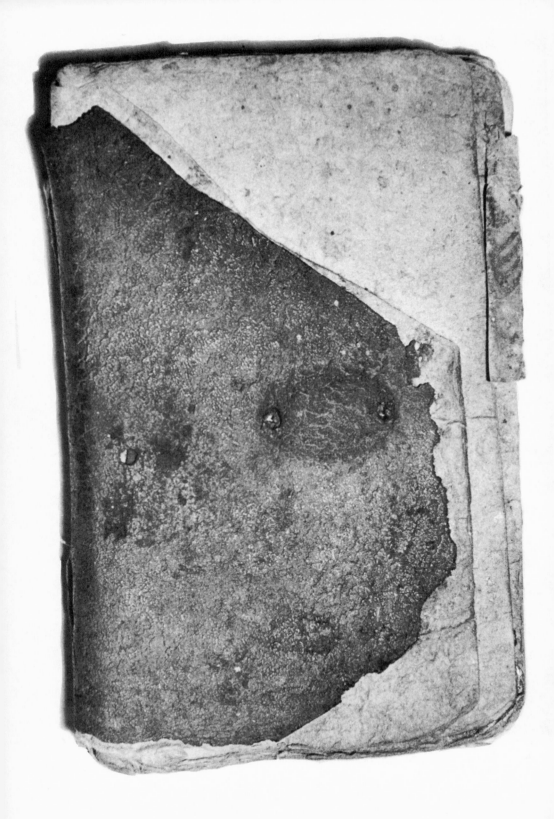

20. *Banneker's Commonplace Book:* (left) *the cover;* (above) *entries relating to household and personal matters*

21. *Mural painting of the Federal Territory survey by William A. Smith, showing Banneker and Major Ellicott in the field, with Ellicott's topographical map of the District of Columbia in the background. The painting is at Maryland House on the John F. Kennedy Highway, Aberdeen, Maryland*

V

THE GREAT ADVENTURE

◊❀◊❀◊❀◊❀◊❀◊❀◊❀◊❀◊❀◊

We but view the scene before us
Strangers to each future stage;
Greater strangers to the glories
Blooming thro' th' eternal age.
"On a Cloud," *Banneker's*
Almanac for 1794

EARLY IN 1791, Banneker became involved in what he considered the greatest adventure in his life—the survey for a federal city which was to serve as the capital of the new republic, on a site chosen by President Washington.

Curiously enough, the record of Banneker's involvement rests on extremely meager documentation, consisting of a statement in a letter written by Thomas Jefferson and two statements made by Banneker himself. There may be other records that mention Banneker in this connection, but they have not yet been found. Consequently, it is well to present the account of that part of the survey with which Banneker was involved in extensive detail based primarily on the papers of Major Andrew Ellicott. Although a great part of it may not seem to relate directly to Banneker's participation, the detail is necessary to evaluate his role in its accomplishment.

The planning for a national capital had been in progress for a long time, and the need to establish it developed from the growing inconvenience to the Congress brought about by its constant move from city to city. The Congress had met in eight different cities during the War of Independence and the following period of the Confederation. Various sites had been offered for the new capital, and the selection was predicated upon the resolution of two major questions which arose in establishing a seat of government: geographical location and jurisdiction. It was considered important that the new capital should be centrally located along the Atlantic seaboard, and a site at Georgetown, Maryland, near the Potomac's lower falls, was finally selected. It was agreed that Congress was to have exclusive jurisdiction over the seat of government.

Discussions in the Congress concerning the establishment of a seat of government began in 1779, but it was not until 1783 that a site was selected. A proposal to establish a national capital city under the jurisdiction of the Congress was included in the draft of the Constitution of the United States, which was adopted by the Congress and ratified by the states in 1787. When the first Congress under the federal Constitution met in 1789, there was much deliberation over the site. In 1790 it reached an agreement, which took the form of a bill that became law that year. The states of Maryland and Virginia ceded portions of their respective territories to form what was to be known as a new District of Columbia, and work was finally to begin. The project was launched by a proclamation made by President Washington on January 24, 1791, in which he directed that a survey be made of a ten-mile square. Two days before the proclamation, the President appointed three Commissioners to oversee the survey and design of the city. These were Daniel Carroll and Thomas Johnson of Maryland and Dr. David Stuart of Virginia.

The region selected for the ten-mile square between Georgetown and the Eastern Branch included two unincorporated "paper" towns known as Hamburgh and Carrollsburgh. Hamburgh consisted of 130 acres fronting on the Potomac River just above the mouth of Tiber Creek (also known as Goose Creek). It was a platted town laid out by Jacob Funk in October 1771 from land purchased from Thomas Johns in 1765. Carrollsburgh consisted of about 160 acres lying between the north bank of the Eastern Branch and James Creek and consisted of land sold by Charles Carroll, Jr., to three purchasers.

The only settled community that existed within the region was Georgetown. This was an active trading center which had been laid out as a town in 1751 and developed with the construction of mercantile houses of Scottish agents of English merchants. Vessels docking at its wharves brought freights of dry goods, wines, and hardware and returned with tobacco and furs. Georgetown served as a port for coastal commerce, from which many brigs and schooners traded with New York, Boston, and other New England ports as well as the West Indies, returning with sugar and molasses. Conestoga wagons rumbled along the dusty streets, bringing wheat and corn from farmers in Maryland and central Pennsylvania to barter for groceries, dry goods, and fish. Meanwhile, products of Maryland were also brought down the Potomac River between Georgetown and Cumberland. This waterway served as the route for flat-bottomed boats, which transported pork, flour, corn, and iron to other ports from Georgetown.

Situated eight miles farther down the Potomac River was the port town of Alexandria, Virginia, which was then one of the three most important seaports in the country.

The site of the new capital city was not only centrally located along the seaboard but would occupy a strategic position in the commercial life of the new republic.

Following the President's proclamation establishing the site, and the appointment of the Commissioners, the next step was to define the area and then design the city itself. The choice of the individual to undertake the survey was an obvious one, and Major Andrew Ellicott was appointed. Ellicott had been a professional surveyor all his adult life and he had achieved distinction in his work. The son of Joseph Ellicott, the eldest of the brothers who founded Ellicott's Lower Mills, Andrew was born in Bucks County in 1753 and arrived in Maryland with his father in 1772. Soon after his father had established Ellicott's Upper Mills several years later, Andrew moved his own young family to the new community.

Ellicott left home to undertake various surveys, such as the boundary between Pennsylvania and Virginia in September 1784. He returned to the Mills in November of that year to find that his family was in poor health; one of his sons was seriously ill and finally died in March 1785. He was unhappy about the Mills, and after his son's death he moved his family to Baltimore. In addition to surveying, he had served in military and political positions. In May 1778 he was commissioned first a captain and later a major in the Elkridge Battalion of Militia for Anne Arundel County. While living in Baltimore, he represented the city in the state legislature for one term, but he refused a second term when offered.

His survey of the islands of the rivers Allegheny and Ohio within the boundaries of Pennsylvania was completed in 1788, and in the following year he moved his family from Baltimore to Philadelphia. This provided him with a better base of operations because the federal government was then centralized there. He was interested in becoming involved in some of the new surveys which were being proposed, and in this connection he asked his friend, Benjamin Franklin, to submit a recommendation on his behalf to the government. Whether derived directly from Franklin's support or not, Ellicott was commissioned to run the western boundary of the State of New York. He undertook the project with his brothers, Joseph and Benjamin, in September 1789. The winter weather made it difficult to work in the field, and Ellicott customarily closed his camp and returned to his family until the spring. However, he managed to complete the survey of the western boundary late in 1790, and retired to Philadelphia for several months' rest and relaxation. It was during this period that he was interrupted in order to commence the survey of the ten-mile square for the new Federal City.

When the preliminaries had been dispensed with, the Commissioners were advised of Ellicott's appointment in a letter from Jefferson conveying the wishes of the President:

> The President thinking it would be better that the outline at least of the City, and perhaps Georgetown should be laid down in the plat of the territory. I have the honor now to send it and to desire that Major Ellicott may do it as soon as convenient, that it may be returned in time to be laid before Congress . . .[1]

Washington expressed himself as being extremely anxious to proceed with the project now that the various problems with the landowners appeared to be resolved,[2] and he so informed Jefferson, urging him to have Ellicott proceed as soon as it could be arranged.*

Ellicott received his formal notification from the Secretary of State in a letter written the following day, February 2, 1791.[3] As could have been expected from Washington, the former surveyor, the instructions conveyed from him by Jefferson were carefully delineated. Ellicott was advised that he was to run the first two lines as mentioned in the President's proclamation to fix the beginning point, and from that to establish the four "lines of experiment" for the ten-mile square. Furthermore,

* See Document 2.

he was to find the true meridian and determine the latitude and map the course of the rivers within the segment surveyed.*

Ellicott was excited by the assignment, and he lost no time in making preparations for a long absence from home. His first concern was for skilled assistance. His two younger brothers were still completing the survey in New York State and it would be several months before they would be able to join him. He then probably remembered his young cousin, George Ellicott, who was a competent surveyor and astronomer, as he had so ably demonstrated in laying out the Baltimore-Frederick Turnpike. He wrote to George and offered him the position of scientific assistant. In addition to the field hands he needed, he required someone with a knowledge of astronomy and an ability to use scientific instruments for making daily observations. George had the ability, although he did not have the field experience.

George was regretful in his reply, explaining that business pressures would not permit such a prolonged absence. Along with operating the grain mills in partnership with his brothers, he was responsible for the several new enterprises which they had developed in the Lower Mills. However, he probably reminded Andrew about Banneker and his mathematical skill, and described the remarkable progress he had made in the study of astronomy. Andrew agreed that Banneker might be useful. The ephemeris which he had reviewed for Hayes the year before indicated that he would be competent, although Banneker was then sixty and might not be able to cope with the hardships of working in the field. Andrew also recalled Banneker's local reputation for drinking. In subsequent conversations with Secretary of State Jefferson, Ellicott mentioned his need for trained assistance and discussed the scarcity of competent persons, none of whom were available for the project on such short notice. Jefferson encouraged Ellicott to employ Banneker for the preliminary survey, and suggested that he would be useful until such a time as Andrew's younger brothers could join

* See Document 3.

him. Confirmation of this discussion is to be found in Jefferson's letter to the Marquis de Condorcet, written in the following year, in which he mentioned: "I procured him to be employed under one of our chief directors in laying out the new Federal City on the Potomac. . . ." [4] Although there is no further substantiation of Jefferson's part in hiring Banneker, and Banneker did not acknowledge it in his communication with Jefferson in the following year, there can be no doubt that Jefferson approved of Ellicott's choice.

Whether Andrew Ellicott communicated with Banneker from Philadelphia before meeting him is not known. He may have asked George to speak to Banneker to find out whether he would consider the opportunity. After making his final preparations for his sojourn, Andrew left Philadelphia on horseback. He planned to break his journey so that he could visit his widowed mother at Ellicott's Upper Mills and at the same time meet Banneker and complete his arrangements.

His negotiations were successful, and Banneker expressed his interest and excitement at the prospect. While Andrew spent the next several days with his mother, Banneker made arrangements for his journey. He asked his two sisters, who lived in the neighborhood, to look after his farm. There were the several farm animals to be looked after, and someone had to keep an eye on the house during his absence to prevent theft or vandalism. Banneker was uncertain about his needs during his absence; he collected and discarded possessions in considerable confusion until the final moment of departure. He rode to the Upper Mills, stopping for a brief visit at the Lower Mills to bid good-bye to his good friend George. The latter was almost as excited by the assignment as Banneker himself. They discussed the nature of the work and the possibilities for the use of astronomical instruments which would not otherwise have been possible. Andrew owned what were probably the finest instruments in the country at that time. Banneker would have been content merely to see Major Ellicott using them, to say nothing of handling them himself. He could hardly believe that he, a farmer sixty years old, with no education other than what he had painfully gleaned from borrowed books, would have the chance to participate in what was unquestionably the most important surveying project in the new republic. One resolution he had made when Major Ellicott offered him the work was that during the course of the project he would do no drinking.

A touching evidence of the great esteem for Banneker which Elizabeth Ellicott shared with her husband is this statement written by her daughter concerning the preparations made for Banneker's sojourn:

> Under the impression that Banneker would fall under the notice of the most eminent men of the country, whilst thus engaged, the lady who has been referred to, as having paid a visit in his cottage in 1790 [Elizabeth Brooke Ellicott], was careful to direct the appointments of his wardrobe, in order that he might appear in respectable guise, before the distinguished personages likely to be assembled there.[5]

The time came when they were ready to proceed to the new Federal Territory. Ellicott was eager to begin and he did not linger more than a few days at the Upper Mills while he waited for Banneker to get ready. Finally, the day of departure arrived. Shortly after dawn, the two men set off on horseback, with their equipment and luggage packed behind their saddles. They made an unusual pair to the few they encountered along the highway. Major Ellicott was tall and big-boned, and despite his youth—he was thirty-eight—he looked much older, possibly owing to his graying hair and portliness. He wore sturdy garments against the winter cold, a snug vest, and a tricorn hat. Riding along beside him, Banneker made a pronounced contrast. He was considerably shorter than his companion, with a heavy frame. His work on the farm had made him extremely muscular, but the advancing years had made him somewhat corpulent. He had a rather short neck, and with his shock of white hair he most resembled Major Ellicott's eminent friend, Benjamin Franklin. He was not as accustomed to riding long distances, and his age and ailments contributed to his weariness. They followed the turnpike, stopping for a meal and a short rest en route before continuing on their way. Ellicott had decided to make his first base at Alexandria, in preference to Georgetown. The base point of the survey was to be at Hunting Creek and it would be most convenient to operate from a spot nearby until the survey was more advanced.

The two travelers arrived at Alexandria on the evening of February 7 and obtained lodging at Wise's Fountain Tavern* on Cameron Street. When they drew up before the tavern, they were directed around the corner to the tavern stables on Pitt Street, where they left their horses and waited until they had been prepared for the night. Banneker was impressed by his surroundings; he had never seen a city of this size before. It was much larger than Joppa or Baltimore. The tavern itself fronted on three streets and was one of the busiest centers in town, with merchants, gentlemen, sailors, and others constantly coming and going.[6]

Despite the excitement of finding himself in new surroundings, Banneker welcomed the opportunity to rest. The last part of the journey had been done in the rain. The skies were overcast and Ellicott was concerned that they might be delayed in beginning their survey. His predictions were justified: they were beset with bad weather, causing them to remain indoors during the next several days.

Banneker was filled with curiosity, however, and after he had been well rested he wandered around the seaport town even

---

* A discrepancy occurs in Ellicott's correspondence. In his letter to his wife dated February 14, 1791, from Alexandria, Virginia, he stated that he had arrived on Tuesday, while in a letter to Jefferson he reported that he arrived on Monday. He probably arrived Monday evening, and the first day actually spent on the scene was Tuesday. The details of the arrangements and the journey to Alexandria are assumed, in view of the absence of Ellicott's diary.

during the drizzle. He found himself in an exciting place, for Alexandria was one of the country's largest commercial centers. It had become a rendezvous for merchants, soldiers, and travelers of all kinds. The wharves teemed with activity as all sorts of cargoes were loaded and unloaded on the ships at anchor in the harbor. As he walked along the streets, he was enthralled by the sounds of the busy city and the voices that spoke in many languages. The city brought to life the magic world of history which he had found in his books, and his eyes and ears and mind were filled with a multitude of exciting impressions.

As Major Ellicott went about making arrangements for the purchase of equipment for his field camp, hired hands and woodcutters, and horses, and completed the many other necessary preparations, he grumbled about the weather and the overcast that prevented him from making astronomical observations. The first step was to set up a surveyor's camp near the apex of the proposed square, somewhere near Jones' Point on the upper cape of Hunting Creek near Alexandria. Ellicott led his surveying party to the site, and they set to work to establish a camp. The party consisted of several men who tended the pack horses, packing and unpacking, and helped clear a route through the dense underbrush and forest.

Ellicott preferred to establish his main encampment on the top of the highest available elevation in the region to be surveyed, and he customarily sought the protection of trees or the edge of a forest for additional protection when possible. The focal point of his operation was the observatory tent, which Ellicott located by tracing a meridian and then laying off an angle from it. It was at this observation point that he set up his large zenith sector and near which he placed his astronomical clock. The clock was a critical factor to all his observations, the one piece of equipment that habitually presented the most problems. It was a precision timekeeper, liable to derangement from many causes. Vibrations from movements upon the ground nearby, changes in temperature, and any contact with it might cause inaccuracy. For this reason he usually set the clock upon the stump of a tree which he had cut down for that purpose. He then erected his observatory tent over the sector and the clock and his other instruments. Other tents for sleeping and for meals were then set up in the vicinity, and an area was provided nearby for tethering the horses.

By far the most important of Ellicott's instruments was the larger of his two zenith sectors, which was nearly six feet long, and by means of which meridional observations were made through an opening in the top of the tent. It had been made for him by David Rittenhouse and he had added his own modifications. It was probably the most accurate scientific instrument in America at that time. It was used for determination of the latitude by observation of stars near the zenith. Observations would be made of six or seven stars as they crossed the meridian at different times of the night, and the observations would be repeated a number of nights over a period of time. Ellicott had remarked in some of his writings that when the stars were so near the zenith they were affected by the different refractive powers of the atmosphere which derived from the varying degrees of density. He found that the error of the visual axis could be reduced to a reasonable minimum by taking zenith distances of the stars with the plane, or face, of the sector alternately facing east or west. The figures derived in this manner were averaged, corrected for refraction, aberration and nutation were applied, and then a comparison was made with the data in published star catalogues. Determination of the latitude was accomplished from this comparison, based on each of the stars observed.

Another of the more important instruments used by Ellicott was his transit and equal altitude instrument, which he had constructed himself in 1789 based on the design illustrated and described by Pierre Charles Le Monnier in his *Histoire Celeste*. Ellicott had already made good use of it in running the western boundary of the State of New York, and in his opinion it was almost perfect and particularly adapted for running straight lines. He also used it for taking equal altitudes of the sun by means of which he could rate his astronomical clock and check it for accuracy at periodic intervals throughout each day.

Ellicott's field equipment also included a smaller zenith sector having a radius of nineteen inches. It was much smaller than its counterpart, and consequently less accurate. Its advantage was in its portability which made it possible to use it elsewhere in the field to which the large sector could not be transported and installed.

For taking horizontal angles Ellicott used a brass circumferentor with a radius of eight inches, made by George Adams of London. He also had a fine plain surveying compass of brass made expressly for him by Benjamin Rittenhouse for use in running the lines. He customarily had several sextants, one with a radius of seven inches, made by Jesse Ramsden of London, which served him in taking lunar distances. Three telescopes were usually on hand, the largest of which was an achromatic instrument with pedestal produced by Dollond of London and equipped with a terrestrial eyepiece having a magnification of about sixty times, as well as several eyepieces for celestial observation which magnified from 120 to 300 times. His two other telescopes were smaller, having sliding tubes for taking signals and used primarily for making observations of the occultations and eclipses of the satellites of Jupiter for determining the longitude.

Ellicott determined the longitude by two separate methods. He recorded the time of the appearance or eclipse of one of Jupiter's satellites with the time that the same event had been observed at Greenwich Observatory, and then converted the differences into the appropriate degrees of longitude. He also employed the observation of lunar distances for the same purpose.

Smaller equipment included an artificial horizon, several thermometers, two stopwatches with second hands, two sets of cased drafting instruments, and two copper lanterns of Ellicott's own design which had special slits for tracing meridians and giving the direction of the lines when he determined them at night by means of celestial observation. Finally, two two-pole chains formed basic adjuncts for his field work.

Banneker soon found that his assignment was not as simple as he had anticipated. He was to assist Ellicott in the observatory tent, and to participate in observations made in the field as well. His most important responsibility was the maintenance of the astronomical clock, which proved to be far more complicated a chore than he had imagined. The clock was an extremely well-made timepiece designed for the maximum precision that could be achieved in that period. It was housed in a simply made wooden tall-case, and Banneker eventually began to understand why Ellicott seemed to be so fretful of its operation. Remembering his own wooden clock, Banneker admired the movement in this one, which was the finest he had ever seen. It was his duty to keep it wound, to check its rate by means of equal altitudes taken of the sun at periodic intervals with the transit and equal altitude instrument, and it was necessary to keep the temperature in its vicinity constant. For this purpose he had several thermometers placed at appropriate points from which he recorded the readings several times each day.

The astronomical clock was a particular concern of Ellicott's, for his experience in previous surveys had made him aware of the numerous and constant problems inherent to keeping the timepiece operating at maximum accuracy. Various types of minor accidents were liable to occur in its vicinity that would affect its rate, and Banneker was constantly on the alert in fulfilling his responsibility.

In the past, when Ellicott's two younger brothers were available, they worked in the field running the lines while Major Ellicott spent most of his time in the observatory tent. Now he was required to reverse his procedures. Since Banneker was neither capable nor qualified to run the lines, and was much more useful with the astronomical instruments, Ellicott supervised the work in the field. He keenly felt the absence of his other experienced assistants as well as of his brothers. Whereas in the past he customarily had a crew of twenty men working with him, he had been able to recruit not more than six men for the Territory, none with any previous field experience.

Ellicott was finally able to make the first of his astronomical observations on the evening of Friday, February 11. He forwarded his first report to Jefferson, describing what he had been able to accomplish and the conditions he had found, in a letter written exactly one week after his arrival at Alexandria.[7] He had been hampered by cloudy weather from making observations earlier in the week, but he had used the interim profitably by buying needed equipment, hiring woodcutters to cut down trees and to work in the field, and in establishing his camp. The first major difficulty he encountered was that according to his instructions the wharfs and harbor of Alexandria would be included within his square. Since this was not desirable, he had adjusted his lines accordingly, and planned to submit them for approval.*

On the same evening he wrote to his wife to advise her that all was well and that he had been able to begin to work at last.[8] He commented that he had been well received in Alexandria during the few days he remained there before moving into the field.†

His procedure for laying out the square was a simple one. Before undertaking the definition of the square, Ellicott traced a meridian at Jones' Point on the west side of the Potomac River and then laid off an angle of 45° from this meridian to the northwest, and continued a straight line in that direction for ten miles. He made a right angle at the termination of this line with a straight line which he carried in a northeasterly direction, also for ten miles, and then from the termination of this second line he carried yet a third line for the same distance at a right angle to it, to the southeast. Finally he carried a line from the terminal point at Jones' Point to meet the termination of the third line. He measured these lines by means of a chain, which he examined and corrected each day to ensure that the links had not

* See Document 4.
† See Document 5.

opened and that there was no other change affecting its accuracy. He plumbed it wherever the ground proved to be uneven, and traced it with his transit and equal altitude instrument.[9]

Ellicott directed all his efforts to making as much progress as possible with the boundary survey, for he knew that President Washington was anxious to have a report of results. However, he encountered one frustration after another, primarily because of the lack of experienced assistants. He was forced to become involved in the countless details of day-to-day operation, which reduced the efficiency of his own efforts and slowed the work. To add to his frustration, he succumbed to a bout of influenza which was distracting and painful. He nevertheless forced himself to continue, but it was mid-March before he fully recovered. He commented on his problems to his wife at that time and noted:

> I have met with many difficulties for want of my old hands, and have in consequence a most severe attack of influenza worked for many days in extreme pain. I am now perfectly recovered, and as fat as you ever saw me. . . . The President will be here next Monday, and after I receive his future orders, you shall hear from me. . . .[10]

By this time Ellicott had found it expedient to establish himself in Georgetown, and he moved from Alexandria to new lodgings at an inn, and set up an office as well, in the home of William Prout. This house was advantageously situated for Ellicott's needs. He may have obtained lodgings at Prout's inn as well, or he may have kept a room at Suter's Tavern. In 1791 this was one of only two inns in Georgetown and it served as the community center as well as a way station for travelers through the area. It was situated on High Street (now Wisconsin Avenue) between Bridge and Water Streets (M Street and the Canal Bridge). Built in 1761, it was kept by several landlords before

John Suter acquired it and obtained his license as an innkeeper in 1783. Although formally named The Fountain Inn, it was locally known by the name of the innkeeper, and favored by gentlemen over the neighboring Sailor's Tavern. It was a long wooden building of one and a half stories with a projecting roof over a long veranda and with large stables. It was at this tavern that President Washington had his accommodations during his visits to supervise the survey.[11]

Meanwhile, Banneker remained with the other men and assistants in the survey camp. Since so much of his time was spent in the observatory tent, he also slept there. He was not accustomed to exposure and the cold but he made the best of it, consoling himself with the uniqueness of his opportunity to work with one of the country's foremost scientists and to use those fine astronomical instruments. Ellicott usually took Banneker to the meetings with the Commissioners; there were also other occasions when Banneker could leave the confines of the camp. He was learning a great deal about astronomy in the course of his work, and he used every chance to familiarize himself with the instruments and the few scientific texts Ellicott had brought along. He realized how relatively simple his own work in calculating ephemerides had been compared with the project in which he was now involved.

Whenever he found time, he returned to his own almanac calculations, drafting an outline for an ephemeris for the following year because he planned to make another attempt to have one published. He saved what little time he could for the purpose, trying to take advantage of the materials available to him. This was not a simple matter, however, for he was required to work long hours, and he was usually exhausted by the time he was able to rest.

Banneker's greatest problem stemmed from the erratic schedule he was forced to follow, owing to the nature of his assignment. His day and night were broken up so that he could rest only during those brief periods when his presence was not required elsewhere. The kind of astronomical observations needed for the survey made the evening and night periods the most important working time for him, so that he could not retire until the morning. As the night ended and he was ready to go to bed, Major Ellicott customarily rode up to the observatory tent as he came into camp from his Georgetown lodgings. Arriving just at sunup, he was in the habit of reviewing the night's work from Banneker's notes before proceeding with the field work. When the other men were beginning their working day, Banneker was about to finish his own, then rest. But not always without interruption, however. From time to time he had to be awake to take observations of the sun with the equal altitude instrument to establish the correct time for the observatory clock. The last of these morning chores took place at mid-afternoon, so that he could sleep for the remainder of the afternoon, unless one of the men had need to come into the tent in the meantime. This schedule, combined with the extreme cold and humidity, aggravated Banneker's aches and pains, often giving him great distress.

The problems encounted by Ellicott and his men were magnified for the older man, but since he did not have to spend much of his time in the field, he consoled himself with the fact that he was gaining new experience with instruments, and a look at his opportunities was enough to ease his discomfort. Nevertheless, he eagerly awaited the arrival of spring weather.

Major Ellicott was a hard taskmaster. Each morning he rose while it was still dark, and by the first light of day he had completed his breakfast and was ready to begin work. Ellicott worked with his men seven days a week not leaving the field until bed time. He recovered slowly from his siege of illness, and with the end of winter, conditions improved somewhat, although the thaw made the ground underfoot less favorable.

The work was made unpleasant by the extreme changes of weather and hazardous by the nature of the undertaking. The situation was best described in the occasional statements included by Ellicott in his letters to his wife. His description of the terrain was fairly vivid:

I have found the weather in this country extremely hot, partly owing I suppose to the want of rain, having had but three small showers since I left you last. The country through which we are now cutting one of the ten mile lines is very poor. I think for near seven miles, on it there is not one house that has any floor except the earth, and what is more strange it is in the neighborhood of Alexandria and Georgetown. We find but little fruit, except huckleberries, and live in our Camp as retired as we used to do on Lake Erie. Labouring hands in this country can scarcely be had at any rate, my estimate was twenty—but I have to wade slowly thro' with six, this scarcity of hands will lengthen out the time much beyond what I intended. . . .[12]

Ellicott also made mention of some of the mishaps which befell his crew. "We have a most eligant [sic] Camp and things are in fine order but where you are not there are no charms—— One of our Hands was killed last week by the falling of a Tree——" [13] Later he noted that this was not in fact an unusual incident and commented: "I have had a number of men killed this summer one of whom was a worthy, ingenious, and truly valuable character, he has left a wife and three small children to lament his untimely fate——" [14]

The project's slow but certain progress was watched with interest by the citizens of Georgetown. On February 23 the *Gazette* noted:

Mr. Ellicott, we learned, finished the first line of his survey of the Federal territory in Virginia yesterday, and crossed below the Little Falls, the river Potowmack, on the second line.[15]

While Ellicott was well underway with his boundary survey, Jefferson notified Major Pierre Charles L'Enfant, in a letter dated early in March.[16] Jefferson's instructions were as precise with L'Enfant as they had been with Ellicott. L'Enfant was to prepare drawings of the grounds best suited to the site for the federal city and for the specific government buildings to be erected there. He was to note roads, streams, and other topographical data, within the area which Ellicott was surveying.*

L'Enfant was a French soldier and engineer who had fought in the Continental Army and later remodeled the temporary quarters for the federal government in New York. He arrived at the scene of the survey on March 9, a month after Ellicott had begun work on the project. President Washington had neglected to specify to L'Enfant that he was to be subordinate to the District Commissioners, so that L'Enfant was led to believe that he was responsible only to the President himself. It was this notion that later caused friction between the Commissioners and the engineer and subsequently led to his dismissal.

It is important to point out at this time that, contrary to popular notion, Ellicott was the first to receive an appointment to produce a survey, and that L'Enfant's appointment was made at least one month later.

Historians have occasionally erroneously reported that Andrew Ellicott and Banneker were L'Enfant's assistants. Ellicott was never appointed as assistant or subordinate of L'Enfant; he worked independently under the jurisdiction of the Commissioners. Banneker was assistant to Ellicott and, as far as can be determined, worked only under his direction and was not involved with other aspects of the project. During the summer of 1791, however, Benjamin Ellicott, Andrew's younger brother and assistant surveyor, was delegated to assist L'Enfant in drawing up the sketch of the city. It is probably from this assignment that the confusion developed.

An interesting commentary on this matter was made by John Saurin Norris in a written statement prepared for Martha E. Tyson, perhaps to provide clarification of the point in her paper which he read before the Maryland Historical Society in 1854.[17] After describing the legislation for creating the Federal

* See Document 6.

Territory and the appointment of Commissioners and the survey of the ten-mile square and the design of the city itself, he made some interesting comments as to whether Banneker was employed to lay out the "District," so called, or whether he worked with L'Enfant in laying out the city. He pointed out that the former required knowledge of astronomy and the use of scientific instruments, whereas the latter could be accomplished merely with a knowledge of engineering, so that it was his conclusion that Banneker was involved with the former. Norris went on to assume that during his sojourn Banneker had met Jefferson, but he was obviously in error, inasmuch as Jefferson is not reported to have visited the site during the period in question.*

The arrival of L'Enfant in the Federal Territory was announced in an article in *The Georgetown Weekly Ledger*, which also reported the presence of Banneker on the one and only occasion in which his participation was publicly noted:

> Some time last month arrived in this town Mr. *Andrew Ellicot*, a gentleman of superior astronomical abilities. He was employed by the President of the United States of America, to lay off a tract of land, ten miles square, on the Potowmack, for the use of Congress;—is now engaged in this business, and hopes soon to accomplish the object of his mission. He is attended by *Benjamin Banniker*, an Ethiopian, whose abilities, as a surveyor, and an astronomer, clearly prove that Mr. Jefferson's concluding that race of men were void of mental endowments, was without foundation.
>
> Wednesday evening arrived in this town, Major *Longfont*, a French gentleman, employed by the President of the United States to survey the lands contiguous to George-Town, where the federal city is to be built. His skill in matters of this nature is justly extolled by all disposed to give merit its proper tribute of praise.

* See Document 7.

He is earnest in the business, and hopes to be able to lay
a plat, of that parcel of land, before the President, upon
his arrival in this town.[18]

This newspaper article has been quoted widely in subsequent
historical accounts of the survey, and it has in fact served as
evidence in the litigation of the Potomac Flats Case relating to
the allocation of lots laid out in the development of Washington.[19] Curiously enough, however, not a single copy of this issue
of the *Ledger* is known to have survived. The same account was
published verbatim with a George-Town by-line and the date of
March 12 in newspapers in other areas, such as *The Maryland
Gazette*.[20] It was also the basis for an abbreviated news item
which appeared in the Philadelphia press a week later:

Mr. Ellicot and Major L'Enfant, are now engaged in
laying out the ground on the Patowmac, on which the
Federal buildings are to be erected.[21]

President Washington arrived at Georgetown on March
28th to inspect the ground and to reach an agreement with the
thirteen original proprietors for the conveyance of such parts
of their farms as was needed for streets without compensation,
and such land as was needed for buildings and public reservations
at a specified amount.

Washington met with the three Commissioners in the morning and then proceeded out of town where he and the principal
citizens dined at Suter's Tavern.[22] There he ". . . examined the
Surveys of Mr. Ellicott who had been sent on to lay out the
district of ten miles square for the Federal seat; and also the
works of Maj. L'Enfant who had been engaged to examine &
make a draught of the grds. in the vicinity of George Town and
Carrollsburg on the Eastern Branch . . ." and the next day he
personally visited the grounds, leaving Georgetown the following day.[23] On March 31 Ellicott was directed by the Commissioners to proceed with the survey of the square as soon as pos-

sible, and he immediately undertook the preliminary work. Within two weeks the Commissioners were informed that he had run a line from the courthouse in Alexandria due southwest one half mile and thence southeast course to Hunting Creek to locate the beginning of "the four lines of experiment." On April 15, 1791, the Commissioners, in company with Ellicott and many spectators, took part in a ceremony by installing the stone marker at Jones' Point. The event was reported not only in the Alexandria press, but as a news item in Baltimore, Boston, and other cities.[24] The accounts noted that on Friday, April 15, after Daniel Carroll and "Dr. David Steward" arrived in Alexandria to supervise the fixing of the Federal District, the mayor, other town officials, and the townspeople turned out to participate in the event. The marker was placed after Ellicott had ascertained the precise point for its installation, and a ceremony followed which was performed according to the rite with the ancient implements of Freemasonry in which the level, as an emblem of equality, the plumb, as the emblem of rectitude of life, and the square, which represents virtue, were all applied in setting the stone. After the stone was in place it was consecrated with corn for nourishment as a symbol of goodness and plenty, wine for refreshment as a symbol of joy and gladness, and oil as a symbol of peace and harmony.*

Although the news item did not mention Banneker's presence, he undoubtedly participated as a spectator.

With the installation of the foundation stone as the first marker, the formal survey of the new national capital city had begun. The temporary marker was replaced by Thomas Freeman, an assistant surveyor at the order of the Commissioners, on June 21, 1794, with a more formal monument lettered with the words "The beginning of the Territory of Columbia." The area surveyed for the district was generally described as a square, yet it was in fact more in the nature of a trapezoid. The northern point is not situated exactly north of the southern point, but bears

* See Document 8.

5′ 19.7″ west of north of it. It is 116 feet west of the meridian through the southern corner. The sides, intended to be exactly 10 miles in length, vary in length as follows:

Southwestern side is 10 miles plus 230.6 feet long;
Northeastern side is 10 miles plus 263.1 feet long;
Southeastern side is 10 miles plus 70.5 feet long;
Northwestern side is 10 miles plus 63.0 feet long.[25]

When the boundary survey was completed, the line was carefully and thoroughly cleared for a distance of twenty feet on either side, making a clear lane forty feet wide through the woods for each ten-mile distance. In this lane stone posts were placed at every mile, and only the fourteen stones set on the Virginia line were completed before the end of the year. They each bear the date 1791, while the twenty-six stones on the Maryland side are marked 1792. Each stone also had the distance from the preceding corner. Occasionally Ellicott's men discovered that the exact number of miles from one of the corners ended in a point ill suited for a monument, such as a swamp area or a stream bed. In such instances they measured back and forth from that point to firm ground and there placed the monument. Since the Commissioners did not reach an agreement on the name of the new city, which was finally resolved as the City of Washington in the Territory of Columbia, the monuments do not bear the chosen name, having been installed earlier.

Ellicott made periodic visits to his family in Philadelphia, and his letters to his wife that have survived express the loneliness he felt during his absence from home. The first occasions on which he made the journey was in the last two weeks of April, at which time he called upon Tobias Lear, President Washington's secretary.*

* Noted in a letter from Lear to Washington dated April 24, 1791. He wrote that "Mr. Ellicott has returned from surveying the federal territory. . . ."

The survey had progressed satisfactorily and Ellicott was now ready to undertake the next phase of the project. His youngest brother, Benjamin, had arrived at the beginning of April, and now his other brother, Joseph, had also appeared on the scene. Both were employed by Andrew in the capacity of assistant surveyors.[26]

It was at this point in time that Banneker decided to return to his farm. He agreed to wait until Ellicott would make another journey to his family in Philadelphia, and then would accompany him part of the way, as far as Lower Mills.

Benjamin Banneker's name does not appear on any of the contemporary documents or records relating to the selection, planning, and survey of the City of Washington. An exhaustive search of the files under Public Buildings and Grounds in the U.S. National Archives, and of the several collections in the Library of Congress have proved fruitless. A careful perusal of all known surviving correspondence and papers of Andrew Ellicott and of Pierre Charles L'Enfant has likewise failed to reveal mention of Banneker. This conclusively dispels the legend that after L'Enfant's dismissal and his refusal to make available his plan of the city, Ellicott was able to reconstruct it in detail from Banneker's recollection. Equally untrue are the legends that Thomas Jefferson as Secretary of State invited Banneker to luncheon at the White House. Jefferson during this period was in Philadelphia, the national capital had not yet been built, and there was no White House.

Nevertheless, Banneker was certainly involved in the project as an assistant to Ellicott during the preliminary survey of the ten-mile square and in establishing lines for some of the major points in the city. On the basis of other evidence, Banneker arrived at the site with Ellicott early in February 1791 and returned to his home at the end of April of the same year.

He may have been mentioned in the field notes, journals, and diaries which Ellicott maintained of his survey, papers which have not been found. Some of them were removed from Ellicott's surveyor's office by order of the Commissioners in 1793. They have not been consulted or quoted by any of the writers on the history of the Federal Territory.

Other critical Ellicott documents of this period have remained in the hands of the family and have not been studied by historians. A notable exception is in the case of his great-granddaughter, Sally Kennedy Alexander, whose use of some of these papers in her biographical sketch of Andrew Ellicott has already been noted.

The basis for Banneker's employment has already been described. The recommendation by other members of Andrew's family who knew Banneker, his own familiarity with Banneker's calculations of an ephemeris for 1791, and the absence of other candidates for the position of a scientific assistant were all factors that led Ellicott to employ Banneker in the historic survey.

In addition to his demonstrated knowledge of practical astronomy and its related instruments, Banneker was also familiar with the science of surveying. He had not had field practice to any appreciable degree, but he had at least some basic training in its principles. Among the books that had been lent to him by George Ellicott, and which were returned to him after Banneker's death, was a second edition of Robert Gibson's famous treatise on surveying.[27]

Balanced against Banneker's scientific knowledge were his lack of field experience, his age, and increasing infirmity.

Obviously, his role was not that of a laborer hired to fell trees to clear the lines of the square, nor a supervisory one of directing others in these chores. He was not capable of serving as a rod man or a chain man, which required wearying hours of tramping through the underbrush and patiently holding the rod or chain for the surveyor. He served in the true sense of an assistant to Ellicott himself, maintaining notes for him, making calculations as required, and using the astronomical instruments for establishing base points. Once the square had been laid out and markers established, Ellicott would have been able to proceed with the finer details of the survey with the participation of the assistant surveyors hired for that purpose some months later.

Although Banneker's involvement in the survey was not noted by Latrobe in his memoir, it was described in the sketch by Martha Tyson from the notes assembled in 1836:

> Banneker was but once absent, at any distance, from his domicil. An appointment having been made after the adoption of the Constitution, in 1789, of commissioners, to run the lines of the District of Columbia—then called the "Federal Territory," they wished to avail themselves of his talents, induced him to accompany them in the work and retained him with them until the service was completed.[28]

Tyson elaborated her report of the incident in her later writings[29] but without any major change in the substance of her account.* She also commented on Banneker's deportment during his sojourn, and his relationship to the other principals involved in the project.[30] She noted that he had won the respect of those with whom he worked to such a degree that they overlooked his color, and that he was able to discourse with them on a variety of topics.†

This episode has been the subject of considerable attention by later writers, many of whom have claimed that it was the Commissioners who invited Banneker to join them at their table during meals. In actual fact, the Commissioners were in the field on rare occasions, and there would have been only infrequent opportunities for issuing such an invitation. In her later account, Tyson clarifies the situation, and explains that it was the members of "the engineer corps" who invited Banneker to dine:

> He was invited to sit at table with the engineer corps, but, as his characteristic modesty induced him to decline this, a separate table was prepared for him in their

* See Document 9.
† See Document 10.

dining-room; his meals being served at the same time
with theirs.[31]

The only surviving mention of his participation in the survey in Banneker's own words occurs in a letter which he wrote
to Thomas Jefferson as Secretary of State after his return from
the Federal Territory.

> And altho I had almost declined to make my calcula-
> tion [of an almanac] for the ensuing year, in conse-
> quence of that time which I had allotted therefor being
> taken up at the Federal Territory, by the request of
> M^r. Andrew Ellicott, yet finding myself under Several
> engagements to printers of this state, to whom I had
> communicated my design, on my return to my
> place of residence I industriously applyed my Self
> thereto. . . .[32]

There is a single entry in Banneker's Astronomical Journal
which may relate to his sojourn in the Territory.[33] This can be
compared with two observations of the annular eclipse made
by Ellicott at the Federal Territory at the same time,[34] and which
were subsequently published.*

Finally, Banneker's presence at the survey was described by
Jefferson in his letter to the Marquis de Condorcet in August
31, 1791, which has already been noted.

When the time came for Banneker to return to Baltimore
County, he was torn by indecision. He would have preferred
to continue in the exciting work with Major Ellicott, particularly
since the most rugged aspects of it had been completed.[35] His
services were not absolutely needed, however, since Ellicott's
two brothers had arrived and Isaac Briggs had been hired as well.
On the other side of the balance, Banneker considered his own
health. The winter months had been difficult, and he was anxious
to get some rest. It had been a serious struggle from time to

* See Document 11.

time to continue in the field, although the major had been as cooperative as the nature of the work permitted. Banneker was eager also to begin the calculation of an ephemeris for another almanac. He had learned a considerable amount about practical astronomy during his few months with Major Ellicott and he was anxious to apply it to his own work. Finally, there was the consideration of his farm, which he could not leave in other hands much longer. It was with mingled regret and relief that he reported to Major Ellicott that on the latter's next journey to Philadelphia he wished to return home. This probably occurred in late April 1791.

Banneker's return to Baltimore County was reported by Martha Tyson based on the account rendered by her parents.

On his return home, he called at the house of his friend George Ellicott to give an account of his engagements. He arrived on horseback, dressed in his usual costume, a full suit of drab cloth, surmounted by a large beaver hat.

He was in fine spirits, seeming to have been reanimated by the kindness of the distinguished men with whom he had mingled.

With his usual humility he estimated his own services at a low rate.[36]

After Banneker's departure and Ellicott's return from Philadelphia, the latter was recalled from his work on the ten-mile square to join his efforts with those of L'Enfant in order to hasten the survey of the city lines. Conflicts developed with some of the proprietors early in May and President Washington and the Commissioners were eager to proceed with a sale of lots. The progress made as a result of the combined efforts of the surveyor and engineer made it possible to render a plan of the city to the President and to report substantial accomplishment.[37] A month later, on June 4, it was reported in the press that on the previous Saturday, Ellicott, "the geographer general of the

United States," had completed the six main lines of the federal city, and was engaged in clearing and bounding the lines of the district or ten-mile square.[38] Ellicott's participation in the design of the city at this time is confirmed by a notice from the Commissioners to property holders on June 30 to submit any information they had about the lines of their land to "Major L'Enfant and Major Ellicott" for the general plat. By this time it had become necessary to establish a surveyor's office in Georgetown from which Ellicott and L'Enfant operated and directed the several aspects of their work.[39] Tradition claims that it was located in the two-story structure at 3049 M Street.*

Following the establishment of the square, Ellicott drew a north-south straight line through the area which was specified by L'Enfant to be occupied by the Capitol, and then crossed it at this point with another line drawn at right angles. He then continued both lines to the outer boundaries of the new city. He attempted to lay off the parallels with a chain, but encountered difficulties because of the cold weather. He became concerned with the degree of expansion and contraction of the links due to heat and cold and the errors due to the bending and straightening of the links. Finally, Ellicott laid his chain aside and used instead a set of wooden rods made with graduations like a carpenter's square and accurately divided. They were accommodated with plummets and sliders to permit the measurements to be made horizontal, and the devices worked successfully.

Ellicott found that one source of error remained, namely, the human element. His line men occasionally made errors in returning the tallies, and Ellicott discovered that the intersections of the major avenues which established the locations of other streets were sometimes moved, leading to much confusion. He firmly suspected that this was being done deliberately. It worried him, and required constant vigilance and re-examination of each point before going on. He used this method to establish all

---

* This building was marked in 1899 with a plaque inscribed "Gen. Washington's Headquarters while surveying the city of Washington in 1791," erected by the Hiram Ripley Society, D.A.R.

the main avenues as well as the parallel streets with the transit and equal altitude instrument.

The work progressed on both projects until the beginning of September, when a series of incidents brought L'Enfant into disfavor with the Commission and with the President. The first was when the Commissioners requested ten thousand copies of the map to be distributed in October for use in the sale of lots in the new city. L'Enfant had arranged with a French printer to produce them. They were never delivered, and the first land sale was done without maps. It was a great disappointment to all concerned, but Washington was convinced that it was not L'Enfant's fault. However, he was quite provoked when L'Enfant refused to permit the original of his general plan to be displayed at the sale.

Then in November L'Enfant discovered that one of the Commissioners was having a house built on the line of Jersey Avenue at E Street which would project out into the street about seven feet. L'Enfant ordered the house destroyed, an action which created hard feelings on the part of Carroll, who was one of the most influential men assisting in the development of the new city. Washington was greatly annoyed, and reprimanded L'Enfant and told him that in future he would have to submit to the orders of the Commission. L'Enfant refused to be subordinate to the Commissioners, and on March 6, 1792, Jefferson wrote to the Commissioners that it was impracticable to keep L'Enfant on the project.

Meanwhile the winter weather made it impossible to continue work in the field, and in December Ellicott closed down his camp and returned to his family in Philadelphia for the rest of the winter. By the beginning of March, as the weather improved, he became concerned about the program of work for the following season. Despite his communications, he had received no reply from the Commissioners, and he wrote to them once more in desperation.[40] He pointed out the scarcity of qualified surveyors and scientific assistants, noted the problems which developed with L'Enfant, and justified the expenses he had incurred with the project.*

This letter is of particular importance because it described the nature of Banneker's role in the survey prior to the arrival of Ellicott's brothers. Ellicott did not receive a satisfactory reply to his letter, and in the interim L'Enfant was discharged. An assistant surveyor named James Dermott had been hired without Ellicott's knowledge or approval. Dermott, a young Irish emigrant who taught mathematics at the Alexandria Academy, had come to the favorable attention of Dr. David Stuart, one of the Commissioners.

The Commissioners placed Ellicott in charge of the overall project on March 14, 1792, and in the following August a young surveyor named George Fenwick was added to his staff. During the rest of the year Ellicott and his party laid out and divided the squares of the city at the same time they were completing the boundary survey. It was an unpleasant period, for several times Ellicott succumbed to influenza and both of his brothers as well as Fenwick and Briggs also came down with it.[41]

Inevitably problems began to arise between Ellicott and the Commissioners with increasing frequency. Pressures developed from proprietors who complained that the project was proceeding too slowly. Ellicott in disgust offered to yield the project to someone else if the Commissioners wished, but he was asked to continue. He submitted his formal report on the completion of the boundary survey on January 1, 1793.[42] A week later, he felt constrained by the increasing number of proprietors' complaints to announce that he planned to resign from the project the following May. Continued harassment from the proprietors and the press led Ellicott at the end of the month[43] to demand that the Commissioners make an investigation of the Surveyor's Office. At the same time he brought to light his dispute with Dermott, who he claimed had removed

* See Document 12.

some of the important papers relating to that office, presumably for the purpose of discrediting Ellicott. Ellicott's exasperation and continuing friction in his relations with the Commissioners led to an open controversy, with the result that on March 12, 1793, the Commissioners discharged Major Ellicott and his assistants. It was only through the intercession of President Washington, during his visit to the site a week later, that Ellicott and his assistants were returned to service on April 3, after a reorganization of the Surveyor's Office. In the course of this development, the Commissioners ordered the confiscation of all of Ellicott's papers from that office, an action which led to another eruption between Ellicott and the Commissioners. Andrew mentioned the incident in a letter to his wife.[44] With a certain measure of satisfaction he reported that he had succeeded in having all of his men reinstated after a month's suspension of work. His contest with the Commissioners was one fraught with difficulty inasmuch as his papers had been seized by their order after his return from Philadelphia, though they were later restored to him.*

Ellicott departed for Philadelphia on July 19, 1793, informing the Commissioners that his services would not be required for the time being and that Briggs and his brother Benjamin would be in charge during his absence. These two assistants carried on through the summer and the autumn, during which period their relationship with Dermott became increasingly worsened. It led to a confrontation between Briggs and Dermott before the Commissioners in October, and Briggs was dismissed. Joseph Ellicott and Fenwick then assumed charge of the project. Andrew returned on December 9 and the Commissioners lost no time in informing him that during his absence the work had progressed satisfactorily and suggested that they had no real need of him during the winter. He incited his brothers to rebellion, and Benjamin Ellicott, half in fun and half in earnest, advertised the theft of the L'Enfant map by Dermott in the press. It was at this point that the controversy became even

* See Document 13.

more heated. The President drew the attention of the Commissioners to letters addressed to Washington by Andrew and Benjamin Ellicott and Isaac Briggs dated June 29, 1793, and February 28, 1794, which described in detail the complaints of the writers against Dermott and the Commissioners. The reply made to the President by the Commissioners in a long letter dated March 23, 1794, went into full detail of the incidents that had occurred, expressed their dissatisfaction with Ellicott's performance, and told of their consequent actions.[45] They admitted the seizure of the surveyor's papers in connection with his accusations against Dermott.* The matter of the confiscation and the restoration of the papers, as well as the eventual loss of some of them, is intimately connected with the problem of documenting Banneker's presence at the Territory, and for that reason has been given in some detail.

Meanwhile, Ellicott had received an appointment from the governor of Pennsylvania to survey a road from Reading to Waterford. He undertook the project upon his departure from Washington, and spent the following two years in its completion. The Commissioners placed Dermott in charge of dividing the squares into lots, and the work progressed.

The second incident in which Ellicott's papers were seized is of particular significance, for it may explain the total absence to the present time of his field notes, journals, and diaries. A reference is made to the loss in his communication to Robert Patterson published several years later, in which he commented: "A number of the eclipses of the first Satellite of Jupiter together with a great proportion of my notes relative to the city of Washington, were privately taken from my lodgings in Georgetown, otherwise they should have appeared in this paper."[46]

Ellicott planned to prepare a paper for presentation and publication by the Society in which he would mention the survey of the City of Washington and "the method pursued in executing that part of the plan in which I have been concerned

* See Document 14.

will be explained," as he wrote to Dr. William Thornton some time later.[47] He registered his objections to the changes made in the plan after his departure, and his conflicts with the Commissioners during the course of the project. Particularly he commented on the pillaging of his office during which the notes of his observations for determining the longitude were lost or destroyed.*

Ellicott's strong statements were a severe indictment of Dermott's intentions and actions, and the statement that he had pilfered Ellicott's papers provides explanation for their mysterious absence from the records of this important survey.

A further comment on the incident was made by Ellicott in a communication to Jefferson some years later:

> Whilst I was engaged in the City of Washington some years ago I made a number of observations to determine its longitude but all those observations with some others relative to the plan of the City were lost when the office was pillaged;—but fortunately two very important observations which I had communicated to our late worthy friend M^r. Rittenhouse have been saved and published in the fourth volume of the transactions of our Society. . . .[48]

Details of the nature of Banneker's participation in the survey of the Federal Territory undoubtedly existed in the field notes, journals, and private diary of Andrew Ellicott. As has been demonstrated, some of these papers were pillaged and never returned to the surveyor. They must be presumed to have been destroyed. Other papers, including correspondence and a personal diary, were owned by Ellicott's descendants into the twentieth century. This material is probably in the possession of some unidentified member of the family at the present time.

---

* See Document 15.

VI

HIS FIRST ALMANAC

❖❖❖❖❖❖❖❖❖❖❖❖❖❖❖❖❖

View yon majestic concave of the sky!
Contemplate well, those glorious orbs on high—
There Constellations shine, and Comets blaze;
Each glitt'ring world the Godhead's pow'r displays!
                              Banneker's Almanac for 1794

As SOON AS HE had settled down once more to the homely routine of his farm, Banneker turned his attention again to his astronomical observations. He had suffered great discouragement
as a result of his experience with publishers in the previous year,
but he now had hopes of achieving his dream. His work with
Major Ellicott on the survey had taught him much about the
use of instruments for making astronomical observations and
he set to work with renewed vigor on an ephemeris for 1792.

He had already completed some of the preliminary work

during his rare leisure moments while in the field camp, and he now finished the projections for the eclipses. Within a short time he had outlined each of the months, and had undertaken the tedious task of inserting his calculations in the columns as he completed each segment of the project. He enjoyed his lonely hours at the telescope at night during the spring and the early summer, and he slept away the hottest part of the day. The arduous months he had spent on the survey had tired him, and he found little energy to do more than work on the ephemeris after his return.

One lesson he had learned in particular from his brief employment with Major Ellicott was the need for orderliness and accuracy in the making and maintenance of mathematical calculations. If the results were to be useful, they must be readily available and identifiable. Accordingly, he came to the conclusion that he needed a special volume for keeping his astronomical records. He found just what he needed in the store of Ellicott & Co. This was a handsome folio journal with several hundred unlined blank pages. For Banneker it proved an expensive purchase, but since astronomy was to be his new work, he considered it a worthwhile investment. Back home again, he worked out the manner in which his new journal would be used.

The manuscript journal took an honored place on the oval table, beside his text books, which he kept in a neat pile at one side, and his telescope and drafting instruments. It was a handsome volume of fine handmade paper, measuring nine by almost fifteen inches, with a sewn binding and parchment wrapper, its three hundred pages fairly beckoning him to begin his work.*

---

* The journal and the borrowed texts are owned by Dr. Robert T. Fitzhugh. Each page of the journal bears a watermark with a design which incorporates a hunting horn and the cipher "G R." The paper appears to have been made in the American colonies, probably the product of one of the two new paper mills which had been established near Baltimore after 1778, or of one of the numerous mills in nearby Pennsylvania. The horn and shield watermark with the G R cipher was quite common in England from just prior to 1750 until a little after 1800, but the cipher has not been known to have been used by

He now spent a part of each day, as well as the major part of his evening hours, in astronomical studies. He enjoyed the new leisure which he had assigned to himself, and he worked alone, with only the company of his own thoughts and the ticking of his clock against the wall near the fireplace. The hours passed quickly, punctuated periodically by the striking of the clock, and time seemed to have become an endless sea with no shore in sight.

After careful consideration of the use he would make of his new journal, Banneker began to copy his final calculations for each month from his work sheets to the recto of the succeeding pages, leaving the reverse side for miscellaneous notes. He had carefully studied the format of the published almanacs and he utilized it for his completed results. He left the first several pages blank and then began the inscription of his finished calculations from his notes:

1792
January First Month hath 31 Days . . .

As was his wont, he wrote carefully, forming his letters slowly and with precision in a beautiful hand, in a style which his grandmother had taught him and of which he was extremely proud.

At the top of the facing page he inscribed the formula for the use of the Dominical Letter, with a reference to his source as Ferguson's work, citing chapter and page.[1] This was followed by "Common Notes and Movable Feasts for the Year 1792," and then a quotation, which was probably also taken from Ferguson's volume:

It is to be observed that the Moon and the five primary planets has the Same Declination as the Sun has, when

---

colonial American papermakers. (Data courtesy of Dr. Arnold E. Grummer, Curator of Museums, The Institute of Paper Chemistry, Appleton, Wisconsin.)

in the Same Sign and Degree that the Moon or planet is in at the given time.*

The first drawing for a projection of an eclipse of the sun which is to be found in the volume is drawn on the page facing the calculations for May 1792. It includes the following notation:

This projection I laid down for April the third 1791 when the Sun rose Centrally eclipsed at the City of Washington this is a back tryal to See how present method would agree with the former.

N. B. Ferguson's Tables make the new abotit [orbit?] 30 minutes to Soon Viz

	d	L	M	
April	3	10	30	
I say	3	11	2	A.M.
			32	

Among the first leaves in his manuscript journal, Banneker made a notation relating to one of his reference works, but it is not completely comprehensible because part of the page is torn away:

. . . Astronomy Explain'd on Sʳ Isaac Newton's principles says . . . Stands in the Same line as Easter Sunday
. . . must Serve for the given year.[2]

In this volume Ferguson repeatedly referred the reader for more specific information to one of his lesser known works entitled *Tables and Tracts* . . . , which Banneker was subsequently able to acquire for his own library, although his copy has not survived.[3] He extracted useful passages from this text and

---

* The remainder of the page is cut away just below this entry.

occasionally added them to his manuscript journal as reminders of procedures as he worked.*

By the beginning of June, Banneker had completed a draft of his manuscript ephemeris; he promptly mailed a copy of it to a printer in Georgetown. Whether he had had previous contact with the printer cannot be determined, but he apparently received some assurance of the acceptance of his work. The Georgetown printer was not identified, but he may have been either Charles Fierer, the printer and publisher of *The Times and the Potowmack Packet,* or one of the partners, Matthias Day and William Hancock,[4] who published *The Georgetown Weekly Ledger.*†

It occurred to Banneker that it would be desirable to obtain the greatest possible distribution for his work, and accordingly he sought printers in both Baltimore and Philadelphia. He had already heard of William Goddard, the patriot and enterprising publisher in Baltimore who printed *The Maryland Journal.* As soon as Banneker was well enough to travel, he made another copy of his ephemeris and took it to him on horseback to Baltimore.

Inasmuch as Goddard was a most significant figure in Banneker's life as well as in the history of American printing, he deserves particular notice. A member of a prominent New England family, he was born in New London, Connecticut, in 1740 and worked with newspapers in Connecticut and

* For an example of these quotations, see Document 16.

† Charles Fierer was a Hessian soldier captured at the Battle of Trenton. He later joined Washington's forces, fought in the southern campaign, was wounded in 1781, and later returned to Europe. He returned in 1788 to Norfolk. He moved to Georgetown where he established a printing office in partnership with Christian Kramer in 1789 which lasted briefly, and then another with Thomas Updike Fosdick. He published *The Times and the Potowmack Packet* from 1789 until the end of 1791.

Matthias Day and William Hancock established *The Georgetown Weekly Ledger* in April 1790 and sold it to Alexander Doyle in August or September 1791. He in turn was succeeded by his brother, James Doyle, in 1792.

then New York City from an early age. He moved first to Providence, Rhode Island, in 1762, then went to work in New York and then in Philadelphia, where he began to publish *The Pennsylvania Chronicle* in early 1767. It was continued until 1773, but its Tory leanings led to its demise. Early in 1773 Goddard visited Baltimore at the urging of some of its citizens to establish the first newspaper in that city. He moved in June and established a printing shop on Market Street in Baltimore. The first issue of his new weekly newspaper, *The Maryland Journal and Baltimore Advertiser*, appeared in August. In October he made a visit to the northern provinces and left the newspaper in the care of his sister, Mary Katherine Goddard. He made a second tour in the following year for the purpose of developing a proposal for an American postal system. His plan for a Continental Post Office proved so successful that it forced the discontinuation of the British postal system. Goddard's system was taken over by the Continental Congress in 1775. He received no compensation, and subsequently returned to Baltimore to assist his sister with the newspaper. His articles brought him much censure, first from the Whigs which led to his banishment to Annapolis, and then from the patriots. As the supply of paper became very scarce, Goddard became involved with the operation of a paper mill at Elk Ridge and with a bookbinding business. After a short partnership with his sister in the publication of *The Maryland Journal*, he entered a short-lived partnership with Edward Langworthy, which ended in 1787.

In 1786 Goddard was married to Abigail Angell, and in 1789 he took as his partner her brother, James Angell. The partnership continued until August 1792, during the period that Banneker's almanac was being considered for publication. Goddard sold his interest to Angell although his name remained in the shop's imprint until February 1793. Angell continued the business alone, including the newspaper, *The Maryland Journal*, until November 1, 1793. In the summer of 1792 Goddard moved permanently to Rhode Island. Angell had another partner in the firm for a brief period before he sold the printing business to

Francis Brumfield in October 1794, and died three years later.[5]

Banneker was impressed by his meeting with Goddard, and perhaps for that reason failed to obtain a definite decision about his work. Goddard had published almanacs in the past and at this point in time he was interested in issuing another, primarily to compete with local printers. He realized that an almanac with an ephemeris calculated by a Negro philomath might be advantageous for marketing at this particular time. Banneker explained that he planned to sell copies of his calculations to one or two printers in other cities and that he believed that such distribution would not affect Goddard's sales. The printer did not comment, but he offered Banneker a small sum for his work, with the promise that if the almanac proved successful it might be possible to render a bonus.

Banneker was rather well satisfied with himself, for he had found two printers who expressed interest in his work and would probably publish it. During the days that followed, his satisfaction gave way to doubt, and he wondered if he might have the almanac published also in Philadelphia, where it would receive the greatest exposure of all, particularly if it were supported by the Pennsylvania Society for the Abolition of Slavery, which had already expressed some interest in his work. He consulted with George Ellicott at the first opportunity and the latter suggested that it was worth the effort. Banneker provided him with another manuscript copy of his ephemeris which George sent on to his brother Elias in Baltimore.* Elias and one of his friends and business associates, Joseph Townsend, had been elected to membership in the Pennsylvania Society for the Abolition of Slavery during the previous summer, and they had become increasingly active in its affairs.[6]

* Elias Ellicott (1759–1827) was a son of Andrew and Elizabeth Ellicott. He married Mary Thomas in 1786 and they became the parents of fifteen children. He was a merchant miller in Baltimore and had his home at the corner of Sharp and Lombard streets. He acted as the agent in the various Ellicott milling interests for himself and his brothers.

The election of Elias Ellicott and Joseph Townsend to membership in the Society was noted in its minutes for June 5, 1790.

Elias was eager to be of assistance, because he saw in Banneker's achievement an opportunity to serve the antislavery cause. During the previous year he had learned from Townsend of James Pemberton's interest in Banneker's first ephemeris, and he lost no time in writing to Pemberton directly[7] to advise him that Banneker had completed the calculations for an ephemeris for 1792 and that he was seeking an interested printer in Philadelphia:

> Understanding that thee wrote to Joseph Townsend expressing a desire to be informed particularly respecting Benjamin Banaker, I take the Freedom to inform Thee that I am personally Acquainted with him. He is a Black Man about 56 Years of Age. His Father was a Guinea Negroe. He is a man of strong Natural parts and by his own Study hath made himself well Acquainted with the Mathematicks. About three Years Ago he began to study Astronomy by the Assistance of some Authors which he with much difficulty procured soon became so far a proficient as to Calculate an Almanac, he calculated one for the Year 1791 and Intended to have had it Published but could not. He hath a Copy now ready for the Press for the Year 1792—and is very desirous of having it Published in Philadelphia. Now if Thee thinks it Worthy thy notice it might be well to make inquiry of the different Printers to know whether any one of them will undertake to Print it. He is a Poor man & Would be Pleased With having something for the Copy but if the Printer is not Willing to give any thing He would rather let him have it for nothing than not to have it Published. He thinks as it is the first performance of the kind ever done by One of his Complection that it might be a means of Promoting the Cause of Humanity as many are of Opinion that the Blacks are Void of Mental en-

dowments. If thee can find any one that will take the
Copy of the Almanac please to inform me by the Post
and I will have the Copy Forwarded.

Elias also added as a postscript:

Said Banaker lives about 10 miles from Baltimore near
Ellicotts Lower Mills, it may be depended upon that
he never had any assistance from any Person in respect
to his Knowledge of Astronomy.

Pemberton replied promptly with an expression of interest
and an assurance that a suitable printer could be found, if the
ephemeris proved upon examination to have been competently
calculated. He urged Elias to forward it as soon as possible,
because the year was already half over and there was relatively
little time to have the calculations reviewed and to negotiate
with a printer.

Elias informed his brother of the results, and George undertook to visit Benjamin for the purpose of obtaining the ephemeris
for forwarding. He found that Banneker had not completed the
copy required—he had been seriously ill in bed for some days.
The elderly man was more concerned about the delay of his
project than he was about his pain and discomfort; once again
it seemed that the fates might keep his work from publication.
As soon as he was able, Benjamin returned to his work table
and completed a clean copy of his work to be forwarded. He
sent it by one of his young relatives to George Ellicott's home,
and the latter forwarded it immediately to Elias in Baltimore.
Fortuitously, John Todd, a Philadelphia businessman and
fellow member of the Society was visiting in Baltimore. Todd
was also a member and secretary of the Pennsylvania Society.[8]

Since the post left much to be desired, Elias made arrangements with Todd to deliver the manuscript ephemeris by hand,

together with his own covering letter to Pemberton* in which he explained the causes of the delay:

> I Now Send by John Todd the copy of Benjn. Banekers Allmanack which wold of been Sent before had we not been waiting for the Introduction & Certifycate which is not yet reddy owing Chiefly to Baneker being indisposed but is now better and I hope we Shall be able to forward them in the course of a few days, but as the Printer can be going on with the Coppy exclusive of them it may not be of Any disadvantage, the Introduction is to Contain Something of the Life and the Situation in Life of the Author, the Certifycate of him being the real Author——.[9]

Meanwhile, an event had taken place in Baltimore which helped to cement Banneker's importance as a man of science and as a free Negro. On the occasion of the July 4 celebration in Baltimore, the Maryland Society for promoting the Abolition of Slavery held a public meeting at which the speaker was Dr. George Buchanan, a distinguished local practicing physician and a member of the American Philosophical Society.[10] A native of Baltimore County, Buchanan had studied medicine in Philadelphia and had continued his studies in Edinburgh and Paris before returning to establish a practice in Baltimore.

The announcement of the meeting brought many members of the public in addition to the Maryland Society's members.

The subject of Buchanan's oration was a daring one, to say the least, particularly in Maryland and only four years after the adoption of the Constitution. In his oration Buchanan included Banneker among those Negroes who had distinguished themselves as outstanding members of their race. He stated that:

* Pemberton had noted on the reverse side that the letter had been forwarded by Todd and received on June 24, "with Banneker Calculations for a Almanac for 1792."

. . . Many instances are recorded of men of eminence among them. Witness Ignacio Sancho, whose letters are admired by all men of taste; Phillis Wheatley, who distinguished herself as a poetess; the Physician of New Orleans; the Virginia Calculator; Banneker, the Maryland Astronomer, and many others, whom it would be needless to mention. . . .

The presentation was extremely successful,* and the oration was subsequently published in a pamphlet of twenty pages with a dedication to Thomas Jefferson, Secretary of State.[11]

The distinction that had come to Banneker as a result of Buchanan's oration made the publication of his almanac all the more desirable to Pemberton and his associates. He considered it necessary, however, to have it reviewed by competent scientists, and Pemberton forwarded a copy of it to David Rittenhouse, unquestionably the foremost scientist in the country at that time; he had recently been appointed president of the American Philosophical Society to succeed Benjamin Franklin who had died in the previous year.

At this time Rittenhouse was in ill health and nearing the end of his active career. In addition to his appointments as a trustee of the University of Pennsylvania and as the new president of the American Philosophical Society, he had recently embarked on a new program of the State of Pennsylvania relating to the improvement of roads and rivers and the construction of a network of canals. Despite his other commitments, Rittenhouse also reviewed and reported on many of the proposals submitted to the American Philosophical Society in this period.[12]

* It was reported in the Society's minutes that ". . . at a special meeting of the Maryland Society for promoting the abolition of slavery and the relief of free negroes and others unlawfully held in bondage, held at Baltimore, July 4th, 1791, unanimously *Resolved*, That the president presents the thanks of the society to Dr. George Buchanan, for the excellent oration by him delivered this day, and, at the same time, request a copy thereof in the name and for the use of the society."

Rittenhouse checked a number of calculations throughout the ephemeris, and reported favorably and promptly with the comment:

> I think the papers I herewith return to you a very extraordinary performance, considering the Colour of the Author. Though I have had leisure to make but few comparisons I have no doubt that the Calculations are sufficiently accurate for the purposes of a common Almanac. Every Instance of Genius amongst the Negroes is worthy of attention, because their oppressors seem to lay great stress on their supposed inferior mental abilities.[13]

Pemberton sought a second authority to whom Banneker's ephemeris could be submitted for review, and finally selected William Waring of Philadelphia. Waring calculated *Poor Will's Almanack* which had been published in Philadelphia each year since 1787 by Joseph Crukshank. He was acknowledged to be a competent astronomer and his almanacs were professionally calculated and popular. He was associated with Pemberton as a fellow member of the Pennsylvania Society, to which he was elected on April 4, 1790, and they were engaged in a cooperative enterprise in which Banneker's work could be useful.

Although his name has not survived in the annals of science, Waring was a popular figure in Philadelphia scientific circles. He was a teacher of mathematics at the Friends' public school on Pear Street, and author of a journal for the use of seamen in making lunar observations for calculating the longitude, which was published in 1791. A few years later he co-authored *The American Tutor's Assistant* in cooperation with John Todd, Zachariah Jess, and Jeremiah Paul. Waring was also concerned with the subject of mill construction; several of his papers on aspects of the subject were read before the American Philosophical Society, to which he was elected in 1793. He was undoubtedly one of the most competent astronomers available at that time to evaluate Banneker's work.[14]

Waring made his report in the form of a general statement which could be published in the almanac if required, and which he submitted to Pemberton:

> I have examined Benjamin Banneker's Almanac for the Year 1792, and am of the Opinion that it well deserves the Acceptance and Encouragement of the Public.
> W^m. Waring.
>
> Phila. 16th. 8th. mo. 1791.[15]

Through the Ellicotts, Pemberton passed back the word to Banneker that he had aroused the interest of Joseph Crukshank in his almanac and that although he had not come to a final decision, the prospects seemed favorable. Banneker was delighted, for Crukshank was one of the foremost printers in Philadelphia. He was a member of the Society of Friends and one of the founding members of the Pennsylvania Society for the Abolition of Slavery. He utilized his press freely on behalf of the Society of Friends as well as in support of the antislavery movement, and he published a number of Negro writings in which he had an interest. In 1786 he produced the first American edition of the poems of Phillis Wheatley, and in 1790 he published a work of his own authorship entitled, *A Poetical Epistle to the Enslaved Africans in the Character of an Ancient Negro Born a Slave*.

Banneker now found himself waiting on three fronts—Georgetown, Baltimore, and Philadelphia, and it was somewhat hard to believe that his own efforts would possibly be published and distributed over such a large part of the country. As he thought about this prospect, an idea began to form in his mind. From his conversations with the Ellicotts and their reports of interest in his work expressed by Friends in Philadelphia, it was the subject of his race that generated the greatest response. He was at first somewhat put out by this attitude, for in his own opinion, the proposed almanac was of interest and value because of the competence of his astronomical calculations. Now he began to realize that he and his work were being used for other purposes.

It was at this point in time that Banneker wrote a letter to Thomas Jefferson, submitting a manuscript copy of his almanac calculations. Banneker's letter to Jefferson has been generally construed as evidence that he realized how he could be cited as an example of the Negro's mental capacity in refutation of Jefferson's statements to the contrary. There is serious doubt that such was indeed the case. A careful study of Banneker's life, and of his correspondence, notes in his journal, and his general attitude as expressed by those who had known him, reveals him as a man of considerable dignity, industry, amateur of the arts and sciences, and deeply religious although not a member of any sect. He was well aware and appreciative of his many opportunities, and in his lifetime he never aimed beyond his reach. He displayed no resentment of his station nor of that of his race. Because of the relative remoteness of his home, work, and leisure from any community, Banneker had little if any experience of oppression and cruelty to Negroes.

Examples of slavery to which Banneker might have been exposed were slaves owned by neighbors along the Patapsco. During his boyhood the adjacent plantation on the one side of his father's farm was owned by Roger Randall, who kept two slaves. Beyond was the farm of Emmanuel Teale, who had one slave only. On the other side of his father's farm but some distance away was John Owings' farm with two slaves, and Thomas Floyd who kept a single slave to help with his work.[16] However, there would have been little communication between the Banneker family and the slaves on these other farms, so that the matter of slavery remained relatively remote during Banneker's boyhood.

The fact that nowhere in his surviving letters and papers did Banneker express any concern for the subjugation of his race, or express interest or willingness to help the antislavery cause, or refer again to his purpose in writing to Jefferson, seems to indicate that the letter may have been suggested to him or urged upon him by the Ellicotts or their associates in the movement who foresaw in such a correspondence the opportunity to advertise the almanacs and the abolitionist movement.

There can be no doubt that Banneker approached the proposal to write to Jefferson with extreme caution. He could easily understand how the publication of such an exchange of letters with the Secretary of State would be beneficial to the advertising of his almanac, but at the same time he could visualize how a letter from an unknown amateur almanac maker could also be offensive to the statesman. He gave careful thought to the suggestion before he began to draft his letter. It was important, he thought, to identify himself with Jefferson's interests, and this he was enabled to do in relation to the survey of the Federal Territory which he mentioned in his letter.

In this connection Banneker was undoubtedly reminded of the newspaper account in the *Georgetown Weekly Ledger* which described his arrival in the new national district ". . . as an Ethiopian whose abilities as surveyor and astronomer already prove that Mr. Jefferson's concluding that that race of men were void of mental endowment was without foundation," and this may have led him to emphasize Jefferson's own involvement in his appointment as Ellicott's assistant, and his further achievement of an ephemeris for an almanac that was about to be published. He gave no indication that he was otherwise informed of Jefferson's expressed opinions or writings on the subject of the Negro, and he did not refer to his Notes on Virginia. Instead, he likened the slavery of Negroes to the enslavement of the colonies by the British Crown and the justification for the correction of one state of oppression on the basis of the other.

Banneker's involvement with the sciences, first in the survey, and then in the calculation of an ephemeris, was designed to appeal to Jefferson's own avid interest in the sciences and in American scientific achievement. The content of the letter was carefully drafted, cautiously written, and deliberately directed to the interests of the recipient.[17] It is too much to believe that Banneker, who had distinguished himself by a lifetime of modesty, prudence, and dignity, could have conceived, without the guidance and encouragement of others, a letter so deliberately planned to evoke a statement of position from the statesman who had avoided a public commitment on the subject whenever possible:

> Maryland, Baltimore County,
> Near Ellicott's Lower Mills August 19th. 1791.
> Thomas Jefferson Secretary of State.
>
> Sir, I am fully sensible of the greatness of that freedom which I take with you on the present occasion; a liberty which Seemed to me Scarcely allowable, when I reflected on that distinguished, and dignifyed station in which you Stand; and the almost general prejudice and prepossession which is so previlent in the world against those of my complexion.
>
> I suppose it is a truth too well attested to you, to need a proof here, that we are a race of Beings who have long laboured under the abuse and censure of the world, that we have long been looked upon with an eye of contempt, and that we have long been considered rather as brutish than human, and Scarcely capable of mental endowments.
>
> Sir, I hope I may Safely admit, in consequence of that report which hath reached me, that you are a man far less inflexible in Sentiments of this nature, than many others; that you are measurably friendly and well disposed towards us, and that you are willing and ready to Lend your aid and assistance to our relief from those many distresses and numerous calamities to which we are reduced.

Now, Sir, if this is founded in truth, I apprehend you will readily embrace every opportunity to eradicate that train of absurd and false ideas and oppinions which so generally prevail with respect to us, and that your Sentiments are concurrent with mine, which are that one universal Father hath given being to us all, and that he hath not only made us all of one flesh, but that he hath also without partiality afforded us all the Same Sensations, and endued us all with the same faculties, and that however variable we may be in Society or religion, however diversified in Situation or colour, we are all of the Same Family, and Stand in the Same relation to him.

Sir, if these are Sentiments of which you are fully persuaded, I hope you cannot but acknowledge, that it is the indispensible duty of those who maintain for themselves the rights of human nature, and who profess the obligations of Christianity, to extend their power and influence to the relief of every part of the human race, from whatever burthen or oppression they may unjustly labour under; and this I apprehend a full conviction of the truth and obligation of these principles should lead all to.

Sir, I have long been convinced, that if your love for yourSelves and for those inesteemable laws which preserve to you the rights of human nature, was founded on Sincerity, you could not but be Solicitous, that every Individual of whatsoever rank or distinction, might with you equally enjoy the blessings thereof, neither could you rest Satisfyed, short of the most active diffusion of your exertions, in order to their promotion from any State of degradation, to which the unjustifyable cruelty and barbarism of men may have reduced them.

Sir I freely and Chearfully acknowledge, that I

am of the African race, and, in that colour which is natural to them of the deepest dye*; and it is under a Sense of the most profound gratitude to the Supreme Ruler of the universe, that I now confess to you, that I am not under that State of tyrannical thraldom, and inhuman captivity, to which too many of my brethren are doomed; but that I have abundantly tasted of the fruition of those blessings which proceed from that free and unequalled liberty with which you are favoured and which I hope you will willingly allow you have received from the immediate Hand of that Being from whom proceedeth every good and perfect gift.

Sir, Suffer me to recall to your mind that time in which the Arms and tyranny of the British Crown were exerted with every powerful effort, in order to reduce you to a State of Servitude; look back I intreat you on the variety of dangers to which you were exposed, reflect on that time in which every human aid appeared unavailable, and in which even hope and fortitude wore the aspect of inability to the Conflict, and you cannot but be led to a Serious and grateful Sense of your miraculous and providential preservation; You cannot but acknowledge, that the present freedom and tranquillity which you enjoy you have mercifully received, and that it is the peculiar blessing of Heaven.

This, Sir, was a time in which you clearly saw into the injustice of a State of Slavery, and in which you had Just apprehensions of the horrors of its condition, it was now Sir, that your abhorrence thereof was so excited, that you publickly held forth this true and invaluable doctrine, which is worthy to be recorded and remembered in all Succeeding ages. "We hold these truths to be Self evident, that all men are created equal, and that they are endowed by their creator with certain

* My Father was brought here a Slave from Africa.

inalienable rights, that amongst these are life, liberty, and the persuit of happiness."

Here, Sir, was a time in which your tender feelings for your selves engaged you thus to declare, you were then impressed with proper ideas of the great valuation of liberty, and the free possession of those blessings to which you were entitled by nature; but Sir how pitiable is it to reflect, that altho you were so fully convinced of the benevolence of the Father of mankind, and of his equal and impartial distribution of those rights and privileges which he had conferred upon them, that you should at the Same time counteract his mercies, in detaining by fraud and violence so numerous a part of my brethren under groaning captivity and cruel oppression, that you should at the Same time be found guilty of that most criminal act, which you professedly detested in others, with respect to yourselves.

Sir, I suppose that your knowledge of the situation of my brethren is too extensive to need a recital here; neither shall I presume to prescribe methods by which they may be relieved, otherwise than by recommending to you, and all others, to wean yourselves from those narrow prejudices which you have imbibed with respect to them, and as Job proposed to his friends "Put your Souls in their Souls' stead," thus shall your hearts be enlarged with kindness and benevolence towards them, and thus shall you need neither the direction of myself or others in what manner to proceed herein.

And now, Sir, altho my Sympathy and affection for my brethren hath caused my enlargement thus far, I ardently hope that your candour and generosity will plead with you in my behalf, when I make known to you, that it was not originally my design; but that having taken up my pen in order to direct to you as a present, a copy of an Almanack which I have calculated

for the Succeeding year, I was unexpectedly and un-
avoidably led thereto.

This calculation, Sir, is the production of my
arduous study, in this my advanced Stage of life; for
having long had unbounded desires to become Acquainted with the Secrets of nature, I have had to
gratify my curiosity herein thro my own assiduous
application to Astronomical Study, in which I need
not to recount to you the many difficulties and disadvantages which I have had to encounter.

And altho I had almost declined to make my calculation for the ensuing year, in consequence of that
time which I had allotted therefor being taking up
at the Federal Territory by the request of M^r. Andrew
Ellicott, yet finding myself under Several engagements
to printers of this state to whom I had communicated
my design, on my return to my place of residence, I
industriously apply'd myself thereto, which I hope I
have accomplished with correctness and accuracy, a
copy of which I have taken the liberty to direct to you,
and which I humbly request you will favourably receive, and altho you may have the opportunity of pe-
rusing it after its publication, yet I chose to send it to
you in manuscript previous thereto, that thereby you
might not only have an earlier inspection, but that you
might also view it in my own hand writing.

And now Sir, I Shall conclude and Subscribe my
Self with the most profound respect,

Your most Obedient humble Servant
Benjamin Banneker.

N.B. any communication to me may be had by a direction to M^r. Elias Ellicott merchant in Baltimore Town.

B.B.

Hopeful of some reply, Banneker then added a second postscript. It provides some insight of his concern in relation to the

publication of his calculations, a concern which he found himself forced to express without wishing to offend his correspondent:

> As an Essay of my calculation is put into the hand of
> M^r. Cruckshank of Philadelphia, for publication I
> would wish that you might neither have this Almanack
> copy published nor give any printer an opportunity
> thereof, as it might tend to disappoint M^r. Joseph
> Cruckshank in his sale
>
> B.B.

Banneker's postscript confirms the fact that the almanac
had been given to Crukshank for publication, and that he was
the Philadelphia printer sought by Banneker and arranged by
Pemberton.

The manuscript copy of the almanac and the letter were
forwarded to Jefferson at Philadelphia, which was then the
seat of government, and it was received by Jefferson exactly a
week later, on August 26. He lost little time in returning a reply.
Within four days' time he had responded. He acknowledged
Banneker's plea for the improvement of the state of the Negro,
and expressed his own hope that a system would be initiated
which would make it possible as soon as circumstances would
permit. Jefferson then went on to add that he had forwarded
the manuscript copy to his friend, the Marquis de Condorcet,
who was Secretary of the Royal Academy of Sciences at Paris,
as evidence of the equal talents of the Negro race. Jefferson's
letter was a relatively short one, which nonetheless gave Banneker immense satisfaction:

> Philadelphia, Aug. 30. 1791.
> SIR, I Thank you sincerely for your letter of the
> 19th instant and for the Almanac it contained. No body
> wishes more than I do to see such proofs as you exhibit,
> that nature has given to our black brethren, talents

equal to those of the other colors of men, and that the appearance of a want of them is owing merely to the degraded condition of their existence, both in Africa & America. I can add with truth, that no body wishes more ardently to see a good system commenced for raising the condition both of their body & mind to what it ought to be, as fast as the imbecility of their present existence, and other circumstances which cannot be neglected, will admit.

I have taken the liberty of sending your Almanac to Monsieur de Condorcet, Secretary of the Academy of Sciences at Paris, and member of the Philanthropic society, because I considered it as a document to which your whole colour had a right for their justification against the doubts which have been entertained of them.

I am with great esteem, Sir your most obed^t humble serv^t.

Thomas Jefferson.

Mr. Benjamin Banneker,
Near Ellicott's Lower Mills, Baltimore Co.[18]

The deliberate intent behind Banneker's letter to Jefferson was demonstrated shortly after Jefferson's reply was received. The two letters were published as a pamphlet by the Philadelphia printer, Daniel Lawrence, and widely distributed soon after the almanac was first published.[19] The letters were also published in at least one popular periodical, the *Universal Asylum and Columbian Magazine* during the following year.[20]

Jefferson forwarded the manuscript ephemeris with a covering letter to de Condorcet as he had promised.[21] After acknowledging receipt of materials relating to the adoption of a unit of measure by France, of which Jefferson admitted he did not approve because of its liability to error, he went on to mention his enclosure and the circumstances that had brought it to his attention:

I am happy to be able to inform you that we have now in the United States a negro, the son of a black man born in Africa, and a black woman born in the United States, who is a very respectable mathematician. I procured him to be employed under one of our chief directors in laying out the new federal city on the Potowmac, & in the intervals of his leisure, while on that work, he made an Almanac for the next year, which he sent me in his own hand writing, & which I inclose to you. I have seen very elegant solutions of Geometrical problems by him. Add to this that he is a very worthy & respectable member of society. He is a free man. I shall be delighted to see these instances of moral eminence so multiplied as to prove that the want of talents observed in them is merely the effect of their degraded condition, and not proceeding from any difference in the structure of the parts on which intellect depends.

Jefferson's letter to de Condorcet reflected a marked mellowing of attitude toward the Negro from that expressed some years earlier in his *Notes on Virginia*. In that work he had indicated his own hatred of the system of slavery in America despite the fact that his own livelihood as a planter depended upon the system. He stated that he hoped to change the status of his slaves to that of tenants, but his own financial status never enabled him to do so except in token instances. Although most of his writings on slavery had been more academic than practical, he admitted the system to be an evil as well as an injustice, but he specified that it was evil primarily because of how slavery affected the masters by appealing to their baser instincts, rather than because of its effect on the slaves themselves.

Much of Jefferson's feeling about slavery was due to his great fear of a slave rebellion. It was only with the greatest reluctance that he permitted his *Notes on Virginia* to be published, and then several years after he had written it. While

Minister to France he refused to become a part of the antislavery movement in the United States or in France because of his honest concern that the involvement of a public figure such as himself might be detrimental to the purpose. To the invitation to become a member of the French Société des Amis des Noirs, Jefferson replied to Jean Pierre Brissot de Warville as follows:

> . . . You know that nobody wishes more ardently to see an abolition not only of the trade but of the condition of slavery: and certainly nobody will be more willing to encounter every sacrifice for that object. But the influence & information of the friends to this proposition will be far above the need for my association. I am here as a public servant; and those whom I serve having never yet been able to give their voice against this practice, it is decent for me to avoid too public a demonstration of my wishes to see it abolished. Without serving the cause here, it might render me less able to serve it beyond the water. . . .[22]

This letter is of interest for another reason. Obviously Jefferson had received information about Banneker other than those facts derived from the latter's letter. The reference to the Secretary's involvement in Banneker's employment confirms the previously unsupported supposition that Major Ellicott had consulted with the statesman before he selected Banneker as his assistant. Perhaps at the same time Ellicott may have described one or more of the mathematical puzzles of which Banneker was fond and concerning which he may have been informed by his cousins.

Jefferson's decision to send Banneker's manuscript ephemeris to de Condorcet demonstrates his intention to provide Banneker with the best possible exposure if his work deserved it. In writing to de Condorcet he was paying Banneker a great honor. Not only was the Académie the foremost body of scientific learning in France, but Marie Jean Antoine Nicholas Caritat, Marquis de Condorcet (1743–1794), was one of that country's foremost scholars. A noted mathematician, philosopher, statesman, and more recently a revolutionary, de Condorcet was a descendant of an ancient aristocratic family. In 1777 he became perpetual secretary of the Académie Royal des Sciences, in 1782 he was elected a member of the French Academy, and in the same year he published an important work on the doctrine of probability. During this period he was inspector-general of the mint. He subsequently opposed the arrest of the Girondists, which led to his own condemnation.

In September 1791 de Condorcet became secretary of the Legislative Assembly, and during the political ferment that followed, he was among the first to support the proposal for a republic. It was he who drew up the memorandum that led to the suspension of the king and summoned the national convention. These events occurred at just the time that he would have received the letter from Jefferson and its enclosure. De Condorcet then went into hiding for a time, during which period he produced some of his most important philosophical works. Believing that he was being watched, he escaped from his refuge but was captured and imprisoned. On the following morning (March 28, 1794), he was found dead; whether death was caused by exhaustion or poison was never determined.

It had been Jefferson's intention to have Banneker's work reviewed by one of the Académie's committees, possibly with the thought that if the report was favorable it would shed honor on the scientific work of the New World. Although Jefferson mailed his letter with the enclosed manuscript at the end of August 1791, it is fairly certain either that it was never received by de Condorcet, or that if it was the marquis did not present it to the Académie. There are several justifications for this conclusion.

First of all, a letter from Jefferson, as a prominent American figure in science and as Secretary of State, would not have been left unanswered. No reply from de Condorcet or from the Académie has been found among the Jefferson papers[23] nor does a draft of such a reply survive among the voluminous papers of de Condorcet which are preserved in the Bibliothèque de l'Institut de France in Paris.[24] Furthermore, a careful search of the manuscript proceedings of the Académie for the period revealed that Banneker's ephemeris had not been presented to that body nor, as a search of the surviving records shows, was it presented to the sister body, the Académie des Inscriptions et Belles-Lettres.[25]

The fact that Banneker's work was not presented to the Académie by de Condorcet is not surprising in view of the events already described. Since the marquis was also greatly concerned with the French antislavery movement and, together with Jean Pierre Brissot de Warville and the Marquis de Lafayette, was among the founders of the Société des Amis des Noirs, the possibility that the Banneker ephemeris might have been submitted to that society was also explored, with negative results.[26]

Had Banneker's achievement been presented to the Académie it would have created a sensation in France at that time, and particularly in pro-Negro circles. The Société des Amis des Noirs would have welcomed this fresh and impressive example of Negro accomplishment, and it would have been widely publicized. That no mention is to be found in any of the literature of the period confirms the conclusion that while it may have been received by de Condorcet, he probably did not have the opportunity to present it himself or to have someone else do so.

Meanwhile, Banneker was highly pleased with Jefferson's reply and with the latter's decision to send the manuscript to the great French body of learning.

A few problems were developing in the plans for publishing the almanac, however. Pemberton and his friends were seeking a leading figure to write an introduction to the new almanac which would help to popularize it. They finally selected James McHenry (1753–1816), Senator to the Congress from Maryland, who agreed to write the preface or introduction. There were many advantages to having McHenry associate his name with the venture. He was popularly recognized as a Southerner, and he was well known throughout the country as a prominent soldier in the Revolution and as an important statesman.

Having emigrated from his native Ireland in 1771, McHenry studied medicine under Dr. Benjamin Rush and later served on the medical staff of the Continental Army. For more than two years he worked as General Washington's private secretary and subsequently he filled the same position with the Marquis de Lafayette. From 1783 McHenry was a member of the Continental Congress for three years, after which he was elected the Maryland delegate to the Constitutional Convention in 1787. At the time in question he was Senator from Maryland to the Congress. From 1796 until 1800 he was to serve as Secretary of War in President Adams's cabinet. But in spite of McHenry's promise, the introduction was not forthcoming, and there was some question whether it would be made available in time for a printer to include it. This concern was expressed by George Ellicott to Pemberton late in August, when the prolonged absence of his brother forced him to act.[27]

As My Bro. Elias Ellicott hath for some time past been out of Town I take the liberty to inform that I am fearfull there will be a disapointment in respect the preface for Banakers Allmanacke but I shall inform more fully on the return of My Brother. D^r. James M^c.Hennery who is now in Philadelphia was to have wrote it. Inclosed is a Coppy of a Letter which Benjamin Banaker wrote to Thos. Jefferson Secretary of State which he wrote himself and desired Me to send to thee it is his wish to have it put into the Allmanacke if its thought proper or in to the publick papers. Their is a small piece of poetry inclosed of Banaker's composing which he desires may be put under the Letter if its published. Their was Something said in respect to a cirtificate being Necessary from sundry people that was acquainted with said Banaker seting forth that He was the Calculator: If it is Necessary their can one soon be had.

Banneker's suggestion that his letter to Jefferson be published as part of the almanac "or in to the publick papers" confirms the supposition expressed earlier that the letter was a deliberate attempt to use the almanac as propaganda for the abolitionist movement, and to involve Jefferson because his published opinions on slavery made him a natural target for any timely expression on the subject.

The "small piece of poetry . . . of Banaker's composing" did not survive in the same repository, but it is probably to be identified with the poem which formed one of the exhibits at the anniversary meeting of the Banneker Institute in 1860, and which a newspaper account of the event[28] described as follows:

> As a curiosity, also, we give the following attempt at versification, written upon a slip of paper almost disintegrated by time.

A copy made at that time bears the date "October 19, 1791" and the following verses:

> Behold ye Christians! and in pity see
> Those Afric sons which Nature formed free;
> Behold them in a fruitful country blest,
> Of Nature's bounties see them rich possest,
> Behold them herefrom torn by cruel force,
> And doomed to slavery without remorse,
> This act, America, thy sons have known;
> This cruel act, relentless they have done.
>
> B. Banneker

While arrangements were being made with haste and concern in Baltimore and Philadelphia, a new obstacle suddenly

presented itself. When Banneker had given a copy of his calculations to William Goddard, it was with the expressed intent that
the almanac could be published by several printers simultaneously
in Baltimore and Philadelphia without conflict of interest, to ensure its widest possible distribution.

Goddard did not agree with such an arrangement, and
chose to understand that in submitting the manuscript to him,
Banneker had given him exclusive rights. He had meanwhile
managed to obtain from Senator McHenry the manuscript of
the introduction which had been solicited, and he planned to
proceed with an exclusive publication. Goddard, who was then
one of the most important printers in the country, had distinguished himself equally by the high quality of his work and
because he was always in conflict with almost everyone he dealt
with or to whom his publications were addressed.

Elias Ellicott reported the situation in detail to Pemberton
with the hope that the latter could exert his influence to solve
the situation:

> William Goddard it seems is really printing Bannakers
> Allmanack and hath the Work in forwardness—Altho
> it does Not Appear that he bought the Coppy Right of
> him he Nevertheless thinks or affects to think himself
> intitled to an exclusive right in it an^d. Refuses to give a
> Coppy of the introduction Written by D^r. M^c.Henry
> —This information I have from the Doctor himself
> Who this day Called on Willm. Godard respecting it—
> However if Joseph Crookshank thinks proper to pro-
> ceed, this Introduction Cannot. I aprehend be Material
> to the Sale of it especially if it was prefaced by a Copy
> of his Letter to the Secretary or Any other Introduc-
> tion explanatory of the Author's Situation etc. etc.—
> Certification of its athenticity May Also be had from a
> Number of Respectable Men at Any Moment—this
> disappointment, I am Sorry for and doe not think
> Godard hath Acted a Generous part, especially as he

had no expectation of Any introduction of the Kind When he purchased the Coppy—he Informed Dr. M^c.Henry that he had Ingaged a Quaker printer in Philadelphia to Make Sale of them in that City.[29]

Goddard's whimsical behavior in this situation did not surprise those who knew him, but proved to be a disappointment to the Ellicott brothers, and Goddard's response to McHenry himself showed that he would not retreat from his position. However, McHenry's letter was not critical to a publication of the almanac if other suitable material could be found to replace it, and Banneker's letter to Jefferson might be sufficient for the purpose.

Elias Ellicott wrote to Banneker to describe the situation, and suggested that it might be useful if he would prepare a statement describing the details of his negotiations with Goddard, which could be used to inform Pemberton and the others.

Banneker was appalled by the situation he had apparently unwittingly created, and he was concerned that his friends the Ellicotts should not be embarrassed by his actions. He was perturbed by the impression his mishandling may have given to the members of the Abolitionist Society, and he set to work to write out an account of the circumstances as he had understood them. This appeared to be an appropriate opportunity also to forward a copy of the reply he had just received from Jefferson and which had impressed him deeply. It now seemed feasible to consider publication of both letters in lieu of the McHenry introduction, in the first issue of the almanac. He made a handwritten copy of Jefferson's reply, and prepared a covering letter. These he forwarded to Elias from the mail room at the store of Ellicott & Co.:

After an inspection of a Letter by you directed to M^r. Elias or George Ellicott, respecting the sale of my essay of an Almanack to M^r. William Goddard, I find myself desirous to reply thereto. It appears that you are apprehensive that M^r. Goddard has purchas'd the Copy Right to my Calculations, of which I can inform you, that he has purchased a Copy, which I have Sufficient reason to believe he will publish; but that I have not an Idea that he has purchased to himself the Sole and exclusive right to the publication, this would be unreasonable in him to expect, after reflecting on my indigence, as also my labour and loss of time in the Calculation, and his compensation to me therefor the Sum of £3, and which in case he is Successful in the sale he will increase to 3 Guineas, but he has lately informed me that there is a probability of my Still being further rewarded and I can Scarcely think that M^r. Goddard considers the Sole right to the Copy to be in himself, for I have in my Conversation with him intimated, that the publication of another Copy in Philadelphia would not be injurious to him with which he expressed neither unwillingness nor dissatisfaction, and as the disposing of the same Copy to different printers is not unprecedented, I have thought it was allowable in me when I had not bound myself by any contract to the contrary, and it was under this Idea that I not only Sold a Copy to M^r. Goddard, But also previous thereto disposed of one to a printer in George Town on Patowmac, and interceded with my friends Messrs. Ellicotts to assist me in endeavoring to have one published in Philadelphia, which anxiety proceeded not so much from a lucrative view as a certainty of its publication, which in the preceding year my utmost exertions were ineffectual to obtain, for having prepared a Copy, I offered it to three printers of this State two of which refused its acceptance, and the third after detaining it in his possession under a promise to publish it until a period to far advanced therefor, when he informed me that he could not. And now Sir, I hope that these Circumstances are Sufficient to Justify my conduct, under which I shall conclude with assuring you, no person can wish more sincerely to regard truth and adhere to reputation than Sir,

Your most obedient humble Servt
Benjamin Banneker

Septr. 3^d. 1791

N. B. I send inclosed the Copy of a Letter which I received from the Secretary of State, in answer to one I sent him, the Copy of which M^r. George Ellicott sent you Some time Since, both of which, if you See proper I have no objection to have published.

N. B. The introduction that D^r. M'Henry wrote, was intended for the Almanac that was to be published in Philadelphia, as also the one that M^r. Goddard was to publish, M^r. Elias Ellicott informs me that M^r. Goddard hath it in his possession and will not give a copy of it, now I have a great desire to have an Allmanack published in Philadelphia as I think it would tend greatly to increase the circulation as I do no expect that M^r. Goddard will circulate his into Pennsylvania. I think that the certificate which M^r. Elias Ellicott will forward, and my letter to M^r. Jefferson and his answer to me, will answer in place of a preface.[30]

Banneker's letter was revealing and informative; it described a financial arrangement with Goddard which is of particular interest. The payment of three pounds for the ephemeris was relatively modest, and his promise of an increase to three guineas if it succeeded was hardly a substantial bonus. Banneker's letter indicated that there had been further communication with Goddard on the subject by personal contact; this probably required a second visit to Baltimore prior to this date.

The letter clarifies yet another point not previously known. His decision to have his ephemeris published in an almanac had not developed as much from the urgings of George Ellicott as has popularly been supposed, but as an independent idea of Banneker's. He had offered his work to several printers before informing George of his desire for assistance in finding a printer in Philadelphia for the purpose of obtaining wider distribution. George was willing to assist, and in doing so, brought the elderly philomath to the attention of his brother Elias and his friends, who recognized in this request an unforeseen opportunity to serve also the antislavery movement.

When Banneker's report reached him, Elias read it with interest. Exasperated by Goddard's action, and determined that the best solution would be to publish an affidavit of Banneker's authorship, he drafted an appropriate statement and circulated it to interested members of his family and to prominent citizens of Ellicott's Lower Mills and Baltimore. Elias then assembled Banneker's report and the certificate and forwarded them to Pemberton with a covering letter:

Since My letter of the 31st. Ultimo. I Wrote to Benjn. Banneker and desired him to write thee a full Statement of Contract between him & William Goddard, which he hath done and forwarded by this post—inclosed is a Certifycate Certifying that Benjn. is the author of the Calculation—that, with his Letter to Jefferson & his answer which Benjamin hath Sent thee—I think will Answer as well as the proposed Preface as Mentioned in My Last—I think You need not hesitate in Respect to the propriety of Publishing the Allmanack, as it is clear that Goddard hath not the Least Shadow of right to the Exclusive privilege of printing his Allmanack— We Shold have discouraged Benjamin's having a copy Printed in Your City had we not good reason to believe that it wold not interfere with any Contracts which he had made—I Recd the Urgent Epistle thee Sent and Shall take proper Care to produce the Same to Our Yearly Meeting.

If You Shold think proper to form an introduction

or preface Your Selves we can furnish You with Something of Baneker's Life & Situation in Life. We Shold be glad to hear your determination.[31]

The "Certificate" was an unusual and impressive document, addressed simply to the public:[32]

> To the Public.
> In Order to clear up any doubt that may Arise as to Benjamin Banneker (a Black man whose Father came from Africa) being the Author of the Prefixed Almanac We whose Names are hereunto Annexed do Certify that we for several Years have been Acquainted with him and that his knowledge in Astronomy and the Mathematicks was of his own Acquiring Assisted only by Astronomical Tables which he with much Difficulty procured.

Andrew Ellicott	Michael Pue, M.D.
James Gillingham	George Ellicott
Daniel Carroll	Gerard Hopkins
Elias Ellicott	Jonathan Ellicott
W^m. Dillworth	James Carey.
Joseph Evans	

To the knowledgeable, the list of signers may have been less than impressive, inasmuch as seven of the eleven names were those of members of the Ellicott family; the others were close friends or business associates. Nevertheless, the list was headed by the signature of none other than the Geographer General of the United States, Major Andrew Ellicott. Of the other signers, in addition to the Ellicott brothers, Joseph Evans was a millwright married to Joseph Ellicott's daughter, Ann, and James Carey was a Baltimore merchant married to John Ellicott's daughter, Martha. Gerard Hopkins was a minister of the Society of Friends whose wife was a cousin of Elizabeth Brooke Ellicott. Daniel Carroll was a merchant in Baltimore; James

Gillingham, later a respected elder in the Society of Friends, was a blacksmith who had lived for a time at the Lower Mills. Dr. Michael Pue was a physician in Baltimore, and William Dillworth was a long-time customer of Ellicott & Co. who later served as a witness for the Ellicott brothers in a lawsuit.

Upon receipt of Banneker's letter and that of Elias Ellicott, Pemberton came to the conclusion that there was no further time to lose if the almanac was to be published in a Philadelphia edition. Since the major obstacle appeared to be William Goddard, the matter had to be settled with him as soon as possible, whether he planned to publish it and what he would do if others issued the almanac. In this communication Pemberton explained how he had become involved in the project:

> Towards the close of last year, I first Recd. information of the Astronomical Genius of Benj. Banniker a Black man in the neighbourhood of Baltimore and that he had made calculations for an Almanac for the pres.t year but he was disappointed in the publication of it which induced me to make enquiry concerning him, and receiving satisfactory information on the Subject from some of his friends one of them Sent me a few weeks past a Copy of his Calculations for the ensuing Year, which I communicated to David Rittenhouse, who after inspection as fully as his leisure would permit Returned the copy with a letter expressing his approbation of the Calculations. I then laid them before another Astronomer who also after an examination Certified in writing to the same effect; I then engaged a printer to publish 4000 Copies on terms very advantageous to Banniker & had made a Collection of some instructive essays to be published as usual in an Almanac expecting it to be prefaced by some account of the Author, which was to be sent up in time, and understanding Dr. McHenry had made such an Essay, I applied to him just before his leaving the city last week

when he informed me that he had left the Essay in thy hands, and that thou had undertaken to publish the Almanac, upon which I conjectured Banneker had sold thee the Copy Right, & therefore thought it improper to proceed in the Publication here, and altho' I do not find that is altogether the case, I have judged it best to decline any further progress in the business, and to inform thee of it, that thou may publish a larger number of Copies than thou might otherwise conclude to be necessary, and being informed of thy attachment to the Cause of humanity, and kindly disposition towards the poor degraded Blacks, whom the prejudices of some men & the Avarice of others have held in estimation equal or inferior to the Brute Creation, while the most extensive Proclamation is made of the uninterrupted enjoyment of Liberty & the Rights of Man under the Constitution of in the United States of America.

Having no interest of my own in this, I now only Sollicit thy attentive benevolence to poor Banniker to make further Compensation as thou may Judge to make up in some measure for the disappointment he will be subjected by the publication of his performance being laid aside here—And I further request thee to send me up a dozen Copies of the Almanac as soon as it is published, the members of our Abolition Society intended to have interested themselves in the sale of the Almanac had it been published, & I have reason to believe a considerable number of Copies will still be taken of by them.[34]

Goddard lost no time in responding to Pemberton, assuring his full cooperation in the project:

Your highly acceptable Letter, rec.ᵈ this Day, merits greater Attention and a more explicit Answer than I

am, at present, able to give it, being suddenly called
from Home to visit a dear Friend in a House of Mourn-
ing. I cannot, however, delay informing you that B.
Banniker's Almanack will be published in a few Days,
and that I Shall not only send the Copies you desire,
but will, most cheerfully, cooperate with you in giving
Success to your benevolent wishes & endeavours—
Tho' I had engaged to send a Number to W. D. Humphreys, yet as M^r. Crukshank hath been at some
Trouble and Expense, I shall consider it an Act of
Justice & Civility to give him the Advantage of selling
the Work, & will, therefore, send him a Number of
the first Impression. I am heartily disposed not only
to be just, but generous to poor Benjamin, and as I
Sincerely respect your Character, your Principles &
Profession, I shall be governed by your Advice and
Opinion as to what would be a liberal ample Compensation to the Sable Astronomer,—I shall give you
an honest Account of my Sales, in which I hope for
the Assistance of the Benevolent, and flatter myself the
Issue will prove advantageous to the ingenious Man
you aim to patronize, and pleasing to yourself and
Fellow Labourers in the same glorious Cause. In great
Haste.[35]

Goddard's response expressed an unusual degree of cooperation, and reflected Pemberton's importance as a leading
figure of his time. The apparent conflict of the several printers
was resolved to the satisfaction of each, although mostly to that
of Goddard, and Banneker's almanac was assured a wide distribution. This was to be a new venture for Goddard for he
had not produced almanacs for some time. In December of 1790
he had acquired a stock of an almanac produced by others and
made them available to his clients, in accordance with a brief
advertisement in his newspaper:

A few Groce of A L M A N A C K S, for 1791, a very interesting and useful Work, and inferior to none on the Continent, may be had of the Printers, if applied for soon.[36]

Now, although he had assured Pemberton that Banneker's almanac would be printed within a matter of days, there was some delay; it was late December before he first announced the publication in his newspaper, and then to advise that it would be available shortly:

BENJAMIN BANNEKER'S highly approved AL-MANACK, for 1792, to be sold by the Printer's hereof, Wholesale and Retail.[37]

It may be significant that although the almanac featured Banneker's race, the advance announcement made no mention of it.

Pemberton's note that he had selected "instructive essays" to include in the almanac is revealing. It confirms the fact that Banneker was not responsible for the literary content of the publication. Contrary to popular belief, the literary content of most eighteenth-century almanacs was not the compilation of the person who calculated the ephemeris; his work was generally restricted to the mathematical data. It was the printer who collected the rest. He gathered prose and poetry from available periodicals, and chose appropriate allegories, proverbs, recipes, and remedies from standard works. To these he added useful information such as would be desired by the reader: a listing of the more important positions in the federal government, including members of the Cabinet, Senate, and federal courts; a calendar of the courts of law holding sessions in areas where the almanac would be distributed; a calendar of meetings of the Society of Friends; roads and distances of cities from the place of publication; and miscellaneous tables of general use, such as the weights and values of sundry coins, of interest rates and a scale of depreciation.

Banneker's almanac had many resemblances to others published at that time. His ephemeris was supplemented by such other of his own work as a list of movable feasts, followed by a calendar of the eclipses for the year, with a page devoted to the Anatomy, or "The Moon's Man." The ephemerides for each of the twelve months were supplemented at the foot of each page with a single item of useful information. A short essay on "The Planetary and Terrestrial Worlds comparatively considered" may have been submitted by Banneker but could have been taken from another unidentified publication.

Goddard and Angell used quotation marks at the beginning and end of many of their essays and other literary contents, indicating that the material was not original. "The Planetary and Terrestrial Worlds" was followed by a two-page essay of "Remarks on the Swiftness of Time," and then with a letter to the editor of the *London Magazine* on the "Origin of the Gray's Mare being the Better Horse." Miscellaneous short subjects included an allegory on "The Two Bees," another "On Health," and what purported to be "Extracts from the Common-Place Book of the Kentucky Philosopher." Other brevities, designed to be instructive and elevating, included "Extracts from the Writings of the Ancients of distinguished fame," "The stings of Poverty, Disease and Violence . . . ," "The Balance of Happiness equal," and a treatise on curing the defects and diseases of trees presented in an address by William Forsyth to the House of Commons. Buried among the poems and remedies was a short excerpt from *The Columbian Magazine*, "On Negro Slavery, and the Slave Trade" in which was quoted a statement on skin pigmentation by none other than David Rittenhouse.

When the arrangements between the respective printers were completed, the almanac finally went to press. It was produced at the press of Goddard and Angell on Market Street in Baltimore. As indicated in the notice of imprint, it was made available for distribution in Philadelphia separately by Joseph Crukshank and Daniel Humphreys, and in Alexandria at the shop of Hanson and Bond. Humphreys was a prominent printer of the period. The son of Joshua Humphreys, he served an apprenticeship as a printer with William Bradford. In 1775 he opened a printing office in partnership with Enoch Story the elder in Norris Alley near Front Street. They undertook to produce a newspaper, but a few months later a fire destroyed their shop and its contents, and the partnership was dissolved. Humphreys opened another printing shop of his own, and from 1783 to 1784 was a partner with Ebenezer Oswald in the publication of *The Independent Gazetteer*. Later he established another newspaper by himself.

The pamphlet bore an impressive title which promised a wide range of useful materials to the prospective purchaser:

BENJAMIN BANNEKER'S
PENNSYLVANIA, DELAWARE, MARYLAND, AND
VIRGINIA
ALMANAC
AND
EPHEMERIS
FOR THE YEAR OF OUR LORD,
1792.

Being Bissextile or Leap Year, and the sixteenth year of American Independence, which commenced July 4th, 1776. Containing the Motions of the Sun and Moon, the true places and aspects of the Planets, the Rising and Setting of the Sun, and the Rising, Setting, and Southing Place and Age of the Moon, etc., the Lunations, Conjunctions, Eclipses, Judgments of the Weather, Festivals, and other remarkable days. Days for holding the Supreme and Circuit courts of the United States, as also the usual courts in Pennsylvania,

Delaware, Maryland, and Virginia; also several useful Tables and valuable Recipes; various selections from the commonplace Book of the Kentucky Philosopher, an American sage; with interesting and entertaining Essays in Prose and Verse, the whole comprising a greater, more pleasing and useful variety than any work of the kind and price in North America.

The initiation of a new almanac calculated by an Afro-American provided the distributors with an unusual opportunity for publicity, and they made every use of the materials at hand. Not only would they be assured of success with the project through the agency of the abolitionist societies, but they had in hand the best evidence yet available that Negro capability was equal to that of other races.

Goddard and Angell took every advantage of the opportunity, as evidenced in the introduction, which appeared on the reverse of the title page:

The Editors of the PENNSYLVANIA, DELA-WARE, MARYLAND, AND VIRGINIA AL-MANACK, feel themselves gratified in the Opportunity of presenting to the Public, through the Medium of their Press, what must be considered an extraordinary Effort of Genius—a COMPLETE and ACCURATE EPHEMERIS for the Year 1792, calculated by a sable Descendant of Africa, who, by this Specimen of Ingenuity, evinces, to Demonstration, that mental Powers and Endowments are not the exclusive Excellence of white People, but that the Rays of Science may alike illumine the Minds of Men of every Clime, (however they may differ in the Colour of their Skin) particularly those whom Tyrant-Custom hath too long taught us to depreciate as a Race inferior in intellectual Capacity—They flatter themselves that a philanthropic Public, in this enlightened Era, will be

induced to give their Patronage and Support to this
Work, not only on Account of its intrinsic Merit, (it
having met the Approbation of several of the most distinguished Astronomers in America, particularly the
celebrated Mr. Rittenhouse) but from similar Motives
to those which induced the Editors to give this Calculation the Preference, the ardent Desire of drawing
modest Merit from Obscurity, and controverting the
long-established illiberal Prejudice against the Blacks.

Though it becomes the Editors to speak with less
Confidence of the miscellaneous Part of this Work,
they yet flatter themselves, from their Attention to the
variegated Selections in Prose and Verse, that their
Readers will find it both USEFUL and ENTER-
TAINING, and not undeserving of that Approbation
which they have had the Happiness of experiencing for
a Series of Years—an Approbation they are still ambitious of meriting, and which, they hope, will crown
their present Wishes and Labours with Success.

The Editors have taken the Liberty to annex a
Letter from Mr. McHENRY, containing Particulars
respecting Benjamin, which, it is presumed, will prove
more acceptable to the Reader, than anything further
in the prefatory Way.

The letter from McHenry, which follows, was a desirable
addition, supporting with its new evidence the arguments against
slavery. It not only described Banneker and his career but left
no doubt concerning the purpose of the publication.

Baltimore, August 20, 1791.
Messrs. GODDARD and ANGELL,
BENJAMIN BANNEKER, a free Negro, has calculated an ALMANACK, for the ensuing year, 1792,
which being desirous to dispose of, to the best advantage he has requested me to aid his application to

you for that purpose. Having fully satisfied myself, with respect to his title to this kind of authorship, if you can agree with him for the price of his work, I may venture to assure you it will do you credit, as Editors, while it will afford you the opportunity to encourage talents that have thus far surmounted the most discouraging circumstances and prejudices.

This Man is about fifty-nine years of age; he was born in *Baltimore County;* his father was an *African,* and his mother the offspring of *African* parents—His father and mother having obtained their freedom, were enabled to send him to an obscure school, where he learned, when a boy, reading, writing, and arithmetic as far as double position; and to leave him, at their deaths, a few acres of land, upon which he has supported himself ever since by means of economy and constant labour, and preserved a fair reputation. To struggle incessantly against want is no ways favourable to improvement:

What he had learned, however, he did not forget; for as some hours of leisure will occur in the most toilsome life, he availed himself of these, not to read and acquire knowledge from writings of genius and discovery, for of such he had none, but to digest and apply, as occasions presented, the few principles of the few rules of arithmetic he had been taught at school. This kind of mental exercise formed his chief amusement, and soon gave him a facility in calculation that was often serviceable to his neighbours, and at length attracted the attention of the Messrs. *Ellicotts,* a family remarkable for their ingenuity and turn to the useful mechanics. It is about three years since Mr. *George Ellicott* lent him *Mayer's* Tables, *Ferguson's* Astronomy, *Leadbeater's* Lunar-Table, and some astronomic instruments, but without accompanying them with either hint or instruction, that might further his studies, or lead him to apply them to any useful result. These books and instruments, the first of the kind he had ever seen, opened a new world to *Benjamin,* and from thenceforward he employed his leisure in astronomical researches. He now took up the idea of the calculations for an ALMANACK, and actually completed an entire set for the last year, upon his original stock of arithmetic. Encouraged by this first attempt, he entered upon his calculation for 1792, which, as well as the former, he began and finished without the least information, or alliance, from any person, or other books than those I have mentioned; so that, whatever merit is attached to his present performance, is exclusively and peculiarly his own.

I have been the more careful to investigate these particulars, and to ascertain their reality, as they form an interesting fact in the History of Man; and as you may want them to gratify curiosity, I have no objection to your selecting them for your account of *Benjamin.*

I consider this Negro as a fresh proof that the powers of the mind are disconnected with the colour of the skin, or, in other words, a striking contradiction to Mr. *Hume*'s doctrine, that "Negroes are naturally inferior to the whites and unsusceptible of attainments in arts and sciences." In every civilized country we shall find thousands of whites, liberally educated, and who have enjoyed greater opportunities of instruction than this Negro, his inferior in those intellectual acquirements and capacities that form the most characteristic feature in the human race. But the system that would assign to these degraded blacks an origin different from the whites, if it is not ready to be deserted by philosophers, must be relinquished as similar instances multiply; and that such must frequently happen cannot well be doubted, should no check impede the

progress of humanity, which, meliorating the condition of slavery, necessarily leads to its final extinction.—
Let, however, the issue be what it will, I cannot but
wish, on this occasion, to see the Public patronage keep
pace with my black friend's merit.

I am, Gentlemen, your most obedient servant,
JAMES McHENRY.

With the best intentions in the world, McHenry's account
was not completely accurate in all details relating to Banneker's
life, but it was an impressive introduction.

Inasmuch as McHenry's introduction was utilized by Goddard in this, his exclusive publication of Banneker's work, Pemberton and his associates reserved the exchange of letters with
Jefferson for another issue. Banneker's poem on slavery was
not published in this or any other of the almanac issues which
were to follow, nor was it necessary to include the certification
of Banneker's authorship which Elias Ellicott had so carefully
prepared.

Banneker's almanac was placed on sale at the end of 1791
and it sold in great numbers. Large stocks of copies were furnished by Goddard to the three other distributors, and it was
not long before the first issue was exhausted, requiring Goddard
and Angell to produce a second edition. One of these editions
bore the title "Benjamin Banniker's Pennsylvania, Delaware,
Maryland and Virginia Almanac and Ephemeris." The mis-
spelling of the author's name was apparently no reason for
recalling the issue, and there is no way of knowing whether this
error was in the first or second of Goddard & Angell's editions.

The unidentified printer in Georgetown whom Banneker
had contacted did not publish an edition of the almanac after
all. If the firm involved was Hancock and Day, it may have
abandoned the project because they had decided to sell out their
printing business during the following months.

A separate edition of Banneker's first almanac was issued
by another of Philadelphia's most prominent printers, William

Young (1755–1829). His firm was one of the most important in Philadelphia during the late eighteenth and early nineteenth centuries. Young was born in Scotland and migrated with his family to the United States in 1784. He settled at Philadelphia and established a printing and stationery shop at the southwest corner of Chestnut and Second streets, where he printed and sold books. The business prospered and in 1793 he established a paper mill at Wilmington, Delaware, which he continued as a second business.

Young's edition of Banneker's almanac was not a reprint of the Goddard & Angell edition but a distinctly separate issue. It was somewhat smaller in overall size and reduced also in content, from twenty-four to eighteen pages.

Banneker was stunned by the sudden fame that came to him. The almanac was an unusual success, although in his own mind he attributed this to the determination and organized efforts of the Pennsylvania and Maryland Societies for the Promotion of the Abolition of Slavery rather than to the significance of his achievement. The fact that so many individuals prominent in public affairs and in business had devoted so much of their time to producing his work led Banneker to a deeper examination of their purpose and of the antislavery movement.

He found that his life was changing almost overnight. Neighbors and occasional travelers through the region called at his home to see him and speak to him, marveling at the accomplishment represented by self-study, undertaken so late in life, which had brought him to national attention. Banneker was hospitable and courteous to all who came. He invited them into his house, where they wished especially to see his clock and his worktable with his calculations. Now that he had to abandon tobacco growing because of his infirmities, he cultivated a small garden just for his own needs, and gave some attention to his beehives and his orchard. He enjoyed the visits. Surprisingly enough, he did not feel that his had been a meager lot. Life had indeed been good to him, and he intended to make the most of the years that remained.

As he whiled away the hours at his worktable or in his garden, he had much time for thinking, and in his solitude his mind turned to the cause in which he had become involved. He often reflected on the exchange of correspondence with Jefferson. As he reviewed his own communication to the statesman, refreshing his memory from the draft of both letters which he had copied carefully into his journal, he was dissatisfied with his own.[38] Many of the statements now sounded stultified and pompous, and he wondered what Jefferson had felt when he first read them. That such sentiments from an unknown Negro farmer could have been expressed to the leading American statesman of his time and elicited a reply was particularly impressive, and to Banneker confusing and distressing. Looking over his draft, Banneker tried to remember the exact wording in some instances, for he recalled that he had made some last-minute revisions in the copy he had forwarded.

The more frequently his mind returned to the letters, however, the more Banneker considered the suggestions made by his friends, the Ellicott brothers, and by Pemberton, to publish the letters in the almanac. The addition of McHenry's introduction eliminated the necessity for such material in the 1792 issue, but now Goddard & Angell and Pemberton were planning next year's almanac in which they proposed to publish the letters. After long consideration, Banneker finally decided that the letters should be published, if indeed they would serve the antislavery movement, and he began his preparations for the next year's almanac.

VII

THE YEARS OF
FULFILLMENT

◇❄◇❄◇❄◇❄◇❄◇❄◇❄◇❄◇

The expanded spheres, amazing to the sight,
Magnificent with stars and globes of light,
The glorious orbs which heaven's bright host compose,
The imprison'd sea that restless ebbs and flows,
The fluctuating field of liquid air,
With all the curious meteors hovering there,
And the wide regions of the land, proclaim
The Power Divine that rais'd the mighty frame.
                        Benjamin Banneker's Almanac for 1792

NOW THAT THE SUCCESS of his first almanac was assured, Banneker lost no time in preparing an ephemeris for the following year. There would be no further reluctance of printers to publish his work, and in fact he found himself faced with having to make a selection among several. Two separate editions of the almanac for 1793 were produced, one by his former publishing firm in Baltimore, Goddard Angell, and another edition issued by Joseph Crukshank in Philadelphia.

Although Goddard Angell undertook to publish the 1793 almanac, the firm was in the midst of an upheaval. The partnership which had been formed between Goddard and Angell in 1789 was dissolved in August 1792, and thereafter Angell continued the business alone. Goddard's name was retained on the imprint of the shop until February 1793, but Banneker negotiated solely with Angell.[1]

Banneker's ephemeris followed the same format as the one he had established in the previous year. Relatively little change was made in the contents of the almanac by Angell, although a greater number of longer stories and essays were included. The contents were organized in a more orderly fashion, and the appearance of the publication as well as its literary quality were somewhat improved.

The almanac was introduced with an enthusiastic statement by the publisher, who certified that the original mission had been successfully accomplished:

From the rapid Sale and extensive Circulation of "BENJAMIN BANNEKER'S PENNSYLVANIA, DELAWARE, MARYLAND, and VIRGINIA AL-MANACK," for 1792, the Editors draw the most flattering Prestiges of the Success of the Calculations, for 1793, of the same ingenious self-taught Astronomer, as they are equally accurate with the former, which excited the Attention, and engaged the Approbation, of Characters highly distinguished for their profound abilities, and alike exalted by their Philanthropy, both in EUROPE and AMERICA—among whom may be mentioned those eminent Orators, Statemen, and Patriots—PITT, FOX, and WILBERFORCE—who produced the Work, in the British House of Commons, with much Applause, as an Argument in favour of the Cause of Humanity they had espoused, and with a View of putting a Period to the diabolical Traffic in human Flesh on the Coast of AFRICA, in which we are happy to observe, they were, in a great Degree, successful—After this Communication, the Editors conceive that an Eulogium from them, on BANNEKER'S Astronomical Talents, would be superfluous if not arrogant.—With respect to the MISCELLANY attached to the present Calculations, they shall only observe, that they have been selected with Care, and with an ardent Desire to combine the USEFUL, INSTRUCTIVE, and ENTERTAINING, which they hope will be found correspondent with the varied Taste of the Public, and deserving of that Encouragement it hath been their condition to merit.

The following Letters will give a further Proof of our sable Brother BENJAMIN'S mental Endowments, in the Approbation he received from a Gentleman very competent to decide on their Extent and Importance.[2]

Banneker's friends and printers had wisely reserved the correspondence with Jefferson for inclusion in the second issue, in which it was given the greatest prominence. Banneker's letter to Jefferson followed the introduction; it was published together with Jefferson's reply without editorial comment.

Another important item in the 1793 almanac was "A Plan Of a *Peace Office* for the United States," which aroused a good deal of comment at the time. It was believed by many to have been Banneker's own work. Even within recent decades its authorship has been debated. In 1947 it was identified beyond question as the work of Dr. Benjamin Rush, in a volume of his writings that appeared in that year.[3]

The publication of Rush's "Plan," presumably for the first time, in Banneker's almanac provided prestige that contributed largely to the almanac's impact on behalf of the anti-slavery movement. For some unexplained reason, it was published without identifying the author. Rush included the "Plan" in a collection of essays published five years later, with substantial additions to the text.[4] An introduction to the volume stated that most of the essays had been previously published in *The Museum, and Columbian Magazine* in Philadelphia soon after the end of the War of Independence, and that a few of them had first appeared in pamphlets. A careful search of the periodical mentioned has failed to bring to light the "Plan" in its pages, however, and it may have appeared as a separate pamphlet, from which it was reprinted in abridged form by Angell.[5]

The essay was most timely, and presented Rush's philosophical opposition to war.* Although he had not expressed his strong feelings on the subject during the course of the War for Independence, nor during the War of 1812, Rush assumed a clearly stated pacifist position in his later writings.

The contents of the Philadelphia edition printed by Joseph Crukshank were particularly directed to the interests of the antislavery movement, and included materials which were not contained in the Goddard & Angell issue. This was a deliberate selection, based on the distribution which was to be made of the several editions. Besides the McHenry biographical sketch, Crukshank's edition contained Rush's "A Plan of a Peace Office," extracts from the debates in the previous session of the British Parliament in April 1792 from the speeches of William Pitt, M. Montague, and C. J. Fox, a passage on slavery from Jefferson's *Notes on Virginia*, and an extract from "Wilkinson's appeal to England on Behalf of the Abused Africans."

Banneker's letter to Jefferson and the latter's reply received additional distribution shortly after the appearance of the almanac for 1793. The letters were published in a pamphlet of fifteen pages by Daniel Lawrence, a Philadelphia printer, late

* See Document 17.

(*187*)

in 1792, and widely circulated. That same year, Lawrence reprinted the pamphlet in a twelve-page format after the first edition was sold out. It was particularly useful for circulation by the abolitionist societies in support of claims for Negro equality.

Banneker derived pleasure from the fact that during these first two years of his endeavors, his almanacs were competing with those calculated by Major Andrew Ellicott and published in Baltimore by John Hayes, Goddard's great rival. He also derived a certain amount of satisfaction from the knowledge that his own publication was now vastly outselling its competitor, since the printer of the latter had refused his first ephemeris.

The appearance of Banneker's almanac, with the Jefferson correspondence and the first printing of Rush's "Plan," made it one of the most important publications of its time. It was distributed in great numbers and became the subject of widespread discussion at all levels. The Pennsylvania Society for the Promotion of the Abolition of Slavery took advantage of this new medium for propaganda and made careful plans for the following year. Arrangements were made by William Young of Philadelphia to publish an edition of his own.

Since the first issues had achieved national importance, Banneker was assured there was no question about an almanac for the following year. He began to make his projections of the eclipses and to compile calculations of an ephemeris for 1794 fairly early in the spring. The printers, as well as his sponsors, planned to start early on this next almanac. It was a bad winter for Banneker, however. In between his bouts of illness he worked as well as he could, but it was the middle of May before he had made substantial progress. Townsend had become anxious about having the materials ready for the printers, and he wrote to Banneker early in May to inquire.[6] Banneker's reply reflected his poor health and poor spirits. His letter was not written in the precise script and with the careful attention to form that distinguished most of Banneker's handwriting, indicating that it had cost him some effort.* He forwarded the letter through Elias Ellicott.[7]

> I received your favour of the 8th instant and can give two reasons that I did not answer till now, the first is I have been very unwell scarce able to Set up. the Second I have been calculated the rising and Setting of the Sun for every Sixth day of the year for the Latitude of London, which I have inclosed Sent unto M^r. Pemberton requesting him to have it inspected by some Judicious person and if the work proves erroneous, I will confess there is many errors in my calculations for London—if otherwise I shall think european printers no better than those of America.
>
> I wrote M^r. Pemberton to remind M^r. Cruckshank of the ballance due me and Send it to you——
>
> I am busy when circumstances permit, making ready copies to put into your hands——
>
> I am your Humble Servt. B. Banneker.

Banneker's calculations for an ephemeris for the latitude of London is surprising, and can be due to only one reason, that Pemberton had suggested that he produce an ephemeris for an almanac to be published in England, presumably to be distributed by the English abolitionist society. During this period the English abolitionists had become a strong and active body, nourished by the enthusiasm and assistance provided by the American societies. Undoubtedly they had become aware of the value of an abolitionist almanac for propaganda purposes, as had been so clearly demonstrated by the first two issues of Banneker's almanac in America. Consequently, a similar publication was being planned in Great Britain. Such a work required an

---

* Evidence of the prolonged illness from which Banneker suffered at this time is to be found in his *Manuscript Journal*. Under date of May 15, 1793, he noted an account with a Doctor Hulse for £5 16s. 8d. of which he recorded a partial payment made of £3 18s. 9d.

ephemeris calculated specifically for the latitude of London or for one of the major cities. If no astronomer was available to the English abolitionists, it was conceivable that Banneker's assistance would have been sought through the Pennsylvania Society. Copies of his almanacs were sent to England to demonstrate achievement by a member of the Negro race, and had been widely distributed. They were presented in evidence in the House of Commons by such great proponents of the movement as Pitt, Fox, and Wilberforce, and the successful sale of an English edition could be readily foreseen.

Banneker's involvement with an ephemeris for England is supported to some degree by a drawing for projection which he included in his manuscript journal, with the statement, "This projection is for an eclips of the Sun for the Vortex of London, June the 24th, 1797." He added the notation: "I find by this Diagram this Eclips at London . . ." followed by data relating to its beginning, greatest obscuration, end, and duration.[8]

The additional burden on Banneker's time imposed by the task of producing an ephemeris, besides the one promised to the Philadelphia printers, was too much for him in view of his poor health. He worked hard, however, and during the next few weeks completed his calculations, which he forwarded to the printer, William Young, in Philadelphia, by the usual circuitous route of Townsend at Baltimore to Pemberton. He delayed in preparing the tide tables, however, as reported in the following communication from Townsend to Pemberton. The same letter indicated that Banneker had not yet received the balance of payment due him from Crukshank.[9]

> This is to acknowledge the receipt of thy favor by Jos. Thornburgh, as also the receipt of G. Sharp's Letter, &c.* Our Committee has since concluded to recom-

* Joseph Thornburgh was a native of Carlisle, Pennsylvania, who moved to Baltimore where he established a dry-goods business. He became a wealthy merchant, and in 1800 he married Cassandra Hopkins Ellicott, the attractive young widow of John Ellicott (1739–1795), one of the founding brothers of Ellicott's Lower Mills.

mend the publication of said Letter to the Society at
their next Meeting which will be on 7th day next—I
have wrote to Benjn. Banneker for the Tide Table for
W^m. Young but have not rec^d. his Answer yet—I am
owing Owen Jones Ju^r. a balance please pay him £5.5
for the Calculation, & I will pay Benjn. that sum by first
conveyance.—We are preparing to meet this Morning
at 9 O'Clock to hear an Oration on the Institution of
the Society by James Winchester—I shall write thee
soon.*

The several editions of the almanac for 1794 went to press
simultaneously, and a large sale was anticipated. James Angell
took the opportunity to include an appropriate preface in his
edition,[10] in which he related Banneker's work to that of another
outstanding American Negro, the poet Phillis Wheatley, as
further evidence that "Africans and their Descendants are capable of attaining a Degree of Eminence in the Liberal Sciences." †

The popularity of the new issue proved to be greater than
the printer's wildest expectations. The almanac sold rapidly and
widely. Banneker was extremely pleased by the growing success
of his venture. He may even have been led to consider having
additional editions of his work published in the next year by
other printers as well. There is some evidence of this in a letter
he wrote to James Pemberton at Philadelphia on March 22,
1794:

I have taken the liberty of writing these few lines
unto you, Sincerely wishing they may find you in perfect health and Strength as I am at this present
writing, I have not heard any thing particular from

* On the reverse side of the letter Pemberton noted that it was from
Joseph Townsend in Baltimore dated July 4, 1793, forwarded via Jacob
Myers, received on July 6, and "Answered the 18th & sent him Owen
Jones, Junr. Rec^t. for £5.5—paid him as desired."

† See Document 18.

you Since the raging of the pestilential disorder in your City, Yet I am in hopes of Seeing a few lines from under your own hand as soon as curcumstances [sic] may permit—

I have to inform you that the rapidity of the Sale of my Almanac for this present Year, has gaven [sic] me encouragement to make a calculation for the ensuing year, and with my own care and diligence, and the assistance of a Nautical Ephemeris I flatter my Self that the work are as correct as any of the kind in common use among us——

And as you have been very friendly to me in time past, I hope that friendship may continue if it be not too burdensome unto you to mention me to your printers and if any of them has an inclination to take a copy of mine, by giving timely notice I can Supply them—

And now I conclude by saying that any Services in my power to do for you, Your reasonable requests shall be armed with the obedience of—

Y^r. Sincere Friend and Hum^b. Servt.
B. Banneker.[11]

Neither Pemberton's reply nor evidence of any assistance he may have provided to Banneker is recorded. The almanac for the year 1795 had a substantially increased circulation, however. Angell published one of the editions shortly before he sold his firm to Brumfield, and two other editions appeared in Baltimore, one printed for John Fisher and another issued by the Wilmington printers, S. & J. Adams, who had recently established a branch printing firm in Baltimore. Five other separate editions were produced by the firm of S. & J. Adams at their Wilmington press, one of which was produced exclusively for Frederick Craig for distribution from his stationery store.

Samuel and John Adams were the sons of James Adams,

a printer of Wilmington, Delaware, who had first established himself in Philadelphia in 1753 and worked for a time with Benjamin Franklin. The Adams brothers had opened a printing office in Wilmington in partnership about 1761 and then added a branch shop at Baltimore late in 1789 in which they featured the printing of almanacs and religious books. Following their father's death, the Adams brothers removed their operation entirely to Wilmington. Their Baltimore printing office was continued thereafter by others.

Meanwhile, editions of Banneker's almanac for 1795 were also produced separately by three other printers in Philadelphia, namely, William Young, William Gibbons, and Jacob Johnson & Co. Finally, yet another edition was published by Matthias Day of Trenton, New Jersey. The total of at least nine known editions of Banneker's almanac for the same year was record-breaking, and not only brought the amateur astronomer considerable renown, but a substantial income as well.

The outstanding feature of the 1795 issue was a portrait of Banneker on the cover of several editions. The best likeness was the one used in the edition printed for John Fisher of Baltimore, which consisted of a woodcut portrait bust of a Negro representing Banneker wearing the typical Quaker garb of the period. The edition published by S. & J. Adams at Baltimore attempted to reproduce the same woodcut portrait but without success. The same strong lines of the woodcut were used in what was unquestionably a copy of the portrait of the Fisher edition, but without delineation of the features or other major details. The artist who produced the portrait is not identified.

The literary and miscellaneous contents of the several editions varied considerably, and were assembled by the respective printers to fill out their publications. Fisher prefaced his version with a page quoting from McHenry's letter about Banneker's life. The Adams brothers, on the other hand, introduced theirs with a short preface:

> The Editors again offer this their periodical Manual to the kind Patronage of a discerning Public. From the

Accuracy of the astronomical Calculations; the pleasing Variety of Essays, of moral Excellence and genuine
Humour; and the numerous useful Receipts, Tables,
&c. contained in this Year's Almanac, we presume,
without further Preface, it will be entitled to the same
Support it has hitherto met with.

> The wisest Men that ever writ
> To please each Taste could never yet;
> What some disdain, others commend;
> Come buy our Book, and there's an End.[12]

The William Young edition in Philadelphia differed from
the others in that it featured "An Account of the Yellow Fever
Lately Prevalent in Philadelphia; With the Number of those
who Died, From the First of August till the Ninth of November 1793." The only other literary content was a poem "Addressed to *Benjamin Banneker*" by an unidentified writer who
signed the work "G. H." [13] The poem extolled the astronomer's
accomplishments despite the color of his skin, and compared
his achievements with those of Isaac Newton. Its theme was sum-
marized in the lines:

> Long may thou live an evidence to shew,
> That Afric's sable race have talents too.

The almanac for 1796 for which Banneker provided an
ephemeris had a much more limited distribution. Only two
editions are known to have been produced, both issued by the
printing firm of Philip Edwards, James Keddie, and Thomas,
Andrews and Butler of Baltimore. Of the numerous partners of
this firm, Edwards was the best known. A native of Baltimore,
he opened a printing office in 1792 and two months later undertook the publication of the *Baltimore Evening Post*, the name
of which was later changed to *Edwards' Baltimore Daily Advertiser*. He also published broadsides, sermons, and the first
magazine with a Baltimore imprint. He was the publisher of

George Buchanan's *Oration* in 1793, and in 1795 he acquired *The Maryland Journal* which he combined with his own newspaper until it became defunct two years later.

Neither of the two editions of Banneker's almanac for 1796 included any material of particular note, but a preface provided the publishers with another opportunity to speak on behalf of the antislavery movement with some clever use of language.[14] The fact was emphasized that the work was the achievement of a man of color, and that a basic lesson to be learned from it was that ". . . although the God of Nature has marked the face of the African with a darker shade than his brethren, he has given him a soul equally capable of refinement." *

This is the first association Banneker had with this printing firm, and it may be assumed that his change of publisher was due to the vagaries of the printing business. Whatever the reason, it was the single issue of the almanac having the smallest distribution.

The sale of this issue is the only record of Banneker's negotiations with his printers that has survived. In his commonplace book he made the following entry of the transaction:

Sold on the 2nd of April, 1795, to Buttler, Edwards & Kiddy, the right of an Almanac, for the year 1796, for the sum of 80 dollars, equal to £30.[15]

From this record it is possible to fix the currency of the time, with the pound equal to $2.67.

Banneker's almanac for the year 1797 was the last issue known to have been published. Two editions were produced in Baltimore by Christopher Jackson, and separate editions were produced in Petersburg and Richmond, Virginia. Jackson printed them for distribution by George Keatinge's Book Store.[16]

Jackson's second issue of Banneker's almanac was for wider

* See Document 19.

distribution, in Pennsylvania, Delaware, Maryland and Kentucky.

The Petersburg imprint, issued by William Prentis and William T. Murray, covered Virginia and North Carolina only, while the Richmond edition, published by Simon Pleasants, Jr., was issued "[by privelege]" for Pennsylvania, Delaware, Maryland, and Kentucky. The size of these editions ranged from sixteen leaves for the Baltimore and Petersburg versions to twenty-two leaves for the Richmond edition. Arrangements for publication by a Petersburg printer were probably made through members of the Ellicott family, who maintained business interests in that community.

Two items of more than usual interest formed part of the 1797 almanac. One was a caution to gentlemen smokers:

Looking over a few old papers the other day, I found the following anecdote, which seems to concern your employment, and as it affords the first, and I believe the last *royal* opinion ever given on the subject of smoaking, I hope you will receive it with all due respect.

Although in this age we see every school boy strut along with his segar and puffing it was most ridiculed in the court of James the 1st. and the courtiers affected to reject it, with horror. The king said that "tobacco was the lively image and pattern of Hell, for that it had in it, by allusion, all the parts and vices of the world whereby hell may be gained, viz.

1st. It was smoak; so are all the vanities of this world.

2nd. It delighteth them who take it; so do all the pleasures of the world delight the men of the world.

3rd. It maketh men drunken, and light in the head; so do all the vanities of the world, men are drunken therewith.

4th. He that taketh tobacco, saith he cannot leave it, it doth bewitch him; even so the pleasures of the world make men loath to leave them, they are for the most part, enchanted with them.

And farther, besides all this, it is like hell in the very substance of it, for it is a stinking loathsome thing; and so is hell."

And farther, his majesty professed that were he to invite the Devil to a dinner, he should have three dishes: first,—a pig; second, a pot of ling and mustard; and, third, a pipe of tobacco for digesture.

Having perused this, gentlemen, I hope you will profit by it, as coming from *the Solomon* of his age; and when you fill your pipes, or illumine with your segars, most gratefully remember the kindness of your affectionate brother.

TOM WHIFF.

Segar Manufactory, Baltimore, 1796.[17]

The second item, entitled "Epitaph on a Watchmaker," appeared in all the four editions.

EPITAPH ON A WATCH-MAKER

HERE lies, in a *horizontal* position,
The *outside case* of
Peter Pendulum, Watch-Maker
Whose abilities in that line were an honour
To his profession.
Integrity was the *main spring,*
And prudence the *regulator*
Of all the actions of his life,
Humane, generous and liberal,
His *hand* never *stopped*
Till he had relieved distress,
So nicely *regulated* were all his *motions,*
That he never *went wrong,*
Except when set a *going,*

By people
Who did not know
His key:
Even then he was easily
Set right again
He had the art of disposing his *time*
So well,
That his hours glided away
In one continual round
Of pleasure and delight,
Till an unlucky *minute* put a period to
His existence.
He departed this life
Wound up
In hope, of being *taken in hand*
By his *Maker,*
And of being thoroughly *cleaned, repaired,*
And set a *going*
In the World to come.[18]

This epitaph, which would have served admirably for Banneker's own gravestone, had he been honored with one, presents a literary mystery. That it was included in each of the four issues of the 1797 almanac, published by three different printers, indicates that it was probably either written or selected by Banneker himself and was not part of the usual miscellany compiled from various repositories.

The most puzzling aspect of the epitaph is that it was used on the tomb of a Devonshire watchmaker in 1802. It is inscribed exactly as presented in the almanac, except that "Peter Pendulum" is replaced by "George Routleigh," and to the line "He departed this life" was added Routleigh's date of death and age, "November 14, 1802, Aged 57, wound up," followed by the remainder of the inscription.

The curious circumstances surrounding this inscription present several possibilities. The inscription may have been of older origin, and Banneker, or his publisher, may have found it in an English journal of unknown identity and date. Again, Banneker may have written it. In any case, Routleigh or a member of his family could have read it in a copy of Banneker's almanac that was circulated in England as well as in the United States, and decided to use it for Routleigh's gravestone five years later.

George Routleigh (also spelled Routledge), was a watch-maker of Lydford who was born in 1745. The survival of his tombstone has been confirmed, and the present rector of Lydford Parish, Okehampton, in Devonshire has affirmed that the epitaph is carved on the flat surface of a slate covering on the top of the tomb of George Routleigh, which stands on a slight bank just outside the main porch of the ancient church. It is constructed with blocks of stone bound together with mortar. The carving has suffered from weather through the years, and may have to be removed to the interior of the church for preservation. It has always been assumed in Lydford that the inscription was original with Routleigh's tomb and had been composed locally.[19] It has been widely quoted and reproduced.[20]

The almanac for the year 1797 was probably the last issue to be published. Banneker nevertheless continued to calculate the ephemeris for each succeeding year through 1802, until the age of seventy-one. His increasing infirmities deterred him, however, and an examination of his manuscript volume shows a progressively increasing shakiness in his handwriting during his later years. Several calculations were made for the years from 1802 to 1805, but then he was no longer able to continue the work he cherished. Almanacs for one or two years after 1797 may have been published, although copies have not been recorded, since Banneker's calculations in his manuscript volume are complete and sound.

The manner in which Banneker's almanacs appeared on the scene so suddenly and then were as abruptly terminated is a subject for speculation. The popularity of the series was unquestioned, for at least twenty-eight known editions of the series were published over a period of six years. Presumably the series was abandoned when Banneker could no longer work. However, his manuscript journal proves beyond doubt that he calculated complete ephemerides for each year from 1798 through 1802.

It is much more likely that Banneker's almanacs were discontinued as a result of the tenor of the times. The first issue had appeared at a moment in history when the emphasis of the almanac as a popular publication was on the verge of change. Whereas almanacs throughout the eighteenth century had been primarily educational and instructive in content, they changed direction during the last decade of the century and became dedicated to national events and local causes. Banneker's almanacs were among the first to reflect the new direction, and they were the first to popularize the theme of antislavery, and contributed substantially to the abolitionist cause. As the scientific effort of a free Negro, his almanacs provided tangible proof of the mental equality of the races, a topic which was central to the antislavery movement. By the second half of the final decade of the century, however, a strong reaction to the cause of abolition had set in, as part of the new national concerns.

This turn in the tide was to persist for a short span of years, but long enough to preclude a possible revival of Banneker's almanacs. Yet another factor contributed to these influences: the increasing competition among printers in the publication of almanacs.

In New England, the almanacs were especially popular. In Massachusetts, eleven to fifteen different almanacs were published each year from 1791 through 1797. In Connecticut during the same period, between ten and thirteen almanacs were published each year, and comparable statistics can be derived for Pennsylvania, Maryland, and other states.

Coincidental with the discontinuation of Banneker's almanacs was the demise of the Maryland Society for the Abolition of Slavery, after seven years of successful achievement. By the latter half of the decade, the antislavery movement had begun to lose its impact. With the end of the American Revolution and the emergence of the new republic, the ideological basis of the war which had included antislavery had begun to be forgotten in the press of many new national endeavors and interests, and particularly the new problems of economic depression and lack of political guidance.[21]

The Society's loss of influence was not due to diminishing membership but to loss of popularity of its mission; this is evidenced by the fact that in 1797 they had 231 members, and were the third largest such organization in the United States.[22]

Among the most important achievements of the Maryland Society were the legislation on manumission and the publication of Banneker's almanacs. Although there is no readily available evidence that Banneker's almanacs owed their publication to the Society, the correspondence between Joseph Townsend and Elias Ellicott with James Pemberton leaves little doubt that the Society and its officers played an important role in their production.

The Society did not mention the assistance provided in publishing Banneker's almanacs among its achievements or interests, although certainly it contributed to this effort. In a report made to the Pennsylvania Society for the Promotion of the Abolition of Slavery, the Maryland Society listed the events of its short history and achievements but the name of Banneker was not mentioned.[23] A curious bit of irony not to be overlooked is that the first of Banneker's almanacs was published shortly after the Maryland Society was founded, and that his last issue appeared shortly before the Society went out of existence.

VIII

SCIENTIFIC

CONSIDERATIONS

✦❀✦❀✦❀✦❀✦❀✦❀✦❀✦❀✦

The most sensible of those who make scientific researches, is he who believes himself the farthest from the
goal, & who whatever advances he has made in his road,
studies as if he yet knew nothing and marches as if he
were only yet beginning to make his first advance.

From "A Scrap," *Banneker's
Almanac for 1795*

A STUDY OF BANNEKER'S ASTRONOMICAL journal and a comparison of his notes with his published almanacs provide a most
revealing documentation of how he taught himself astronomy.
It is possible to follow, step by step, many of the essays he made
in the calculation for eclipses and of the numerous other computations required in preparing an ephemeris. One can de-
tect the errors he occasionally made, and how in the laborious

(202)

process of self-instruction he was able to correct them. His notes remain as a monument to his love of astronomy and of his unflagging determination to master every aspect of the task he had set himself. An adequate evaluation of Banneker's attainments cannot be made without reviewing his astronomical notes and almanacs.

The page format for the monthly ephemerides which was selected by the publisher was identical to that used in the almanacs calculated by Andrew Ellicott and printed by John Hayes of Baltimore. Although the printing style and layout of content otherwise varied considerably in the editions produced by different printers, the ephemerides remained constant in form. The one minor difference is Banneker's use of Arabic numbers instead of Roman numerals for months and days at the top of each page.

An ephemeris is calculated from a series of basic computations required to establish the positions of the sun, moon, and planets each year, from which other calculations may be made: the solar and lunar eclipses, the times of rising and setting of the sun and moon, identification of remarkable days, weather forecasting on a daily basis, tide tables for the region, and similar data.

A comparison of Banneker's manuscript journal with his published ephemerides reveals his method. First, he had to make a reckoning of the calendar, which was one of the major preoccupations of the almanac-maker. He then entered the times of sunrise and sunset, and listed the important religious and noteworthy days of each month in an outline he had previously prepared. These figures could be entered long in advance, once the pattern of the page had been established.

The listing for the remarkable days included the most important religious and saints' days, and anniversaries in American history, such as the surrenders of General Burgoyne and General Cornwallis. Weather prognostications were noted in addition to miscellaneous astronomical information.

Before proceeding with the remainder of the calculations,

Banneker customarily awaited the arrival of the new edition of the *Nautical Almanac*, from which he extracted some of the preliminary data. He then listed the figures of reference and the necessary notes for calculating the ephemeris for each year. These "Common Notes," as he called them, he placed aside in a separate box on his page, wherein he included the dominical letter, the golden number, the epact and the cycle of the sun.

He also listed the longitude and anomaly of the sun for every sixth day of each month, together with the logarithms of the sun's distance from the earth, the longitude and anomaly of the moon at the beginning of each year, as well as the position of the moon's node for the first month of each year. The word "anomaly," which is used frequently, is the distance that the sun or the moon has traveled from its apogee, or farthest point from the earth. It is reckoned by the twelve zodiacal constellations, each of which is allocated thirty degrees along the ecliptic.[1]

Certain mathematical computations had to be made before the calculations of the eclipses for that year could be undertaken. These were to establish the positions of the sun and the moon. For this it was necessary to determine the times of the new and full moon for each of the twelve months, and list them in a column. That done, he then calculated the sun's position for each of these times during the year, and compared them to determine in which months an eclipse might occur. After he had identified the months, Banneker made detailed calculations and prepared a projection or geometrical diagram of the eclipse on the nearest page of the journal that remained blank.

The column of "New and Full Moons" was used also as the basis for the date and time of the new, first quarter, full, and last quarter moons, information usually found at the top of each page of an almanac.

A vast amount of work was required to calculate a single eclipse, which makes Banneker's accomplishment in this field all the more impressive. He had to make at least sixty-eight mathematical calculations to produce the ten elements required to construct a single eclipse diagram.[2]

The results of his calculations, which were in each instance computed to the nearest second, were entered on a blank journal page, including the semi-diameter of the earth, and of the sun's and moon's disks. Also included were the sun's distance from the nearest solstice, the declination of the sun and the moon, and the moon's latitude.

After Banneker had obtained the results of these preliminary calculations, he then utilized them to project the eclipse, which he customarily drew on the next blank page with a sector and dividers. The illustration drawn, he labeled it with a brief statement describing the eclipse. After all the eclipses for the year had been projected, he combined the descriptive statements into a single text to be entered in the space provided for notes for the coming year. This statement, in addition to a listing of the times of the eclipses, would be inserted in the published almanac. Sometimes Banneker was uncertain of his results, so he reconstructed a given eclipse a second time, which would be found elsewhere in the pages of the journal.

In columns following those listing the times of sunrise and sunset, he would enter the position of the moon with respect to the constellations for each day of the month, the times of the rising or setting of the moon, and a particularly interesting column designated "Moon's Southing" which indicated the time that the moon crossed the meridian each day. The last column listed the "age" of the moon with relation to the days of the month.

Banneker's ephemeris included the changing length of the days, the times of the rising and setting of the bright stars, and other astronomical phenomena. His monthly tables were modeled upon those published in the *Nautical Almanac*, and his completed data, with the exception of his times for the principal phase of the moon, were generally in agreement with the British publication. In most instances where discrepancies occurred, the error or difference was seldom more than for one day. However, for the year 1793 Banneker predicted that Jupiter would be stationary on March 15, whereas the *Nautical Almanac* indicated that this occurred on March 17, two days later.

Although the British publication provided the longitude and latitude of the moon and information on planets, Banneker had to work out the times of moonrise and moonset and those of sunrise and sunset for the region where the almanac would be sold. Likewise, the *Nautical Almanac* listed the times for the eclipses of the sun and moon when they occurred for the latitude and longitude of London, and Banneker had to compute all the data for each eclipse—including time of beginning, total, and end of the eclipse—for the region of his ephemeris.

His published almanacs included certain phenomena and data not available to him in the *Nautical Almanac,* Moore's *Practical Navigator,* or other published sources. Such data could only be derived from his own mathematical calculations and use of his instruments, and included the southings, risings and settings of the bright stars, and the changing length of days. The calculations for the moon were somewhat less accurate than those for the sun. Banneker probably used an incorrect eccentricity of the moon's orbit or he may have applied the change of eccentricity incorrectly. The moon's ascension varied by as much as three degrees, plus or minus, from the correct position in some of the calculations for 1794.

For the first several years, he computed the moon's position in his manuscript journal by assigning the numbers from zero through eleven to each of the twelve zodiacal constellations. For the table of the moon's longitude for January 1, 1792, for example, the figures were inscribed as 0-16-8, the 0 representing the first of the constellations, Aries, and the other figures the moon's position as sixteen degrees and eight minutes; as each constellation was allocated thirty degrees along the ecliptic, this placed the moon near the center of the constellation. In the published version the astronomical symbols replaced the numbers. The manuscript journal reveals that by 1795 Banneker had become sufficiently familiar with the process so that he inscribed the symbols directly instead of the numbers assigned.

During the first years of his astronomical endeavors, Banneker attempted to calculate and project eclipses by several different methods until he finally selected one which suited him best. He occasionally tested one method against another, as seen in an example which he drafted in the pages of his journal for 1792. This was the projection for the solar eclipse of April 3, 1791, which he performed by means of Ferguson's method and termed a "back tryal." His previous calculation for the same eclipse may have been done by using Leadbetter's method. He noted in a short text near the projection that he was performing the test to determine whether ". . . this present method will agree with the former." [3] After finishing the drawing, Banneker made a mathematical calculation in the margin as a comparison of his conclusions with those published in Ferguson, and noted that his results differed by thirty-two minutes!

He attempted to make a "back tryal" on other occasions as well, in order to compare construction techniques during some of the later years. For example, he projected an eclipse of the moon for May 8, 1762, an event that took place twenty-nine years before his first ephemeris. [4]

As he worked with his texts, he occasionally made an annotated illustration in his journal of a problem he might encounter again and for which he needed some means to help him remember, particularly when the astronomical relationships required for calculations of future eclipses were involved.

In preparing his ephemeris for 1793, for example, he drew an unusual diagram of the several possible positions of the axis of the moon's orbit to the axis of the earth that might be encountered when plotting a lunar eclipse during the course of a lunar cycle. Without realizing it, Banneker inscribed the terms incorrectly. Where he should have written "North Ascending" he wrote "North Descending" in the upper part of the drawing, and he also inadvertently exchanged the proper places for "South Ascending" and "South Descending." He used the terms correctly in his individual predictions of eclipses in later pages, however, and he must have become aware of his error in the interim.[5]

At first Banneker found the task somewhat confusing and he made projections for eclipses which were not at all times useful to his purpose. After the first few years, however, he learned to conserve his efforts and thereafter he made few constructions for eclipses that were not for the latitude of London, or visible in the Baltimore-Washington area in which his almanacs would be sold. He had obviously become sufficiently adept in making an analysis of his initial calculations so that it was no longer necessary to waste his efforts on projections that were not essential for the published almanacs.

In the standard works by Ferguson and Leadbetter, the calendar was reckoned by the Old Style, or the Julian calendar, while in Banneker's time the New Style, or Gregorian calendar, had come into use. In the latter system, only those century years which are divisible by the number 400 may be considered as leap years. By the year 1800 a discrepancy of nearly two weeks had developed between the two calendars, a situation which had been anticipated by Ferguson.[6]

The problems caused Banneker exasperation from time to time, and he was occasionally forced to choose one form of calendar over the other. In 1796 he noted:

> According to the Nautical Ephemeris, if the moon changes in the morning of any given day, the succeeding day is the third day of her age because it begins the day at noon, but according to the common way of reckoning, if the moon changes in the morning of any given day, the succeeding day is the second day of her age but if in the afternoon it is allowed to be the first day of her age.[7]

In that year Banneker recorded a decision he had made in reckoning the calendar:

In 1800 This Year in obtaining the planets places I shall keep by the old Stile with the addition of 12 days according to the method prescribed by Doc^r. Ferguson, but I had like to forgot the Sun and Moon had only 11 days added to the old Stile.[8]

On the blank pages opposite the entries for the monthly calculations Banneker occasionally noted how he had derived his results. One example is the following:

To obtain the Latitude of the above places [that is, Baltimore] I took the point where the path of the penumbral center intersected the Earth's axes and the center of the projection. In my compasses from the line of Sines, the Sector being first set to the radius of the disc that subtracts from the Sun's declination being of contrary names, leaves the Latitude of the place where the Sun is centrally eclipsed and the declination greatest.[9]

Before venturing to make calculations of his own, a competent philomath must have mastered a good deal of the text of an authoritative writer on the subject, such as Ferguson or Leadbetter. Banneker had both available to him. He not only studied them thoroughly but compared the procedures described by each author.

He suffered from an embarrassment of riches, however, for he became confused by the apparently conflicting instructions occasionally presented by the two authors for the same type of computation. At first he convinced himself that one or the other was at fault. After further study he discovered that the results achieved were the same, but that the methods differed.

The methods used by Ferguson and Leadbetter to construct the diagrams for the solar eclipse differed substantially. A reader who undertook to construct a diagram for a solar eclipse according to the method described by Ferguson would draw the axis of the earth to the right of the axis of the ecliptic. Leadbetter's instruction for the same eclipse, on the other hand, specified that the earth's axis should be placed to the left of the axis of the ecliptic. Banneker described his confusion resulting from this diversity of procedure in a letter to George Ellicott dated October 13, 1789 (see pages 82–83).

Again and again during the years that followed he experienced the same problem of having apparently conflicting instructions not only from Ferguson and Leadbetter, but from the *Nautical Almanac* as well.[10]

This important work was first conceived by Rev. Nevil Maskelyne in 1765 and the first issue was published in 1766 for the year 1767. At the same time Maskelyne published his *Tables Requisite to be Used with the Astronomical and Nautical Ephemeris* which served as a handbook for the *Almanac*. The latter included the lunar tables of Tobias Mayer for determining the longitude at sea and compilations of other astronomical data which were useful for the seaman. The work was published annually with relatively little change until 1834, when it underwent major revision with the replacement of the apparent time with mean time as the argument of the ephemerides.

The conflict in the methods used by the various authors repeatedly forced Banneker to make a decision in favor of one over the other. Frequently he was uncertain, and went on to attempt the computation with the other method prescribed as a check on his results. He occasionally found apparent discrepancies in the works and he noted them in his journal if he could not resolve them immediately. An example occurred in 1796:

> It appears to me that the wisest of men may at certain times be in error, for instance Doctor Ferguson informs that when the Sun is within 12° of either Node at the time of full, that moon will be eclipsed, but I find according to the method of his projecting a Lunar Eclipse there will be none by the above Elements, and

yet the Sun is within 11° . 4′6 . 11″ of the Moon's Ascending Node— But Moon's being in her Apogee pre-
vents the appearance of this Eclipse.[11]

Ferguson was exonerated of the presumed mistake which
Banneker attributed to him in a footnote which Ferguson added
to his published description, in which he indicated that if the
full moon is in apogee, the eclipse will not occur if the sun is
more than ten degrees and thirty minutes from the node.[12]

Elsewhere in his journal Banneker made another notation
for his own guidance in future calculations, again based on
errors he had discovered in the published sources he was using:

> Errors that ought to be corrected in my Astronomical
> Tables are these 2 Vol Leadbetter, page 204, when ♄
> Anomaly is 4ˢ 30°, the equation 3° 38′ 41″ which
> ought to have been 3° 28ˢ 41″. In ♂ equation page 155,
> the Logarithm of his distance from ☉ ought to have
> been as thus, in the 2nd place from the Index, instead
> of 7, that is from the time that his Annomally is 3ˢ 24°
> until it is 4ˢ 0°.
>
> In ☿ Node Novemb. 30th where 66″ read 46.″ [13]

Another example of the confusion Banneker experienced
is to be found in his notations relating to the times of the moon
for the year 1795:

> In the year 1795, according to the Nautical Almanac
>   the Moon was full that year in the month of
>   February .... 3.12.32.
> But according to Doc. Leadbetter the moon
>   was full .... 3. 9.44.
> By the Nautical Almanac New Moon in
>   February .... 19.1. 5.
> By Leadbetter's method New Moon in
>   February .... 19.3.16.

1795 By the Nautical Almanac Full Moon
in March .... 5. 5. 6.
By Leadbetter's method full Moon
in March .... 5. 2.44.
1795 By the Nautical Almanac New Moon
in March ....20.11.42.
By Leadbetter's method New Moon
in March ....20.13.40.[14]

Still another interesting entry is the following:

It is Said and generally believed that when the Moon
is changing that she is in conjunction with the Sun, viz,
in the Same Sign, the Same degree and minute with
him, likewise when the Moon is full that she is in
direct opposition to the Sun, being in the opposite Sign,
degree and minute to him, but it will not be the case,
Calculations tho' made by the best of Calculators—
I have taken all the fulls and new Moons from the
Nautical Almanac for the year 1781 and have given
the difference at each time in motion.[15]

Banneker then added a table of differences in the positions of the
sun and moon for the twelve months. This was followed on a
later page by a listing:

New and Full moons for the year 1781 by the Nautical
Almanac and by a method prescribed by M^r. Leadbetter[16]

which showed substantial variation in every single example
listed for the twelve-month period.

Banneker studied his texts with considerable care, as is evident in some of the notations he made from them. In one instance
he noted:

For discovering how many Luminarian Eclipses may happen in any year, See a Compleat System of Astronomy Vol. 1 page 413 precept 14.[17]

The note which follows on the same page, "To find the time the Moons Southing See Doctrine of the Sphere page 264," relates to the same work by Leadbetter.[18]

An almanac-maker was required to commit to memory a good deal of information derived from his texts in order to develop the necessary calculations. Such a question as the direction that the axis of the earth would point in relation to the axis of the ecliptic would have to be kept constantly in mind while preparing a projection for a solar eclipse.*

No less important were the small subsequent changes required, depending on whether his calculations revealed the sun's declination to be north or south.[19]

Occasionally, published astronomical tables suggested the possible occurrence of an eclipse, and Banneker proceeded to make a detailed projection just to ascertain whether such might be the case. He did not want to leave the matter to a hasty judgment. The published tables, regardless of their source, sometimes provided data so close that a decision unsupported by calculations could not be made, and a projection was required. As an example, he figured that for 1797 there would be a solar eclipse on November 18, beginning at 7:44 A.M., and would be visible at Baltimore. Later he made new calculations and found that he was in error, and he noted in his journal that "This diagram is corrupt—Moons Lat[itude] thr[ough] mistake is too great North—" and he then crossed out the description of this eclipse in the appropriate section for that year, reducing the number to four. The specific information concerning this eclipse

---

* Ferguson noted that "If the Sun's declination had been south, the diurnal path of 'London' would have been on the upper side of the line VI-K-VI [of his diagram included] and would have touched the line D-L-E in L. . . ."

was deleted from the published ephemeris, but an error remained nonetheless, for the published text read:

ECLIPSES for the year 1797 are five in number, to wit, three of the Sun and two of the Moon[20]

although the listing actually included only four eclipses.

Banneker occasionally encountered similar problems in the years that followed. He calculated and projected a solar eclipse for April 23, 1800, and then came to the conclusion that it would be "invisible at the City of Washington." Later he crossed out this statement and wrote instead that it would be "partly visible in the United States."[21] He was not satisfied, however, and reconstructed the diagram for the eclipse, to which he added the note ". . . by projection it begins some minutes before the true conjunction and Sun sets before the general observation so it is partly visible in the United States."[22]

A similar difficulty arose with the second solar eclipse for that year, which occurred on October 18. He plotted this eclipse three separate times, and after looking in vain for confirmation in Ferguson's *Astronomy*, he remarked with some dismay:

. . . Ferguson speaking of all visible eclipses at London says nothing of this so that the mistake may be in me.

Ferguson provided some measure of caution to those of his readers who planned to become prospective almanac-makers with the following advice:

But these suppositions do not exactly agree with the truth; and therefore, supposing the Elements given by the Tables to be accurate, yet the times and places of the Eclipse, deduced from its construction, will not answer exactly to what passeth in the Heavens; but may be at least two or three minutes wrong, though done with the greatest care.[23]

From this statement it may be assumed that an error of two or three minutes, which was inherent in the construction of an eclipse, could lead to a difference as great as five or six minutes for any single eclipse which was being predicted by two different almanac-makers, even though they employed the identical method.

Further down the same page, Ferguson went on to compare his tables with those prepared by others, and commented on the differences which the reader could expect:

> According to Mayer's Tables, this eclipse [April 1764] will be about a quarter of an hour sooner than either these Tables, or Mr. Flamstead's or Dr. Halley's makes it; and Mayer's Tables does not make it annular at London.

Consequently, if Banneker relied on Mayer's *Tables* instead of employing Ferguson's, he could have introduced an appreciable discrepancy into the time of the eclipse. In general, he preferred to use Ferguson's tables instead of those of Leadbetter or Mayer.

Banneker's problems were not derived only from the use of various sources, however. In calculating the lunar eclipse for February 25, 1793, for instance, he plotted it incorrectly. A mistake in the setting of his drafting compass resulted in placing the moon at mid-eclipse in the wrong portion of the earth's shadow; while he had correctly plotted the moon's path at the beginning and end of the eclipse. Later he recalculated the same eclipse and arrived at a time difference of approximately one minute.

Banneker demonstrated in his notes that he was greatly concerned with the accuracy of his work. This was proved by the fact that after having made calculations for the first five months for his ephemeris for 1795, he came to the realization, perhaps after having studied other almanacs, that his method for calculating the "rising," "setting," and "southing" of the moon was erroneous. Evidence of this is found in the notes for January of that year, which were apparently extracted from a published source, relating to the meridian of Baltimore:

> As the Moons Diurnal motion in Degrees and minutes is to that motion turned into time, So is 2° 44′ the Moons obit motion between the Meridian of Greenwich and that of Baltimore to a fourth proportional number which must be added to the moon's apparent Southing to reduce it to the mean time of Southing.
>   N.B. The above must be farther examined before I can pass it for the truth—[24]

His comment expressing his doubt is significant. He apparently discovered, however, that the statement was correct, and he then proceeded to rewrite the equation for the longitude of Baltimore in addition to a list of figures to be added to the moon's monthly calculations.[25]

> As the Moons Diurnal motion turned into time is to 24 hours so is 5 hours, the difference between the meridian of Greenwich and that of Baltimore, to a fourth proportional number which must be added to the moon Southing on the Meridian of Greenwich to reduce it to meridian of Baltimore

When the Moons Diurnal motion	Min.
is 11°, add to her Southing	9
When 12°, add	10
When 13°, add	11
When 14°, add	12
When 15°, add	13

Banneker then crossed out all of his figures relating to the moon for the first five months, with the statement that they were "Corrupt," and added new corrected figures in the margin.

Some of the pages of Banneker's journal reveal other occasional slight errors which then led to a number of others. An example is his work on the lunar eclipse for July 31, 1795, which he had to calculate twice. In his preliminary eclipse data, he had provided information required for the solar eclipse for July 16 and the lunar eclipse for July 31, and for both of these he had calculated the moon's motion as being "South Ascending." That is to say, at the time of the eclipse, the moon would be crossing the ecliptic (the path of the sun) traveling from south to north. This was an obvious error because if the moon is ascending in one node, it must be descending when it reaches the opposite node two weeks later. The first time that he constructed the projection, he plotted the moon's path as "South Ascending" as he had just done for the solar eclipse. Although he had already mathematically determined that the eclipse would be about two and a half digits eclipsed (one digit is one-twelfth the diameter of the orb of the moon or sun), he proceeded to construct a diagram which showed the moon to be about three-fourths eclipsed. When he became aware of his mistake sometime later, he reconstructed the figure and recalculated it with the moon's path now "South Descending" and the eclipse plotted for Greenwich time, the moon shown properly eclipsed about two and a half digits. This was Banneker's first attempt to calculate an eclipse as seen from Greenwich rather than from the Baltimore-Washington area.

It was during this year that Banneker changed his method for presenting solar eclipse information. Instead of merely stating that the eclipse was visible or invisible from Baltimore, as before, he now provided the precise latitude and longitude of the location from which an eclipse could be most centrally observed. The usefulness of his almanacs was thus considerably broadened in geographical scope, and led to his production of simultaneous calculations of eclipses not only for the United States but for England as well.

Other mistakes that were made and corrected are recorded in the journal. For an eclipse which was to occur on January 10, 1796, he indicated variously that the time of occurrence would be 10:15 A.M. and later on the same diagram to be 11:15 A.M. Seeing his error, he crossed out the projection, labeled it "corrupt," and then proceeded anew. His new computation indicated that the correct time for eclipse was 1:15 A.M., which later appeared in the published ephemeris.

In addition to his other texts, Banneker also used John Hamilton Moore's *Practical Navigator*, a world-renowned basic and encyclopedic work, containing detailed descriptions of the principal navigational instruments and practices.[26] Moore was a native of Edinburgh, educated in Ireland, who established an academy at Brentford in which he taught navigation to young men. Later, with his sons and son-in-law, he established a shop at Little Tower Hill in London, where he sold charts and instruments and advertised himself as a hydrographer. His *Navigator* went into more than nineteen editions and continued to be published long after his death. It appeared in the United States in 1799 in an edition revised by Nathaniel Bowditch.

An example of the material which Banneker copied from Moore's volume is the following:

Wind may be Culled, by the explosion of a vigorous Cannonade. See Hamilton Moore's practical Navigator, p. 241.

Another notation from Moore's work is found among the first pages of the Manuscript Journal:

To Find the Moon's Rising

We must Subtract the Sun's Right Ascension from the Moon's Oblique Ascension then Enter the Table Shewing the time of the planets Setting when they have North Declination, and their rising when they have South Declination. Enter this Table I say with the Moon's Declination at the head and your Latitude in the Side Column and in the Common Angle is the hours and minutes that is to be added to the difference of the Sun's and Moon's Ascensions if it be less than Six Hours but Subtracted if more—the Sum or Difference is the time of rising—Practical Navigator.

And on the same page:

> In Calculating the Moon's place, we must observe to add 2°44″ to the Longitude that is given by the Table, to compensate for the Difference in the Meridians, as the Tables was Calculated to the Meridian of Greenwich.

In an adjoining table, he noted that "To find the Mean Changes of the Moon, See practical Navigator, p. 150."

Some evaluation of Banneker's calculations may be derived by comparing them with the ephemerides for the same months prepared by Major Andrew Ellicott and published by John Hayes in 1792. Generally, Ellicott listed several more entries of remarkable events for each month in his almanacs than did Banneker. A comparison for each of the twelve months of the two almanacs for 1792 shows that Ellicott included twenty-two entries each month whereas Banneker had no more than twenty. The only tables that agreed were the ones for sunrise and sunset. These were computed from the apparent instead of the mean sun time. The differences in time of the various phases of the moon for each month varied as much as three hours and as little as fifteen minutes. This discrepancy can be illustrated by the time provided for the moon's first quarter for April 29, 1792. According to Banneker's calculations, this would occur at 1:37 A.M. whereas Ellicott indicated that it would occur at 4:57 A.M., a difference of three hours and twenty minutes.

The figures presented in the *Nautical Almanac* and those which appeared in Banneker's ephemeris for that year suggest that Banneker probably did not have published tables available for comparison, and that he was forced to compute his own times for the phases of the moon in that year. In contrast, Ellicott's figures for Baltimore are consistently six hours and fifty-four minutes later than those published in the British publication, suggesting that he merely applied a calculated correction factor.

Differences of several minutes also occur in the time given for the moon's "southing," or its highest elevation for that day, when the moon is on the observer's meridian.

The moon's position among the constellations, or "moon's place," never varied more than one whole degree between the two almanacs, which leads one to the conclusion that both philomaths derived their figures from the same source, which may have been a printed book of tables. The error of one degree may have resulted from the rounding off of numbers.

In Banneker's almanac the positions of the planets frequently differ by as much as one and two degrees from those noted in the *Nautical Almanac*. He may have derived his data from other tables, inasmuch as the planets come to a stationary point at the same time but not at exactly the same place. The same error occurred in the tables for the moon's position, in which the error could have become greater.

A variation of several minutes occurred in virtually every other astronomical entry included in the two series of almanacs. For instance, although Banneker and Ellicott both indicated that winter and summer would begin on the twentieth day of the appropriate month of that year, they differed by one day for the beginning of spring and autumn. Banneker indicated that spring would begin on March 20 and autumn would commence on September 23, while Ellicott listed March 19 as the beginning of spring and September 22 as the first day of fall. Ellicott indicated that Jupiter would be 90 degrees from the sun on July 14; Banneker indicated that it would occur on July 16. There were numerous other disparities in the two ephemerides. Banneker stated that the bright star Arcturus would be on the meridian on April 17 at the 12th hour and twenty-third minute, while Ellicott listed the same time but on April 16. Banneker noted the hour 8:48 P.M. as the time of the rising of the bright star Sirius on December 4, while Ellicott gave the time as 8:42 P.M. on the same day.

In the almanacs for 1792 there is a major discrepancy in the times for the solar eclipse for March 22. Banneker calculated that it would begin at 1:22 P.M., twenty-nine minutes later than predicted by Ellicott. Banneker went on to calculate that some of the other phases of the eclipse would lag behind Ellicott's prediction by as much as thirty-two minutes. Similar comparisons can be made with the calculations published by William Waring in his "Poor Will's Almanac" for the same year:

	BANNEKER	ELLICOTT	WARING
Beginning time	1:22 P.M.	0:54 P.M.	1:01 P.M.
Greatest eclipse	2:15	1:51	1:58
End	3:15	2:43	2:49

The purpose in identifying Banneker's mistakes is not to show that he was a poor mathematician, nor to compare him unfavorably with the other astronomers of his day who also calculated almanacs. Instead, these errors have been described to demonstrate the laborious process by which he was forced to teach himself, without guidance from others—actually by trial and error. Again and again Banneker must have faltered in his work, wondering if he had assumed a project beyond his capabilities. These pages prove beyond doubt that by his method of self-instruction he emerged as a most competent mathematician and amateur astronomer and that his published results were of equal caliber with those of most of his contemporaries.

No basis can be identified for the method Banneker used for weather predictions, since no working notes or clues relating to them have survived. A survey of the literature among the almanac-makers of England and America has not revealed standard formulae for making such prognostications, but many were presumably based on astrological sources. According to the preface of a work published in England at the end of the eighteenth century:

> Many ingenious gentlemen in different and distant places, at home and abroad, have kept journals of the weather, air and its temperature, and their monthly and yearly quantities of rain; several abstracts of all which I have perused and computed at monthly mediums between the highest and lowest of mercury, or spirits in their tubes, or rain in its receiver; but these being fitter for speculation and amusement than any other useful purpose yet known, though if collected, compared and improved, might afford some not contemptible hints, therefore such journals should be deposited in some public museums where the curious might have access to them.[27]

Such a source may indeed have served Banneker for his forecasts, for as a farmer most of his life, he would have purchased an almanac each year to guide him in his farming and tobacco growing, as was then the custom. Because of the dearth of reading matter, he undoubtedly preserved these copies carefully through the years and consulted them from time to time for the literary content. When he undertook to produce his own almanacs, he may have referred to this collection once more, and made a comparative study of the predictions for each day of the year. If, for instance, he discovered that for eight of twelve years a cold spell of several days was predicted for the second week of January, or rain for the fourth of July, it was reasonably safe, he may have assumed, that the same weather would prevail in the following year. Certainly such predictions would be quite as legitimate as those produced by other almanac-makers during and before his own time.

Prior to the nineteenth century not only were there no methods, instruments, or institutions for weather forecasting; there was no actual knowledge of the laws which governed the weather. There was, however, an accumulation of miscellaneous information on specific aspects of the subject. For instance, it was known that northerly winds in the Northern Hemisphere were ordinarily attended by low temperature and southerly winds were usually followed by rising temperature, and that in the middle latitudes snow or rain followed easterly winds and that clearing or fair weather followed westerly winds. Observations of clouds led to information that specific cloud formations and movements were usually indications of certain types of weather, and that changes of atmospheric moisture could be used to predict anticipated weather changes.

No compilations of weather observations were available in published form in the eighteenth century in the United States, although several records of the climate in the region of the Chesapeake had been made and published in England. It is doubtful, however, that Banneker had access to them, and if he did, that they would have served any useful purpose in the day-to-day compilation of forecasts required for his almanacs.

The earliest account was that of Captain John Smith published in his *History of Virginia* at the beginning of the seventeenth century in which he described the climate of the Chesapeake Bay area as reported by the first English settlers during the winters of 1606 and 1607.[28] Similar records were maintained by John Campanius from 1644 through 1645 at Wilmington and Philadelphia, and reported by his grandson, Thomas Campanius Holm, early in the eighteenth century.[29] In 1667 Thomas Glover reported on storms in Virginia and the lower Chesapeake Bay.[30] His work was followed by a much more detailed account of observations made by John Clayton about 1685 and reported to the Royal Society.[31] This report of the climate around Jamestown and the lower Potomac region was the first scientific report which included details of weather conditions.

Among eighteenth-century published records of weather phenomena must be included Benjamin Franklin's observations in 1747 relating to northeast storms and the observations on storms described by Lewis Evans in his *Map of Pensilvania,*

New Jersey, New York and the three Delaware Counties, which was published in 1749. The map included "Several Useful Remarks in Physicks & Commerce" which were probably derived from Franklin's observations.[32]

Undoubtedly the most useful records of weather were those maintained in the field notes and journals of such professional surveyors as Charles Mason, Jeremiah Dixon, David Rittenhouse, and Andrew Ellicott, but these were not published or made available to almanac-makers.

Also of interest were the weather observations, probably the first made with meteorological instruments, by Dr. Richard Brooke between 1753 and 1757. Dr. Brooke was born near Nottingham in Prince George's County in Maryland and lived at Brookfield, the family estate, where he presumably made his studies. These were communicated to the Royal Society and published in its *Transactions* over several years. These observations may have been available to Banneker but it is doubtful that he used them.[33]

Another method Banneker could have used, and he may have attempted, was the traditional belief that the moon was the weather breeder, and that prognostications could be made from astronomical analysis of the moon's positions. Although the concept of lunar control of weather has been discarded in modern times, it prevailed strongly in the eighteenth century.

The concept is simply stated. The appearance of the moon to a terrestrial observer is determined by its relative position to the sun in relation to the earth. As the moon progresses from a new moon to a full moon, the orb gradually develops in appearance from a slim crescent to a full circle, and then reduces gradually from a full circle back to a slim crescent. It is visible because it reflects the light of the sun back to the earth. The time of day that it can be seen changes, as the moon progresses in its monthly journey around the earth.

Numerous traditions concerning the moon and the weather have developed over the centuries, the most prevalent of which relates to the positions of the "horns" or cusps of the new moon.

When the moon is in such a position that an invisible line connecting the cusps is nearly horizontal, it is considered to be a "wet moon," presaging rainy weather. When such a line is nearly vertical, it predicts a "dry moon" and dry weather. Doubtless these and other traditions arose from a natural and frequent coincidence between selected moon phases and specific weather changes. For instance, the moon enters a new phase every seventh day, and in the middle latitudes the weather normally changes once or twice within the same period. This led to many coincidences and formed the basis for a system of prediction in which only the agreements are considered and the disagreements are ignored.

This system could be further refined by consideration of the time of day that the moon enters into any one of its four phases. Presuming that the moon entered a new phase between 12 midnight and 2 A.M., it indicated fair weather if it occurred during the summer, and presaged fair weather with hard frost if it occurred in winter. If the moon entered a new phase between 12 noon and 2 P.M. in summer, it indicated rain; or rain and snow in winter. Such a system was developed and produced in tabular form by John Gruber in *The Hagerstown Almanac* for all the hours to indicate the affinities of the sun and moon, and was utilized in the almanac published from 1797 to the present.

The tables were said to have been compiled by Friedrich Wilhelm Herschel (1738–1822), although the astronomer later repudiated them. The system was in fact developed by Gruber's assistant, Charles Flack, for making the weather prognostications which were published annually in the almanac.

John Gruber (1768- ?) of Lancaster County, Pennsylvania, worked as an apprentice with Carl Cist in Philadelphia and moved to Hagerstown, Maryland, in 1795, where he established several newspapers, all of them short-lived. He published several books and then in 1797 printed the first issue of *Neuer Hägerstauner Kalendar*, an almanac in the German language, which he continued for a quarter of a century. He added an English edition in 1822.

There are other considerations which have been applied in predicting weather. Generally a full moon is associated with clear and cold weather, perhaps because it is more noticeable when the skies are clear, and the nights are generally cooler when there are no clouds due to the more rapid radiation of the earth's heat. Furthermore, in winter the moon's path, which is inclined to the ecliptic, is elevated higher above the southern horizon and therefore to the observer is rising earlier and setting later than in other seasons.[34]

Long-term weather forecasts were a traditional component of the almanac in the American colonies. They were first instituted by John Tulley in the almanacs he produced late in the seventeenth century. Tulley was a teacher of astronomy and navigation, and had a reasonably good training in these subjects for his time. His prognostications were deliberately vague, hardly useful by modern standards. As an example, he advised in his forecast that during the week of December 26–31, 1692, there would be "Perhaps more wet weather, after which cold winds and frosty weather may conclude the year." In general, however, Tulley's astrological and meteorological prognostications were considered to be extremely skillful compared with the absurd predictions generally found in English almanacs of his time. His forecasts became such a successful feature of his almanacs that it was adopted by his successors and became standard procedure. Owners of almanacs frequently interleaved the pages and added a record of events for the year, including daily weather reports, political and national events, and family data. It has been suggested that these written comments may have been noted and assimilated by other almanac-makers.

In planetary meteorology as applied by long-range weather forecasters, the moon was given the primary responsibility for weather changes. A nineteen-year lunar cycle, during which the new and full moons were repeated on corresponding days of the month, was believed to form the basis of the rotations of certain types of weather. The daily change of the moon's aspect was correlated with the daily changing weather, and the weekly change of the lunar phases was also related to the prevalence of storms.

The weather and seasonal conditions, as well as the results of human endeavors, have been foretold from ancient times from the relative positions of the planets, and the practice of astrology for this purpose was continued into the nineteenth century by almanac-makers.[35]

Although it may not be related to his forecasts, an intriguing entry in Banneker's journal describes an unusual relationship between the moon and the weather which he observed and recorded on March 8, 1796:

A Chronological Observation

1796 March 8 Snow Moon in ♓ her Latitude South
March 14th Thunder and rain Moon in ♊ her Lat. South
16th High wind ☽ in d°——[36]

In this notation Banneker seemed to have explored the possible existence of yet another connection between the moon with the weather, depending on whether the moon's latitude was north or south of the ecliptic.

No system presently known can be identified as the one used by Banneker for his weather prognostications, but it is certain that he did not use the table employed by Gruber. A comparison of a compilation of the weather conditions described in his almanacs for a period of several years with the phases of the moon indicates that the phases did not provide a basis for the forecasts. The same is true of Ellicott's almanac for 1792, in which there is no correlation between the prognostications and the moon's phases. Nor does there appear to be any similarity between the weather data shown in the almanacs of Ellicott and Banneker for the same year, 1792.

Besides, Banneker's manuscript and published prognostications are not the same in any of the months for the years 1792 through 1795. This fact suggests that he may have attempted to develop his own system of forecast as an experiment, but his printers had a prepared system or systems of their own which they preferred.

The occurrence of weather phenomena on certain days was used to indicate the weather for specific subsequent days, as the basis of another system. A common saying, for instance, is that if it rains on the first Sunday of a month, it will rain on every Sunday of that month. The six- or seven-day period of recurring weather is usually based on the supposed influence of the moon.

A great body of proverbs has developed over the centuries which provide formulas for forecasting weather based on the behavior of clouds, winds, temperature, and humidity. Often there is some basis for such conclusions, but in general they are not reliable.

Yet another ancient system of prediction was derived from the supposed effect of sun spots upon meteorological conditions.[37]

Observations of the habits and conditions of animals, birds, and plants, particularly undomesticated animals, were traditionally used as another basis.

Several of the systems described were embodied in an interesting compilation of *"Prognosticks of the Weather"* included by the Adams brothers in their issue of Banneker's Almanac for 1795:

> Those who look after cattle observe when they go together in troops or herds; or whether the swine grub the earth with their heads turned to the *north;* and if they find it so, let them take care to provide store of fuel, for it generally proves a hard and long winter.
>
> Take notice of the 24th of November, and as the day is, so the winter is like to prove; and as you find the 25th of the same month, so will the month of January be.
>
> You may easily know what sort of a winter it will

be, by observing the last days of the moon between November and December; for as they prove, so will the winter.

And to know what sort of a summer you will have, those who are nice observers of the seasons say, that the three last days of the moon between April and May, are infallible presages how it is like to prove. A great plenty of acorns are a certain presage of a severe winter.[38]

It has been scientifically established that the moon has no significant effect on the weather, but until a system of systematic weather records could be compiled, and means for observing weather throughout the world could be established, the almanac provided the only source of information. The predictions were cast in flexible language, and the words most frequently encountered were "moderate," "changeable," "variable," and "unsettled," which left room for much variation from the prediction.

In 1830 and earlier, skeptics who made a study of the weather forecasts in almanacs concluded that one correct guess in every ten was a reasonably good record for the almanac-maker. The bits of evidence that have survived seem to support the conviction that in general the almanac-makers merely made guesses of the weather conditions for each of the days of the forthcoming year, with no other basis except possibly reference to guesses made during the previous year by other almanac-makers.

Among the desirable features of Banneker's almanacs was a tide table for Chesapeake Bay. This item made the almanac particularly useful for the pilots as well as the fishermen and others who lived and made their living along the shores of the Bay and its many rivers. The other almanacs of his time and region did not include a tide table, a factor which contributed to the popularity of his work.

The form and content were identical in the first three issues of Banneker's almanacs. It included listings for the high water or high tide at Cape Charles, Point Look-out, Annapolis, and

Baltimore. It was simple enough to calculate, for the high tide at Annapolis was two hours later than at Point Look-out, and at Baltimore and Head-of-the-Bay the high tide was five hours later than at Point Look-out. The table bore the caution that:

> The times of High-Water in Chesapeake-Bay are very uncertain, and depend much upon the circumstances— the distance between Cape-Charles and Cape-Henry being small, in comparison to the extent of the Bay, and therefore not capable of admitting a sufficiency of water during the time of flood at Cape-Charles, to make any considerable tide toward the Head of the Bay, without being assisted by a smart S.S.E. wind; and in time of a N.N.E. wind, the tides from Patuxent, upwards, will be very small.

The table was simplified considerably in the almanacs for 1795 and 1796, which also provided facilities for determining tides in a wider range of ports as far north as Halifax and Boston. It was entitled "Rule to find the Time of HIGH WATER at the following Places" and consisted simply of an additive for each of the places listed to be combined with the day of the moon's age.

Banneker changed the format once again in 1796 and utilized that same form in the following and last issue. This was entitled "TABLE Shewing how much should be added to, or subtracted, from the moon's southing, for the time of high water at the several places following; this mark * directing to add and this + to subtract." Twenty-five ports were listed alphabetically from Albany to Wilmington and ranging as far north as Quebec and Plymouth.

The tide tables for the almanac were provided by Banneker himself, not by the printer. The data were simple to acquire and there was no mathematical achievement involved. The changing of the tides had been associated with the motions of the moon for centuries; the earliest surviving tide tables were compiled in the thirteenth century by the monks of St. Albans in England. Once the time of the highest tide or spring tide was known at a particular point at the age of the full and new moon, it was a simple matter to derive a table for each day of the month at the same place. Banneker applied the standard daily retardation of forty-eight minutes or ⅘ of an hour. This determination of the highest tide waters or spring tides on the days of the full and new moon were known as "the establishment of the port" and was generally marked on the charts for the port in question.[39]

As Banneker undoubtedly knew from his lifetime on the Patapsco River, the tides of Chesapeake Bay were considerably less than those at other points along the Atlantic coast. They were relatively small in the Bay, and considerably affected by wind direction. The tides were particularly high with a southerly wind. As the tidal current began to flood, water flowed into the Bay through the opening between the Virginia Capes. Only a small amount of water passed these points before the sea tide began its ebb because the opening between the Capes was relatively small in proportion to the size of the Bay itself. As the sea tide began its flood, the water spread itself over the wide span of the Bay and its many rivers, so that the flood was dispersed and the rise of the tide within the Bay area was relatively small. The same was true of the ebbing tide. As the waters of the Bay slowly receded through the opening between the Capes, the sea tide was again rising so that there was comparatively little change.

The tidal waters were swept up into the river openings by strong tidal currents, however, until they reached their fall lines. The width of the rivers generally decreased in proportion to the distance from the mouth of the river, so that it had the effect of making the tide change at the fall line higher than occurred at the mouth of the river.

A curious characteristic of the rivers which emptied into the Chesapeake Bay were the half tides, which ran opposite to the main current on either side. Some of them were relatively strong and provided an advantage to pilots when the channel current was adverse.

Banneker occasionally noted in the pages of his Manuscript Journal unusual atmospheric phenomena which he had observed. On the very first page he noted under the date of December 23, 1790:

> About 3 o'clock, A.M. I heard a Sound and felt the Shock like unto heavy thunder. I went out but could not observe any Cloud about the Horizon. I therefore Conclude it must be a great Earth Quake in some part of the Globe.[40]

The notations were few and interspersed apparently at random through the journal, frequently inserted between mathematical calculations. Two years later he recorded another observation:

> May the 4th 1792. In a Squall from the N.W. I observed the Lower regions of the Clouds to move Swiftly before the wind, and the upper region Slowly against it.[41]

Six years later Banneker noted another of his observations:

> 1798 November 16. Between 8 and 9 O'clock I saw a bur or some Condensed particles of the Atmosphere, of divers colours gather round the moon, and that which was first and nearest to her center appeared white, the Second of an orange, the third blue, and the fourth red, nearly coloured like unto the rain bow, this small circle was in breadth, about seven times the moons apparent Diameter.
>
> B. Banneker.[42]

The weather was a subject of considerable interest to him in his later years, as evidenced by still another entry in his journal:

> 1803, Februr 2nd in the morning part of the day, there arose a very dark Cloud, followed by Snow and haile a flash of lightning and loud thunder crack, and then the Storm abated untill after noon, when another cloud arose the Same point, viz, Northwest, with a beautiful Shower of Snow, but what beautyfyed the Snow was the brightness of the Sun, which was near Setting at the time. I looked for the rain bow or rather Snow bow, but I think the snow was of too dense a nature to exhibit the representation of the bow in the Cloud.
>
> N.B. The above was followed by very cold weather a few days.[43]

He noted several observations which related to the meridian of Baltimore, Maryland, in his journal. In addition to a carefully drawn projection for a solar eclipse, and its description,[44] he included the following reference to the Federal Territory in his manuscript journal:

> 1793 January the first day at noon, we find the Sun's Longitude at the Meridian of Greenwich to be 9-11°-39′ and as his mean motion is 59′ 8″, and the Difference between the Meridian of Greenwich and that of the Federal District is about 5 hours west Longitude, we must say by Trigonometry As 24 hours in time is to 59′ 8″ motion, so is 5 hours time to 12-7/24ths minutes motion which must be added to the Greenwich Longitude, to make it right at the Federal District.[45]

The pages of Banneker's journal served as the repository for numerous exercises in mathematics and astronomy. Among these was an unfinished table of "The days of year returned from the beginning of January" which was completed only through the month of July, and may have been done in 1802.[46] Another was a table of the moon's longitude and anomaly compiled for the years 1806 through 1820. This table, which appears on a separate sheet of paper folded four times and bearing Banneker's signature in pencil at the top, was probably one of the last compilations he made before his death.

The journal also provides ample evidence of Banneker's diminishing ability to pursue his astronomical endeavors in his final years. The last ephemeris for which he completed and entered all the required calculations was for 1800. He finished the outlines of the ephemerides for the next two years, 1801 and 1802. He completed all the calculations and entered them for the months of 1801 but did not add the important days or the weather prognostications for that year. In 1802 he succeeded in calculating all the eclipses as well as the times for sunrise and sunset and moonrise and moonset, and he entered a few of the remarkable days in the outline. Presumably he was unable to complete the remaining data.

The contents of Banneker's Manuscript Journal and his commonplace book are unique records of an eighteenth-century almanac-maker in which are combined invaluable data about his way of life and events of major and of only passing importance, with a clear exposition of the method by which almanacs were calculated during this period of American scientific history. Few, if indeed any, similar repositories have survived in which the evolution of a philomath can be traced through the entire span, from the beginning of his self-instruction, encompassing his work from his basic computations to the published product, year after year, for the entire period of his scientific involvement. This important resource has provided the means for making an analysis and evaluation of the work of Benjamin Banneker.

IX

THE
FINAL YEARS

❖❖❖❖❖❖❖❖❖❖❖❖❖❖❖❖❖❖

Presumption should never make us neglect that which appears easy to us, nor despair make us lose courage at the sight of difficulties.

Banneker's Almanac for 1794

DURING THE LAST DECADE and a half, from the time that he calculated his first ephemeris, Banneker's life underwent a marked change. Following the death of his mother some years earlier, he had become accustomed to living alone on his farm. Two of his sisters, who lived with their own families within walking distance, visited him regularly and took turns attending to his household needs. He prepared his own meals, but his sisters did his laundry and the other household chores his mother had performed all her lifetime.

With age, Banneker's health deteriorated considerably,

(235)

and it became increasingly difficult for him to pursue his accustomed activities. He discontinued tobacco growing with a sense of great relief, and limited his labors to the maintenance of a garden for his own use, to his beekeeping, and to the cultivation of his fruit orchard, of which he was most fond. The almanacs provided a modest source of income which enabled him to buy whatever he could not produce on his land, and he had few other requirements. He reorganized his life on this new modest scale and managed his daily existence on an orderly basis.

Banneker remained a bachelor all his life. No evidence of a love interest exists, a circumstance which may be explained by the solitude with which he clothed himself throughout his lifetime. As a young man, he lived and worked on the farm with his parents and his sisters. The only others with whom he associated with frequency were his grandmother and his aunts and their families. The peculiar circumstances of his family would have kept them apart from their neighbors, and Banneker never spoke of close friends in his childhood or adult life. His father's death, when Banneker was twenty-eight—an age when he would have been seeking a wife—left him with the responsibility for his mother and the farm, all of which he assumed with his accustomed seriousness. His sisters had already married and left the farm one by one. Later, his mother developed an independent source of income from sales of farm produce and other staples to Ellicott's Lower Mills.

Several factors may have influenced his decision to remain single. His grandmother and his mother had shown themselves to be women of considerable dominance, and Banneker had always lived within the shadow of matriarchal supervision. His increasingly casual manner of existence, along with his weakness for liquor, became deterrents to thoughts of a family of his own. His consuming interest in reading and mathematical studies, and his jealous preservation of the little leisure he had for pursuing them, disinclined him to seek a wife.

As he grew older, his reliance on the Bible and its teachings as a guide to daily living made itself more and more manifest, and perhaps in itself was a deterrent to marriage. Among the few pieces published in his first almanac without the quotation marks indicating another source was a short essay, perhaps of his own composition, containing the words: "Assemble all the evils which poverty, disease, or violence can inflict, and their stings will be found, by far, less pungent than those which guilty passions dart into the heart." [1]

The opening up of the whole new field of astronomy was like the beginning of a new life for Benjamin. He regretted that the opportunity had come so late, but now that he had it in hand, he was not about to let it elude him. It was at this point in his career that he paused to take stock of himself and the course he would pursue. He was sixty years of age when the first almanac was finally published; he lived alone, with no responsibilities to anyone or anything other than himself. [2] He had made his home with his mother until her death, which occurred some time after July 1775. Curiously enough, the tax list for 1773 listed Banneker only as the single adult living at that time on his property, yet there is no evidence that his mother was living elsewhere at the time. [3] The children of his sisters, who lived within walking distance, were grown up, and he felt reasonably reassured that their families were in good circumstances. It may be assumed that Banneker's sisters had inherited shares in Molly Banneky's farm, or that their husbands pursued some sort of trade in the neighborhood.*

A true farmer at heart, he was distressed at first to see his land lie fallow and unused. When some of his neighbors asked for its use, he divided it into several small holdings which he rented to them. This project proved to be less than successful. He repeatedly encountered problems with collection of the

* Exhaustive research of land records and vital statistics in the Hall of Records at Annapolis, the City Hall at Baltimore, the files of the Maryland Historical Society, and other related repositories, have failed to bring to light any documentation relating to property owned by Molly, her daughters, or granddaughters.

rents. Occasionally he would forget when the time came for collections, and at other times his tenants were unable or unwilling to pay the small amounts due. They would often deliberately
quarrel with him to avoid payment. This source of unpleasant-
ness was distressing. He had lived a lifetime of cooperative
endeavor, always at peace with everyone he knew, and it was too
late in life to suffer these new annoyances. If he insisted on
payment, which he did infrequently, his tenants took the opportunity to annoy him or threaten him so that he dared not return.
To add insult to injury, they sometimes prevailed upon him to
lend them small sums, then refused to repay them.

Unpleasant incidents increased. On December 18, 1790,
Banneker noted on the first page of his manuscript journal:

> ——— ——— informed me that ——— Stole my
> horse and Great Coat, and that the said ——— in-
> tended to murder me when opportunity presented.
> ——— ——— and further gave me Caution to let no
> person in my house after Dark.[4]

The names of the individuals were later carefully obliterated by overwriting, and the entire entry was crossed out. He
became concerned that such a record might bring reciprocal
action to others, a possibility to be avoided at all costs. His plan
to retire from active farming so that he could devote all his time
to his studies did not come easily, for his solitude was periodically jarred by further attempts to annoy him. Seven years
later he recorded another incident of violence in his journal:

> August 27, 1797. Standing by my door, I heard the dis-
> charge of a gun, and in 4 or 5 Seconds of time after the
> discharge, the Small Shot came rattling about me, one
> or two of which Struck the house, which plainly
> demonstrates that the Velocity of Sound as [sic] much
> greater than that of a Cannon-Bullet.[5]

He did not say whether this was another attempt to annoy him or whether the shots about his house might have come from a careless hunter. The persecution, however, did not cease. Less than a year later he reported another violent incident directed against him:

> April 29, 1798. Came two Black men with a gun in my inclose and discharged it a few perches from door, I being very unwell I could not persue them to find out who they were.[6]

A few years later he recorded still another disturbance:

> On the night of the 27th November 1802 my house was violent broke open and Several articles taken out.[7]

These incidents might have developed from several causes. First, there were the disgruntled tenants who resented his requests for rent. His almanacs had made him a person of note in the region. Travelers who had heard of him wished to see this unusual man of achievement. He was held in high esteem by his neighbors and friends at Ellicott's Lower Mills. There may have been those who assumed that his fame had also brought him fortune, and that he had money stored away in his cabin. Then there may have been those of both races who were envious and resentful of his accomplishments and fame. Banneker, who had devoted a lifetime of living by the best Christian standards, was often uneasy during his final years because of these disturbances.

Annoyances came from all levels. The orchards adjacent to his house, which he loved, were well known in the neighborhood, especially to youngsters. They particularly favored his cherries and pears, which were of outstanding quality. As the population increased, boys of varying ages learned about Banneker's orchards. Several of them would call at his door, and with the utmost respect they would ask permission to pick some of the fruit. Banneker always graciously agreed, then returned to his work at his table. Later, the boys would return and strip the trees bare. He frequently scolded the boys and even attempted to negotiate with them. If they would leave him half of his crop, he suggested they could take the rest, but this had no effect. To a friend who called on him once during the summer, he apologized that he had no fruit to offer, adding: "I have no influence with the rising generation. All my arguments have failed to induce them to set bounds to their wants." [8]

As Banneker's studies and daily routine were interrupted again and again, he wished more than ever for peace of mind. He wasted many hours in this dilemma and finally came to the conclusion that his problem was mostly derived from his only valuable possession—his land. Perhaps if he disposed of it his troubles would disappear. He owned more than a hundred acres, since with his father's death in 1759 he had taken title to the farm in its entirety. He was greatly saddened at the prospect of selling his land. He remembered the fierce joy his father had expressed again and again when he had first acquired the farm and while he was building his home. He remembered with how much love his father had nurtured the orchard, built the tobacco sheds, and cared for the whole place. Banneker had been a small boy when the land was purchased, but he still remembered the walks with his father during the leisure hours on Sunday afternoons, during which Robert Banneky expressed his pride of possession. Again and again he had told young Benjamin that it was the land that made the difference between independence and slavery. And Benjamin was stirred by his father's words, so that he devoted the major part of his life to developing and preserving what his father had created. Now came the time of decision. Should he sell the land, or should he convey it by deed to his nephews and nieces? It was a hard decision, and he considered it for many days before he made up his mind.

Some years earlier, in 1785, he had already given thought to his obligations to his sisters and their families in the event of his own death, and particularly to his favored young nephew,

Greenbury Morten. Young Greenbury had reached manhood and had shown a determination to develop a farm of his own. Accordingly, Banneker had sold him a tract of twenty acres for twenty-five pounds in common currency. The price was modest and designed to meet Greenbury's circumstances. It gave Banneker pleasure to help assure his future.[9]

Morten came to public attention in a somewhat unusual manner several years after Banneker's death. Although the right of suffrage had been granted to all freemen of Maryland by the Constitution of 1776 if they owned a certain amount of property, a law enacted in 1783 specified that "no colored person freed thereafter, not the issue of such, should be allowed to vote, or to hold any office, or to give evidence against any white, or to enjoy any other rights of a freeman than the possession of property and redress at law or equity for injury to person or property." An amendment to the Constitution was adopted in 1810 which further limited the right of suffrage to white men. Greenbury Morten had voted regularly, and was not aware of the new law of 1810. When he reported to the polls in Baltimore County in that year, his vote was rejected. He became incensed, and addressed the crowd gathered at the polls "in a strain of true and passionate eloquence" which is said to have kept his audience at breathless attention.[10]

Banneker had given careful consideration to the other children of his sisters and finally came to a conclusion. Any attempt to partition the farm among them would serve no purpose, for none of the portions would be adequate because of the quality and nature of the land. Presumably none of the other nephews, the number and identity of whom are not presently known, was in a position to purchase the land as Morten had done. If Banneker conveyed his land to several of them, such a decision might engender envy and ill feeling in his immediate family.

In addition to the full one hundred acres of the original farm called "Stout," Banneker owned another tract of approximately ten acres adjoining the main farm. This may have been his share of Timber Poynt or his mother's share of Molly Welsh's land. No records of its acquisition can be found, and it is not mentioned as a separate parcel, but its existence came to light in compiling a total of the land sold by Banneker during the next decade.

It was at this time, probably about 1790, that he divided his land. He set aside certain portions that he planned to sell individually in the next few years as he had need, and kept intact the largest segment consisting of seventy-two acres. The Elli-cott brothers had expressed an interest in acquiring this tract, since it would supplement their own holdings in the area, and when Banneker broached the subject again they suggested that he sell them the land and retain life residence on the premises. They offered him £180 for the land, or £2½ per acre. This seemed to be a practical solution and he agreed.

The offer was completely acceptable, and Banneker was greatly relieved. The suggestion may have been made that the sum was to be paid in annual increments to assure that Banneker would not invest it foolishly and that he would have a constant income.

Banneker could not resist the opportunity to apply his mathematical exercises to such an intriguing arrangement, and he set about to calculate his life expectancy, and to determine the amounts of the annual payments accordingly. The results of his computations were recorded as part of his agreement with the Ellicott family:

> I believe I shall live fifteen years, and consider my land worth £180 Maryland Currency; by receiving £12 a year, for fifteen years I shall in the contemplated time, receive its full value; if on the contrary I die before that day, you will be at liberty to take possession.[11]

The sale was made by verbal arrangement, not then formal-ized with a deed. There is some confusion about the date of the transaction, because Tyson as well as Latrobe stated that for once in his career Banneker erred, and that he lived beyond the period that he had estimated.* Banneker frequently expressed concern over his error, but the Ellicott firm continued to pay his annuity without question, dismissing his worry with the reassurance that in the interim his land had increased in value and that his continued use of it was no burden to them.

The sale to Ellicott & Co. provided Banneker with security for the rest of his days, but there still remained five small parcels of land, which he proceeded to sell from time to time. The income provided him with those extra luxuries which he could not otherwise enjoy, such as books, and other needs for his studies.

The first of these sales was to John Barton, a neighbor, of ten acres "including all the Improvements thereon and appertainances thereto belonging, effected in April 1792, for the sum of thirty pounds." [12]

Later that year Banneker disposed of a second parcel, consisting of sixty-four perches, or 2½ acres, of the original farm, to John Nimiy, a cooper of Baltimore County and presumably a near neighbor. The sum paid by Nimiy was two pounds and ten shillings. It is interesting to note that, in the indenture of this sale, the seller is identified as "Benjamin Banneker of Baltimore County in the State of Maryland astronomer. . . ." John Nimiy may have been one of Benjamin's relatives, possibly a cousin or nephew. [13]

Two years later, in December 1794, he once again agreed to sell part of his patrimony to a certain Edward Shugar, this time a small parcel of two acres, for the sum of five pounds. [14]

Benjamin sold two more portions of land during the next several years, both of them to the same purchaser, a cooper of Baltimore County named Thomas Gibbons. The first tract consisted of a parcel of undetermined size described as "parts of tracts" which were approximately two acres and sold for the sum of ten dollars in June 1797. [15]

* Latrobe in his *Memoir* (p. 361) stated that Banneker lived eight years longer than he had estimated he would, but Tyson in *A Sketch* (p. 11) noted that "he lived several years beyond the calculated period."

The second parcel of one acre was sold in October 1799 for the sum of five pounds.[16]

At this time Greenbury Morten also appeared in Baltimore to formalize the sale of land he had acquired from his uncle, to the self-same cooper, Thomas Gibbons.[17]

At the same time Banneker finally transferred his remaining land to Ellicott & Co. By an indenture dated October 23, 1799, he conveyed in equal shares to Jonathan, Elias, George, and John Ellicott his remaining seventy-two acres of land for the sum of 180 pounds which he stated he had received to his full satisfaction.[18]

It is to be presumed from this transaction that Banneker had received a number of payments in either cash or goods purchased from the Ellicott brothers in annual amounts of twelve pounds or equivalent, leaving a balance of some seventy pounds, or that he had received varying amounts totalling the entire price specified—180 pounds. Whichever may have been the case, after the formalization of the sale by indenture, a new procedure for payment was instituted. Thereafter Banneker was given a charge account at the Ellicott & Co. store whereby he would make his purchases during the year. In Mid-November his indebtedness would be totaled, subtracted from the twelve pounds due him annually, and the balance rendered to him in cash by one of the Ellicott brothers.

Banneker kept a running account of his expenditures on blank pages of his manuscript journal. The contents of this volume were well organized in that each right-hand page was carefully inscribed with the calculations for the ephemeris for each month, set down as it would appear in a printed almanac, and constituted Banneker's master copy. The left-hand page was used for various other purposes, not always in chronological order. Many of the left-hand pages were filled with projections for eclipses with related notes. Occasionally they were used for formulas for making calculations, often copied from some of the sources he used, and for tables and records of observations. Here also he made personal notations, records of dreams, proverbs, and quotations.

The listing of expenditures for each year was headed "Articles Received of Ellicott & Co." and variously "for the fourth payment [1802]," or "for the fifth payment [1803]," and so on.

There may have been several reasons for such an arrangement whereby Banneker was not required to keep substantial amounts of cash on hand. Possibly his drinking might tempt him to spend his money. On the other hand, the anxiety he expressed concerning incidents which ranged from threats on his life to thefts from his home increased his uneasiness when he had money at hand.

The first recorded payment made to Banneker by Ellicott & Co. was for the year from November 1798 to November 1799, although he identified it as "Second Payment," probably in error. He charged purchases against his account at the firm's store and received the balance in cash. The second payment began with three entries,-two of them dated December 29, 1798:

> By Cash received of them in
> part Pay^t £0.1.10½
> ~~To Cash paid for Signed a~~
> ~~Deed~~ .... ———— £ [illegible]
> 1799 January 12 by an Alma-
> nac .... 0.0.11.[19]

The almanac, because of the price paid, was not a current copy of the *Nautical Almanac* but a common one of the region.

Although of no great historical importance, these accounts are interesting because they provide a clear picture of how Banneker lived. The most frequent purchase was of pork; he bought between seven and ten pounds each month. He averaged approximately two pairs of shoes every year at a cost of 11s. 3d. each. He bought corn on a monthly basis a half bushel at a time, and molasses and candles.

He occasionally indulged in the purchase of clothing. On December 23, 1801, two days before Christmas, he paid the tailor for making him a new pair of breeches, and on the following April 15 he recorded the purchase of "A fine hat for 4 dollars (£1 10s.0d.)." On June 25 he bought 3¼ yards of Irish linen, in addition to 3½ yards of other linen as well as thread and buttons. Presumably the cloth was for shirts and handkerchiefs which his sisters may have sewn for him. During the course of the year he listed other purchases for cloth including sheeting, nankeen, muslin, as well as thread. One item noted the payment to a tailor for making him a jacket. He purchased stockings separately. Unusual items were "a paper of ink powder, one quarter pound of gunpowder, as well as some shot." The balance due him for the year was four dollars or £1 10s.0d. There were several unusual expenses as well. On May 20, 1802, he purchased a gunlock for 9s. 4½d., and on August 4 he invested two shillings for a padlock and ¼ pound powder (probably gunpowder) as well as two pounds of shot. Each year he listed a payment to the sheriff in the amount of 4s.6d. for taxes.

Several purchases were recorded for scholarly materials. On July 8, 1802, he listed "cash payd for a Book 3 Dollars (1 £ 2s.6d.)" and in November 1803 he purchased an ink stand for three shillings.

At the end of each November Banneker's account was totaled and any unexpended balance was rendered to him in cash. On November 16, 1802, he received the amount of £1 18s.8d. For some reason not apparent, a departure from this procedure was made in 1803. On November 14, George Ellicott paid him £5 17s.4d. in cash leaving a balance £6 2s.8d.

An unexplained item is a payment made by Banneker in June 1803 to Nanny Hall in the amount of 6s.3d. Was she perhaps a housekeeper who came in to care for his house?

Various minor entries made in Banneker's journal and in his commonplace book provide some insight into the manner of his existence during his final years. One purchase, which he recorded and later crossed out because he wished to use that page of his journal for drawing a lunar projection, was the following:

1796.   John Barton D[r]
July 3   To 1 Candles.[20]

On a separate sheet of paper which he had added to his journal he had drawn two horizontal lines intersected by five vertical lines. The whole was part of a notation of his purchases of cider, for it was labeled "The long marks are barrels Cyder for B.B." and below the diagram were the words "for (or per) Barton & Samson."

In 1795 he kept a separate set of accounts in a small book which he called his commonplace book. This little volume appears to have been of his own construction, utilizing the leather-bound hard covers of an old account book into which he sewed, folded, and trimmed sheets with discarded astronomical calculations.*

The entries relate primarily to miscellaneous purchases and loans he made of small sums of money. The first item on the first page which was later crossed out is the following:

April 30th, 1795
Cash lent John Ford
Five Dollars £1.17.6

This was followed by

1797 Dec.[r] 12th
bought a pound of candles
at ⅛ p. ——

---

* The commonplace book measures 3½ × 6 inches and is bound in heavy boards with blue marbelized linings and a leather cover. It includes thirteen sheets, and there is evidence that other sheets were removed. Eleven of the twenty-six pages are filled with ephemerides in draft form; six pages are blank. (Privately owned; used with permission.)

An undated notation lists several names followed by a calculation:

    Henry Ball
    Sam¹ Harlan
    Rowan Hugh
    John Lyons

    d h   m   d   h   m
    4 8   11   twenty times added together give   19   1   50
    thirty times added gives 4   6   0

The second page has a draft of significant days for an unidentified month, and the following entries appear on the third page:

    1795)   Received of John Henderson
    June 1) £0.2.0

                    1803
    April 13th planted Beans and Sowed Cabbage Seed

On the eleventh page is noted in a shaking hand the name "Harriet Ministry," and on the seventeenth page there is the following item:

    1799 Harriet Ducket D^r.
    Novr 17   To ½ pint honey   £0.0.7½

Banneker used the pages from both ends of the volume rather than in a continuous manner from front to back. On the last page is the following:

    1795)   Sold Butler, Edwards and Kiddy the right of
    Ap 2)   a copy of an almanac for the year 1796, for
              the Sum of 80 dol. equal to 30 £.

1795) June 5, answered James
Marr £0-1-6

On the 26th day of March 1798 came Joshua Sank with 3 or 4 Bushels turnips to feed the Cows. B. Banneker

On one page there are calculations for the moon's longitude for the month of January 1804, as well as the following entries made in 1795:

William Hubbard Dʳ.
April 30 [1795] Cash lent him £0. 0. 10
R 2 b 2 C 1   C 1 b 1 2   Dʳ.

1795   )
) Cash lent her   £0.7.6
May 23)
June 22   Cash of her   £0.1.6
Aug. 27   Cash lent her—0.4.2 ½

Both entries were later crossed out, indicating that they had been settled.

Another page stated:

1796   Tho.ˢ Finton Dʳ.
May 4 To a watch 4 dol. £1.10.0.

This entry deserves particular attention. The purchase of a pocket watch was a notable event in Banneker's life and marked a milestone in his career. During the many decades since he had made a wooden clock, he undoubtedly had occasion to see and examine a number of other clocks and watches, but he never had money enough to buy one. Now, in the sunset of his life, such a purchase would still have constituted a major luxury but one that he felt he deserved. Perhaps he even justified it on the basis of need, for an accurate timepiece would have been useful in astronomical observations. The old wooden clock would have sufficed for measuring the mere passage of time but would not have served for his observations. Banneker's income from the several sales of property and the payments for the various editions of his almanacs now provided him with sufficient funds for an occasional unusual expenditure during this period, and the investment was relatively modest. Curiously, the watch was not noted among the memorabilia that survived his death some years later, nor was there evidence of any scientific use he may have made of it. There can be no doubt, however, that it was a new addition to the cherished materials that occupied the place of honor on his oval table, which was his observatory. The watch entry was canceled at a later date with a line drawn through it. On the same page were the following:

1799 Contra C^r.
Sept. 18 Reced of John Collins
at Sundry times £1.15.11
Receded fodder 0.11. 3
_____
2. 7. 2
Nov. 23 Cash of wife 0.11. 6
~~Novr. 2~~

1799 John Collins D^r.
To house and Grounds Rent £3. 0. 0
June 24 lent yr. wife 0. 2. 6
Sep^t. 7 Cash lent you 0. 0.11
Cyder at Sundry times 0. 4. 9
2 Quarts dry peaches 0. 0. 6
~~Nov. 27 To ½ peck Apples .... 0. 0.11½~~
Dec. 31 To a Quart mead 0. 0. 4
1800)
) Cash lent y^r. wife 0. 1.10½
Jan. 2)

Banneker never fully lost his concern over how his decision to dispose of his land would appear to his family, his neighbors, and others. For a time at least, he felt the need to provide justification, which was in fact not required. As he grew older, his health began to fail, and he no longer looked forward to the all-consuming labors of the farm. His infirmities were increasing, and he no longer had the strength and tenacity for work which had marked his younger years. He feared the censure of his family and his neighbors perhaps more than he was willing to admit, should his land no longer be adequately cultivated and fall into disuse. Bad enough that he drank—a weakness since his youth but kept under control by his mother while she lived. After her death, Banneker's will power often failed. In this respect he was no different from anyone else of his time, white or black, wealthy or poor. His addiction, along with his seemingly slothful existence, caused him concern. He justified his retirement from farming and the sale of his land on the basis of his desire to develop his scientific knowledge; previously he had neither the time nor the means.

Despite the possible criticism of others, he was greatly relieved when he could stop working, except for his own pleasure in his garden and orchard. At last he was able to spend the hours of the night, as late as he wished, contemplating the celestial wonders through his telescope. Often he wrapped himself in his cloak and lay on the ground to observe the stars, experiencing the greatest pleasure in the nocturnal solitude, drinking in the beauty which in the past he had been too preoccupied to appreciate.

Banneker went to bed at dawn, when the light obliterated the night sky, and he spent part of each day sleeping and resting indoors. He did not need very much sleep; in this respect he was quite unusual. Later in the day he would work around his house. He was often seen by passing neighbors hoeing his corn, pruning the fruit trees in his orchard, or weeding his garden. With all the leisure now at his command, he took the time to observe the wonders of nature so close at hand. He would sit for hours and watch his bees, for instance, as they departed and returned to their hives.

At the end of each day Banneker customarily relaxed with music. He brought out his violin and flute and would alternate in playing them with a certain amount of skill. He often sat in a favorite place under a chestnut tree near his doorway playing until sunset passed into twilight. Passersby sometimes observed his figure silhouetted against the tree and heard the soft sounds of his music, before he resumed his nightly astronomical observations.

Banneker had few other diversions besides his studies and his music. He hunted on occasion, in search of small game for the table. He was at home in the woods. As a young boy he had learned to identify every shrub and tree in his woods: prickly ash, spice wood, alder, red bud, tulip tree, elder, dogwood, as well as the great chestnuts, oaks, ash hickories, maple, and gums. He was familiar with the small game, and he frequently startled herds of deer and flocks of wild turkeys as he wandered through the trees. He went after larger game only when an occasional wildcat ventured from its haven to plunder his farmyard of a young pig or poultry. He made no mention of hunting in his writings, but in his later years his accounts with the Ellicott & Co. store now and then included purchases of gunpowder and shot.

Banneker probably enjoyed smoking. Tobacco was widely used as snuff and for smoking in clay pipes from the earliest days of the province. The cigar did not come into popularity until late in the eighteenth century, and cigarettes did not follow until much later. He probably smoked the common clay pipe, for the same accounts from the Ellicott & Co. store listed periodic purchases of tobacco by the half pound. On July 13, 1803, he purchased one pound of tobacco, and another half pound on November 11 of the same year.

He apparently enjoyed reasonably good health during his life until his final years. The earliest record of illness occurred in the spring of 1793 while he was in the midst of preparing an ephemeris for the printers and was delayed in submitting his materials. He noted his account with his doctor in his Manuscript Journal. The amount due leads to the conclusion that he had been ill for some time:

1793
May 15   Due Doc^t. Hulse £5. 16. 8
         Cash paid him ....   3. 18. 9[21]

Approximately six years later Banneker was stricken with an illness that brought him close to death. The nature of his ailment was not recorded, but it lasted a long time. It was probably then that he reviewed his estate and decided its disposition. Tyson reported the illness as having occurred some years prior to Banneker's death. Convinced that he would not recover, he instructed his family in the specific disposition to be made of his personal possessions, but he did not put these instructions in writing.[22]

The illness probably occurred about 1799. The general concern for his health led the Ellicott brothers to complete a transfer of his land after his recovery in October of that year.

Banneker's weakness for liquor undoubtedly had undermined his health. This was remarked by several writers, among them Martha Tyson.[23] Concerning Banneker's mother, she wrote:

Being much attached to her son, she had watched over his best interests with prudent care; a care, which we regret to record, became necessary, from one great weakness that occasionally appeared in this, in other respects fair character. Inebriety was the ruling vice of the day, and he had sometimes been the victim of its influence.

Elsewhere she spoke again of his excesses, mentioning that he

. . . had not always refrained with prudence from intoxicating liquors. No one appeared to be more sensible of their debasing effect, than the subject of our notice; and, as to "know ourselves diseased is half a cure," he lamented his weakness, and gradually relieved himself of its fetters, not, however, until excess had impaired his strength, given him the appearance of premature old age, and produced the diseases which shortened his days.[24]

Another reference to this problem is mentioned in connection with Banneker's sojourn in the Federal Territory:

One matter, personal to himself, gave him great pleasure in the retrospect. *He had not, during his absence, tasted either wine or spiritous liquors.* He had experienced the fact that it was unwise for him to indulge, ever so slightly, in stimulating drinks. On this occasion he said, "I feared to trust myself even with wine, lest it steal away the little sense I have." He was a noble example of what may be accomplished by a firm resolve.[25]

A contemporary reference is found in an unpublished manuscript journal of the Reverend William Colbert, a Methodist Episcopalian minister who rode the Chester and Strassburg circuit in September 1799.[26] An entry for Sunday, September 22, reads as follows:

I preached at John Hagerty Paper Mill on Acts 3rd 19. Bro. Neel gave an exhortation. It appears to me, that if there was proper attention paid to the people in this place some might be brought to the knowledge of the truth. In the afternoon brother Neel preached at Benjamin Banneker's, this black man has acquired so much knowledge in the science of Astronomy as to attract the public notice in the calculation of several Almanacs but has become a great drunkard, for while bro. Neel was preaching on Rom. 6 & 23rd he was so drunk that he could hardly stand. I spoke a little at the grave as it was a funeral sermon.[27]

This passage brings to light certain facts that are of considerable interest in reconstructing Banneker's life. First, the presence of the Reverend Colbert and Brother Neel at his home to officiate at a burial implies that the deceased belonged to the Methodist Episcopal faith. Presumably, the person being buried was a member of Banneker's family, perhaps a nephew or niece. He might have been overcome with emotion over the loss, and grief rather than overindulgence could have accounted for his state at the graveside.

Perhaps too much of an issue has been made by past writers about Banneker's drinking. One possibility not previously suggested is that his occasional inebriate appearance may have been a symptom of the unidentified illness which eventually led to his death rather than of a weakness for liquor. Furthermore, if drinking to excess was indeed his failing, it was one common in his time at every level of society.

From his boyhood Banneker had a great love for mathematical puzzles, and he collected them at every opportunity. Several of these puzzles he copied into his astronomical journal. The first of them he recorded shortly after his return from the survey of Washington.[28] He identified the originator of the puzzle, or at least the person he acquired it from, as Major Andrew Ellicott, presumably during the period of their association in the Federal Territory.*

Another puzzle of somewhat different form was one Banneker seems to have recorded for Gerard Hopkins, as its title indicates.† Hopkins was a close friend and associate of George Ellicott, and his wife was the cousin of Elizabeth Brooke Elli-

---

* For the puzzle and Banneker's solution, see Document 20.
† For the problem and Banneker's solution, see Document 21.

cott. He was a learned man and a minister of the Society of Friends, associated with George in the latter's endeavors to improve the condition of the Indians; he accompanied George on a visit to the Indians at Fort Wayne in 1804. The puzzle was entered in the early part of the Manuscript Journal.[29]

The puzzles which Banneker collected and recorded in his journal were of varied type, but most of them were based on algebra.[30] They often dealt with farm animals and simple objects found around the home,[31] and also with subjects relating to his new scientific interests.*

The elderly farmer's interest in mathematical puzzles was well known to his acquaintances. They would bring examples of them to the store of Ellicott & Co. to give to Banneker when opportunity arose. This interest was described in an account of Banneker by Charles W. Dorsey, who recorded one such puzzle.† Dorsey worked as a clerk in the Ellicott store as a boy, from 1800 until he resigned to become a planter in Elkridge. He was about fifteen when he was first employed at the store. He had known Banneker during the last six or seven years of his life. Furthermore, he was a neighbor and lived with his family on the tract called "Three Brothers" near the Old Frederick Pike, about a mile west of Ellicott's Lower Mills. He later became a lifelong friend of the Ellicotts. In his recollections, Dorsey provided an interesting description of Banneker:

> He was fond of, and well qualified to work out, abstruse questions in arithmetic. I remember he brought to the store one which he had composed himself and presented to George Ellicott for solution. I had a copy, which I have since lost, but the character and deportment of the man were so wholly different from anything I had ever seen in one of his color; his question made so deep an impression on my mind that I have

* For other examples, see Documents 22 and 23. For the latter Banneker did not record a solution.

† See Document 24.

ever since retained a perfect recollection of it, except two lines, which do not alter the sense.

I remember George Ellicott was engaged in making out the answer, and cannot now say how he succeeded, but have no doubt he did. I have thus briefly given you my recollections of Benjamin Banneker. I was young when he died, and doubtless many incidents, from the time which has since elapsed, have passed from my recollection.[32]

The puzzle which Dorsey recorded was not included in Banneker's journal and may have been one that came to his attention near the end of his life.[33] His pursuit of arithmetical exercises throughout his life—from boyhood, he continued to collect them in his journal as late as 1801[34]—provides a circumstantial linking of his early attraction to mathematics with his later achievements with almanacs.*

Other than members of his family and his neighbors, visitors to Banneker's home, particularly strangers, were the exception rather than the rule. When a member of the "gentry," so-called, came to see him, it was an event to be remembered. One such visit was made in the summer of 1796 by Susanna, the wife of George Mason of Chester County, Pennsylvania.[35] During the great yellow-fever epidemic they lost a son and a daughter and a slave child, and Mrs. Mason suffered from the fever as well. Mason set out upon an expedition to the western territory to find a suitable place to establish his family, and upon her recovery Susanna moved with her children to the home of a sister in St. George's County near Baltimore. She was not destined to move westward, however, for one illness after another prevented the journey, and instead she moved about with her children from one friend's home to another, in Chester County, Philadelphia, and Baltimore. Meanwhile she took a great interest in the problems of those around her, and she established "a female association for the relief of the poor and afflicted of Baltimore."

* See Document 25.

Among Susanna's close friends was a distant cousin, Cassandra Hopkins Ellicott, the wife of John Ellicott of Lower Mills.[36] Cassandra had been widowed a few months before, and she welcomed Susanna's visit. It was during her prolonged stay with Cassandra that Susanna Mason learned about Benjamin Banneker and his meteoric career from tobacco farmer to almanac-maker. Her daughter, writing from notes that her mother had made after her visit to the Mills, reported:

> My mother, who ever felt a deep interest in this department of the human family, had a desire to see him. Accordingly she, her cousin C. Ellicott, and a number of young friends, walked thither. We found the venerable star-gazer under a wide-spreading pear tree, laden with delicious fruit; he came forward to meet us, and bade us welcome to his lowly dwelling. It was built of logs, one story in height, and surrounded by an orchard. In one corner of the room was suspended a wooden clock of his own construction, which was a true herald of departing hours.
>
> As no "thrifty wifie's" smile had ever enlightened his abode, I have no remembrance that neatness and comfort were conspicuously depicted there.
>
> He took down from a shelf a little book, wherein he registered the names of those by whose visits he thought himself honoured, and recorded my mother's upon the list; he then diffidently, but very politely requested her acceptance of a manuscript almanack, which she received with evident marks of gratification, derived from this interview with him.[37]

Susanna Mason reacted warmly to the aged almanac-maker. Several days after her visit, she addressed a poetic letter to him which her daughter subsequently included in her *Selections*.[38] She was particularly impressed with his scientific skill and concerned that

Thou need'st to have a special care
Thy conduct with thy talents square.
That no contaminating vice,
Obscure thy lustre in our eyes,
Or cast a shade upon thy merit
Or blast the praise thou might'st inherit. . . .*

Banneker was obviously greatly impressed by the compliment, particularly from a member of the gentry, and for a time he did not attempt a reply. Finally, he wrote to Mrs. Mason at the end of the following summer. He explained that his delay was due to ill health, and he begged excuse for his poor penmanship.

The letter in fact provides concrete evidence of his growing infirmity, for he was no longer able to write in the beautiful script of which he had always been so proud.[39]

August 26th 1797

Dear Female Friend
I have thought on you every day Sinc I saw you last, and on my promise in respect of composing Some verses for your amusement, but I am very much indisposed and have been ever Since time, I have a constant pain in my head, a palpitation in my flesh, and I may Say I am attended with a complication of disorders at this present writing, So that I cannot with any pleasure or delight gratify your curiosity in that particular at this present time, yet I Say my will is good to oblige you if I had it in my powers because you gave me good advice and edifying language in that piece of poetry which you was pleased to present unto me, and I can but love you and thank you for the same, and if ever it should be in my power to be Serviceable to you in

* For the poem in its entirety, see Document 26.

any measure, your resonable requests shall be armed
with the obedience of your Sincere well wisher—

B. Banneker

M.ʳˢ

Susanna Mason

N.B. the above is mean writing done by trembling hands

BB

Susanna died in 1805, a year before Banneker, after a long
illness, at the age of fifty-seven. The exchange of correspondence
was a touching one, and one that meant much to Banneker in
his final years.

During his later years, as Banneker found it increasingly
difficult to move about, he no longer was able to ride his horse
to Ellicott's Mills, and it was too great an effort to walk the
distance. Jacob Hall's young grandson came frequently, served
as his messenger and ran his errands. The boy was impressed
by this gentle old man who worked so assiduously among his
books and papers on the great table opposite the fireplace, and
he would find many excuses to run over to the Banneker farm
to spend time with him. He often helped with the milking of
the solitary cow which Benjamin kept and sometimes shared his
meals.

Banneker cooked his own meals, which were simple indeed.
He kept a fire in his hearth most of the time, and a two-gallon
iron kettle hung from the crane at all times. He would cut a
large piece of salt pork which was hung from one of the rafters
nearby and throw the piece into the kettle and let it simmer
away. When it had been boiled sufficiently, he would make
some corn dumplings, shaping the cornmeal in his hands until it
was hard, throw the dumplings into the kettle, and return to
his work. When finally the pangs of hunger, induced by the
odors from the bubbling kettle, drove him to eat, he would put
his work aside, clear a space on the table, and have his meal. The
fare was relatively constant, except for occasional greens from
his garden added to the menu.[40] He drank only milk with his
meals and never used coffee or tea.

This insight into Banneker's mode of life during his last few years was given to Bishop Payne almost half a century after Banneker's death by "Mr. H—, one of the local preachers residing at the Mills, who used to be his [Banneker's] messenger and errand boy." "Mr. H—" was probably the grandson of Jacob Hall, Benjamin's old schoolmate who later worked as caretaker of the Ellicott family cemetery at the Lower Mills until his own death in 1843.*

Despite his new preoccupation, Banneker found in his garden and his orchard the necessary relaxation from his nocturnal studies. He made various notations of these efforts.[41]

> 1798 November the 30th, planted 170 pare [sic] tree Sprouts.
> 1798 March 6th I planted in garden Nursery Some young pare [sic] trees, in the [part of page torn away]
> . . . in the same row 15 red kind grew near the old pare.[42]

In his Commonplace Book Banneker recorded that on April 24, 1802, he worked in his field holing corn; there were also several entries of charges to his tenants for pasturage. Entries made in the following year included:

> On the 26th of March, came Joshua Sanks with 3 or 4 bushels of turnips to feed the cows.
> 13th of April, 1803, planted beans and sowed cabbage seed.[43]

In general, however, in his last decade and a half Banneker enjoyed life as never before. He had found an outlet for his scientific instincts which was rewarding financially as well as

---

* Members of the Hall family continued to live in the vicinity of Banneker's farm to the present time, and a short distance from the site of Banneker's house there is an old abandoned family cemetery of the Hall family.

mentally, and each succeeding day and night became a new adventure.

His easy existence now permitted him to devote more time and thought to natural phenomena. He commented in his journal on the common things about him, with which he had been familiar all his life but which he now observed from a different point of view, because he had become more acutely aware of them, and reported these when he considered them sufficiently unusual.

One of his observations which was published and later widely reprinted, was a short paragraph on robber bees:

In the month of January, 1797, on a pleasant day for the Season I observed my honey bees to be out of their hives and Seemed very busy all but one hive, Upon examination I found all the bees had evacuated the hive and left not a drop of honey behind them, and on the 9th day of February ensuing, I killed the neighbouring hives of Bees, on a Special occasion, and found a great quantity of honey considering the season, which I imagine the Stronger had violently taken from the weaker and the weaker had persued them to their home resolved to be benefitted by their labour or die in the contest.[44]

The hives for beekeeping used in Banneker's time were skeps, which resembled inverted baskets made of plaited straw with two wooden cross-members inserted into the domed top of the structure, in which the bees built their comb. The bees commonly cultivated in Maryland in the eighteenth century were black German bees and were known and used for more than two centuries. It was virtually impossible to remove the honey from a skep without destroying the hive. The risk of angering the bees was overcome by blowing smoke, which is lethal to bees, into the hive, and killing the bees before removing the comb.[45]

Banneker's brief statement on bees, which appeared in the accounts by Latrobe and Tyson,[46] seems to have led later writers to the conclusion that Banneker had published a treatise on bee culture.[47] The assumption may have been strengthened by the inclusion in the almanac for 1792 of a short parable about "The Two Bees." [48] That Banneker was actually the author of the parable is doubtful, inasmuch as most of the literary content of his almanacs was provided by the printers. A careful search of Banneker's correspondence and writings and of the published literature has failed to bring to light any treatise on the subject.

Banneker inherited his interest in beekeeping from his father, who had established several hives on his farm soon after he acquired it. Whereas Robert's interest in bees was primarily for the production of honey, which was then one of the few, and perhaps only, sweetening agents available for his family, Benjamin's interest was more extensive. In addition to the practical aspects of apiculture, Banneker had demonstrated that he was also an amateur naturalist, and he took great pleasure in watching the bees at work.

Of equal interest was a somewhat longer observation on the subject of "locusts" which Banneker reported in his journal approximately three years later:

The first great Locust year that I can Remember was 1749. I was then about Seventeen years of age when thousands of them came and was creeping up the trees and bushes, I then immagined they came to eat and destroy the fruit of the Earth, and would occation a famine in the land, I therefore began to kill and destroy them, but soon saw that my labor was in vain, therefore gave over my pretension. Again in the year 1766, which is Seventeen years after their first appearance, they made a Second, and appeared to me to be full as numerous as the first. I then, being about thirty-four years of age had more sense than to endeavour to destroy them, knowing they were not so pernicious to the fruit of the Earth as I did immagine they would be. Again in the year 1783 which was Seventeen years Since their Second appearance to me, they made their third; and they may be expected again in the year 1800, which is Seventeen years Since their third appearance to me. So that if I may venture So to express it, their periodical return is Seventeen years, but they, like the Comets, make but a short stay with us—The female has a Sting in her tail as sharp and hard as a thorn, with which she perforates the branches of the trees, and in them holes lays eggs. The branch soon dies and fall, then the egg by some Occult cause immerges a great depth into the earth and there continues for the Space of Seventeen years as aforesaid.

B. Banneker.[49]

Banneker signed a number of his entries with his full signature, which may mean that he had intended to include them in the published almanacs, and thus distinguished them as his original work and not copied from other sources. The entry on the locusts, which was complete as written, was followed by this insert which he added some years later:

I like to forgot to inform, that if their lives are Short they are merry, they begin to Sing or make a noise from the first they come out of Earth till they die, the hindermost part rots off, and it does not appear to be any pain to them for they still continue on Singing till they die.

Banneker's account described not the true locust or migratory grasshopper which periodically caused devastation in large sections of the American colonies recorded for several years in the mid-eighteenth century and again at the end of the century, [50] but the seventeen-year locust or periodical cicada (*Tibi-*

cina septendecim) which is prevalent on the North American continent.[51]

Ever since his childhood, Banneker was a deeply religious man, though he never joined any denomination. He favored the Society of Friends, however, and he frequently attended their meetings. He was especially interested in attending when ministers or speakers came from other places. The Ellicott family made certain that he was informed of such occasions, and they habitually sent a messenger to notify him. Mrs. Tyson remarked:

> We have seen Banneker in Elkridge Meeting house, where he always sat on the form nearest the door, his head uncovered . . . in quiet contemplation.[52]

Later he attended the Friends Meeting House, constructed at Ellicott's Lower Mills by the Ellicott family. Tyson, in her second account, expanded on the subject somewhat:

> His life was one of constant worship in the great temples of nature and science. In his early days, places of worship were rare. As they increased in number during his later years, he would occasionally visit those of the various denominations. He finally gave a decided preference for the doctrines and form of worship of the Society of Friends, whose meeting-house at Ellicott's Mills he frequently attended.
>
> The author well remembers Banneker's appearance on these occasions, when he always sat on the form nearest the door. He presented a most dignified aspect as he leaned in quiet contemplation on a long staff, which he always carried after passing his seventieth year. "And he worshipped leaning on the top of his staff." His reverent deportment on these occasions added to the natural majesty of his appearance.[53]

The Meeting House at Ellicott's Lower Mills had been built by the Ellicott family in 1800 to accommodate the local residents of their own faith. It stood on the top of Quaker Hill on the western side of the Patapsco River and was named Elkridge Meeting House. That same year, the old Elkridge Meeting House, which had been used as a place of worship since 1670, was abandoned. The building was located in an attractive rural setting but it was old and small and uncomfortable, and access was made by crossing the Patapsco River. It was situated at Elkridge, about a mile from Ilchester. At the time that the new building was opened at the Mills, the congregation numbered 120 Friends, and meetings were held on the first day of each week and again on the fourth day following. The members attended the monthly meetings at Indian Spring in what is now Prince George's County, near the Pawtuxent River.

Familiar with the Bible from earliest childhood, when he spent hours reading from its pages to his grandmother, he kept a Bible of his own to the end of his life. He was thirty-two years of age when he acquired it, and it served him for his lifetime. Inscribed in the volume, in addition to a record of his own birth and his father's death, was the statement:

I bought this book of HONORA BUCKANAN, the 4th day of January, 1763.[54]

Interspersed throughout his manuscript journal are passages which he apparently copied from his Bible for later reference and possibly for use on appropriate occasions.

The religious notes were made at random. One which he considered worthy of preservation was the following:

2 Kings Chap. 23, verse 11, And he took away the horses that the kings of Judah had given to the Sun.[55]

The passage relates to Josiah, the king of Jerusalem, who as a young man responded to the call of God and set about to reform the city.

On the same page Banneker inscribed a quotation from II Samuel 12:31, which was concerned with the same theme:

And he brought away the people that were therein and
put them under Laws, and under harrows of iron, and
under axes of iron, and made them pass through the
brick-kiln.

Here again the theme was the curse of cities, when Jerusalem
was as full of sorrow and strife as any other city, caused by sin.

Banneker also liked proverbs, and he occasionally copied
them into his notes, again with the idea of using them in the
almanacs, although these particular ones were never included.

Our distilled Spirits are like unto the water of the river
of Phrygia, which, if drank sparingly, purges the brains
and cures madness, but otherwise it infects the brains
and creates madness. See Enticks Dictionary page 458.[56]

Another proverb or maxim which Banneker found of interest was the following:

Evil Communications Corrupts good manners, I hope
to live to hear that Good Communications Corrects
bad manners.[57]

Banneker was able to consider religion from a humorous
point of view, as the following anecdote preserved among his
other notations shows:

A very melting Sermon on being preached one day
which caused all the Congregation to weep but one
man, which attracted the notice of the people, after
Sermon, a curious inquirer demanded his reason for not
weeping as well as the rest of the congregation, he
pertinently reply'd I do not belong to the parish.[58]

At various times during his adult life Banneker attempted
to produce literary essays which purported to be accounts of
his dreams. Whether they actually were dreams cannot be de-

termined; he described them as such, but they seem rather his fantasies, which may have been the result of his preoccupation with religion. The earliest of these has survived in a manuscript entitled "A Remarkable Dream" and dated October 1762.[59] This was written almost a decade before Banneker's association with the Ellicott family, and even longer before his inclination toward scholarly pursuits had evidenced itself.*

Several other examples of these dreams or fantasies were recorded by Banneker in his journal; for the most part they seem to have been added during the earlier part of his so-called scholarly period. This continued preoccupation with developing a literary style as well as the emphasis on macabre subjects may have some significance beyond the apparent text of the written examples, of which four others occur elsewhere in his manuscript journal.† Pervasive throughout these "dreams" is the feeling that Banneker was attempting to develop a form of self-expression. Were these actually dreams, or were they literary efforts? Is it not more likely that they were mystical fantasies, ranging from the search for Rasannah Crandolph's soul,[60] his skirmish with "the Infernal Spirit," [61] the touching language of his encounter with a white fawn,[62] and finally his great distress over a child that had hurt its head? [63]

Of equal interest are the occasional glimpses of Banneker's way of life, seen in some of his other notes, such as the following:

> "Some say that it is dangerous to let blood in the Dog days, but I question it, because that, on the 30th Aug.ᵗ 1796 which was 4 days before the expiration of the Dog Days, no harm ensues.—I bled John Minney——" [64]

The identity of John Minney is uncertain, but it is noted that on August 10, 1792, he had sold to John Nimiy, a cooper of that region, a section of sixty-four perches or two and a half

* See Document 27.
† See Documents 28 through 31 inclusive.

acres of land of his farm, Stout. The resemblance of the names suggests that they were one and the same, and that the recorder of the indenture may have been in error. For Banneker to have parted with a small section of his beloved farm at this time indicates that it must have been to a relative. It is not too farfetched to assume that John Minney, or Nimiy, was the son-in-law of one of his sisters living nearby. The fact that he bled him also implies that Minney may have been a close relative.

As the years wore on, Banneker reduced his farming to the most necessary chores, and even his astronomical endeavors diminished, although his interest continued as strong as ever. His physical infirmities increased, and it became difficult for him to keep his long nightly vigils observing the stars. This is reflected in the pages of his manuscript journal. He continued to make his calculations through the year of 1803 and he completed those for January 1804. Random calculations for that year occur in the journal, but the ephemeris was never completed. The latest entry which appeared in the journal was the inscription "January 1805."

Despite his reduced activity, Banneker continued to maintain a daily schedule. Each morning he set forth from his house for a walk to observe his beloved hills, some of which rose nearby almost as guardians of his house and orchard and provided a windbreak from the winter winds, and others that were visible in the distance over the Patapsco River, where they provided a picturesque frame for the view.

He took his final walk on the morning of October 9, 1806. It was a Sunday. The crisp autumn air was invigorating and he enjoyed the bright sunshine as he followed his accustomed route. He met an acquaintance, and for a short interval they stopped to talk. Suddenly, Banneker felt unwell, and excused himself. His acquaintance walked with him back to his house, and waited until Banneker stretched himself out on his couch in the large room. He never spoke again, and in a short while he was dead.

His family was summoned immediately. His sisters and

nephews soon arrived on the scene. His death did not come as a surprise, for Banneker had lived exactly a month short of his seventy-fifth birthday. His family remembered his instructions and followed them to the letter. One of his nephews was delegated to carry the news to Ellicott's Mills. Banneker's instructions for the disposition of his personal property were also recalled, and the nephew hitched up a horse to a cart and loaded thereon all of those items which were to be given to his old friend George Ellicott. These included the old oval table, all of his scientific instruments, and a collection of several books including the references on surveying and astronomy. These items had all been gifts or lent him from time to time by George, and it was only fitting that they should be returned to him. To these were added the only treasures that Banneker owned, his Manuscript Journal of astronomical calculations and his daily commonplace book.[65]

The remainder of his possessions he left to be divided equally between his two sisters, Minta Black and Molly Morten. Of these, only two items survived. Several months prior to his death, he had presented a featherbed to one of his sisters. Some years later she felt a hard object among the feathers, and upon examination she discovered it to be a purse of gold coins. Banneker had apparently saved this small hoard for a rainy day in anticipation of his growing disability. He may have forgotten its existence at the time he gave his sister the bed. At any rate, apparently there was cause for fear of robbery in his lifetime, as proved by several attempts on his life and property.

The only other possession known to have been preserved was Banneker's Bible. It was removed from his house at the time of his death and before the funeral, probably by one of his sisters. It may in fact have been used at his burial. It remained in the possession of his family well into the nineteenth century.

Banneker's funeral was held two days after his death, on Tuesday, October 11. Just as his body was being lowered into the grave a few yards away, his house caught fire. The old wooden building blazed away rapidly, and before help arrived, the entire structure had burned to the ground. Nothing of its contents was saved. His clothing, the few bits of furniture, his manuscript copies of his almanacs, and his personal library were all consumed, as well as the well-worn wooden striking clock that had served him for more than forty years. It seemed almost as if an act of fate was determined to destroy every earthly vestige of the Negro sage with the extinction of his life.

Banneker's death did not pass unnoticed. An obituary appeared in the *Federal Gazette* on October 28, 1806, which well described Banneker's way of life—modest, like his contributions.

On Sunday, the 9th instant, departed this life at his residence in Baltimore county, in the 73d [sic] year of his age, Mr. BENJAMIN BANNEKER, a black man, and immediate descendant of an African father. He was well known in his neighborhood for his quiet and peaceable demeanor, and among scientific men as an astronomer and mathematician. In early life he was instructed in the most common rules of arithmetic, and thereafter, with the assistance of different authors, he was enabled to acquire a perfect knowledge of all the higher branches of learning. Mr. B was the calculator of several almanacs which were published in this, as well as some of the neighboring states, and although of late years none of his almanacs were published, yet he never failed to calculate one every year, and left them among his papers, prefering solitude to mixing with society, and devoted the greatest part of his time in reading and contemplation, and to no books was he more attached than the scriptures. At his decease he bequeathed all his astronomical and philosophical books and paper to a friend.

Mr. Banneker is a prominent instance to prove that a descendant of Africa is susceptible of as great mental improvement and deep knowledge into the mysteries of nature as that of any other nation.[66]

X

THE MAN REMEMBERED

❖❀❖❀❖❀❖❀❖❀❖❀❖❀❖❀❖

> There is no reputation so great but requires a little
> indulgence.
> "Extracts from the Common-Place Book of the Ken-
> tucky Philosopher," *Banneker's Almanac for 1794*

BANNEKER THE MAN is remembered in five descriptions written
by those who knew him during his lifetime, one portrait claimed
to have been drawn from life, and numerous biographical
sketches and published references, of which only four were based
on contemporary sources.

The several physical descriptions of Banneker are based
on personal observation, and are consistent in their portrayal
of the amateur astronomer during the last decade of his life.
The earliest of these was by an unnamed correspondent in a

letter to Benjamin H. Ellicott* in 1844 or 1845, as reported
by Latrobe:

> His head was covered with a thick suit of white hair,
> which gave him a very venerable and dignified appear-
> ance. His dress was uniformly of super fine drab broad
> cloth, made in the old style of a plain coat, with
> straight collar and long waistcoat, and a broad brimmed
> hat. His colour was not jet black, but decidedly negro.
> In size and personal appearance, the statue of Franklin
> at the Library in Philadelphia, as seen from the street,
> is the perfect likeness of him. . . .[1]

The statue of Franklin to which Ellicott's correspondent
referred was the one installed in 1790 in a niche on the façade
of the building housing the Library Company of Philadelphia.[2]
Curiously enough, the statue was not an accurate representation
of Franklin. The figure had been based on sketches, not drawn
from life, although the features were based on a head of Franklin
by Caffieri. The implication in the statement, therefore, is not
that Banneker resembled Franklin, but that he resembled the
statue.†

Some comments on Banneker's appearance were recorded
also by Charles Worthington Dorsey, who recalled:

> He was very precise in conversation and exhibited deep
> reflection. His deportment, whenever I saw him, was
> perfectly upright and correct, and he seemed to be

---

* Benjamin H. Ellicott (1796–1867) was the son of Elias and continued
the family mills and merchandising operations of Ellicott & Co. There
are several other members of the family with the same name in the same
period, including Benjamin Ellicott (1809–1863), the son of Jonathan,
but the correspondent appears to be the first named.

† The statue was replaced in 1959 with an exact copy by Lewis
Iselin, Jr., and the original is presently preserved in the collection of
the Library Company of Philadelphia.

acquainted with everything of importance that was passing in the country. . . . He was a large man and inclined to be fleshy. He was far advanced in years when I saw him. . . .[3]

Another member of the Ellicott family, Thomas,* described the amateur astronomer to his niece, Martha Tyson, in the following words:

I remember Benjamin Bannekers personal appearance very well. I remember much that was said about him by my elder Brothers, and other persons, at times, when I visited them at Ellicotts Mills; but as I never lived at that place, during Bannekers life term, I can say nothing that ought to be incorporated in to a Biographical memorial of his life.—I recollect he was quite a black man, of medium stature, of uncommonly soft and gentlemanly manners, and pleasant coloquial powers, and like *other* gentlemen of that day had not abstained from the use of intoxicating drink—though I think I never saw him improperly influenced by it. He owned I think about 50 acres of Land, about half a mile from the mills, which he conveyed to Ellicott & Co., a few years before his death, reserving to himself a life estate in it, and a yearly payment, during his life, of a Sum of money sufficient to supply his wants. How much that sum was, I do not remember, nor the time of his death.[4]

Finally there was the memory of him retained by Martha Tyson, who had seen him at the Elkridge Meeting House when she was a young woman. She remembered:

* Thomas Ellicott was a son of Andrew Ellicott [III] by a second marriage, and a younger half-brother of George Ellicott.

His ample forehead, white hair, and reverent deportment, gave him a very venerable appearance, as he
leaned on the long staff (which he always carried with
him) in contemplation.[5]

Later, in her posthumously published account, she described him again in virtually the same words, but at greater
length:

> The countenance of Banneker had a most benign and
> thoughtful expression. A fine head of white hair sur-
> mounted his unusually broad and ample forehead,
> whilst the lower part of his face was slender and slop-
> ing towards the chin. His figure was perfectly erect,
> showing no inclination to stoop as he advanced in
> years. His raiment was always scrupulously neat; that
> for summer wear, being of unbleached linen, was
> beautifully washed and ironed by his sisters. . . . In
> cold weather he dressed in light colored cloth, a fine
> drab broadcloth constituting his attire when he de-
> signed appearing in his best style.[6]

Although details are meager, these descriptions create a
general impression of Banneker in his later years from which
it is possible to visualize his appearance. They are somewhat at
variance, however, with the only contemporary portrait which
was purportedly drawn from life. This first portrait appeared
as a woodcut on the title page of the Banneker almanac for
1795 printed for the Baltimore distributor, John Fisher. There
is no comment concerning the portrait in the almanac's contents, nor is any mention of it made in the papers of Banneker
or of those involved in the almanac's publication. The artist has
not been identified but the portrait may have been the work of
John Fisher, who was also an engraver. Little is known about
him, other than that he had lived in Philadelphia at the time of the

Revolution. The Journals of the Continental Congress recorded on June 26, 1773, that John Fisher was owed twenty dollars for renewing copper plates for loan-office certification and making two letters for the device utilized in thirty-dollar bills.[7]

A number of the persons involved in various aspects of the book trade in Philadelphia moved to Baltimore, and Fisher may have been one of these.

The woodcut constitutes a representation of Banneker drawn with a tendency to idealize his appearance. It represents a Negro male in his late youth or early middle age, of medium frame. At this time Banneker was sixty-three years of age, and his physical appearance undoubtedly already reflected to some degree his past illnesses and discomfort. He was described as being relatively fleshy, which leaves no doubt that the portrait was in fact no more than an artist's conjecture of his appearance.*

A portrait of Banneker in another edition of his almanac for 1795 was considerably less successful. On the cover of the edition published by Samuel and John Adams at their Baltimore print shop was what seems to be a copy of the portrait as it appeared on the Fisher edition. The outline of the figure is identical in almost every detail but presumably the printers did not have a competent artist or draftsman, for the space within the outline is filled with vague, meaningless lines. It seems as if the portrait had been copied in an effort to make the purchaser assume that the almanac was the one published for Fisher.

The earliest account of Banneker's life and achievements was the letter from Senator James McHenry which was published in the almanac for 1792. In addition to serving as an introduction to the work of the almanac-maker, the letter was published separately again and again through 1793, usually without editorial comment or explanation.

The first acknowledgment made of Banneker in print other

---

* Although Shirley Graham stated in her fictionalized biography of Banneker that the portrait was executed at the Mills by an artist named Timothy Wood, no information about an artist of that name can be found.

than the McHenry letter was a brief reference in a work by Gilbert Imlay, published in 1793 in London, in which, however, he was not mentioned by name.[8] The reference was made in relation to an attack upon Thomas Jefferson's position on slavery, and it was in this connection that Banneker's name was repeatedly brought to public notice within the next decade. It is necessary to recapitulate briefly the question of antislavery for a fuller understanding of its importance at this time.

The cause of slaves in the New World had engendered a growing sympathy even from the end of the seventeenth century, particularly in New England. Samuel Sewall had published his work on *Selling of Joseph* in 1729, which was a criticism of the slavery traffic, at a time when legislation against slavery was being prepared in Boston. This was followed by a growing opposition in the Society of Friends against the purchase of slaves, and during the next century Quaker leaders such as John Woolman and Anthony Benezet popularized the concept that slavery was unchristian. With the advent of the War of Independence, the doctrine of natural rights which led to the Revolution helped to emphasize the evils of slavery. Once again the Society of Friends assumed the burden of a national conscience. An exchange of correspondence between Quakers on both sides of the Atlantic developed into an antislavery movement which erupted into positive action in the new republic at the end of the war.

Leaders of the American abolitionist movement exerted a strong effect on English Quakers who were leading the British antislavery movement. The American colonies' war to overthrow the British yoke was being compared with the enslavement of the Negro. Thomas Paine's tract in 1775 appeared the same year in which the first American antislavery society was formed in Philadelphia with Benjamin Franklin as its president. During the next several years, while some of the American colonies were enacting laws to prevent future importation of slaves, motions were being introduced into the British Parliament against the slave trade. By the end of the war, the English

Quakers had developed sufficient strength to launch an organized attack, and succeeded in consolidating the abolitionist forces in Great Britain sufficiently to present an Abolition Act in Parliament by 1787. This won the support of William Wilberforce, William Pitt, and Granville Sharp. During the next few years the cause of abolition became of increasing importance throughout the British Empire until it reached a climax with the great battle in Parliament led by Wilberforce in the spring of 1792. Considerable influence on the movement in England was derived from events that took place elsewhere throughout the world during the previous year. The French Revolution had developed into its most violent phase in 1791 and the ensuing events in the conflict in France brought about a violent reaction in England. At the same time the French Revolution affected its colonies overseas, and in 1791 the uprising of the mulattoes in Santo Domingo resulted in massacres of white men on the island and the destruction of considerable property. A chain reaction developed, and slaves of other French islands revolted. Pitt seized the opportunity and changed his position from advocacy of gradual abolition of slavery to urging immediate abolition. The House of Commons followed his lead and recommended the termination of the slave trade by 1796.

The wild enthusiasm for the antislavery movement which developed in England in 1792 did not sustain itself, however, and the deliberations of the House of Lords succeeded in diminishing its support in the following year. The movement dwindled by 1800, and it was not until four years later that the campaign for the abolition of the slave trade was renewed.

During this period the abolitionist societies were avidly seeking candidates to demonstrate the Negro's intellectual endowments as justification for his receiving equal rights. Dramatic examples of Negro achievement were difficult to find in any numbers. Dr. Benjamin Rush had discovered James Derham, a Negro physician in New Orleans, and he also brought to light an untutored mathematical prodigy in Alexandria named Thomas Fuller. Phillis Wheatley had demonstrated her genius as a poet, and to the list could be added the Negro ministers Richard Allen and Absalom Jones, of Philadelphia, and Prince Hall, a publicist of Boston. It was thus with considerable interest that the Maryland and Pennsylvania Abolition Societies made every possible attempt to bring Benjamin Banneker to public notice after they discovered him, for he was the unique example of achievement in the sciences.

It was no accident that, with the assured publication of his almanac for 1792, Banneker forwarded a manuscript copy of his ephemeris for that work to Thomas Jefferson, then Secretary of State. Jefferson's interest in persons of scientific achievement was well known, and his sincere desire to promote the sciences was undisputed. His position on the subject of slavery was also well known, and any comments he might make about Banneker's accomplishment would be useful to the abolitionist movement.[9]

Banneker provided no indication in his letter to Jefferson that he was aware of the latter's position or writings relating to Negro slavery, and gave no hint that he had read the latter's *Notes on Virginia*. It seems unlikely, on reviewing the situation after the passage of almost two centuries, that Banneker's patrons would not have been aware of the impact of the incident. Knowing his nature and integrity, however, he would not have been party to a deliberate plot to place the statesman in an embarrassing position. Banneker wrote his letter from the heart, meaning every word, but perhaps with the encouragement of others who were aware of how the ensuing correspondence could be used. It was not in Banneker's character, as shown in those reported events prior to and following this correspondence, to seek Jefferson's attention. He was at all times pleased with his own achievements and the acknowledgment made of them, and he at no time sought to solicit praise. Nor had he shown any particular concern for the cause of slavery, despite his own family's involvement. Other than his letter to Jefferson, Banneker's awareness of slavery was evident only in a brief poem he wrote during the same period. Martha Tyson's observation about this aspect of Banneker's career was the following:

He appears to have been the pioneer in the movement in this part of the world, towards the improvement of his race; at a period of our history when the negro occupied almost the lowest possible grade in the scale of human beings, Banneker had struck out for himself a course, hitherto untravelled by men of his class, and had already earned a respectable position amongst men of science.[10]

Jefferson's reply to Banneker was straightforward and written very much in the same manner in which he responded to the many others who submitted their proposals or evidence of achievement in the field of science. The publication of the two letters in the Banneker almanac of 1793, as well as in a separate pamphlet, must have brought realization to Jefferson of the trap into which he had fallen and the use that would undoubtedly be made of it by his political enemies. In the controversy that ensued over Jefferson's candidacy for the presidency a few years later, he was attacked simultaneously from both sides, by those who foresaw in the liberation of Negro slaves a danger to the entire property system in the Southern states, and by those who supported the abolition of slavery. Banneker emerged from these attacks as the symbol of the oppressed Negro. In fact, he was far from oppressed, and had lived a half century and more in peaceful content.

Jefferson's critics lost no time in pointing out the apparent inconsistencies between the statements in his reply to Banneker and the position he had taken on the subject of the Negro in his *Notes on Virginia* some years earlier. William Loughton Smith was among the first to comment:

> What shall we think of a *secretary of state* thus fraternizing with negroes, writing them complimentary epistles, stiling them *his black brethren*, congratulating them on the evidences of their *genius*, and assuring them of his good wishes for their speedy emancipation?[11]

Smith's attack on Jefferson as a presidential candidate was vicious, and not at all times rational. He launched his barbs in both directions, for he described Banneker as "the *reputed* author of an Almanac," implying that he might have been given the credit for the work of others.

Again in 1800 Jefferson was the subject of an attack by Henry W. De Sassure in a public statement which was subsequently printed. As a candidate for the presidency, De Sassure found Jefferson vulnerable on a number of points, including his reply to Banneker, and he attempted to prove that Jefferson's election would be detrimental to the interests of the Southern states.[12]

The attacks continued, and in 1806 Thomas Green Fessenden added his comments on the President's attitude on the subject, again using his letter to Banneker to illustrate his position.[13]

In general, the published attacks on Jefferson because of his position on Negro slavery sought to point out that his error may have been in not having endorsed Banneker's achievement as an example of intellectual activity but rather as evidence of moral eminence. If he had acknowledged Banneker's work as an example of scientific accomplishment, as had such other prominent American figures in the field of science as David Rittenhouse and Andrew Ellicott, the presumed implication of Negro inferiority claimed in Jefferson's reply would not have emerged as a major issue.[14]

Following the occasional references which appeared in connection with the attacks on Jefferson, Banneker was first memorialized in a work on Negro literature by Henri Gregoire, Bishop of Blois, which was published in Paris in 1808. Gregoire was a great libertarian who devoted his lifetime to the politically and socially oppressed. He produced the first study made of Negro literature, in which he presented each of the arguments being made against the mental and moral faculties of the Negro, with his own rebuttal to each of them. Gregoire collected biographical sketches of fifteen Negroes of note, including Banneker. This brief account featured Jefferson's reply to Banneker, and incorporated a number of factual errors. The author's sources were the McHenry letter and the brief references he had found in the works of Imlay and Fessenden. He was not aware of Banneker's death two years earlier.[15]

Gregoire's presentation of Banneker's life tends to support the possibility that Jefferson's letter to the Marquis de Condorcet with Banneker's manuscript was not submitted to the Académie des Sciences. The bishop would have been the first to have been informed of it, and would have exerted every effort to publicize it. As an active member of the Société des Amis des Noirs he would have found Jefferson's communication particularly valuable as propaganda for the French antislavery movement. Even more conclusive is the fact that Gregoire would have mentioned the letter and the manuscript in his correspondence with Jefferson on the subject of his book, a copy of which he had forwarded to him as President of the United States. The latter acknowledged the gift and closed his letter with the expressed hope that the Bishop would ". . . accept my thanks for the many instances you have enabled me to observe of respectable intelligence in that race of men, which cannot fail to have effect in hastening the days of their relief." [16]

Jefferson's politeness to Gregoire was not completely sincere, and in a letter to his friend Joel Barlow, which he wrote shortly thereafter, he commented on his correspondence with Gregoire and on his book in rather uncomplimentary terms.[17] He described the work as having been assembled without discrimination or relation to truth or fiction. Furthermore, despite his own reply to Banneker, Jefferson had apparently had cause to reflect further and had come to the conclusion that he could not, after all, entertain a high opinion of either the amateur astronomer's work or his mental ability:

Bishop Gregoire wrote to me on the doubts I had expressed five or six and twenty years ago, in the *Notes on Virginia*, as to the grade of understanding of the negroes. His credulity had made him gather up every

story he could find of men of color (without distin-
guishing whether black, or of what degree of mixture),
however slight the mention, or light the authority on
which they are quoted. The whole do not amount in
point of evidence, to what we know ourselves about
Banneker. We know he had spherical trigonometry
enough to make almanacs, but not without the suspicion of aid from Ellicot, who was his neighbor and
friend, and never missed an opportunity of puffing
him. I have a long letter from Banneker, which shows
him to have had a mind of very common stature indeed. It was impossible for doubt to have been more
tenderly or hesitatingly expressed than that was in the
Notes on Virginia, and nothing was or is further from
my intentions, than to enlist myself as the champion of
a fixed opinion, where I have only expressed a doubt.
St. Domingo will, in time, throw light on the question.

Jefferson's comments about Banneker come as somewhat of
a surprise after having read his letter acknowledging receipt
of the manuscript ephemeris and the one to the Marquis de
Condorcet. His reference to "the suspicion of aid from Ellicot
who was his neighbor and friend, and never missed an opportunity of puffing him" deserves some comment. The Ellicott
who was Banneker's neighbor and friend, namely, George, did
not calculate ephemerides for almanacs, while Andrew Ellicott,
who did make such calculations for a series of almanacs, was
neither a neighbor nor particularly Banneker's friend. It is true
that Jefferson had expressed himself on the Negro question most
tenderly and hesitatingly in his *Notes on Virginia*, but there is
considerable question whether Banneker was aware of this work
and had read it.

In 1836 the first American account of Banneker's career
was published in a volume of collected letters and manuscripts
of Susanna Mason which included a memoir of her life by
her daughter Rachel.[18] In this work Rachel related that while

she was visiting friends at Ellicott's Mills a short time before the book's publication, she was reminded of her mother's visit to Banneker. With several of her friends, she set out across the countryside to revisit the site of the farm, only to discover that "memory has not chart whereby to direct our steps," and they failed to find it. Others in the region told her that the pear tree and the orchard still remained, although all evidence of the log house had perished.*

Social and political events of the decades that followed had the desirable effect of periodically reviving Banneker's name as an outstanding member of his race. In 1844 John H. B. Latrobe of Baltimore was chiefly responsible for the founding of the American Colonization Society, and was instrumental in the establishment of the Maryland Historical Society in the same year. He compiled a memoir of Banneker which he read before the members of the Maryland Historical Society and then published it in the *Maryland Colonization Journal* during the following year.[19]

Latrobe utilized such original materials as Banneker's Manuscript Journal and commonplace book, which had been loaned to the Maryland Historical Society, and in addition to assistance from Martha E. Tyson, he had the benefit also of a compilation of information about Banneker made by Benjamin H. Ellicott from those who remembered him.

His *Memoir* was one of the most important source works and provided the first comprehensive account of Banneker's life and work. It proved to be a popular account, and was reprinted again and again in books and periodicals in the years that followed.

At about the same time Banneker became the subject of preoccupation of yet another prominent figure in Baltimore. The Reverend Daniel Alexander Payne had been assigned to the Bethel Church of the African Methodist Church in 1845. In the early part of that first year in his new parish the Reverend

* For the full account see Document 32.

Payne learned about the self-taught astronomer and was intrigued with the story of his life. He prepared a lecture about Banneker's life and work which he delivered at his church with the purpose of inspiring the young men of his parish to pursue the sciences. At the same time he used the lecture, when opportunity presented itself, to raise funds for erecting a monument over Banneker's grave.

On July 9, 1845, Payne headed a committee of three men of his church that set out to find the site of Banneker's burial place. At Ellicott's Lower Mills they were conducted by residents in the area across the fields of Banneker's farm to the spot which had served as the Banneker family graveyard. Payne subsequently reported:

> Beneath two tulip-trees, so grown as to seem one, lay the mortal remains of the black astronomer of Maryland. A few yards to the north-west of the grave was the site of his house, not a vestige of which could then be seen. It was marked only by a shallow cavity, at the south-eastern end of which stood a tall Lombardy poplar, said to be that which overshadowed the gable end of his house. . . .[20]

Payne, who later become a bishop of the A. M. E. Church, did not succeed in raising sufficient funds for erecting the monument. However, with the assistance of John H. B. Latrobe, a design for such a monument was prepared by R. Cary Long, Jr., a prominent architect of Baltimore. It is impressive to learn that Long's assistance had been enlisted for designing the modest little monument, inasmuch as he had succeeded his father as the foremost architect of Baltimore. His specialty was church architecture and he distinguished himself with the use of a military Gothic style. For a brief period, during which he had been contacted by Payne and Latrobe in relation to the Banneker monument, he had become interested in an Egyptian style of design, particularly for cemetery structures.[21] The design he produced for the Banneker monument was in the form of an Egyptian obelisk.*

Bishop Payne's interest in Banneker did not diminish despite his unsuccessful attempt to memorialize his grave. During the years between 1858 and 1862 he served as editor of the periodical *Repository of Religion, Science and Literature*, and during that period he wrote a series of articles on Banneker which he published in the *Repository*.[22]

Another effort to revive the name and accomplishments of Banneker was made several decades after his death by the Baltimore philanthropist, Moses Sheppard, who spent a large part of his fortune on behalf of free Negroes who had been manumitted by their masters but had not been set free by the heirs. He donated in funds and in books and by other means to Negroes in Africa. Sheppard (1771–1857) was a well-known Quaker philanthropist who, although a native of Philadelphia, lived most of his life in Baltimore. The espousal of the Loyalist cause by his father, Nathan Sheppard, resulted in the forfeiture of his property and caused young Moses to seek his own career at an early age. He worked as a clerk with John Mitchell and later became his partner and finally his successor. After his retirement from business in 1832 he devoted all his energies and much of his wealth to the antislavery movement, and he was a supporter of the American Colonization Society.[23] He provided funds also for the education of Samuel McGill and other Negroes who played an important role in the development of Liberia, and he was instrumental in preventing the passage of a law to banish free Negroes from Maryland. Upon his death in 1857 his estate was bequeathed to the founding of the Sheppard asylum for the insane in Baltimore.

He was a member of the Maryland Historical Society and spent much of his time almost daily in its reading rooms as well

* The drawing was preserved by Bishop Payne among his papers at Wilberforce University Library, but it seems not to have survived.

as at the Baltimore Library. He became interested in Benjamin Banneker from reading the memoir by Latrobe.

It was during the same period that Sheppard found Banneker's manuscript astronomical journal in the Society's collections in which, in 1852, it had been deposited by a member of the Ellicott family. Martha E. Tyson noted that "the manuscripts . . . were enclosed in a rustic cover of parchment of antique appearance" and that Sheppard "had them bound in Russia leather." [24] She pointed out further that the manuscripts comprised two separate volumes, one being a large volume of astronomical and other notations, the second described as "his common-place book." [25] Latrobe had furthermore commented on the old farmer's writing in these volumes,[26] noting that it ". . . is very good and remarkably distinct, having a practised look, although evidently that of an old man, who makes his letters and figures slowly and carefully." *

When Sheppard discovered the journal, he was particularly intrigued with the copies of the correspondence with Jefferson and undertook to have the two letters reproduced in a large lithograph for distribution. In addition to the reproduction of the two letters, a short descriptive text was added, which may have been prepared for him by Latrobe.†

This project was recorded in some detail in a series of letters from Sheppard written to several significant figures of the day. The earliest, dated January 20, 1852, was addressed to Latrobe, with whom he worked closely over a period of years in the antislavery cause.

> I agreed with Hoen & Co to Lithograph Bannaker and Jefferson's letters, they got the original when you were absent. I wanted you to edit it, thier shop is in one of Hopkins's row 2nd Street, will you take the trouble to call and give them any directions that you

* See Documents 33, 34, and 35 inclusive.
† See Document 36.

may see proper, would it not be well to insert that it is Bannaker's writing. I want a handsome Job.[27]

This communication explains in great part the circumstances under which the lithograph was produced, and Latrobe's co-operation. Early in May Sheppard sent a copy of the lithograph to Charles Sumner, congressman from Maryland, noting that perhaps the Banneker-Jefferson correspondence would not be unacceptable to the author of the "Law of Human Progress" which Sheppard stated he had read with considerable interest. Exactly a week later, he again wrote to Sumner,[28] commenting on the latter's speech on the Iowa land grant, and then went on to remark that "I know that a single case proves nothing as to a race, there was Newton and I have internal evidence that all his race are not Newtons." *

In July, Sheppard wrote to Dr. Samuel F. McGill at Cape Palmas in Liberia and described the lithograph he had had produced, which he noted had cost him sixty dollars.[29] He expressed a deep disappointment in the reaction he had received in some quarters to his purpose in publishing the lithograph, and noted that white people seemed to have taken more interest in his project than members of Banneker's own race.† Sheppard's disappointment was understandable, in view of his great investment in the advancement of the Negro, and he was unable to understand the failure of the Afro-Americans to express an interest in such an outstanding member of their race. The apparent lack of appreciation of Sheppard's endeavors is reflected to some degree in a brief typewritten account of Banneker, undated and not identified as to the author, in the files of the State Hall of Records in Annapolis. The account states that the Reverend John T. Raymond, a distinguished colored Baptist clergyman, issued an edition of the Latrobe memoir with the comment:

* See Document 37.
† See Document 38.

I have snatched it from their (the Colonizationalists)
foul purpose, in order to produce a contrary effect.—
Our people are now too wise to be entangled in their
meshes.

Later in the same year Sheppard again corresponded with
Dr. McGill, and provided some valuable data concerning his
interest in the self-taught astronomer.

On the same day Sheppard forwarded a copy of the lithograph to George M. Justice at Baltimore, with the note that it
was done "To preserve from accident and oblivion something
of a man who may be termed the Newton of his race." He
speculated particularly on the possible effect the knowledge
that he was of mixed blood may have had upon Banneker's own
attitudes.*

It is important to note that the lithograph was a reproduction of the correspondence copied in Banneker's hand into his
manuscript astronomical journal, and not the originals of the
letters. There are several distinct differences between the originals and the copies in Banneker's journal. For instance, in the
latter Banneker did not spell out his name in full as he had in
the original, and he omitted both the footnote concerning his
father's African origin as well as the second postscript concerning Crukshank.

A limited edition of the lithograph was published at Sheppard's cost, and he forwarded copies to appropriate libraries as
well as to many prominent individuals. Among the latter were
General John G. Chapman of Port Tobacco, Maryland, Judge
Chambers of Chestertown, and Edward Everett at the State
Department in Washington.[30] Dorothy Dix in Washington
wrote to Sheppard requesting a half dozen copies of the lithograph which she planned to distribute to several members of
Congress and public institutions.[31]

* See Document 39.

At the same time Sheppard undertook to have the Manuscript Journal bound in order to protect it. The binding was of fine Russia leather, with marbled end-papers and six blank sheets added to the front and back of the manuscript. Banneker had begun a separate set of astronomical calculations, and the six additional pages of these notes were bound in at the end of the larger volume. The separate sheets were of smaller size, measuring 7½ by 12⁹⁄₁₆ inches on paper watermarked with the cipher "McC" and the date "1798."

The front cover is decorated with an elaborate border of blind stamping in gilt, with the name BANNEKER printed in the upper center. Pasted inside the front cover is a bookplate of the Maryland Historical Society. The notation of gift or donation has since been erased, but the date 1845, remains. The binding was consequently done before that date.[32]

Banneker's manuscript volume had not originally been intended as a gift to the Society by the family, but more probably as a deposit or loan so that Latrobe could use it at the time he was preparing his *Memoir* in 1844. It is not recorded among the gifts in the Society's records, and the circumstances of its removal from the collections are almost as mysterious as those relating to its appearance in them. It was returned to a member of the Ellicott family or collateral descendant, and has since remained in the possession of the family.[33]

The Maryland Historical Society again inadvertently became the cause of Banneker's commemoration. A biographical sketch of Banneker by an unidentified author was read before a meeting of the Society on October 5, 1854, by J. Saurin Norris, the president of the First National Bank of Baltimore.* On that occasion he presented to the Society two original letters

* John Saurin Norris (1813–1882) was born in Baltimore and served as secretary of the Merchants Fire Insurance Company as well as treasurer of the Savings Bank of Baltimore. He later served in several positions with the First National Bank and became its president. He was an avid reader, a supporter of the Maryland Historical Society and an intimate friend of the philanthropist Moses Sheppard and was the second president of the Sheppard Asylum and Enoch Pratt Hospital.

from Banneker, one to George Ellicott and the other to Susanna Mason, both of which have been quoted in the foregoing. As part of the gift was the copy of the Banneker almanac for 1792, owned by George Ellicott, on which he had inscribed his name. These were gifts from the family of George Ellicott, donated by the unidentified author of the sketch, who was in fact Martha Ellicott Tyson. Norris was the husband of Henrietta Tyson, the niece of Nathan Tyson, and thus related to the author by marriage.

The sketch was one of the most important contributions to Banneker's memory. It was a compilation of facts collected from those who had known him during his life, or their descendants. Martha Tyson had begun collecting this information in 1836 at the suggestion and with the encouragement of her mother. Because of her valuable contribution to the memorialization of Banneker, it is appropriate to dwell briefly on Martha Tyson and her unusual career.

A daughter of George and Elizabeth (Brooke) Ellicott, she was born at Ellicott's Lower Mills on September 13, 1795. More than any other member of her family, she became interested in family history and even as a child was observant of the events at the Mills. She was eleven when Banneker died, so that her memories of him were few, but she remembered and treasured the accounts of him she heard from her father and her mother, as well as from other relatives and friends at the Mills. On September 27, 1815, she married Nathan Tyson, a merchant miller and one of the sons of the celebrated philanthropist and advocate of antislavery, Elisha Tyson. They had twelve children and were important members of the Society of Friends in Baltimore. Martha became an acceptable minister of the Society, remaining active in the organization until her death in 1873. She was the author of several small works, including the paper read by Norris in 1854 and later published and the longer work published after her death by her daughter.

A foreword to the paper read by Norris about Banneker described the author:

. . . a lady, who, from motives of delicacy, had chosen
to withhold her name, and therefore a word of explanation might be proper to relieve it from the appearance
of an anonymous communication. The Authoress was
an immediate descendant of that branch of the Ellicott
family, of Ellicott's Mills, from whom Banneker received much assistance in the prosecution of his
studies. . . .[34]

In the same work, Martha Tyson noted about the compilation of notes from which it was derived:

All were designed for the use of one of our citizens,
a writer of acknowledged merit, who believed that the
astronomer's example of mental application, and subsequent attainments, might have a useful influence on
his brethren, both in the United States, and in the African Colonies, and therefore wished to draw up a
narrative of his life. But discouragement in the prosecution of the plan, having occured, the work was abandoned, and its intended author died in 1849.

The notes were returned to Mrs. Tyson, who prepared
them in the paper that was presented to the Society. The "writer
of acknowledged merit" was Rachel Mason, who in 1836 had
completed a volume of her mother's letters with a memoir. She
was a distant cousin of Martha, and they corresponded frequently in the several decades preceding her death. In one letter
to Martha, Rachel wrote:

I received a message from thee through H. McPherson
[a relative] respecting B. Banaker. I have not materials
to complete anything worth giving to the public, I
think if I had, I should not feel competent to do it.[35]

This was written long after Martha Tyson had begun to
collect data for her cousin's use. Rachel had the impression that

the advantage to the Negro race of a publication about Banneker would be enhanced if he could be represented therein to be "of strictly African parentage," but her failure to find that such was the case apparently dissuaded her from attempting it.[36] Furthermore, the local political scene in relation to the abolitionists had become such that the appearance of such a work would have been untimely.* Rachel Mason died in 1849 without having even begun the project, and it remained for Martha Tyson to fulfill it.[37] When the latter undertook the preparation of the sketch for the Maryland Historical Society, she had several aims in mind.[38] She had noted in an unpublished manuscript that Latrobe's *Memoir* had misrepresented Banneker's parentage, and it was in an effort to correct this misinformation, in addition to bringing to fruition Rachel's plan, that led her to have her *A Sketch* presented to and published by the Society.†

It was not until almost a decade after the appearance of *A Sketch* that Martha Tyson sent a copy of it to Latrobe, along with other related materials. He replied graciously,[39] noting that he had not seen her work before its arrival and that he now stood corrected in the matter of Banneker's parentage.‡

Martha Tyson was extremely thorough in her research, and over the years she personally interviewed a number of the people still living who had known Banneker in his lifetime, and those of his relatives who survived. Among the latter were Banneker's cousin, John Henden, and his boyhood friend, Jacob Hall. According to her own account, late in December 1851:

> Just before completing the "Sketch" which had been presented to the Historical Society I sent for a niece of Banneker, named Harriet Henderson, in order to find if her account of her Mother's grandmother would coincide with John Henden's statement. She was young at the time of Banneker's death, and was living

* See Document 40.
† See Document 41.
‡ See Document 42.

as a small servant at the house of Ennion Williams at Elkridge Landing. Her account of Molly Welsh was similar to that I have given above with a few additional particulars, respecting the cause of her leaving England. Harriet Henderson lives at present in Washington, she sometimes visits Baltimore. Moses Sheppard's servant George* sent her to me and could say where she might be found. It was in George's family I found the old Bible which contains the records of Benjamin Banneker's birth.[40]

When the *Sketch* was published for the Maryland Historical Society, some question arose about some of the statements therein, and Mrs. Tyson was asked to make some revisions. A letter from Brant Mayer, the Society's librarian, to Norris expressed concern as to whether the article was strictly factual in matters dealing with race.[41] He emphasized that opinions on the subject of slavery should be deleted to avoid giving further fuel to the Society's critics.† A comparison of the original manuscript with the published version reveals that considerable material was deleted for this purpose.

Meanwhile, Banneker's name and fame were perpetuated in still another manner, by the establishment of The Banneker Institute, of the City of Philadelphia. This organization was founded in a meeting of the incorporators held on September 9, 1853, who voted to form a "Young Men's Mutual Instruction Society." The name was not a satisfactory one, and several changes were made soon after. The next name chosen was the "Alexandrian Academy," and later it became "Alexandrian Institute." There was no evidence in the minutes for the first year that the organization was limited in membership to

* Sheppard's servant was named George Barton. He may have been a grandson of Banneker's aunt, Katherine, who had married James Boston [or Baslon?] in 1735, his name perhaps erroneously derived over the years, as had happened with Banneker's own.
† See Document 43.

Negro youth, but at a meeting late in 1853 a motion was made "that a memorial be presented to the committee of the Institute for Colored Youth." At the meeting of April 13, 1854, the organization was named the "Banaker Institute." [42]

The Institute flourished. Within the decade it published a constitution and by-laws which stated that the objective of the organization was primarily:

> . . . the mental improvement of its members by means of lectures, debates and the formation of such committees in the various branches of knowledge, as may be deemed most effectual in carrying out the designs of the Institute; secondarily, the diffusion of useful knowledge among all who may come within the pale of its influence.[43]

Meetings were held on the second Wednesday of each month at eight o'clock in the evening and membership consisted usually of about thirty young Negro men of Philadelphia. The Institute received important press notices in November 1860 when it celebrated the eighth year of its existence on the 128th anniversary of Banneker's birth.[44] The event was held at the colored Masonic Hall on South Eleventh Street, below Pine Street, and drew the elite of the Negro population of Philadelphia.*

The article then went on to describe how in honor of the occasion a bundle of Banneker's letters, in the possession of the Anti-Slavery Society, were exhibited to the audience.[45]

The Banneker papers presented on the occasion were not in fact original documents but transcriptions made by hand and later deposited in the files of the Banneker Institute. Included among them were a number of letters sent by Townsend and Elias Ellicott to Pemberton concerning Banneker and the publication of the almanac for 1792, the comments of David Rittenhouse and William Waring on the first almanac, and the certifi-

* See Document 44.

cate of its authenticity. Also included was the short poem by Banneker.[46]

The Institute continued to meet over the years in various public places in Philadelphia, including the Masons Hall, the Library Company of Philadelphia, and others.

Banneker's memory was revived once more in 1863, during the Civil War, in a detailed account by Moncure D. Conway, published first in *The Atlantic Monthly* and subsequently reprinted several times. Conway was the son of a slave owner in Virginia who later achieved considerable note as an author and preacher. During his career he changed his position on slavery from his earlier writings, in which he supported it, to becoming such an outspoken exponent on antislavery that he was dismissed as pastor of the Unitarian Church in Washington in 1856. He was the editor of an antislavery newspaper called *The Commonwealth*. After publishing several books and pamphlets, he lectured on the subject in England.[47]

Conway's article about Banneker was one of the most substantive publications and was reprinted widely in the United States. In 1864 it was published in London as a separate tract by the Ladies' London Emancipation Society and became a useful work in supporting the Northern interests in Great Britain.

It was shortly before the close of the nineteenth century that the first book-length biography of Banneker, and the most authoritative study of his life and work, was published. This tiny volume was based on notes compiled over a period of many years by Martha Ellicott Tyson. It was intended to be an expansion of an earlier paper she had prepared, and was read by John Saurin Norris before the Maryland Historical Society in 1854. Martha Tyson did not succeed in bringing the work to publication before her death in 1873; it was posthumously compiled and edited by her daughter Anne Tyson Kirk.[48]

During the preparation of the manuscript for a publisher, Mrs. Kirk wrote for advice to Frederick Douglass, the Negro lecturer and writer. Although her own letters to Douglass have not survived, a clear account of the discussion of the book can be derived from his replies. Inasmuch as these letters have not previously been studied or published, and since they relate so closely to the perpetuation of the image of Banneker, the complete texts of the three letters are presented herewith.[49]

In the first of the letters, dated March 4, 1878, Douglass replied in a most cooperative manner, encouraging Mrs. Kirk in her project:

> You have made me greatly obliged to you for your note and the Sketch of the life of Benjamin Bannecker. In answer to your question as to the probable Sale of his Biography, I do think that the Book, if small and not made to cost more than fifty cents per copy, could sell and sell well among my newly emancipated people. We as a people are especially in need of just such examples of mental industry and success as I believe the life of Bannecker furnish. The sooner you give us the work the better and more timely it will be. With great respect for your own and for your grand father's sake.[50]

Mrs. Kirk proceeded with her intention to have her mother's manuscript published and she spent considerable time in editing the material. Her negotiations with a publisher proved to be less promising than she had anticipated, however. Possibly the times were not propitious and the publisher's initial enthusiasm may have been dampened. This may have been reflected in her letter to Douglass a year later. He continued to be encouraging, but took the opportunity to specify that his own interest in the subject would be lessened under certain conditions:

> I can speak for myself—for one I believe that a full narrative of the life of So exceptional a character as Bannecker will find a ready sale both in the North and

in the South among colored and among white readers. I wish I could see the Manuscript before you publish it. I would not, however, have its publication delayed a week longer. The country needs it today. It will, I believe help my race immensely both as an incentive and a vindication. I remember your family as friendly to the enslaved in my early childhood—and have no doubt you have been just to Bannecker. There has been an attempt lately to make him son of a white woman by black father, and thus to credit the white race with whatever ability he possessed. I confess that my interest in him would would [sic] be measurably diminished if this should turn out to be true.

You may depend upon me to do my full share in getting the Book before the public. I propose soon to write a lecture on Bannecker and deliver it in many places—I am the more anxious therefore to get just such material in the way of facts as your Story of his life and work in the world will supply.

Anne Kirk struggled on with the manuscript for the next several years, and was finally able to report to Douglass in 1882 that the little book was ready for publication. His response reflected his interest and willingness to provide some limited assistance:

I am glad to know that you have not abandoned the purpose to publish a Biography of Benjamin Bannecker. I predict for the Book a larger sale among the colored people of the country than any Book yet published. I think every colored man who reads will want it and those who cannot will want their children to read it. Bannecker has been much talked about of late, and many are curious to know all about him. It will, however, not be easy to dispose of the Book in advance of its publication. People want to see before they purchase. If the Book could be retailed at one dollar it can be sold at wholesale for fifty cents a copy. If I am right in this I will take fifty copies of the first Edition for gratuitous circulation. If a few others will do the same the Book can easily be set well afloat.

My own Book is selling very well— notwithstanding my many offences to popular sentiments—and the prejudice and envy excited by my success in life. The Story of Bannecker will not encounter any jealousies. He has been dead too long for that.

Of how many pages do you intend to make the Book? A great many in buying books look [for] quantity as well as quality, and determine to buy or not to buy as they are suited or not suited by the former, without thinking of the latter.

The book was finally published, and once more there was the promise that the story of Banneker properly told would be available and that his name would come to public attention as the nineteenth century approached its close.

The project was not yet free of problems, however. After the manuscript had been completed and submitted to the publisher in Philadelphia, in 1884, Mrs. Kirk suddenly died. Consequently the literary property passed with other assets into the hands of a trustee, and relatively little distribution of the work was made. It had been, in effect, privately printed for the author, who was presumably responsible for its distribution. The edition remained relatively intact, and although it received several impressive reviews in 1884 in *The Critic* (New York), *The Friends' Intelligencer*, and in *The Baltimore Sun*, it remained almost unknown to the reading public. Within the following year or two, a relative of the author, Dr. Henry M. Fitzhugh, issued a modest broadside which he forwarded with copies of the book to a number of publishers. After describing the content and the reasons the edition was never distributed, he made this offer:

The trust having now expired, the whole "BANNE-KER" property, consisting of copyright, stereotype plates and several hundred printed copies like the one attached, is offered for sale to any publisher disposed to bring it before the world.

These various events substantially reduced the reading public's awareness of Martha Tyson's work, thereby largely defeating its purpose.

Martha Tyson's posthumous book was the last work about Banneker to be based on original materials. During the next several decades numerous articles in periodicals and newspapers mentioned Banneker's life and work, but each was based on earlier publications without contributing any new materials. Several were articles of some substance, such as a paper read by Philip LePhillips before the Columbia Historical Society in 1916 and published in its *Records* the following year, and a biographical sketch by Henry E. Baker published in the *Journal of Negro History* in 1918. A similar work was produced by Will W. Allen in 1921. Each of these was based almost entirely on earlier works from which they extracted freely. Finally, in 1949, another biography of Banneker appeared. This work by Shirley Graham was highly fictionalized and written for young people. It became popular, but the lack of distinction between fact and fiction in its presentation, while a compliment to the writing skill of Shirley Graham, has resulted in yet more confusion concerning Banneker's achievements and their importance.

The search for the site of Banneker's home and grave, first undertaken by Rachel Mason in 1836 and then pursued by Bishop Payne and his A.M.E. Church committee in 1845, was forgotten until 1953. It was in that year that the State Roads Commission of Maryland considered erecting an appropriate marker to memorialize Banneker. In cooperation with the Maryland Historical Society, the Commission collected and reviewed all available data relating to the location of Banneker's farm.[51]

The Man Remembered

In February 1954 a marker was installed on the premises of the Westchester Grade School on Westchester Avenue in Oella. It bore the following inscription:

BENJAMIN BANNEKER

1731–1806

SELF-EDUCATED NEGRO
MATHEMATICIAN—ASTRONOMER
HE MADE THE FIRST MARYLAND ALMANAC IN 1792.
ASSISTED IN SURVEY OF DISTRICT OF COLUMBIA.
HIS ACHIEVEMENTS RECOGNIZED
BY THOMAS JEFFERSON.
WAS BORN, LIVED HIS ENTIRE LIFE AND
DIED NEAR HERE.

State Roads Commission.*

The location of Banneker's home is derived primarily from a deed of partition made at the time of George Ellicott's death in 1832 and executed three years later by his executors and partners.[52] The property bounds described in this document include some of those defined in the indenture executed by Banneker with Ellicott & Co. in 1799. A number of common points can be identified which verify that Banneker's remaining tract of seventy-two acres was unquestionably included in the former.[53]

Of particular interest is a parcel of land which originally adjoined a corner of Banneker's farm, owned in his lifetime first by William Williams, a merchant who maintained a store near the Patapsco River in the little community that is now Oella.

---

* The marker proved to be not impervious to vandalism. It had to be replaced twice, in 1968 and again in 1969. A new plaque of cast aluminum was provided with a revised inscription (See Document 45.) The new installation proved to be quite as liable to the hazards of vandalism as the earlier ones. Not long after it was installed it was broken from its standard, leaving the site unmarked.

After his death the land was owned by his widow, Mary M. Williams. In her last will and testament dated August 23, 1786, she included an unusual bequest, which may be unparalleled in the annals of slavery in Maryland. She bequeathed to the Quarterly Meeting of the Society of Friends of Baltimore "all my right of thirteen negroes," whom she named individually. She then went on to add as part of her bequest, ". . . also ten acres of Land where James and Margaret [two of the Negroes previously listed] now live, being part of a tract of land called Mount Gilboa laying in Baltimore County for the use of the aforesaid Thirteen Negroes."

This was in itself an unusual gift and reflected the concern and interest of the testator. Mary Williams had more to add to her bequest, however. The remainder of her land she bequeathed to her brother-in-law, John Teale, who was also a neighbor, enjoining him ". . . to hold in possession until such time as any Lawfull heir or heirs do claim any part of the aforesaid negroes as his or their property and my will is that at such times the aforesaid Quarterly Meeting do take from the aforesaid John Teale or any person claiming under him the aforesaid tract of Land and sell the same and apply the Money to the Setting at Liberty the aforesaid negroes which are at any time any otherwise Inthralled . . ." [54]

No evidence can be found that it became necessary to purchase the freedom of the slaves to whom Mary Williams had been so loyal. Undoubtedly Banneker must have been acquainted with some of their number, since his log house was within walking distance from the ten acres where James and Margaret lived.

It was probably on this tract of ten acres that a Negro community survived through the first half of the nineteenth century, for at the present intersection of Oella Road and Westchester Avenue there still stands the Mount Gilboa Chapel, erected in 1859. An abandoned graveyard on the grounds still bears a number of headstones, many overturned and overgrown, dating from the early decades of the nineteenth century and presumably marking the graves of this early Negro community.

The modern pilgrim to the scene where Banneker lived out of his life will find little to remind him of the self-taught astronomer or of his time. Throughout the entire region, he will find ample evidence of the advent and departure of modern technology and of the wasteland that inevitably replaced it. Not more than a mile away to the southwest is Ellicott City, a picturesque, slumbering community which lies in wait for the arrival of the weekend tourist and collector of antiques. Many of its old buildings of gray granite still stand, a reminder of its past as a thriving mill center of national importance. Through the center of the city and proceeding along the route of the National Turnpike flows the once mighty Patapsco River, whose roaring stream provided the power for the myriad turning mill wheels. The visitor will find little resemblance between the storied river and the present docile stream which murmurs along the worn-out river bed passing within a half mile of where Banneker once lived. This was the untamed Patapsco which again and again flooded its banks bringing death and disaster to the region. At the north is the little factory community of Oella which had its beginnings early in the nineteenth century as the Union Manufacturing Company. In addition to its tired mills are the rows of houses which retain the flavor of an old-world factory town. At the right are the suburbs of Catonsville, another manufacturing community which also emerged during the nineteenth century and developed in sprawling suburbs through the old plantation region.

A study made within recent times has succeeded in identifying the salient bounds from related land records and established with a fair degree of certainty the seventy-two acres of land that Banneker sold to Ellicott & Co. where his home and burial ground were located, and which later was resurveyed as a tract named "West Ilchester." [55] These bounds include Cooper's Branch, the Old Frederick Road, the road leading to the Union Manufacturing Company Works, now called Oella Road, the second and third boundaries of "Stout," the first and second lines of "Stout," a corner of the land sold by Banneker to John Barten [sic], and a corner of the remainder of the original tract called "Stout" resurveyed in 1761 for William Williams and bequeathed by Mary Williams to her Negro slaves.

From these points of reference the final segment of Banneker's farm can be determined to have included the land on both sides of Oella Road, between the Old Frederick Road and the line of the Electric Railway and extended as far as the head of Cooper's Branch.

Forming a juncture of these three manufacturing centers is the land Banneker used to farm for tobacco. The farm lies between the little-traveled section of the Old Frederick Road from Ellicott City toward Catonsville and extends on both sides of Oella Road, which twists and curves precariously northward after crossing Westchester Avenue and drops tortuously into the hollow that is now Oella. The line of the abandoned electric railway follows the diminished muddy brook called Cooper's Branch, which skirts the ravine at the foot of the plateau as it trickles westward to join the Patapsco at Ellicott City. Along part of the foot of the slope the old railway line was laid, and the Old Frederick Road runs along a wide plateau which commands a fine view of the region for a great distance on all four sides. The land slopes gently toward Oella Road and it was on the ridge overlooking it that Banneker's log house once stood. The land drops more abruptly toward the ravine of Cooper's Branch. It is there that the family burial ground was located, according to local legend. The plateau which formerly consisted of open fields now lies in the deep shade of tall second-growth trees of many varieties, thickly covered with dense undergrowth that admits only occasional glimpses of sunlight. High up on the knoll are the ruins of an old house. The remaining foundations with its great hearth consist of blocks of the gray granite quarried at Ellicott City. According to local legend, a Negro cabin stood on this site in the nineteenth century but burned many years ago. Banneker's log house stood on the same knoll, although its foundations cannot be identified.

A search for the old burial ground also proves vain, for neither can the two old tulip trees which grew so close together now be identified, nor the old willow which shaded the Banneker spring a short distance away. One now seeks in vain for the tall Lombardy poplar which marked the gable end of the house little more than a century ago, and for the great old pear tree under which Banneker sought shade when he rested from his labors. It is a peaceful setting still, however, and there is little modern intrusion to disturb one's contemplation from this vantage point from which in his lifetime Banneker "commanded a prospect of the near and distant hills of the Patapsco River, which have always been celebrated for their picturesque beauty." [56]

The land on which Robert and Mary Banneky, and later Benjamin, toiled and lived for almost a century resisted the advances of modern technology and succeeded in returning to nature little less primeval than when they first found it. Yet significant memorabilia survives to perpetuate Banneker's memory as well as his name, preserved by the generations of the family that provided his original inspiration and assistance. These constitute, in fact, many of those self-same items which he charged his sisters to return to his benevolent neighbor after his death. Preserved with loving care is the old heavy oval gateleg table before which he sat for so many hours of his later years, the stretchers well worn by the scraping of his feet. His impressive volume of manuscript astronomical notes which represented the study of a lifetime capsulated into his final fifteen years, his little common-place book, the candlesticks that illuminated his nightly vigils of the stars as he noted his calculations, and finally a handful of borrowed texts which formed his fount of knowledge. Surviving also are a modest number of letters, which like his journal provide windows into the heart and mind of the aging philomath. Finally, copies of most of the numerous editions of his almanacs, which blazed so brightly for so brief a time, have found their way into various public collections.

Meager this material heritage is indeed, but it is nonetheless impressive and considerably greater in substance and significance than that which exists for many of his peers. For the past century and a half Benjamin Banneker has been memorialized primarily as a member of the Negro race who achieved distinction. A study of the surviving memorabilia now makes it possible for him to be remembered instead, and for all time to come, for his achievements as an American man of science.

He retained always those characteristics which distinguished him among his contemporaries—a mild and philosophic temperament that never deserted him, a deep sense of religion without alignment to a particular creed, a pride in cleanliness and neatness of personal appearance that clad him always in dignity, a habitual kindness and generosity, and a gentlemanly mien which marked him throughout his life.

In spite of the public acknowledgment which came to him in his final years, Banneker remained always a modest man. His success pleased him, because it enabled him to indulge his avocation in which he found such pleasure. He was appreciative of his opportunities, and grateful to those who contributed to his pursuits. He did not believe that his attainments made him great, nor that renown was due him.

> The pomp of honors may by kings be given
> To men, all equally the make of heaven:
>   But true nobility's confin'd to none;
> It gilds the cottage and may leave the throne.[57]

DOCUMENTS

DOCUMENTS

◇❀◇❀◇❀◇❀◇❀◇❀◇❀◇❀◇❀◇

THE MAJOR PORTION of the original materials upon which this biography is based, including the manuscripts and correspondence relating to Benjamin Banneker and to the survey of the Federal Territory, are either privately owned or form part of large collections for which no convenient catalogue or index exists. To make this work as useful as possible, complete texts of some of the documents quoted, and more extensive excerpts from others, are presented here. Each of the documents is fully identified in the Reference Notes. Those excerpted from published sources are listed in section II of the Bibliography.

Document 1. Letter from Joseph Townsend to
James Pemberton, July 7, 1790.
(See Reference Notes, IV, 15.)

George Mathews intending for your City I am desirous of embracing the Opportunity to inform thee that I rec.d by Elias Ellicott my Acceptable favour of the Pamphlets which is allowed by some of our Judges to be the first piece on the subject they have yet met with.—I was in hopes to have found amongst them some of Pinkney's Speech, as I have been often applied to for them by some of our Members—I think our Society would Cheerfully pay the exepence of some of them if they are to be had—The bearer will be

a safe hand [to send] them by—On 17th day last was our Stated
Meeting where we rec^d. an Acct. from our Acting Committee of
a large number of Slaves being liberated since last Meeting as likewise a very considerable number more whose cases are under the
Consideration of the Court—One of the Committee informed me
that there are nearly fifty Cases that will depend on the Determination of one [case] cause now in Court which I am in hopes will be
so Handled as to be rendered Clear & the freedom of the whole
obtained—Our Society continues to increase considerably, being
now near two hundred Members, notwithstanding we have not
as yet been a body form'd ten Months——

We have concluded to address our next General Assembly respecting the situation of the Negroes in the manner of last Year—
And I expect it will be the case of our Approaching Yearly Meeting
concerning which as we proceed therein I shall inform thee. . . .

Document 2. Excerpt from President Washington's letter to Thomas Jefferson,
February 1, 1791, with instructions
for Major Andrew Ellicott.
(See Reference Notes, V, 2.)

Nothing in the enclosed letter superceding [sic] the necessity of
Mr. Ellicott's proceeding to the work in hand I would thank you,
for requesting him, to set out on Thursday; or as soon after as can
make it convenient: Also for preparing such instructions as you
may conceive it necessary for me to give him for ascertaining the
points we wish to know; first, for the *general* view of things and
next for the more accurate and final decision.

Document 3. Excerpt from Thomas Jefferson's
letter to Andrew Ellicott, February
2, 1791, with instructions for beginning the survey of the Federal Territory.
(See Reference Notes, V, 3.)

You are desired to proceed by the first stage to the Federal territory
on the Potomac, for the purpose of making a survey of it. The first

object will be to run the two first lines mentioned in the enclosed proclamation to wit:—the S.W. line 160 poles and the S. E. line to Hunting Creek or should it not strike Hunting Creek as has been suggested then to the River. These two lines must run with all the accuracy of which your art is susceptible as they are to fix the beginning either on Hunting Creek or the River, if the second line should strike the River instead of the Creek take and lay down the bearing and distance of the nearest part of the creek and also of any of its waters if any of them should be nearer than the creek itself; so also should either of these two lines cross any water of Hunting Creek let it be noted. The termination of the Second line being accurately fixed, either on the creek or river proceed to run from that at a beginning the four lines of experiment directed in the proclamation, this is intended as the first rough essay to furnish data for the last accurate survey. It is desirable that it be made with all the dispatch possible and with only common exactness, paying regard however to the magnetic variations. In running these lines note the position of the mouth of the Eastern Branch, the point of your first course there will receive the S. W. line from the Cape of the Eastern Branch—the Canal and particular distance of your crossing it from either end the position of Georgetown, and mouth of Goose Creek, and send by Post, A plat of the whole on which ultimate directions for the rest of the work shall be sent you, as soon as they can be prepared. Till these shall be received by you, you can be employed in ascertaining a true Meridian, and the latitude of the place, and running the meanderings of the Eastern Branch, and of the River itself, and other waters which will merit an exact place in the map of the Territory. You will herewith receive a draft on the Mayor of Georgetown to cover your expenses.

Document 4. Report of the survey's progress from Andrew Ellicott to Thomas Jefferson in a letter dated February 14, 1791.
(See Reference Notes, V, 7.)

I arrived at this town on Monday last, but the cloudy weather prevented any observations being made until Friday which was very fine. On Saturday the two first lines were completed. You will see by the enclosed plat that the second line does not touch any part of Hunting Creek unless the spring drain noted in the plat is to be considered a part of it. It appears to me that in order to make the plan as complete as possible it will be proper to begin the survey of the ten miles square at the Eastern inclination of the upper cape of Hunting Creek, marked on the plat. This plan will include all the Harbor and wharfs of Alexandria, which will not be the Case if the two first lines mentioned in the proclamation are to remain as now. I shall submit to your consideration the following plan for the permanent location which will I believe embrace every object of advantage which can be included within the ten miles square. [Many erasures follow and writing is indistinct.] . . . as marked in plat A. The magnetic variations at this place is somewhat uncertain, arising no doubt from some local cause. It was 20 easterly when the second line struck the river and at the end of the first line, it was nearly as much Westerly. The Latitude of Alexandria, I find to be about 33 48 20 N. This afternoon I intend beginning the rough survey which shall be executed with all possible dispatch, [more erasures]. You will observe by the plan which I have suggested for the Permanent Location a small deviation with respect to the compass from that mentioned in the Proclamation, the reason of which is that the Coup's in the Proclamation, strictly adhered to, would neither produce straight lines, nor contain quite the ten miles square, besides the utmost impropriety of running such lines without tolerable exactness.

Document 5. Excerpt from a letter from Andrew Ellicott to his wife, February 14, 1791.
(See Reference Notes, V, 8.)

I arrived at this Town on Tuesday, last in good health but in consequences of bad weather, could not proceed to business till Friday last. I have been treated with great politeness by the inhabitants, who are truly rejoiced at the prospect of being included in the Federal district. I shall leave this town this afternoon to begin the rough survey of the ten miles square.

Document 6. Excerpt from a letter written by Thomas Jefferson to Pierre Charles L'Enfant dated March [no day], 1791.
(See Reference Notes, V, 16.)

You are advised to proceed to Georgetown, where you will find Mr. Ellicott employed in making a survey and map of the Federal territory. The special object of asking your aid is to have drawings of the particular grounds most likely to be approved for the site of the federal town and buildings. You will therefore be pleased to begin on the eastern branch, and proceed from thence upwards, laying down the hills, valleys, morasses, and waters between that and the Potomac, the Tyber, and the road leading from Georgetown to the eastern branch, and connecting the whole with certain fixed points of the map Mr. Ellicott is preparing. . . .

Document 7. Communication from J. Saurin Norris to Martha E. Tyson, undated, concerning Banneker's role in the survey of the Federal Territory.
(See Reference Notes, V, 17.)

Whether Banneker went to the Federal Territory to assist the Commissioners to lay out the "District," or L'Enfant to lay out the City, is immaterial,—as in either case it is highly probable he must have met with all parties.—

The laying out of the District necessarily involved astronomical observations & calculations, as well as defining geographical position; while the survey of the City was merely a matter of engineering (after some initial point had been obtained),—and as Banneker's talent for astronomy was so predominant, it is natural to infer that it was to aid in the former work that he was retained—

The above considerations, with the recollection of Mrs. Eliz^h Ellicott as corroboration, leave no doubt with me that it was especially to aid in the survey of the "District" that Banneker was employed,—and that while on that duty he made the acquaintance of Thos. Jefferson, then Secretary of State. His letter to that Statesman is dated August 19, 1791, which was after his return from the District as he alludes to it in his letter.

Document 8. Excerpt from an account of the installation of the Marker at Jones Point in *The Alexandria Gazette*, April 21, 1791.

(See Reference Notes, V, 24.)

The mayor and the commonality, together with the members of the different lodges of the town, at 3 o'clock waited on the commissioners at Mr. Wise's, where they had arrived. After drinking a glass of wine to the following sentiment, viz., "May the stone we are about to place in the ground remain an immovable monument of the wisdom and unanimity of North America", the company then moved on the Jones Point in the following order:

"First, the Town Sergeant; second, the Hon. Daniel Carroll and the Mayor, third; Mr. Ellicott and the recorder; fourth, such Aldermen and Councilmen as were not free Masons; fifth strangers; sixth, the master of Lodge No. 22, with Dr. David Steward at his right and Rev. James Muir at his left. Lastly the citizens, two by two."

When Mr. Ellicott had ascertained the precise point from which the first line of the District was to proceed, the master of the lodge and Dr. Steward, assisted by some of the other brothers, placed the stone; after which a deposit of corn, wine and oil was made upon it and the following observations were delivered by the Rev. Muir:

"Of America it may be said as it was of Judea of old, that it is a good land and large, O America, and prosperity within thy palaces. May jealousy, that green-eyed monster, be buried deep under the work which this day we have completed, brethren and gentlemen."

Document 9. Account of Banneker's selection as assistant to Major Andrew Ellicott. From Tyson, *A Sketch*, pp. 11–12.

(See Bibliography, Part II, Item 22.)

Major Ellicott selected Benjamin Banneker as his assistant upon this occasion, and it was with his aid that the lines of the Federal Territory, as the District of Columbia was then called, were run.

It was the work, also of Major Ellicott, under the orders of

General Washington, then President of the United States, to locate the sites of the Capitol, President's house, Treasury, and other public buildings. In this, also, Banneker was his assistant.

Document 10. Account of Banneker's behavior during the survey. From Tyson, *Banneker* . . . , p. 36.
(See Bibliography, Part II, Item 37.)

. . . Banneker's deportment throughout the whole of this engagement, secured their respect, and there is good authority for believing, that his endowments led the commissioners to overlook the color of his skin to converse with him freely, and enjoy the clearness and originality of his remarks on various subjects. . . .

Document 11. Projection of a solar eclipse made by Banneker during the survey of the Federal Territory, from his Manuscript Journal.
(See Reference Notes, V, 33.)

This projection I laid down for April the third 1791 when the sun arose Centrally eclipsed at the City of Washington this is a back tryal to See how my present method would agree with the former

NB Ferguson's Tables make the new
Moon abbtit 30 minutes to Soon, Viz.

	d	h	m
April	3	10	30
I say	3	11	32 A.M.

Document 12. Letter from Andrew Ellicott from Philadelphia to the Commissioners, March 7, 1792.
(See Reference Notes, V, 40.)

Not hearing one syllable from you since I left George Town last December I am at a loss to know what preparations will be necessary for me to make in order to compleat such work as you may think advisable the ensuing season.—I shall at least want one assistant acquainted with practical astronomy and expert in the use of Instruments.—If you know of any person who has had practice in that way and who may be engaged at a moderate price in my opinion you will essentially serve the business by employing him.—M^r. Rittenhouse of this City and my Brothers are all whom I could undertake to recommend.—the former has never had less than eight dollars p^{er} day since 1786 and neither of the later [sic] will return to the City of Washington for less than three dollars p^{er} day which is the same they were offered by the Jenesco Company for all last season and a dollar short of what they are offered by the same Company to superintend their business the ensuing season.— In consequence of Maj^r. L'Enfant withdrawing himself from the business as soon as he arrived in this place we have been constantly employed in drawing a correct plan of the City and copying it for the Engraver and had we but have joined with him in withholding materials the whole expense of last summer would probably have been thrown away.——

Since I have been in this City I have heard the expense incurred of last season frequently complained of but without offering to vindicate the necessity of every expense I will undertake to say that a piece of work of such magnitude was never executed in that manner so reasonably in this country before—of this I shall produce such proof when I come to George Town as I am sure will satisfy you.——As M^r. Jefferson is now waiting for a small sketch of the City, I am under the necessity of closing this before I intended.——

Document 13. Excerpt from Andrew Ellicott's letter to his wife, April 10, 1793.
(See Reference Notes, V, 44.)

The singular situation into which I was thrown immediately on my arrival at this place and the doubtful issue prevented my writing until a final determination which was had yesterday. My victory was complete; and all my men reinstated in the City, after a suspension of one month. As my reputation depended on the determination, I neglected nothing in my power to defeat the Commissioners, but had to contend very unequally, owing to all my papers being seized by their order the day after I returned from Philadelphia. And this day they were all restored to me again. This victory has cost me at least £75. . . .

Document 14. Excerpt from the Commissioners' letter to President Washington dated March 23, 1794.
(See Reference Notes, V, 45.)

On Major Ellicott's evading the delivery of the papers we went with Colo Deakins to Prouts house where he then kept his Office and made a personal demand of them. He then told us that Dermott had stolen a plan of the City, describing it. Mr. Johnson remarked it was a severe charge for which he ought to be well grounded before he made it. Major Ellicott said he had stolen it, that it was in his Trunk and he could prove enough to obtain a Search Warrant, and if we could break open his Trunk we should find it.

Document 15. Letter from Andrew Ellicott to Dr. William Thornton, February 23, 1795.
(See Reference Notes, V, 47.)

It is with pleasure that I congratulate you on your appointment in the City of Washington. I am in hopes the change of the commissioners will have a good effect, and restore that confidence which the other commissioners by their strange conduct had forfeited.

I have been some time past engaged in drawing up a very long astronomical paper, which will be published the ensuing season, (for the philosophical society), in which I shall have occasion to mention the City of Washington.—The method pursued in executing that part of the plan in which I have been concerned will be explained: But I shall object to the injudicious alteration made since my expulsion from the City, in the street passing by the west end of the Hotel.—The centre of that street, was intended by the plan to pass thro' the centre of the market; but by this alteration will be thrown to the west of it, and the symmetry in that case, and in a great number of squares wholy destroyed.—

To understand the plan of the City some degree of science is certainly necessary, which I am confident is the reason why it was never comprehended by the former commissioners—They never could be taught to distinguish between the President's House, Hotel, and Capitol, on the plan.—Mr. Carroll, however, was enabled to point out Notley Young's, and Daniel Carroll's plans; which are much less conspicuous!!—The former commissioner's total ignorance of the subject, left them an easy prey to the duplicity of the designing, and their pride, and petulance, precluded them from receiving information.—They confided in the tales of one Dermott, who had plundered the office of my valuable papers, and from strong presumptive evidence had moved some very important signal stakes,—made erasures, and alterations on the general plan, and returned them as the errors of others!——These facts were offered to be substantiated, but the commissioners refused to hear anything to his prejudice, fearing that he would either destroy one, or more of them, or that it would imply their fallibility, in attaching themselves to such a character. He is ignorant of the plan, and may therefore from that cause, or perhaps from vilany [sic], pretend to disown many mistakes: But my Friend be upon your guard, for I assure you, that there is not a piece of work of equal magnitude in the universe, presented with equal accuracy.

> *Document 16.* Notation from James Ferguson's *Tables and Tracts, Relative to Several Arts and Sciences* (London, A. Miller and T. Cadell, 1767) copied by Banneker into his Manuscript Journal. The entry is not a verbatim quotation.
> (See Reference Notes, VI, 3.)

In the Calculation of New and full moons it is to be observed that when the Sun's distance from the Antibazon or North node of the Moon's obit [sic], it is more than 11 Signs, 18 degrees at time of the new Moon, since the Sun will be Eclipsed at that time. And when the Sun's distance from the Node is less than 0 Signs, 12 degrees or anything between 5 Signs 18 degrees and 16 Signs, 12 degrees, at the time of full moon, the Moon will be Eclipsed at that time.

Document 17. "A Plan for a *Peace Office* for the United States." A proposal formulated by Dr. Benjamin Rush and published in Banneker's Almanac for the year 1793.
(See Reference Notes, VII, 5.)

Among the many defects which have been pointed out in the federal constitution by its antifederal enemies, it is much to be lamented that no person has taken notice of its total silence upon the subject of an office of the utmost importance to the welfare of the United States, that is, an office for promoting and preserving perpetual peace in our country.

It is to be hoped that no objection will be made to the establishment of such an office, while we are engaged in a war with the Indians, for as the War-Office of the United States was established in time of peace, it is equally reasonable that a Peace-Office should be established in time of war.

The plan of this office is as follows:

I. Let a Secretary of Peace be appointed to preside in this office, who shall be perfectly free from all the present absurd and vulgar European prejudices upon the subject of government; let him be a genuine republican and a sincere Christian, for the principles of republicanism and Christianity are no less friendly to universal and perpetual peace, than they are to universal and equal liberty.

II. Let a power be given to this Secretary to establish and maintain free schools in every city, village and township of the United States; and let him be made responsible for the talents, principles, and morals of all his school-masters. Let the youth of our country be carefully instructed in reading, writing and arithmetic, and in the doctrines of a religion of some kind; the Christian religion should be preferred to all others; for it belongs to this religion exclusively to teach us not only to cultivate peace with all men, but to forgive, nay more—to love our very enemies. It belongs to it further to take away human life, and that we rebel against his laws, whenever we undertake to execute death in any way whatever upon any of his creatures.

III. Let every family in the United States be furnished at the public expense, by the Secretary of this office, with a copy of an American edition of the Bible. This measure has become the more necessary in our country, since the banishment of the Bible, as a school-book, from most of the schools in the United States. Unless the price of this book be paid for by the public, there is reason to fear that in a few years it will be met with only in courts of justice or in magistrate's offices; and should the absurd mode of establishing truth by kissing this sacred book fall into disuse, it may probably, in the course of the next generation, be seen only as a curiosity on a shelf in Mr. Peale's museum.

IV. Let the following sentences be inscribed in letters of gold over the door of every home in the United States:

The Son of Man Came into the World, Not To Destroy Men's Lives, But To Save Them.

V. To inspire a veneration for human life, and an horror at the shedding of human blood, let all those laws be repealed which authorize juries, judges, sheriffs, or hangmen to assume the resentments of individuals, and to commit murder in cold blood in any case whatever. Until this reformation in our code of penal jurisprudence takes place, it will be in vain to attempt to introduce universal and perpetual peace in our country.

VI. To subdue that passion for war, which education, added to human depravity, have made universal, a familiarity with the instruments of death, as well as all military shews, should be carefully avoided. For which reason, militia laws should everywhere be repealed, and military dresses and military titles should be laid aside: reviews tend to lessen the horrors of a battle by connecting them with the charms of order; militia laws generate idleness and vice, and therby produce the wars they are said to prevent; military dresses fascinate the minds of young men, and lead them from serious and useful professions; were there no uniforms, there would probably be no armies; lastly military titles feed vanity, and keep up ideas in the mind which lessen a sense of the folly and miseries of war.

In the seventh and last place, let a large room, adjoining the federal hall, be appointed for transacting the business and preserving all the records of this office. Over the door of this room let there be a sign, on which the figures of a lamb, a dove, and an olive-branch should be painted, together with the following inscriptions in letters of gold:

Peace on Earth–Good-Will To Man.

Ah! Why should Men Forget That They Are Brethren? Within this apartment let there be a collection of ploughshares and pruning-hooks made out of swords and spears; and on each of the walls of the apartment the following pictures as large as life:

1. A lion eating straw with an ox, and an adder playing upon the lips of a child.

2. An Indian boiling his venison in the same pot with a citizen of Kentucky.

3. Lord Cornwallis and Tippo Saib, under the shade of a sycamore-tree in the East-Indies, drinking Madeira wine out of the same decanter.

4. A group of French and Austrian soldiers dancing arm in arm, under a bower erected in the neighborhood of Mons.

5. A St. Domingo planter, a man of color, and a native of Africa, legislating together in the same colonial assembly.

To complete the entertainment of this delightful aparement, let a group of young ladies, clad in white robes, assemble every day at a certain hour, in a gallery to be erected for the purpose, and sing odes, and hymns, and anthems in praise of the blessings of peace.

One of these songs should consist of the following beautiful lines of Mr. Pope:

> Peace o'er the world her olive wand extends,
> And white-rob'd innocence from heaven descends;
> All crimes shall cease, and ancient frauds shall fail,
> Returning justice lifts aloft her scale.

Document 18. Preface to Banneker's Almanac for the year 1794 published by James Angell in Baltimore.
(See Reference Notes, VII, 10 and Bibliography, Part I, Item 8.)

Encouraged by the liberal Patronage bestowed, by an enlightened and philanthropic Public, on BENJAMIN BANNEKER's PENNSYLVANIA, DELAWARE, MARYLAND, and VIRGINIA ALMANACK, for the Year 1793, the Editor now presents them with one, for the Year 1794, calculated by his sable Friend, BENJAMIN, who, penetrated with Gratitude for the distinguished Approbation with which his former Astronomical Labours were received, has applied himself with redoubled Assiduity to bring the Calculations, now presented, to the greatest Degree of Accuracy a Work of the Kind is susceptible of.

That Africans and their Descendants are capable of attaining a Degree of Eminence in the Liberal Sciences BENJAMIN is not the only Proof—Among many which might be produced (without recurring to past Ages) we shall only mention PHILLIS WHEATLEY, who, in her eighth Year, was brought from Africa to Boston, and though labouring under the complicated disadvantages of Poverty and Slavery, and without the Benefit of School Education, before she had attained her 20th Year, composed a Number of Poems, which were published, in a small Volume, in 1772, from which the following, *"On the* WORKS *of* PROVIDENCE," is extracted:

"CREATION smiles, in various beauty gay, While day to night, and night succeeds to day: That Wisdom, which attends Jehovah's ways, Shines most conspicuous in the solar rays: Without them, destitute of heat and light, This world would be the reign of endless night: In their excess how would our race complain, Abhorring life, how hate its lengthen'd chain! From air adust what num'rous ills would rife! What dire contagion taint the burning skies! What pestilential vapours, fraught with death, Would rife, and overspread the lands beneath!"

No Pains having been spared to render the present Publication complete, the Editor, for himself and the *African descended* self-taught Astronomer, solicits a Continuance of that Encouragement which **BANNEKER**'s **ALMANACK** has hitherto experienced, and flatters himself its Patrons will find the Miscellany it contains not only entertaining but at the same time useful and instructive.

Document 19. Preface to Banneker's almanac for 1796 published by Edwards, Keddie, and Thomas, Andrews and Butler at Baltimore.
(See Bibliography, Part I, Item 25.)

GENTLE READER,

To make an **ALMANAC** is not so easy a matter as some people think—like a well furnished table, it requires to have a variety of dishes to suit every palate, besides considerable skill in the cooking— Now, as it is impossible to suit all the dishes to every particular taste, we hope you will not be offended, should you find any not entirely to your liking, as we are certain there are a great many which will suit you to a hair. We are persuaded you will not only be entertained but instructed by our Almanac for we have ransacked all the repositories of learning to cull a few flowers for your amusement. Moreover, Kind Reader, as we believe, you would think the better of a man for having a decent coat on his back, so we have exerted ourselves to make our Almanac appear in a more respectable dress, than some other Almanac mongers have done, who, it would seem, have thought their Almanacs not worthy a good coat.

But there is one dish we invite you to partake of, and we are prouder of it than of all the rest put together; and to whom do you think are we indebted for this part of our entertainment? Why, to a *Black Man*—Strange! Is a *Black* capable of composing an Almanac? Indeed, it is no less strange than true: and a clever, wise, long-headed Black he is: it would be telling some whites if they had made as much use of their *great school learning*, as this sage philosopher has made of the little teaching he had got.

The labours of the justly celebrated *Bannaker* will likewise furnish you with a very important lesson, courteous reader, which you will not find in any other Almanac, namely that the Maker of the Universe is no respecter of colours; that the colour of the skin is no ways connected with strength of mind or intellectual powers; that although the God of Nature has marked the face of the African with a darker shade than his brethren, he has given him a soul equally capable of refinement. To the untutored Blacks, the following elegant lines of GRAY may be applied.

> "Full many a gem of purest ray serene,
> The dark unfathom'd caves of ocean bear:
> Full many a flower is borne to blush unseen,
> And waste its fragrance on the desert air."

> Nor you ye proud, impute to these the blame
> If Afric's sons to genius are unknown,
> For Banneker has prov'd they may acquire a name
> As bright, as lasting as your own.

Document 20. Mathematical puzzle recorded by Banneker in his Manuscript Journal

Question by Ellicott Geographer General

Divide 60 into four Such parts, that the first being increased by 4, the Second decreased by 4, the third multiplyed by 4, the fourth part divided by 4, that the Sum, the difference, the product, and the Qutient [sic] shall be one and the Same Number—

Ans. first part 5.6 increased by 4 ( ) 9.6
　　Second part 13.6 decreased by 4 ( ) 9.6
　　third part 2.4 Multiplyed by 4 (is) 9.6
　　fourth part 38.4 divided by 4 ( ) 9.6
　　　　　　　　　　　$\overline{60.0}$

Document 21. Puzzle of the Dog and the Hare recorded by Banneker in his Manuscript Journal.

Question for Hopkins

> When fleecy skies have Cloth'd the ground
> With a white mantle all around

Then with a grey hound Snowy fair
In milk white fields we Cours'd a Hare
Just in the midst of a Champaign
We set her up, away she ran,
The Hound I think was from her then
Just thirty leaps or three times ten
Oh it was pleasant for to see
How the Hare did run so timorously
But yet so very Swift that I
Did think she did not run but Fly
When the Dog was almost at her heels
She quickly turn'd, and down the fields
She ran again with full Career
And 'gain she turn'd to the place she were
At every turn she gain'd of ground
As many yards as the greyhound
Could leap at thrice, and She did make,
Just Six, if I do not mistake
Four times She Leap'd for the Dogs three
But two of the Dogs leaps did agree
With three of hers, nor pray declare
How many leaps he took to Catch the Hare.

[Answer]

Just Seventy two I did Suppose,
An Answer false from thence arose,
I Doubled the Sum of Seventy two,
But still I found that would not do,
I mix'd the Numbers of them both,
Which Shew'd so plain that I'll make Oath,
Eight hundred leaps the Dog did make,
And Sixty four, the Hare to take.

```
4 :   72   :  :  48
        48
       ───
      576
    288
    4)3456
      ────
      864    ans.
```

Document 22. A Puzzle about Cattle, noted by Banneker in his Manuscript Journal.

A gentleman Sent his Servant with £100 to buy 100 Cattle, with orders to give £5 for each Bullock, 20 Shillings for cows, and one Shilling for each Sheep, the question is to know what number of each sort he brought to his master.

Answer   19 bullocks at £5 each   £95
            1 cow at 20s   1
            80 sheep at 1s each   4
                                      100 proof

Document 23. Puzzle about triangles, noted by Banneker in his Manuscript Journal.

Suppose ladder 60 feet long be placed in a Street so as to reach a window on the one Side 37 feet high, and without moving it at bottom, will reach another window on the other side of the Street which is 23 feet high, requiring the breadth of the Street.
[No solution recorded.]

Document 24. The Puzzle of the Cooper and the Vintner described by Charles W. Dorsey and published in Tyson, *A Sketch.* . . .
(See Bibliography Part II, Items 22 and 37.)

A cooper and vintner sat down for a talk,
Both being so groggy that neither could walk;
Says cooper to vintner, "I'm the first of my trade,
There's no kind of vessel but what I have made,
And of any shape, sir, just what you will,
And of any size, sir, from a tun to a gill."
"Then," says the vintner, "you're the man for me.

Make me a vessel, if we can agree.
The top and the bottom diameter define,
To bear that proportion as fifteen to nine,
Thirty-five inches are just what I crave,
No more and no less in the depth will I have;
Just thirty-nine gallons this vessel must hold,
Then I will reward you with silver or gold,—
Give me your promise, my honest old friend."
"I'll make it tomorrow, that you may depend!"
So, the next day, the cooper, his work to discharge,
Soon made the new vessel, but made it too large;
He took out some staves, which made it too small,
And then cursed the vessel, the vintner, and all.
He beat on his breast, "By the powers" he swore
He never would work at his trade any more.
Now, my worthy friend, find out if you can,
The vessel's dimensions, and comfort the man!
[No solution recorded.]

Document 25. The Puzzle of Three Ages recorded by Banneker in 1801 in his Manuscript Journal.

A, B and C, discoursing about their ages, Says A, if from double the Cube Root of B's age, double the biquadrate root of C's age betaken the remainder will be equal to the Squared Root of my age, says B, the square root of my age is equal to one fourth part of A's, and says C, the Square root of my age is one more than the Square root of B's, Required their several Ages——

A's)   (32 The Squared Root of which is 2
)   (
B's) Age (64 The Cube of Root of which is 4
)   (
C's)   (84 The biquadrate root of which is 3.

[No solution recorded.]

Document 26. Poem about Banneker written by
Susanna Mason and published post-
humously by her daughter.
(See Bibliography, Part II, Item 13.)

*An Address to Benjamin Banneker, an African Astronomer, who
presented the author with a manuscript Almanack.*

Transmitted on the wings of Fame,
Thine eclat sounding with thy name,
Well pleas'd I heard e'er was my lot
To see thee in thy rural cot,
That genius smil'd upon thy birth,
And application call'd it forth;
That time and tides thou couldst presage,
And traverse the celestial stage,
Where shining globes their circles run
In swift rotation round the sun;
Could'st tell how planets in their way,
From order ne'er were known to stray;
Sun, moon, and stars, when they will rise,
When sink below the upper skies;
When an eclipse shall veil their light,
And hide their splendor from our sight.
Now we'll apply thy wond'rous skill,
The wise may oft be wiser still.
Though saving knowledge to impart,
To guide the life and mend the heart,
Belongs to Him who rules the spheres,
Whose potent Arm all nature bears,
Whose sovereign wisdom governs all
If worlds consume or sparrows fall.
Yet nature in its wonted course
Some useful lessons may enforce.
A little star, like speck appears,
Scarce obvious 'mid the mightier spheres,
Into the wondrous field of space,
Eludes thy sight and runs its race,
Yet no account thou make'st of it,

Its waxing, waning, or exit;
What time it pass'd from mortal sight,
Or when again 'twill come to light'
But brighter orbs thou mark'st their way,
Observ'st their motions night and day;
Describ'st the speed at which they run,
And what their distance from the sun:
A speck in these is quickly seen,
If opaque bodies intervene,
Their native brightness to pervade,
And o'er their lustre cast a shade.
Now, as I've said, though thou art wise,
Permit me here to moralize.
Some men who private walks pursue,
Whom Fame ne'er ushered into view,
May run their race and few observe,
To right or left if they should swerve,
Their blemishes would not appear
Beyond their lives a single year.
But thou, a man exalted high,
Conspicuous in the world's keen eye,
On record now thy name's enrolled,
And future ages will be told,
There lived a man called Banneker,
An African astronomer.
Thou need'st to have a special care
Thy conduct with thy talent square,
That no contaminating vice,
Obscure thy lustre in our eyes,
Or cast a shade upon thy merit
Or blast the praise thou might'st inherit:
For folly in an orb so bright,
Will strike on each beholder's sight:
Nay, stand exposed from age to age,
Extant on some historian's page.
Now as thy welfare I intend,
Observe my counsel as a friend.
Let fair examples mark thy round
Unto thine orbit's utmost bound.

"The good man's path," the scriptures say,
"Shines more and more to perfect day."

Document 27. "A Remarkable Dream, 10th Mo. 1762." A manuscript of Benjamin Banneker.

(See Reference Notes, IX, 59.)

I thought I was dead and Beheld my Body lay like a corps, there seem'd to be a person in the appearance of a Man his Raiment somewhat of a sheep skin or bright fawn colour, who said follow me, he ascended a Hill on the Top of which was a Large Building, the outside appeared strongly Built, of Large rough Stone, I follow'd my guide into the House, but did not at first see the Beauty of it, to the full, it seem'd white and Bright, and a Large Company sitting, such a number as I never beheld, the farther we went in, the Brighter it appear'd, and more like the reflection of the Sun, the first step my guide made, seem'd to be more than half way the House, by what I Judg'd from the appearance of the length of the Building on the outside, while the guide stop'd I look'd at the Countenance of those I could see, which were many, but could not see the farther end, for the reflection of the Light, which appear'd brighter than when the Sun shin'd in its fullest Luster on a Summers day, there appeared a sweetness & composure in every countenance, far beyond what I ever seen in any person, while in the Body, and the luster reflected from the light, which extended to the Shirts of their Garments, which appeared like a plain robe or covering, in one piece; so that I was filled with admiration, I look'd to see if I could Distinguish Men from Women but could not, likewise if I could see any one I knew but knew none, on my first entrance into the House, I thought I had been at a Meeting of solid Friends, I looked to see from whence the Light came, but could not discern either Window or opening I then ask'd my guide what is this place he answered Heaven, then I looked to see what they sat on, but could not discern either seats or form the more I look'd, the more I admired and wanted to sit with 'em, but could not tell how, my guide Turned about to go out and look'd at me said follow, but I was so much delighted, that I was unwilling to follow he then Beckon'd and said Come, we had not gone far, before I stoped again, he stoped a little for me, and said again come, I followed, after halting, and Admiring the beauty I saw! in every countenance untill we got out, then the guide turn'd on the left hand, and we seem'd to I did not perceive the road we went, but could see my guide until we were where I beheld a Lofty grand arch of great width where we Entered into a Large Room, which I could not see to the end of, till we passed through: this Room appear'd grandly Wainscoted, and beautifully painted with different Collours, the first sight of this beautiful Room, abated my sorrow, which was very great, while we came down the descent, from leaving the other, I had but Just time to take a view of this fine place before a Number of persons, richly dressed passed us, who smell'd so strong of Brimstone, that I seem'd allmost suffocated all of them were talking to themselves, and before they came to us they look'd well, but when they came near, there appeared a Blackness on their lips, and seem'd to mutter to themselves, which was allso the manner of some that walked alone, I was seized with horror, and asked my guide what is this place and what are these, he Answered this place is Hell, and them are Miserable forever, they were when in the Body in Tumutts and will be so Everlastingly, at some distance sat an old Gentlewoman in a chair like a Bath Chair, a fine person very white and powdered and Grandly dress'd, I made up to her, to see if there was the same appearance of Misery in her, and was more shock'd than before, her lips were moving and from her Eyelids came small flames of fire, and Immediately after this as I look'd roun'd there appeared in my view a Woman Friend, plainly dress'd in a green apron, whom I remembered well when I was young, I often took notice of her, for the Solidity of her Deportment, particularly in Meeting, I eagerly made up to her, and said what art thou among the Miserable, tell me, tell me what brought the hither, she wept and said, no wrong that I have done between Man & Man, but unfaithfulness and disobediance to my God, brought me hither, I thought I wept as much as she, when I first look'd on her, she look'd sorrowful, then I turn'd to my guide, and said, let me go, he walked slowly on, and we met many like the other, in appearance, and smell, that I seem'd allmost suffocated with Brimstone, I then in great bitterness of spirit said to my guide, tell me am I to remain here forever, I thought a little time past, if I had died I had secured an Inheritance among the first we saw, my guide stood, and looking steadfastly at me said thou art not to remain here, but to return to the World again, if thou art faithful to thy God, thou mayest have an Inheritance among the first, but I have something else to show thee he went a little farther, when another arch appear'd, which divided, this place from a Large one, like a Chapple wherein abundance of people were assembled, to worship, and saying Amen, Lord have mercy upon us, Christ have Mercy upon us, these appear'd more plane in their dress and looked whiter, I said to my guide, these are not Miserable too, he said these are Miserable, these are they who thought to be saved by a profession of Religion, but have not the white robes of Righteousness they all came in by the way of this Room, some stop'd among the Worshipers, others went on to those who smell so strong of Brimstone, my distress now greater than before, for I thought I knew many of these who allso look'd at me, as if they knew me, and thought they appeared as if they worshiped, they looked to and fro, and seem'd much discompos'd, I again Intreated my guide to let me go, he walked gently out of this place and came again into the entrance of this House which is wide with a Large Gate, here stood a number in Black or dark Clothes, who did not seem to move forward to the others, when we came to the outside of the gate, I saw an Intimate Friend whom I much loved (this friend died in About a Month after) coming towards the Gate and two persons conducting him he look'd very Sorrowfull on me, and I on him, I asked him art thou agoing amongst the Miserable, what is thy offence, what hast thou done, Tell me, he Answered beware of Covetousness, and the love of Money, that brought me hither, we both wept much, and were greatly troubled, but I wanted to be gone, and followed my guide, and on looking back, saw some pulling, others pushing him, we were now in a large Enclosed field, in the field I saw many persons, some of whom are since Dead, out of it I could see no road, but my guide had me to a place, where there was just room to go Out, he stood and look'd at me, and earnestly said thou art now going into the World again Remember what thou hast seen, it is not enough to be honest to Man, thou must be honest and faithful to thy God Allso on this the thoughts of returning to the World affects me much for it seemed a Matter of doubt, whether I should be able to steer my Course, so as to be deemed worthy of admitance Amongst the first I had a sight of, but standing speechless, and my guide standing still Faith suddenly sprung up in my mind, and I seem'd to say these Words: Lord those can'st if thou wilt preserve me thro' all, then I awoke, but the horror & distress I felt on my mind I am not capable of Expressing, I seem'd as if I fetch'd my breath in a room where Sulphur & Brimstone were Burning, often saying to my Nurse and those about me, I seem as if the smell of Brimstone was in my stomach.

Thought I could not live many Hours, nor do I believe I should if the Almighty in the Extendings of his Boundless—Goodness—had not had Reguard to me a poor unworthy Creature and caus'd that Suffocating smell to pass from me, and gave me to trust in that melted my spirit into contrition before him & Enabled me to vent my Sorrow in many Tears, after which my Toss'd mind was favoured with a Calm.

Document 28. The "Quincunx" Dream, noted in
Banneker's Manuscript Journal.
(See Reference Notes, IX, 61.)

On the night of the fifth of December 1791, Being a deep Sleep, I dreamed that I was in a public Company, one of them demanded of me the limits Rasannah Crandolphs Soul had to display itself in, after it departed from her Body and taken its flight. In answer I desired that he shew me the place of Beginning "thinking it like making a Survey on Land." He reply'd I cannot inform you, but there is a man about three days jorney from Hence that is able to satisfy your demand, I fortwith went to the man and requested of him to inform me place of beginning of the limits that Rasannah Crandolph's Soul had to display itself in, after the Separation from her Body; who gave me the answer, *the Vernal Equinox*, When I returned I found the Company together and I was able to Solve their Doubts by giving them the following answer Quincunx.

Document 29. A Dream, dated "December 13, 1797," from Banneker's Manuscript Journal.
(See Reference Notes, IX, 62.)

I Dreamed I saw some thing passing by my door to and fro, and when I attempted to go to the door, it would vanish and reapted [sic] it twice or thrice, at length I let in the infernal Spirit and he told me that he had been concerned with a woman by the name of Beckey Freeman (I never heard the name as I remember) by some means we fell into a Skirmish, and I threw him behind the fire and endeavored to burn him up but all in vain—I know not what became of him but he was an ill formed being—Some part of him in Shape of a man, but hairy as a beast, his feet was circular or rather globular and did not exceed an inch and a half in diameter, but while I held him in the fire he said something respecting he was able to stand it, but I forget his words.

B. Banneker.

Document 30. Dream, dated "The night of December 25, 1797," from Banneker's Manuscript Journal.
(See Reference Notes, IX, 63.)

I dreamed I had a fawn or young deer; whose hair was white and like unto lamb's wool, and all parts about it beautiful to behold. Then I said to myself I will set this little captive at liberty, but I will first clip the tips of his ear that I may know him if ever I should see him again. Then taking a pair of shears and cutting off the tip of one ear, and he cried like unto a child hath the pain which grieved him very much altho then I did not attempt to cut the other but was very sorry for that I had done I got him at liberty and he ran a considerable distance then he stopped and he looked back for at me I advanced toward him, and he came and met me and I took a lock of wool from my garment and wiped the blood of wound which I had made on him (which sorely affected me) I took him in my arms and brought him home and hold him on my knees, he asked the Woman if she had any trust and she answered him in the affirmative and gave him Some, which he began to eat and then asked for milk in a cup She said the dog had got the cup with milk in it under the house but there is milk in the cup-board.——

My dream left me. B. Banneker.

Document 31. Dream, dated "April 24, 1802," from Banneker's Manuscript Journal.
(See Reference Notes, IX, 64.)

Being weary holing for corn, I laid down on my bed and fell into a deep sleep and dreamed I had a child in my arms and was viewing the back part of its head where it had been sore, and I found it was healed with a hole through the skin and Scull bone and came out at forehead, that I could see very distinctly through the child's head the hole being large enough to receive an ordinary finger——

I called some woman to see the strange sight, and she put her spectacles on and Saw it, and she asked me if I had previously lanced that place in the Child's head, I answered in the affirmative.

N.B. the Child is well as any other.

Document 32. Account of Rachel Mason's visit to Banneker's farm.
(See Reference Notes, X, 18.)

In a late visit to Ellicott's Mills, two beloved friends and myself, who alike enjoy converse with Nature in her deepest solitudes, essayed to find the spot where the mental eye of this sable son of science had often pierced into futurity, and where his hand had recorded events as yet buried in its vast abyss. After mounting and descending successive hills, high and steep, and sometimes winding along the banks of the little streamlets that crossed our way, we found that memory had no chart whereby to direct our steps, and returned without accomplishing our purpose.

But I have heard from those who have passed that way, that a fire kindled by some unknown hand had consumed the cottage, and wasted every vestige belonging thereto. The pear tree and the orchard have not yet yielded to that Sovereign Power, which continued to inscribe this motto upon every terrestrial thing, "It shall perish."

Document 33. Description of Banneker's Manuscript Journal, from Martha E. Tyson's manuscript "A Memoir of Benjamin Banneker."
(See Reference Notes, X, 24.)

All the manuscripts [of Banneker] were presented to the Maryland Historical Society in 1852, and were enclosed in a rustic cover of parchment of antique appearance. With a view to their preservation a member of the Society, the late Moses Sheppard, the founder of the Sheppard Asylum of Baltimore, had them bound in Russia leather.

Document 34. Description of Banneker's Manuscript Journal, from Martha E. Tyson's *Banneker, The Afric-American Astronomer.*
(See Reference Notes, X, 25, and Bibliography Part II, Item 37.)

. . . It was a large volume of his manuscript and his common-place book. The former volume contains Banneker's observations on various subjects and copies of all his almanacs, as well as copies of his letter to Thomas Jefferson, and the reply of that statesman. We have extracted freely from these books. . . .

Document 35. Description of Banneker's Manuscript Journal, from J. H. B. Latrobe's "Memoir."
(See Reference Notes, X, 26, and Bibliography, Part II, Item 14.)

. . . the folio already referred to and now before the Society, contains the calculations clearly copied, and the figures used by him in his work. The hand-writing, it will be seen, is very good and remarkably distinct, having a practised look, although evidently that of an old man, who makes his letters and figures slowly and carefully.

Document 36. Engraved inscription appearing on facsimile of the Banneker-Jefferson letters published by Moses Sheppard as a broadside.
(See Reference Notes, X, 30.)

The Letters, from which this facsimile is taken, are in the handwriting of Banneker, who copied them into the volume of Manuscripts, in which they have been preserved. His house and manuscripts were burnt soon after his decease, except this book which was at a neighbor's, at the time.

Document 37. Excerpt from a letter written by Moses Sheppard to Charles Sumner May 3, 1852.
(See Reference Notes, X, 28.)

Bannaker . . . soon after his death his house and all his manuscripts were burned, except one book which was at a neighbors. I have had it bound. There is no Institution here in which it will not be subject to the same casualty as his other papers. I therefore had the two letters lithographed to preserve as much of Banneker in his own hand writing. I know that a single case proves nothing as to a race, there was Newton, and I have internal evidence that all his race are not Newtons. Pope's remark on Newton might with a little alteration be made applicable to Banneker. The Celestials "admire" such wisdom in an earthly shape and show a Newton as we show an ape.

Document 38. Excerpt from a letter written by Moses Sheppard to Dr. Samuel F. McGill in Liberia, July 5, 1852.
(See Reference Notes, X, 29.)

. . . the whites take more interest in them than the blacks. After Latrobe published his biography of Bannaker, the colored people made a move to erect a monument to his memory, that died away. I then proposed to them to place a cenotaph of either marble or wood painted in each of their churches, they talked that off. I offered them a Lithographed copy of Bannaker's and Jefferson's letters to have framed and placed in their meeting houses, they have not accepted.

Document 39. Excerpt from a letter by Moses Sheppard to George M. Justice, November 18, 1852.
(See Reference Notes, X, 29.)

The number of years in which Bannaker published almanacs is not known; a quantity of them were found in a loft at Ellicott's Mills used as waste paper; a new roof was put on the house and the rest of them were destroyed.

My investigations have convinced me that Bannaker's grandmother was a Scotch woman, he says in his letter to Jefferson that his color is of deepest dye, this must be understood in reference to those of the same mixture, a friend who lived near him and knew him well told me his color was "light black" or a dark mulatto, alieas a mulatto of "the deepest dye," strictly a quadroon reveres [sic].

Bannaker had two reasons to keep his mixture out of sight, one was that he was pleading the cause of the blacks, and he doubtless knew that it would be best to appear as one of them, and the other that his grandmother was a convict, this explanation is not designed to detract, as it cannot detract from the merits of the man, and his being rather intemperate, are circumstances that his biographer might omit, as his talents are the only question before the public. I send thee two of his Almanacs of 1792 and 96. I believe that one of 96 was the last one he published. . . . After Latrobe published his memoirs of Bannaker, the colored people sent a deputation to ascertain the spot where his remains lay, about 15 miles from Baltimore, with the avowed intention of erecting a monument over him, but it was not done, they then talked of placing one in a cemetery near town, that ended in talk also. . . .

Latrobe's Memoirs were printed on a flying sheet that soon may disappear. Should that be its fate, the only Memorial or Monument of Bannaker will be the lithograph.

When we remember that Bannaker was destitute of all the means thought to be essential to the acquisition of astronomical knowledge, his asperations to understand the organization of the Solar system must have been sustained by a mind of unusual force, which places him in the case of great men of his age, and of every age. His case confirms the opinion of my own, if I may quote from myself, "That the Diety in the Creation of man did not restrict himself to any shade or form in which to wrap the ethereal essence that we call mind."

Document 40. Account of Rachel Mason's interest in Banneker, from an unsigned and undated manuscript in the hand of Martha E. Tyson.
(See Reference Notes, X, 36.)

After Rachel Mason had finished her Memoirs of her mother in 1836, she wished to prepare a narrative of the life of Benjamin Banneker, in order that the example of his fine talents, studious habits and ultimate attainments as an astronomer might be made useful to the people of color here as well as elsewhere; but aware at the same time that the value of such a work would be much increased if she could represent him, (according to a concise account which had appeared in print) as being of strictly African parentage, she was anxious to procure proofs to that effect, and by the assistance of her friends made many inquiries on the subject, and I regret to say without the desired success. . . .

Document 41. Note made by Martha E. Tyson concerning J. H. B. Latrobe's "Memoir."
(See Reference Notes, X, 38.)

An able and interesting account of Ben Banneker was read before the H. S. [Historical Society] in 1845 by H. B. Latrobe, was published and extensively circulated—In this first memorial that had ever been prepared of him, appeared some details of his parentage which had then been misrepresented to the author and which were well known by many of the residents of Baltimore and its surrounding vicinity to be quite erroneous. The author of the following essay [A Sketch] who had often seen the old astronomer, and who had taken many notes connected with his history from aged persons who had known him well, yielded to the solicitation of influential members of the Society and prepared for them a new memorial which was read and published by them in the year 1854. . . .

Document 42. Excerpt from a letter written by John H. B. Latrobe to Martha E. Tyson, Septemper 19, 1864.
(See Reference Notes, X, 39.)

I have your note, with the Memoir of Banneker and the returned newspapers. You were quite right in supposing I had not seen the former. I stand corrected, now, on a point, which, I could have wished, for the argument, had been otherwise.—But the truth is the truth: and the capacity of the black color indicated, as us lawyers say, *aliunde*—I mean, of the native race without white admixture. The memoir I will put away as a valuable one, all the more so, because this particular copy has the autograph of a lady I very sincerely admire and respect.

Document 43. Excerpt from a letter by Brant Mayer, Librarian of the Maryland Historical Society, to J. Saurin Norris concerning the manuscript of *A Sketch . . .* by Tyson, dated January 20, 1854.
(See Reference Notes, X, 41.)

I think Mrs. Tyson's amendment of the sentence not only the best that has been made, but the best that could be made. My only desire in this matter was to have the fact explicitly stated that *Madame* Bannecker was a *white* woman. Whether her color is displayed at the *head* of the page or at its *foot*, matters very little. The tact of woman, in this, as in all other matters, has overcome the difficulty.

In regard to other alterations I have only to say that my chief anxiety is to have every thing omitted that can in any way connect our Society with *opinions* about Slavery or anti-Slavery. We may develop as many facts as we please about "the institution," but, as you know, there are so many "carpers and cavillers" about our Society, that I am anxious to give them no topic for fault finding.

You will oblige me very much if you will explain or show this to Mrs. Tyson, in order that she may understand exactly my position, and how much I was gratified by the perusal of her lucid and interesting narrative.

Document 44. Excerpt from a newspaper account of the anniversary celebration of the Banneker Institute held on November 9, 1860, in Philadelphia, from an unidentified Philadelphia newspaper, dated November 15, 1860.
(See Reference Notes, X, 44.)

Among the colored people of the country generally, few names are more honored than that of Benjamin Banneker, of Ellicott's Mills, Baltimore County, the 128th [actually 129th] anniversary of whose birth was celebrated last night by the elite among the colored people of Philadelphia, at the colored Masonic Hall, south Eleventh street, below Pine.

The occasion was the eighth anniversary of the Banneker Institute, a literary society comprising a membership of thirty young men, who meet at Benezet Hall, south Seventh street, and have amply illustrated the capacity of the colored people for a high degree of intellectual advancement. . . .

Document 45. Text of the public marker installed on Banneker's farm in Oella, Maryland, by the State Historical Sites Commission.
(See Reference Notes, X, 51.)

BENJAMIN BANNEKER
(1731–1806)
THE SELF-EDUCATED NEGRO
MATHEMATICIAN AND ASTRONOMER
WAS BORN, LIVED HIS ENTIRE LIFE
AND DIED NEAR HERE.
HE ASSISTED IN SURVEYING THE
DISTRICT OF COLUMBIA, 1791, AND
PUBLISHED THE FIRST MARYLAND
ALMANAC, 1792. THOMAS JEFFERSON
RECOGNIZED HIS ACHIEVEMENTS.

Maryland Historical Society.

REFERENCE
NOTES

REFERENCE
NOTES

✧❈✧❈✧❈✧❈✧❈✧❈✧❈✧❈✧

I. The Heritage and the Land

1. Charles Weathers Bump, "Indian Place-Names in Maryland." *Maryland Historical Magazine*, vol. II, no. 4, December 1907, pp. 287–291.

2. Henry J. Berkley, "Extinct River Towns of the Chesapeake Bay Region," *Maryland Historical Magazine*, vol. XIX, no. 2, June 1924, pp. 125–141.

3. *Laws of Maryland*, 1763, Chapter XVIII.

4. Abbot Emerson Smith, *Colonists in Bondage, White Servitude and Convict Labor in America 1697–1770* (Chapel Hill; University of North Carolina Press, 1947), pp. 89–151. See also James Davie Butler, "British Convicts Shipped to American Colonies," *The American Historical Review*, vol. II, 1897, pp. 12–33; and Abbot Emerson Smith, "The Transportation of Convicts to the American Colonies in the Seventeenth Century," *ibid.*, vol. XXXIX, 1934, pp. 232–249.

5. Basil Sollers, "Transported Convict Laborers in Maryland During the Colonial Period," *Maryland Historical Magazine*, vol. II, no. 1, March 1907, pp. 17–47.

6. [Martha E. Tyson], *Banneker, the Afric-American Astronomer. From the Posthumous Papers of Martha E. Tyson. Edited*

by Her Daughter (Philadelphia: Friends' Book Association, 1884), p. 10. (hereinafter cited as Tyson, *Banneker*). See also Sollers, *op. cit.*, pp. 17–29.

7. Henry F. Thompson, "An Atlantic Voyage in the Seventeenth Century," *Maryland Historical Magazine*, vol. II, 1907, pp. 319–326.

8. *The Maryland Gazette*, July 16, 1767.

9. *The Maryland Gazette*, November 24, 1768.

10. "Transportation of Felons to the Colonies," *Maryland Historical Magazine*, vol. XXVII, no. 4, December 1932, pp. 263–274.

11. For a discussion of the Indians of Baltimore County, see William B. Marye, "The Baltimore County 'Garrison' and The Old Garrison Roads," *Maryland Historical Magazine*, vol. XVI, no. 2, June 1921, pp. 125–127.

12. Robert Sutclife, *Travels in Some Parts of North America, in the Years 1804, 1805, & 1806.* 2nd ed. (New York, 1815), pp. 107–108, 207.

13. Tyson, *Banneker*, p. 10.

14. *Ibid.*, pp. 9–11.

15. *Maryland Laws*, 1752, Chapter I.

16. Jeffrey R. Brackett, *The Negro in Maryland. A Study of the Institution of Slavery* (Baltimore: N. Murray, 1889), pp. 32–33, quoted from *Archives of Maryland*, Proceedings of the General Assembly, 1637–1664, pp. 533–534.

17. Carter G. Woodson, "The Beginnings of the Miscegenation of the Whites and Blacks," *The Journal of Negro History*, vol. III, no. 4, October 1918, p. 341.

II. Home and Family.

1. Tyson, *Banneker*, p. 25.

2. No record of the marriage can be found in the registers of St. Paul's Parish.

3. St. Paul's Parish, Baltimore, Maryland, *Parish Register*, Folio 102, p. 153, No. 27. The entry merely listed the marriage of "James Boston [or Baslon] to Katherine Banneker, May the 22nd, 1735, Negroes."

4. St. Paul's Parish, Baltimore, Maryland, *Parish Register*, Marriages, Folio 111, p. 168. The entry merely states "William Black & Esther Banneker was married September 22, 1744." For a history of the parish, see Helen W. Ridgeley, "The Ancient Churchyards of Baltimore," *The Grafton Magazine of History and Genealogy*, vol. I, no. 4, March 1909, pp. 8–14, and *Historic Graves of Maryland and the District of Columbia* (New York: Grafton Press, 1908).

5. [Martha E. Tyson], *A Sketch of the Life of Benjamin Banneker, From Notes Taken in 1836* (Baltimore: John D. Toy, 1854), p. 4 (hereinafter cited as Tyson, *A Sketch*).

6. William B. Marye, "The Baltimore County 'Garrison' and the Old Garrison Roads," *Maryland Historical Magazine*, vol. XVI, no. 3, September 1921, p. 245. See also Colonel J. Thomas Scharf, *The Chronicles of Baltimore; Being a Complete History of "Baltimore Town" and Baltimore City from the Earliest Period to the Present Time* (Baltimore: Turnbull Brothers, 1874), pp. 12, 202.

7. Scharf, *op. cit.*, pp. 50–51.

8. Hall of Records, Annapolis, *Baltimore County Land Records*, HWS #IA, folio 58–59.

9. Maryland Historical Society, Baltimore County Rent Roll, Calvert Papers No. 883, folio 162. ". . . 27 Mar. 1701 for Capt. Tho. Bales. . . ."

10. Additional Rent Roll of the Western Shore, Baltimore County, 1764, Scharf Papers, Manuscripts, Maryland Historical Society. See also Marye, *op. cit.*, pp. 244–246.

11. The Tax List, 1737, Baltimore County–Upper Patapsco Hundred listed "James Bannacar [sic] and his wife . . . 2 taxables." See also Debt Book, Baltimore County, Calvert Papers No. 904, p. 69, in the collection of the Maryland Historical Society.

12. "Narrative of a voyage to Maryland 1705–1706" (Sloane MS. 2291, vol. 1, British Museum).

13. Thomas Glover, "Account of Virginia, 1671," in Lowthorp, *Philosophical Transactions and Collections*, vol. II, p. 574. See also William Tatham, *Essay on the Culture and Commerce of Tobacco* (London, 1800).

14. J. E. McMurtrey, *Tobacco Production*, Agricultural Information *Bulletin* No. 245, December 1961, pp. 27–29, 57.

15. Also see Lewis Cecil Gray, *History of Agriculture in*

the Southern United States to 1860 (Washington, D.C.; Carnegie Institution, 1933), vol. I, pp. 218–219.

16. *Maryland Archives* (Acts of the Assembly), vol. XIII, p. 552; vol. XXII, p. 560; vol. XXIV, p. 106; and vol. XXVI, p. 331.

17. Aubrey C. Land, "Economic Base and Social Structure: The Northern Chesapeake in the Eighteenth Century," *The Journal of Economic History*, vol. XXV, no. 4, December 1965, pp. 642–646.

18. Tyson, *Banneker*, pp. 13–14.

19. James Eaton, *A Treatise on Arithmetic* (Boston: Brown & Taggard, 1861), p. 203. On "Double Position," see also John J. White, *Arithmetic Simplified: Being a Plain, Practical System, Adapted to the Capacity of Youth, and Designed for Use in The Schools, in the United States* (Hartford: Geo. Goodwin & Sons, 1819), pp. 330–331; and David Eugene Smith, *History of Mathematics* (Boston, Ginn & Co., 1925), vol. II, pp. 437–440.

20. Paul Wilstach, *Tidewater Maryland* (Indianapolis: Bobbs, Merrill Co., 1931), passim.

21. Tyson, *Banneker*, p. 32.

22. *Ibid.*, pp. 12–13.

III. FRIENDS AND NEIGHBORS

1. Charles W. Evans, *Biographical and Historical Accounts of the Fox, Ellicott, and Evans Families, and the Different Families Connected with Them* (Buffalo, N. Y.: Press of Baker, Jones & Co., 1882), pp. 10–74. See also Milton Drake, *Almanacs of the United States* (New York: The Scarecrow Press, 1962), Part I, pp. 135–136, 218–220; Part II, pp. 987, 991, 993, 1321–1322.

2. Martha E. Tyson, *Settlement of Ellicott's Mills, with Fragments of History therewith Connected, Written at the Request of Evan T. Ellicott* (Baltimore: Maryland Historical Society, 1871), p. 9.

3. *Ibid.*, p. 26.

4. Ledger of Ellicott & Co., 1774–1775 (owned by Mrs. Henry M. Fitzhugh III and Mrs. Charles E. Wilde III), pp. 91, 103, 120, 523.

5. John S. Tyson, Sketches of the Settlement of Ellicott Mills for the Howard District Press, May 15, 1847. (Typewritten manuscript is privately owned and used with permission.)

6. Robert Gibson, *A Treatise of Practical Surveying; Which Is Demonstrated From Its First Principles*, 2nd ed. (Dublin: Printed for William Ross, 1768). This copy in its original leather binding is owned by Dr. Robert T. Fitzhugh. On the flyleaf is the signature of George Wall, Jr., with the date 1781; the inscription, "James Hamilton, His Book," also appears and on the title page are the signatures "Geo. Ellicott 1784" and "M. E. Tyson 1854."

7. Ferdinand-M. Bayard, *Voyage Dans l'Intérieur des Etats-Unis, à Bath, Winchester, Dans la Vallée de Shenandoah, etc., etc., Pendant l'Eté de 1791* (Paris, 1797), pp. 5–10. Detailed descriptions of the clock appear in Tyson, *Settlement of Ellicott's Mills, op. cit.*, pp. 57–58; Richard E. Norton, "The Ellicott Clock," *Horology*, vol. VII, no. 5, August 1940, pp. 28–33; and George H. Eckhardt, "The Masterpiece of Joseph Ellicott, American Clockmaker," *Antiques*, July 1934, pp. 50–53.

8. George Wright, *Description and Use of Both the Globes, the Armillary Sphere, & The Orrery* (London, 1783). In the copy owned by George Ellicott (privately owned and used with permission.) the title page has been torn out, but on the second half title are the notations; "Elizabeth Ellicott to her daughter M. E. Tyson 1852" and "Purchased by George Ellicott in 1790," and the note by Martha Tyson quoted is pasted inside the front cover. Bound into the same leather-covered volume are three tracts by Joseph Priestly, "L.L.D. F. R. S. and a Lover of the Gospel," all published in 1784.

9. James Ferguson, *An Easy Introduction to Astronomy, For Young Gentlemen and Ladies: Describing the Figure, Motions and Dimensions of the Earth; the Different Seasons, Gravity and Light; the Solar Systems, the Transit of Venus, and its Use in Astronomy; the Moon's Motions and Phases; the Eclipses of the Sun and Moon; the Cause of the Ebbing and Flowing of the Tides, &c.* 4th ed. (London; Printed for T. Cadell in the Strand, MDCCLXXIX). The Ellicott copy, owned by Dr. Robert T. Fitzhugh, carries on the front flyleaf the story of its associations with the Ellicott family, and on the title page the words "Presented to

M. E. Tyson by her Mother, EE., 1832," both in the handwriting of Martha E. Tyson.

10. Tyson, *Settlement of Ellicott's Mills, op. cit.,* p. 47.

IV. Work and Study

1. James Ferguson, *Astronomy Explained Upon Sir Isaac Newton's Principles, and made easy for those who have not studied Mathematics* (London, 1756, reprinted by J. F. and C. Rivington in at least nine editions. The copy used by Banneker has not been found.

2. [The Reverend Nevil Maskelyne, ed.] *Tabulae Motuum Solis et Lunae Novae et Correctae. Auctore Tobia Mayer: Quibus Accedit Methodus Longitudinum Promota, Eodem Auctore. Editae Jussu Praefectorum Rei Longitudinariae* (London, William and John Richardson. Sold by John Nourse, John Mount, and Thomas Page, 1770). Written on the title page are the words "Presented by George Ellicott to B. Banneker and in the possession of the astronomer at his death. Martha E. Tyson 1854," and an earlier inscription, "George Ellicott 1784." A note attached to the inner cover, signed "W. Kenworthy 1810," gives a formula for correcting "Geo. Ellicott's Tables to agree with Nautical Almanac 1811."

3. Charles Leadbetter, *A Compleat System of Astronomy. In Two Volumes, Containing the Description and use of the Sector, the Laws of Spheric Geometry; the Projection of the Sphere Orthographically and Stereographically upon the Planes of the Meridian, Ecliptic and Horizon; the Doctrine of the Sphere, and the Eclipses of the Sun and Moon for thirty-seven years. Together with all the Precepts of Calculation. Also new Tables of the Motions of the Planets, fix'd Stars, and the first Satellite of Jupiter; of right and oblique Ascensions, and of Logistical Logarithms. To the whole are prefix'd Astronomical Definitions for the Benefit of young Students* (2nd ed., London: J. Wilcox, 1742). The copy used by Banneker has not been found.

4. Letter from Benjamin Banneker to George Ellicott, dated October 13, 1789. Manuscript Division, Maryland Historical Society. The letter was donated to the Society in 1854 by Martha E.

Tyson, together with a later letter to Susanna Mason and George Ellicott's personal copy of Banneker's almanac for 1792.

5. Ferguson, *Astronomy Explained . . .* , *op. cit.* (9th ed., London: J. F. & C. Rivington, 1794), pp. 335–340; Leadbetter, *op. cit.*, pp. 5, 457, 458.

6. Moses Coit Tyler, *History of American Literature* (New York: G. P. Putnam's Sons, 1878), vol. 2, p. 120.

7. Tyson, *Banneker*, p. 31.

8. A. Rachel Minick, *A History of Printing in Maryland 1791–1800* (Baltimore, Enoch Pratt Free Library, 1949), pp. 74–87. See also Joseph Towne Wheeler, *The Maryland Press, 1777–1790* (Baltimore, The Maryland Historical Society, 1938), pp. 43–44, 51–55.

9. Letter from Benjamin Banneker to Andrew Ellicott dated May 6, 1790. Historical Society of Pennsylvania, Pennsylvania Abolition Society Manuscripts, vol. II, folio 145.

10. Letter from Joseph Townsend to James Pemberton dated November 28, 1790. Pennsylvania Abolition Society Manuscripts, vol. II, p. 233.

11. W. E. B. Du Bois, *The Suppression of the African Slave-Trade to the United States of America, 1638–1870* (New York, Schocken Books, 1969), pp. 39–91.

12. Pennsylvania Abolition Society Manuscripts, Minutes of the Society, vol. I (1787–1800), p. 133.

13. Joseph Townsend, "Some Account of the British Army, Under the Command of General Howe, and of The Battle of Brandywine, on the Memorable September 11, 1777 . . . ," *Proceedings of the Historical Society of Pennsylvania*, September 1846, vol. I, no. 7. Includes a biographical sketch of Joseph Townsend by Townsend Ward. See also *Minutes of the Proceedings of a Convention of Delegates From the Abolition Societies Established in Different Parts of the United States, Assembled at Philadelphia, On the First Day of January, One Thousand Seven Hundred and Ninety-Four, and Continued, by Adjournments, Until the Seventh Day of the Same Month, Inclusive* (Philadelphia: Zachariah Poulson, Jr., 1794).

14. The constitution is quoted in its entirety, together with the first slate of officers and committee members, in William

Frederick Poole, *Anti-Slavery Opinions Before the Year 1800* (Cincinnati: Robert Clarke & Co., 1873), pp. 50–54. The constitution is also quoted in John S. Tyson, *Life of Elisha Tyson, the Philanthropist* (Baltimore: B. Lundy, 1820), p. 20.

15. Letter from Joseph Townsend as Secretary of the Maryland Society to the Pennsylvania Society, dated December 28, 1795, Pennsylvania Abolition Society Manuscripts, vol. IV, pp. 197 ff. The Pennsylvania Abolition Society Manuscripts include periodic reports from most of the other antislavery societies in the various states at that time.

16. Letter from Joseph Townsend to James Pemberton dated July 7, 1790. Historical Society of Pennsylvania, Pennsylvania Abolition Society Manuscripts, vol. II, folio 169, AM802. Noted by Pemberton on the cover of the letter was the statement, "Answ^d. the 9th & sent 50 of Pinkney's Speech."

17. The copy of the Banneker letter made by Pemberton for Ellicott is in a collection of Andrew Ellicott Papers in the Manuscript Division of the New-York Historical Society. The original letter was filed by Pemberton among the papers of the Pennsylvania Abolition Society (see note 9 for this chapter).

18. The letter from Joseph Townsend to James Pemberton dated November 14, 1790, is in Pennsylvania Abolition Society Manuscripts, vol. II, p. 223. In the same letter Townsend acknowledged the receipt of books and other materials for the Maryland Society, as well as a circular letter relating to antislavery activities.

19. Letter from James Pemberton to Joseph Townsend dated November 21, 1790. This letter has not been found, but Pemberton noted the date of his reply on the reverse of Townsend's letter of November 14.

20. Letter from Joseph Townsend to James Pemberton dated November 28, 1790, Pennsylvania Abolition Society Manuscripts, vol. II, p. 233.

V. The Great Adventure

1. Letter from Thomas Jefferson dated January 15, 1791, to Messrs. Johnson, Stuart, and Carroll. U.S. National Archives. *Record Group 42.*

2. Letter from George Washington to Thomas Jefferson dated February 1, 1791, U.S. National Archives, *State Department Papers*, D.C. Miscellany.

3. Letter from Thomas Jefferson to Andrew Ellicott dated February 2, 1791, U.S. National Archives, *State Department Papers*.

4. Letter from Thomas Jefferson to the Marquis de Condorcet dated August 31, 1791, Paul Leicester Ford, ed., *The Works of Thomas Jefferson* (New York: Federal Edition, 1904), vol. V, p. 379; quoted in full, vol. VI, pp. 310–312. Jefferson's draft copy is in the Library of Congress, Manuscripts Division, The Thomas Jefferson Papers, ff. 11477–11478.

5. [Martha E. Tyson], A Memoir of Benjamin Banneker, the Negro Astronomer. And Some Account of the People of The Times in Which he Lived, With Historical Extracts of Sketches of Primitive Maryland. Manuscript first draft written in 1865, of the work published as *Banneker, the Afric-American Astronomer op. cit.* Manuscript privately owned; used with permission. (Hereinafter referred to as Tyson, Memoir.)

6. Gay M. Moore, *Seaport in Virginia, George Washington's Alexandria* (Richmond: Garrett and Massie, Inc., 1949) pp. 99–111; and Dorothy H. Kabler, *The Story of Gadsby's Tavern* (Alexandria, Virginia: Newell-Cole Company, 1952), pp. 9–19. The original hostelry was also known as the City Tavern during its early period.

7. Letter from Andrew Ellicott to Thomas Jefferson dated February 14, 1791. From a draft in the possession of descendants, quoted in Sally K. Alexander, "A Sketch of the Life of Major Andrew Ellicott," *Records of the Columbia Historical Society*, vol. 2, 1899, pp. 172–173.

8. Letter from Andrew Ellicott to Sarah Ellicott dated February 14, 1791. Quoted in Alexander, *op. cit*, p. 173.

9. "A Letter from Andrew Ellicott, to Robert Patterson, in Two Parts. Part first contains a number of Astronomical Observations . . . April 2nd, 1795," *Transactions of the American Philosophical Society*, 1799, vol. IV, pp. 49–51.

10. Letter from Andrew Ellicott to Sarah Ellicott dated March 20, 1791. The letter, which is in the possession of the family, is quoted in Alexander, *op. cit.*, p. 173.

11. Ben: Perley Poore, *Perley's Reminiscences of Sixty*

Years of the National Metropolis (Philadelphia, Hubbard Brothers, 1886), vol. I, pp. 480–482. See also Harold Donaldson Eberlein and Cortlandt Van Dyke Hubbard, *Historic Houses of George-Town & Washington City* (Richmond: Dietz Press, 1958), pp. 7–13; and W. B. Bryan, "Hotels of Washington Prior to 1814," *Records of the Columbia Historical Society*, vol. 7, 1904, p. 88.

12. Letter from Andrew Ellicott to Sarah Ellicott dated June 26, 1791, from the "Surveyors Camp, State of Virginia." Quoted in Alexander, *op. cit.*, p. 174.

13. Letter from Andrew Ellicott at Georgetown to Sarah Ellicott dated August 9, 1791.

14. Letter from Andrew Ellicott to Sarah Ellicott dated November 9, 1791, Curtis Collection of Andrew Ellicott Papers, Manuscripts Division, Library of Congress.

15. *Gazette of the United States*, issue of March 5, 1791. The item bears the dateline from Georgetown, February 23.

16. Letter from Thomas Jefferson to Major Pierre Charles L'Enfant dated March 1791, Andrew A. Lipscomb, ed., *The Writings of Thomas Jefferson* (Washington: Thomas Jefferson Memorial Association, 1904), vol. VIII, p. 162.

17. Handwritten statement signed "J S N" and addressed to "Mrs. Tyson." (Privately owned; used with permission.)

18. *The Georgetown Weekly Ledger*, March 12, 1791.

19. "U.S. versus Martin F. Morris *et al.*," *Records of the Supreme Court of the District of Columbia*, Washington, 1898, vol. 7, pp. 2171–2173.

20. "George-Town News," *The Maryland Gazette*, March 18, 1791.

21. *Gazette of the United States*, Philadelphia, March 26, 1791.

22. J. C. Fitzpatrick, ed., *The Diaries of George Washington* (Boston: Houghton Mifflin Co., 1925), vol. IV, p. 152. Diary entry for March 28–30, 1791.

23. William Tindall, *Standard History of the City of Washington from a Study of the Original Sources* (Knoxville, Tenn.: H. W. Crew & Co., 1914), p. 93.

24. *The Alexandria Gazette*, April 21, 1791; also, under a dateline of April 26, 1791, from Alexandria in *The Maryland Journal* and *The Boston Advertiser*.

25. Marcus Baker, "Surveys and Maps of the District of Columbia." *The National Geographic Magazine*, vol. IV, November 1, 1894, pp. 149–178. See also John Stewart, "Early Maps and Surveyors of the City of Washington, D.C.," *Records of the Columbia Historical Society*, vol. 2, 1899, pp. 57–60; and E. F. M. Faehtz and F. W. Pratt, with the assistance of Brainard H. Warner, *Washington in Embryo; Or, The National Capital from 1791 to 1800. The Origin of All Rights and Titles to Property in Washington, D.C.* (Washington, D.C.: privately printed, 1874).

26. These statements are based on Andrew Ellicott's letter to his wife from Georgetown dated April 8, 1791, in the Curtis Collection.

27. Robert Gibson, *A Treatise of Practical Surveying*, 2nd ed. (Dublin: Printed for William Ross, 1768). Owned by Dr. Robert T. Fitzhugh.

28. Tyson, *A Sketch*, pp. 11–12.

29. Tyson, *Banneker*, p. 36.

30. Tyson, *A Sketch*, pp. 11–12; repeated almost verbatim in Tyson, *Banneker*, pp. 36–39.

31. Tyson, *Banneker*, p. 37.

32. Letter from Benjamin Banneker to Thomas Jefferson dated August 19, 1791. Massachusetts Historical Society, Manuscripts Division, Jefferson-Coolidge Papers.

33. Banneker, Manuscript Journal, page facing calculations for May 1792.

34. Letter from Andrew Ellicott to Thomas Jefferson dated April 13, 1801, Curtis Collection.

35. "A Letter from Andrew Ellicott to Robert Patterson. . . ," *Transactions of the American Philosophical Society*, 1799, vol. IV, pp. 49–51.

36. Tyson, *Banneker*, pp. 38–39.

37. Letter from Pierre Charles L'Enfant to Thomas Jefferson dated May 10, 1791, U.S. National Archives, *State Department, D.C. Papers.*

38. *Maryland Journal and Baltimore Advertiser*, June 10, 1791.

39. Wilhelmus Bogart Bryan, *A History of the National Capital From Its Foundation Through the Period of the Adoption of the Organic Act* (New York: MacMillan, 1914), vol. I, p. 165.

40. Letter from Andrew Ellicott to the Commissioners dated March 7, 1792 at Philadelphia, U.S. National Archives, *Record Group 42*, vol. I, *Public Buildings and Grounds*, No. 81½.

41. Letters from Andrew Ellicott to Sarah Ellicott, dated September 3 and 11, 1792, Curtis Collection.

42. Report on the completion of the survey dated January 1, 1793, from Andrew Ellicott to the Commissioners, Library of Congress, Manuscript Division, D.C. Miscellany. The same collection contains a letter from Andrew Ellicott to the Commissioners dated January 8, 1793.

43. Letter from Andrew Ellicott to the Commissioners dated January 29, 1793, U.S. National Archives, *Record Group 42, Public Buildings and Grounds*.

44. Letter from Andrew Ellicott to Sarah Ellicott dated April 10, 1793. Presumed to be owned in the family. Quoted in Alexander, *op. cit.*, p. 191.

45. The details of Ellicott's position in the controversy were set forth in two letters he addressed to President Washington, dated June 29, 1793, and February 28, 1794, and the Commissioners' reply dated March 23, 1794. U.S. National Archives, *Record Group 42, Public Buildings and Grounds*.

46. "Letter from Andrew Ellicott to Robert Patterson, in Two Parts. Part first contains a number of Astronomical Observations. Part second contains the Theory and Method of calculating the Aberration of the Stars, the Nutation of the Earth's Axis, and the Semiannual Equation. Philadelphia, April 2nd, 1795," *Transactions of the American Philosophical Society* (Philadelphia, Thomas Dobson, 1799), vol. IV, pp. 32–66.

47. Letter from Andrew Ellicott to Dr. William Thornton dated February 23, 1795, Library of Congress, Manuscript Division, J. Henley Smith Papers, folio 174V2–175V2. The text is quoted *in extenso* inasmuch as it has never been previously cited in relation to the survey of the city of Washington.

48. Letter from Andrew Ellicott to Thomas Jefferson dated April 13, 1801, Curtis Collection.

Reference Notes

VI. His First Almanac

1. Ferguson, *Astronomy Based on Sir Isaac Newton's Principles* . . . , *op. cit.*, Chapter 21, par. 389.

2. *Ibid.*

3. James Ferguson, *Tables and Tracts, Relative to Several Arts and Sciences* (London, printed for A. Millar and T. Cadell, 1767).

4. Frederick R. Goff, "Early Printing in Georgetown (Potomak) 1789–1800," *Records of the Columbia Historical Society*, vol. 51–52, 1955, pp. 105–111.

5. For an account of Goddard's earlier career, see Joseph Towne Wheeler, *The Maryland Press 1777–1790* (Baltimore: Maryland Historical Society, 1938), pp. 1–10, 43–47, 72. Goddard's later work is described in A. Rachel Minick, *A History of Printing in Maryland 1791–1800* (Baltimore: Enoch Pratt Free Library, 1949), pp. 1–5, 27–32, 74–78.

6. Historical Society of Pennsylvania, Pennsylvania Abolition Society Manuscripts, Minutes of the Society, vol. I, p. 133.

7. Letter from Elias Ellicott to James Pemberton dated June 10, 1791, Pennsylvania Abolition Society Manuscripts, vol. III, p. 55.

8. Edward Needles, *An Historical Memoir of the PENNSYLVANIA SOCIETY FOR PROMOTING THE ABOLITION OF SLAVERY: The Relief of Free Negroes Unlawfully Held in Bondage, and For Improving the Condition of the African Race. Compiled from the Minutes of the Society and Other Official Documents* (Philadelphia, Merrihew and Thompson, 1848), pp. 31–33.

9. Letter from Elias Ellicott to James Pemberton dated July 21, 1791, Pennsylvania Abolition Society Manuscripts, vol. III, p. 75.

10. Colonel J. Thomas Scharf, *The Chronicles of Baltimore* . . . (Baltimore, Turnbull Brothers, 1874), pp. 256–259.

11. *An Oration Upon the Moral and Political Evil of Slavery. Delivered at a public meeting of the Maryland Society for promoting the Abolition of Slavery and the relief of free Negroes and others unlawfully held in Bondage.* Baltimore, July 4, 1791. By

George Buchanan, M.D., Member of the American Philosophical Society. Baltimore, Printed by Philip Edwards, MDCCXCIII, 20 pp. Only a few copies are known, including one in the New-York Historical Society Library, and the copy from the personal library of George Washington preserved at the Boston Athenaeum. The Oration was described and reproduced in its entirety as an appendix in William Frederick Poole, *Anti-Slavery Opinions Before the Year 1800* (Cincinnati: Robert Clarke & Co., 1873).

12. Brooke Hindle, *David Rittenhouse* (Princeton, N.J.: Princeton University Press, 1964), pp. 316–330.

13. Letter from David Rittenhouse to James Pemberton dated August 6, 1791, Pennsylvania Abolition Society Manuscripts, vol. III, p. 81.

14. Pennsylvania Abolition Society Manuscripts, minutes, vol. I, p. 115.

15. Statement by William Waring dated August 16, 1791, Pennsylvania Abolition Society Manuscripts, vol. III, p. 83.

16. "A List of taxables of the Upper Hundred of Patapscoe 1737," City Hall, Baltimore, Maryland, Department of Legislative Reference, *Court Records of Baltimore City and Baltimore County*.

17. Letter from Benjamin Banneker to Thomas Jefferson dated August 19, 1791. Massachusetts Historical Society, Manuscript Collection, Jefferson–Coolidge Papers, 7S. I. 38–43.

18. Letter from Thomas Jefferson to Benjamin Banneker dated August 30, 1791, Paul Leicester Ford, ed., *The Works of Thomas Jefferson* (New York: G. P. Putnam's Sons, 1904), vol. IV, pp. 309–310. Jefferson's draft copy is in the Library of Congress, Manuscripts Division, The Thomas Jefferson Papers, f. 11481.

19. *Copy of a Letter from Benjamin Banneker, to the Secretary of State, with his Answer.* Philadelphia: Printed and Sold by Daniel Lawrence, No. 33, North Fourth-Street, Near Race. MDCCXCII. 15 pp.

20. "Letter from the famous self-taught ASTRONOMER, BENJAMIN BANNEKER, a black man, to THOMAS JEFFERSON, Esq. Secretary of State," *Universal Asylum and Columbian Magazine*, vol. 2, no. 9, October 1792, pp. 222–224.

21. Letter from Thomas Jefferson to the Marquis de Con-

dorcet dated August 30, 1791, Ford, ed., *The Works of Thomas Jefferson, op. cit.*, vol. VI, pp. 310–312.

22. Letter from Thomas Jefferson to Jean Pierre Brissot de Warville dated February 11, 1788, Ford, ed., *The Works of Thomas Jefferson, op. cit.*, vol. V, p. 388.

23. Private communication from Dr. Julian P. Boyd, Editor of *The Papers of Thomas Jefferson*, dated January 29, 1970.

24. Letters from Mme. L. Hautecoeur, Conservateur en chef, Bibliothèque de l'Institut, dated February 17, 1970, and from Jean-Claude Nardin, dated March 14, 1970.

25. Private communications with R. Courier and Louis de Broglie, secretaries of the Académie des Sciences, dated March 17, 1969, and January 8, 1970; from Roger Pierrot of the Bibliothèque Nationale, dated May 12, 1969, and December 29, 1969; from Marcel Thomas of the same repository dated January 27, 1970; and from Jean-Claude Nardin, dated March 14, 1970.

26. The papers of the Société des Amis des Noirs have not been preserved as a whole. The private papers of Brissot are preserved by heirs and are not available for study. Those papers of the Société which have survived are in the collections of the Bibliothèque de l'Institut de France and in the Bibliothèque de l'Arsenal, but the Jefferson letter and enclosure are not among them. Nor are they to be found in the files of "Sequestered Papers," the personal papers seized at the homes of individuals condemned by the revolutionary courts, and which are preserved in *Serie T* of the Archives Nationales.

27. Letter from George Ellicott to James Pemberton dated August 24, 1791, Pennsylvania Abolition Society Manuscripts, vol. III, p. 87.

28. Poem signed by Benjamin Banneker and bearing the date October 19, 1791, Historical Society of Pennsylvania, Leon Gardner Collection on Negro History, Banneker Institute Papers. This poem is one of a number of holographic copies of original documents relating to Banneker in the Pennsylvania Abolition Society Manuscripts. The copies were made by an unknown individual for presentation at the November 9, 1860, meeting of the Banneker Institute. Quoted in an article, "The Banneker Institute," in an unidentified Philadelphia newspaper, issue of November 15, 1860.

29. Letter from Elias Ellicott to James Pemberton dated August 31, 1791, Pennsylvania Abolition Society Manuscripts, vol. III, p. 93.

30. Letter from Benjamin Banneker to James Pemberton dated September 3, 1791, Pennsylvania Abolition Society Manuscripts, vol. III, p. 95.

31. Letter from Elias Ellicott to James Pemberton dated September 5, 1791. Pennsylvania Abolition Society Manuscripts, vol. III, p. 97.

32. "Certificate in Regard to Genuineness of Banneker's Calculations," Pennsylvania Abolition Society Manuscripts, vol. III, p. 115.

33. These accounts are part of the ledger of Ellicott & Co. owned by Mrs. Henry M. Fitzhugh III and Mrs. Charles E. Wilde III. Letters relating to suits for collection of debts owed to a William Dilworth are in the Historical Society of Pennsylvania, Stauffer Collection, vol. 21, p. 1618 (letter of William Dilworth to Garrit D. Wolf dated July 14, 1808, and a copy of Dilworth's letter of the same date to T. Hollinshead), and in the Society's Edward Carey Gardiner Collection, Miscellaneous Section (letter from Benjamin Wilson to Samuel Shoemaker re Dilworth's suit against a certain Marks, dated November 27, 1813).

34. Letter from James Pemberton to William Goddard dated September 9, 1791 (corrected draft), Pennsylvania Abolition Society Manuscripts, vol. III, p. 103.

35. Letter from William Goddard to James Pemberton dated September 13, 1791, Pennsylvania Abolition Society Manuscripts, vol. III, p. 101.

36. *The Maryland Journal and Baltimore Advertiser*, December 21, 1790.

37. *Ibid.*, December 21, 1791.

38. Banneker's Manuscript Journal, pages facing the ephemerides for October, November, and December, 1792 (hereinafter referred to as Manuscript Journal).

VII. The Years of Fulfillment

1. Early in November 1793 Angell took as his partner Paul James Sullivan. The partnership was dissolved in June 1794 and

Angell again continued his business by himself until the end of October 1794 when he sold it to Francis Brumfield. See Joseph Towne Wheeler, *The Maryland Press 1777–1790* (Baltimore, The Maryland Historical Society, 1938), pp. 43–47.

2. *Banneker's Almanac for 1793* (Goddard and Angell), p. 2.

3. Dagobert D. Runes, ed., *Selected Writings of Benjamin Rush* (New York: Philosophical Library, 1947), pp. 19–23.

4. Benjamin Rush, *Essays, Literary and Moral* (Philadelphia: Thomas and Wiliam Bradford, 1798), pp. 183–188.

5. In a private communication dated February 10, 1970, Dr. Lyman H. Butterfield, editor of *Letters of Benjamin Rush*, stated that he had no knowledge of any printing of the essay prior to its appearance in Banneker's almanac for 1793. See *Letters of Benjamin Rush* (Princeton, N.J.: Princeton University Press, 1951), vol. II, p. 542. Dr. Henry J. Cadbury, in private communications dated November 7 and November 14, 1969, also expressed his belief that the essay had been published in an earlier form before its inclusion in the almanac but he had not been able to find such a published version despite an exhaustive search. The essay is mentioned also by Nathan G. Goodman in his biography, *Benjamin Rush, Physician and Citizen 1746–1813* (Philadelphia: University of Pennsylvania Press, 1934), p. 284, as well as by John Hope Franklin in *From Slavery to Freedom, A History of Negro Americans*, 3rd ed. (New York: Alfred A. Knopf, 1967), p. 158.

6. Letter from Joseph Townsend to Benjamin Banneker dated May 8, 1793. This letter has not been located.

7. Letter from Benjamin Banneker to Joseph Townsend dated May 14, 1793, Historical Society of Pennsylvania, Dreer Collection, Astronomers and Mathematicians. A brief description of this letter was published in the *Catalogue of the Collection of Autographs Formed by Ferdinand J. Dreer* (Philadelphia, 1890), vol. I, p. 28.

8. Manuscript Journal, reverse of page with calculations for January 1798.

9. Letter from Joseph Townsend to James Pemberton dated July 4, 1793, Historical Society of Pennsylvania, Pennsylvania Abolition Society Manuscripts, vol. III, p. 246.

10. *Benjamin Banneker's Almanac for 1794* (James Angell), p. 2.

11. Letter from Benjamin Banneker to James Pemberton dated March 22, 1794, New York Public Library, Manuscript Division, Miscellaneous Papers.

12. *Benjamin Banneker's Almanac for 1795* (Baltimore: S. & J. Adams), Preface, p. 2.

13. *Banneker's Almanac for 1795* (William Young), reverse of cover.

14. *Benjamin Banneker's Almanac for 1796* (Edwards, Keddie, and Thomas, Andrews and Butler of Baltimore), Preface, p. 2.

15. This entry from Banneker's Commonplace Book is quoted by Tyson, both in *A Sketch*, p. 16, and in *Banneker*, p. 62.

16. Keatinge, a prominent Irish-born bookseller, bookbinder, and publisher of Baltimore, contracted with Jackson for the printing of a number of books and pamphlets with his imprint in 1796 and 1797. See A. Rachel Minick, *A History of Printing in Maryland 1791–1800* (Baltimore: Enoch Pratt Free Library, 1949), pp. 120–125.

17. *Banneker's Almanac for 1797* (Baltimore: Christopher Jackson), pp. 27–28.

18. *Banneker's Almanac for the Year 1797*, Richmond ed., p. 27; Baltimore eds. p. 26.

19. Private communication from B. J. S. Watkins dated March 1969. In a communication from a reader to *The (British) Horological Journal*, published in March 1959, p. 162, the same inscription was stated to have been found in Aberconway Churchyard in the same form in which it was published in the almanac. A private communication from Gwilyn Berw Hughes, Rector of Conway Parish in Caernarvon, Wales, however, stated that the epitaph does not appear on any of the graves of that churchyard or of other village burial grounds in that area.

20. See, for example, Edward J. Wood, *Curiosities of Clocks and Watches From the Earliest Times* (London: Richard Bentley, 1866), p. 382; C. A. O. Fox, ed., *An Anthology of Clocks and Watches* (London: privately printed for the author, 1947), p. 29.

21. For a discussion of the reasons for the weakening of the antislavery movement by the turn of the eighteenth century,

Reference Notes

see Winthrop D. Jordan, *White Over Black, American Attitudes Towards the Negro 1550–1812* (Baltimore: Penguin Books, 1969), pp. 349–356.

22. Colonel J. Thomas Scharf, *The Chronicles of Baltimore . . .* Baltimore: Turnbull Brothers, 1874), pp. 255–260.

23. "Report of Important Events in the History of the Maryland Society" [compiled by Joseph Townsend, Secretary], 1794, Pennsylvania Abolition Society Manuscripts, vol. IV, p. 31.

VIII. SCIENTIFIC CONSIDERATIONS

1. James Ferguson, *Astronomy Explained . . .* (London, 1794), p. 147.
2. *Ibid.*, Chapter XVIII, "To Project an Eclipse of the Sun Geometrically."
3. Manuscript Journal, page facing calculations for April 1792.
4. *Ibid.*, page facing calculations for the year 1802.
5. *Ibid.*, page facing calculations for the month of April 1793. See Ferguson, *Astronomy Explained . . .* (1794), Plate XII, Figure 2, and pp. 344–345.
6. Ferguson, *Astronomy Explained . . .* (1794), p. 368.
7. Manuscript Journal, page facing calculations for January 1796.
8. *Ibid.*, page facing calculations for March 1800.
9. *Ibid.*, page facing calculations for May 1799.
10. *The Nautical Almanac and Astronomical Ephemeris* (London: H.M. Nautical Almanac Office, 1795). For an account of its history, see Eric G. Forbes, "The Foundation and Early Development of the Nautical Almanac," *Journal of the Institute of Navigation*, vol. 18, no. 4, 1965, pp. 391–401.
11. Manuscript Journal, page facing calculations for June 1796.
12. Ferguson, *Astronomy Explained . . .* (1794), Chapter XVIII, "Of Eclipses: Their Number and Periods," p. 234. Since it is not presently known which edition of Ferguson's work was used by Banneker, it is not possible at this time to determine whether this footnoted material appeared in his copy.

13. Manuscript Journal, page facing calculations for February 1794. The reference is to Charles Leadbetter, *A Compleat System of Astronomy* . . . , 2nd ed. (London, J. Wilcox, 1742), vol. 2, p. 204. The planetary symbols are, in order of their appearance, for Jupiter, Mars and the sun, and Mercury.

14. Manuscript Journal, page facing calculations for February 1802.

15. *Ibid.*, page facing the emphemeris for November 1801.

16. *Ibid.*, opposite ephemeris for May 1802.

17. *Ibid.*, page facing the calculations for January 1798; the reference is to Leadbetter, *op. cit.*, "Precept XIV. To Find in any Year, how many Eclipses there will be and in what Months they happen."

18. Leadbetter, *op. cit.*, Section IV, The Doctrine of the Spheres.

19. See Ferguson, *Astronomy Explained* . . . , Chapter XVIII, "To Project An Eclipse of the Sun Geometrically," p. 337.

20. *Banneker's Almanac for the Year 1797* (Baltimore, printed by Christopher Jackson for George Keatinge's), p. 2.

21. Manuscript Journal, page facing calculations for May 1800. The eclipse notes are inscribed on the page facing calculations for April 1800. The longitude of the eclipse is given as 92½° west and the latitude as 52°50′ north, placing the eclipse center in central Canada, northwest of Lake Superior.

22. *Ibid.*, page facing calculations for July 1800.

23. Ferguson, *Astronomy Explained* . . . , p. 340.

24. Manuscript Journal, page facing calculations for January 1795.

25. *Ibid.*

26. John Hamilton Moore, *The New Practical Navigator; Being an Epitome of Navigation; Containing the Different Methods of Working the Lunar Observations, and All the Requisite Tables Used with the Nautical Almanack, in Determining the Latitude and Longitude, and Keeping a Complete Reckoning at Sea* (London, J. Crowden, 1772). The first American edition was not published until 1799; Banneker used one of the numerous English editions. His copy has not survived.

27. The work is not identified; the quotation appears in Oliver L. Fassig, "A Sketch of the Progress of Meteorology in

Maryland and Delaware," *Maryland Weather Service* (Baltimore: Johns Hopkins Press, 1899), vol. I, p. 331.

28. Captain John Smith, *History of Virginia*. The Sixth Voyage, 1606. *The Works of Captain John Smith*, edited by Edward Arber (Birmingham, 1884).

29. Thomas Campanius Holm, *Kort Beskrifning om Nya Sverige* (Stockholm, 1702).

30. Thomas Glover, "An Account of Virginia," *Philosophical Transactions of the Royal Society*, vol. LXVII, 1667, p. 450.

31. John Clayton, "An Account of Several Observables in Virginia, more particularly concerning the Air," *Philosophical Transactions of the Royal Society*, 1668, vol. XVII, pp. 781 ff.

32. John Bigelow, ed., *Works of Benjamin Franklin*, 1897, vol. II, p. 76, 161–164. Letters to Jared Eliot dated July 16, 1747, and February 13, 1750.

33. Richard Brooke, "Thermometrical Account of the Weather in Maryland for one year from September 1753," pp. 58 ff.; "Thermometrical account of the weather in Maryland for three Years from September 1754," pp. 70 ff.; and "Observations in Virginia and in his Voyage Thither, Particularly concerning the Air," pp. 79–82, *Philosophical Transactions of the Royal Society*, 1759, vol. LI.

34. Weather forecasting based on the influence of the moon is discussed in Fassig, *op. cit.*, p. 347 ff.; F. J. Walz, "Fake Weather Forecasts," *Popular Science Monthly*, vol. XLVII, no. 6, October 1905, pp. 503–513; and E. B. Garriott, "Long Range Weather Forecasts," U.S. Department of Agriculture, *Bulletin No. 35*, Weather Bureau, 1904, pp. 37–43. See also A. J. Prahl, "The Hagerstown Almanack," *The American-German Review*, vol. VIII, June 1942, pp. 7–10.

35. For examples of such predictions see *Moore's Almanac* by Francis Moore, M.D., London, for the years 1791–1800, and an almanac by the Reverend I. R. Hicks called *Word and Works*, January 1904.

36. Manuscript Journal, page facing calculations for August 1797.

37. For discussion of weather prognostication prior to the development of instruments and institutions for the purpose see

James Berry and W. F. R. Phillips, *Proceedings of the Second Convention of Weather Bureau Officials Held at Milwaukee, Wisconsin, August 27, 28, 29, 1901,* U.S. Department of Agriculture, Weather Bureau, *Bulletin No. 31,* pp. 111–167; *passim;* Edward B. Garriott, "Weather Folk-Lore and Local Weather Signs," U.S. Department of Agriculture, *Bulletin No. 33,* Weather Bureau No. 294, 1903; and Garriott, "Long-Range Weather Forecasts," *op. cit.*

38. *Banneker's Almanac for 1795* (Baltimore: S. & J. Adams).

39. D. Gernez, "Les Indications relative aux Marées dans les anciens livres de Mer," *Archives Internationales d'Histoire des Sciences,* no. 7, 1949, pp. 571–591.

40. Manuscript Journal, first page.

41. *Ibid.,* page facing calculations for March 1792.

42. *Ibid.,* page facing calculations for December 1798.

43. *Ibid.,* page facing the ephemeris for October 1802.

44. *Ibid.,* page facing the calculations for May 1792.

45. *Ibid.,* page facing ephemeris for January 1793.

46. *Ibid.,* page facing calculations for the month of November 1802.

IX. THE FINAL YEARS

1. "The stings of Poverty, Disease, and Violence, less pungent than those of guilty passion," *Banneker's Almanac for 1792* (Goddard & Angell), p. 28.

2. Shirley Graham, *Your Most Humble Servant* (New York, Julian Messner, 1949), p. 139, states that Benjamin's mother and oldest sister, Tillie, died in the summer of 1781, but no documentation for this fact has been found.

3. "A List of Taxables for Patapsco Upper Hundred for the Year 1773 Taken by Abraham Walker Constable."

4. Manuscript Journal, first page.

5. *Ibid.,* page facing ephemeris for March 1799.

6. *Ibid.,* page facing calculations for April 1799.

7. *Ibid.,* page facing calculations for August 1802.

8. Tyson, *A Sketch,* p. 13, fn. 1.

9. Indenture for sale of land by Benjamin Banneker to

Reference Notes

Greenbury Morten dated December 20, 1785, witnessed on the following day and recorded on June 19, 1786. State of Maryland Hall of Records, *Baltimore County Land Records*, 1785, WQ#Y, ff. 653–654.

10. Jeffrey R. Brackett, *The Negro in Maryland. A Study of The Institution of Slavery* (Baltimore: N. Murray, 1889), p. 187, fn. 1, and John Slattery, "Benjamin Banneker, The Negro Astronomer," *The Catholic World*, December 1883, p. 351.

11. Agreement between Banneker and Ellicott & Co., quoted in Tyson, *A Sketch*, p. 10.

12. *Baltimore County Land Records*, Liber W. G. # H. H., folios 341–342. Indenture of sale by Benjamin Banneker to John Barten [sic], dated April 2, 1792.

13. *Ibid.*, Liber W. G. # M. M., folios 244–245. Indenture of sale from Benjamin Banneker to John Nimiy dated August 10, 1792, witnessed May 7, 1793, and recorded October 17, 1793.

14. *Ibid.*, Liber W. G. # P. P., folios 606–608. Indenture of sale of land by Benjamin Banneker to Edward Shugar dated December 10, 1794, recorded December 18, 1794.

15. *Ibid.*, Liber W. G. # 51, folios 197–199. Indenture for sale of land from Benjamin Banneker to Thomas Gibbons dated June 8, 1797, recorded June 26, 1797.

16. *Ibid.*, Liber W. G. # 60, folios 139–140. Indenture for sale of land from Benjamin Banneker to Thomas Gibbons dated October 22, 1799, recorded November 4, 1799.

17. *Ibid.*, Indenture for sale of land by Greenbury Morten to Thomas Gibbons dated October 22, 1799.

18. *Ibid.*, Liber W. G. # 60, ff. 408–410. Indenture for sale of land by Benjamin Banneker to Jonathan Ellicott *et al.* dated October 23, 1799.

19. Manuscript Journal, page facing calculations for November 1799.

20. *Ibid.*, page facing calculations for January 1798.

21. *Ibid.*, page opposite the calculations for January 1795.

22. Tyson, *Banneker*, p. 70.

23. Tyson, *A Sketch*, p. 10.

24. *Ibid.*, p. 12.

25. Tyson, *Banneker*, p. 38.

26. Manuscript Journal of the Reverend William Colbert,

p. 81. Collection of the Garrett Theological School, Evanston, Ill.

27. Romans, 6:23: "For the wages of sin is death, but the gift of God is life everlasting in Christ Jesus our Lord."

28. Manuscript Journal, page facing calculations for March 1792.

29. *Ibid.*, page facing the calculations for February 1792.

30. *Ibid.*, page facing calculations for February 1797.

31. *Ibid.*, page facing calculations for August 1798.

32. Tyson, *Banneker*, p. 54.

33. *Ibid.*, pp. 55–56.

34. Manuscript Journal, page facing calculations for March 1801.

35. [Rachel Mason], *Selections from the Letters and Manuscripts of the Late Susanna Mason; With a Brief Memoir of her Life, By Her Daughter* (Philadelphia, Rackliff & Jones, 1836), pp. 16–17.

36. Charles W. Evans, *Biographical and Historical Accounts of the Fox, Ellicott, and Evans Families . . .* (Buffalo: Baker Jones & Co., 1882), pp. 32–33.

37. Mason, *op. cit.*, pp. 242–246.

38. *Ibid.*, pp. 244–246.

39. Letter from Benjamin Banneker to Mrs. Susanna Mason dated August 26, 1797, The Maryland Historical Society, Manuscripts Division.

40. Daniel Alexander Payne, *Recollections of Seventy Years* (Nashville, Tenn.: Publishing House of the A.M.E. Sunday School Union, 1888), p. 78.

41. Manuscript Journal, page facing calculations for December 1798.

42. *Ibid.*, page facing calculations for December 1799.

43. Banneker's Commonplace Book.

44. Manuscript Journal, page facing calculations for June 1798.

45. Everett Franklin Phillips, *Beekeeping* (New York: Macmillan, 1928), pp. 263–264; A. I. Root, *The ABC and XYZ of Bee Culture* (Medina, Ohio: The A. I. Root Co., 1966), pp. 343–345, 568–570, 579.

46. John H. B. Latrobe, "Memoir of Benjamin Banneker, Read Before the Historical Society of Maryland," *Maryland Coloni-*

zation Journal, new series, vol. 2, no. 29, May 1845, p. 360, and Tyson, *Banneker,* p. 62.

47. Such a treatise is mentioned in the entry about Banneker in *Who Was Who in America 1607–1896,* rev. ed. (Chicago: A. N. Marquis Co., 1963), p. 39, as well as in Lerone Bennett, Jr., *Before the Mayflower: A History of the Negro in America 1619–1962* (Chicago: Johnson Publishing Company, 1962), p. 332, and Wilhelmena S. Robinson, *Historical Negro Biographies* (New York: Publishers Co., 1968), p. 9.

48. *Banneker's Almanac for 1792* (Baltimore: Goddard and Angell), pp. 24–25.

49. Manuscript Journal, page facing calculations for June 1800.

50. A. S. Taylor, "Grasshoppers and Locusts of America," *Annual Report of the Board of Regents of the Smithsonian Institution of the Year 1858* (Washington, 1859), pp. 203 ff. See also John T. Schlebecker, Jr., "Grasshoppers in American Agricultural History," *Agricultural History,* vol. 27, no. 3, July 1953, pp. 85–93.

51. J. G. Myers, *Insect Singers: A Natural History of the Cicada* (London: G. Routledge and Sons, 1929).

52. Tyson, *A Sketch,* p. 14.

53. Tyson, *Banneker,* p. 67.

54. Tyson, *A Sketch,* p. 4, and *Banneker,* p. 12.

55. Manuscript Journal, page facing calculations for October 1800.

56. *Ibid.,* page facing calculations for November 1795.

57. *Ibid.,* page facing calculations for August 1800; quoted in Tyson, *A Sketch,* p. 13, and *Banneker,* p. 64.

58. Manuscript Journal, page facing calculations for August 1800.

59. A four-page manuscript written in Banneker's hand but unsigned. (Privately owned; used with permission.)

60. Manuscript Journal, page facing calculations for March 1793.

61. *Ibid.,* page facing calculations for February 1797.

62. *Ibid.,* page facing calculations for December 1799.

63. *Ibid.,* page facing calculations for August 1802.

64. *Ibid.,* page facing calculations for February 1798.

65. Tyson, *A Sketch*, pp. 17–18, and *Banneker*, pp. 70–72.

66. *The Federal Gazette, and Baltimore Daily Advertiser*, October 28, 1806.

X. The Man Remembered

1. John H. B. Latrobe, in "Memoir of Benjamin Banneker . . ." , *Maryland Colonization Journal*, new series, vol. 2, no. 29, May 1845, p. 362.

2. Charles Coleman Sellers, *Benjamin Franklin in Portraiture* (New Haven: Yale University Press, 1962), pp. 203–205.

3. Tyson, *A Sketch*, p. 19, and *Banneker*, p. 54.

4. Thomas Ellicott replied to Martha Tyson's request for information about Banneker in a letter dated "Avondale 12 mo 21st. 1857" addressed to "My dear Niece Martha E. Tyson," now in the possession of Dr. Robert T. Fitzhugh.

5. Tyson, *A Sketch*, p. 14.

6. Tyson, *Banneker*, pp. 67–68.

7. Mantle Fielding, *Dictionary of American Painters, Sculptors and Engravers* (Philadelphia, privately printed, 1926). Fisher is described as a "renewer of copper plates for certificates" in H. Glenn Brown, *A Directory of the Book Arts and Book Trade in Philadelphia to 1820. Including Painters and Engravers* (New York: New York Public Library, 1950).

8. Gilbert Imlay, *A Topographical Description of the Western Territory of North America*, 2nd ed. (London, 1793), pp. 212–213.

9. For a clear analysis of Jefferson's position on Negro slavery see Daniel J. Boorstin, *The Lost World of Thomas Jefferson* (New York: Holt, 1948), Chapters 2 and 4. See also Winthrop D. Jordan, *White Over Black, American Attitudes Towards the Negro 1550–1812* (Chapel Hill: University of North Carolina Press, 1968), Chapter XII.

10. Tyson, *A Sketch*, p. 7.

11. [William Loughton Smith], *The Pretensions of Thomas Jefferson to the Presidency Examined; And the Charges Against John Adams Refuted* (Philadelphia, 1796), pp. 7–14. The passage quoted appears on page 10.

12. Henry W. De Sassure, *Address to the Citizens of South Carolina* (Charleston, S. C.: For W. P. Young, 1800), p. 16.

13. Thomas Green Fessenden, *Democracy Unveiled or Tyranny Stripped of the Garb of Patriotism by Christopher Caustic* (New York, 1806), vol. II, p. 52.

14. An enlightening discussion of Jefferson's position in relation to Banneker is to be found in Jordan, *op. cit.*, pp. 449–457. See also "Thomas Jefferson's Thoughts on the Negro," *The Journal of Negro History*, vol. III, 1918, pp. 55–89.

15. Henri Gregoire, *De la littérature des Negres, Ou Recherches sur leurs facultés intellectuelles, leurs qualités morales et leur littérature* (Paris, Chez Maradan, 1808), pp. 211–212. An English translation appeared two years later with the title, *An Enquiry concerning the Intellectual and Moral Faculties and Literature of Negroes; Followed with an Account of the Life and Works of Fifteen Negroes and Mulattoes.* Translated by D. B. Warden (Brooklyn, N. Y.: Thomas Kirk, 1810).

16. Letter from Thomas Jefferson to Bishop Henri Gregoire, dated February 25, 1809, Paul Leicester Ford, ed., *The Works of Thomas Jefferson* (New York: G. P. Putnam's Sons, 1904), vol. XI, pp. 99–100.

17. Letter from Thomas Jefferson to Joel Barlow dated October 8, 1809. H. A. Washington, ed., *The Writings of Thomas Jefferson* (Washington, D.C.: Taylor & Maury, 1853), vol. V, pp. 475–476. The letter is included also in Ford, *op. cit.*, p. 261.

18. [Rachel Mason], *Selections from the Letters and Manuscripts of the Late Susanna Mason; With a Brief Memoir of her Life, By Her Daughter* (Philadelphia: Rackliff & Jones, 1836), pp. 242–246.

19. Latrobe, "Memoir," pp. 353–364.

20. Bishop Daniel Alexander Payne, D.D., L.L.D., *Recollections of Seventy Years.* Compiled and arranged by Sarah C. Bierce Scarborough, edited by Rev. C. S. Smith (Nashville, Tenn.; Publishing House of the A.M.E. School Union, 1888), pp. 77–78. See also Josephus R. Coan, *Daniel Alexander Payne, Christian Educator* (Philadelphia: The A.M.E. Book Concern, 1935), p. 78.

21. See T. Buckler Ghequiere, "The Messrs. Long, Architects," *The American Architect and Building News*, vol. I, June 24, 1876, p. 207; Richard Hubbard Howland and Eleanor Patterson

Spencer, *The Architecture of Baltimore* (Baltimore: Johns Hopkins Press, 1953), pp. 54–59, 97–99; and Wilbur H. Hunter, Jr., "Robert Cary Long, Jr., and the Battle of the Styles," *Journal of the Society of Architectural Historians,* vol. XVI, no. 1, March 1957, pp. 28–30.

22. *Repository of Religion, Science and Literature,* vol. 4, no. 7, mentions the articles by Bishop Payne.

23. For biographical sketch of Moses Sheppard see *Appleton's Cyclopedia of American Biography* (New York, 1894), vol. V, pp. 496–497. Sheppard's interest in Banneker is mentioned in Bliss Forbush, *Moses Sheppard, Quaker Philanthropist of Baltimore* (Philadelphia: J. B. Lippincott, 1968), pp. 241–243.

24. Martha E. Tyson's comment occurs in her 1865 manuscript entitled, A Memoir of Benjamin Banneker, the Negro Astronomer . . . , p. 108.

25. Tyson, *Banneker,* p. 71.

26. Latrobe, "Memoir," p. 358.

27. Letter from Sheppard to John H. B. Latrobe dated January 20, 1852, The Friends Historical Library, Swarthmore College, The Moses Sheppard Papers, RG 5, Box 2, folder Ser. 3,h.

28. Letter to Charles Sumner dated May 3, 1852, The Moses Sheppard Papers, RG 5, Box 2, Ser. 3,h.

29. Letters to Dr. Samuel F. McGill at Cape Palmas, Liberia, dated July 5, 1852, and November 18, 1852; also letter to George M. Justice, dated November 18, 1852, the Moses Sheppard Papers, Letter Book A, RG 5, Box 2, folder Ser. 3,h.

30. Copies exist in the Historical Society of Pennsylvania, Maryland Historical Society, New York Public Library, and other collections, Sheppard maintained a record of the copies of the lithograph which he distributed in his Letter Books, now preserved among the Moses Sheppard Papers.

31. Letter from Miss Dorothy Dix to Sheppard dated June 29, 1852, the Moses Sheppard Papers, Letter Book A, RG 5, Box 2, folder Ser. 3, h. a.

32. A note made in 1910 by Martha Ellicott Tyson's daughter, Lucy Tyson Fitzhugh, on the reverse side of a letter from Frederick Douglass to Anne Tyson Kirk dated March 4, 1878, stated that "Moses Sheppard had bound in Russia leather a large manuscript book of Bannekers, containing calculations & many interesting things —we also have it. L T F 1910 Westminster, Md."

33. The journal is presently owned by Dr. Robert Tyson Fitzhugh.

34. Tyson, *A Sketch*, p. 2. A manuscript copy in the hand of Martha E. Tyson, presumed to be the original paper read before the Society, is privately owned.

35. Letter from Rachel Mason to Martha E. Tyson, dated December 5, 1847, privately owned.

36. Statement without topical heading, signed by Martha E. Tyson and undated, privately owned.

37. Martha E. Tyson manuscript, privately owned; see note 34.

38. Unsigned and undated statement by Martha E. Tyson, privately owned.

39. Letter from John H. B. Latrobe dated September 19, 1864, to Martha E. Tyson, privately owned.

40. From a handwritten statement signed by Martha E. Tyson but not dated, privately owned.

41. Letter from Brautz Mayer of the Maryland Historical Society to J. Saurin Norris dated January 20, 1854, privately owned. Eight hundred copies of *A Sketch* were published, of which 200 were forwarded to Mrs. Tyson, according to a letter to her dated January 15, 1855, from Lewis Mayer, Assistant Librarian of the Maryland Historical Society, privately owned.

42. Historical Society of Pennsylvania, Leon Gardner Collection of American Negro History, "Minute Book of the Banneker Institute (Literary) 1854," Ams 32.

43. *Constitution and by-Laws of The Banneker Institute of the City of Philadelphia*, Philadelphia: G. T. Stockdale, 1864, 15 pp. Copy in Leon Gardner Collection of American Negro History, Ams 32.

44. An article entitled "The Banneker Institute" in an unidentified Philadelphia newspaper for November 15, 1860, in the collection of the John Carter Brown Library.

45. The Minutes of the Banneker Institute for the years 1854–1859, in addition to four other volumes of rolls, receipts, etc., are in the Manuscripts Department of the Historical Society of Pennsylvania.

46. These transcriptions are in a folder marked "Banneker Institute Papers" in the Leon Gardner Collection on Negro History.

47. Moncure D. Conway, "Benjamin Banneker, The Negro Astronomer," *The Atlantic Monthly*, vol. XI, no. LXIII, January 1863, pp. 79–84; reprinted as Tract No. 9, *Benjamin Banneker, The Negro Astronomer. Reprinted from The Atlantic Monthly*. By M. D. Conway. London, Printed and Published for the Ladies' London Emancipation Society, by Emily Faithfull, Printer and Publisher in Ordinary to Her Majesty, Victoria Press, April 1864, 15 pp.

48. [Martha E. Tyson], *Banneker, The Afric-American Astronomer. From the Posthumous Papers of Martha E. Tyson. Edited by Her Daughter*. Philadelphia, Friends' Book Association, 1884, 72 pp.

49. These three letters from Frederick Douglass to Anne Tyson Kirk are part of the Tyson family papers owned by Dr. Robert T. Fitzhugh.

50. The following note is inscribed on the reverse side of the letter by Martha Tyson's daughter Lucy Tyson Fitzhugh; "The book to which Frederic Douglas [sic] refers in this letter, was edited by Anne Tyson Kirk from the posthumous papers of her mother, Martha E. Tyson. It was published by the Friends' Book Association, 1020 Arch Street, Philadelphia, in 1884. The table upon which Banneker made his calculations & mathematical books were loaned him by my grandfather George Ellicott & are now in my possession. L T F 1910—"

51. The research was directed by John H. Scarff with the assistance of William B. Marye of Baltimore, who contributed a comprehensive study of Baltimore County land records. The statement that Banneker produced the first almanac in Maryland is in error.

52. State of Maryland Hall of Records, *Baltimore County Land Records, Liber T. K. No. 260*, folios 1–46, dated May 2, 1835. Roger Brooke, Joshua Pearce and Nathan Tyson, Trustees for the Estate of George Ellicott, deceased, and Jonathan, John, and Elias Ellicott.

53. *Ibid.*, Liber W. G. No. 60, folio 410, dated October 23, 1799. Benjamin Banneker to Ellicott & Co.

54. Maryland Hall of Records, *Baltimore County Wills*, Liber 4, folios 392–393, filed December 3, 1789. Mary Williams was a sister of Thomas Johnson.

55. A study made by William B. Marye for the Historical Sites Commission, now filed in the Maryland Historical Society.

56. Tyson, *Banneker*, pp. 64–65.

57. From "Worth Superior to meer Birth and Title," *Banneker's Almanack and Ephemeris for* . . . *1794* (Crukshank, Philadelphia) [p. 10].

BIBLIOGRAPHY

BIBLIOGRAPHY

◊❀◊❀◊❀◊❀◊❀◊❀◊❀◊❀◊❀◊

I. Banneker's Letters and Almanacs

1. *Copy of a Letter from Benjamin Banneker, to the Secretary of State, with his Answer.* Philadelphia, Printed and Sold by Daniel Lawrence, No. 33. North Fourth-Street, Near Race, MDCCXCII.

Letter to Thomas Jefferson dated August 19, 1791 transmitting a copy of the writer's almanac, and discussing the subject of slavery. Jefferson's reply is dated August 30, 1791.

2. *Benjamin Banneker's Pennsylvania, Delaware, Maryland, and Virginia Almanack and Ephemeries, For the Year of Our Lord, 1792; Being Bissextile, or Leap-Year, and the Sixteenth Year of American Independence, which commenced July 4, 1776. Containing, the Motions of the Sun and Moon, the true Places and Aspects of the Planets, the Rising and Setting of the Sun, and the Rising, Setting and Southing, Place and Age of the Moon, &c.—The Lunation, Conjunction, Eclipses, Judgment of the Weather, Festivals, and other remarkable Days; Days for holding the Supreme and Circuit*

(379)

Courts of the United States, as also the usual Courts in Pennsylvania,
Delaware, Maryland, and Virginia.—Also, Several useful Tables and
valuable Receipts.—Various Selections from the Commonplace-Book
of the Kentucky Philosopher, an American Sage; with interesting
and entertaining Essays, in Prose and Verse—the Whole comprising
a greater, more pleasing, and useful Variety, than any Work of the
Kind and Price in North-America. Baltimore: Printed and Sold,
wholesale and Retail, by William Goddard and James Angell, at
their Printing-Office, in Market-Street.—Sold, also, by Mr. Joseph
Crukshank, Printer, in Market-Street, and Mr. Daniel Humphreys,
Printer in South-Front Street, Philadelphia—and by Messrs. Hanson
and Bond, Printers in Alexandria. [1791].

3. *Benjamin Banniker's* [sic] *Pennsylvania, Delaware,*
Maryland and Virginia Almanack and Ephemeris for 1792. Baltimore: William Goddard and James Angell [1791].

4. *Banneker's Almanac for 1792.* By Benjamin Banneker.
Philadelphia: Printed for William Young, Bookseller, No. 52, the
Corner of Chestnut and Second Streets [1791].

5. *Banneker's Almanack, and Ephemeris For the Year of*
our Lord, 1793; Being the First After Bissextile or Leap-Year: Con-
taining The Motions of the Sun and Moon; The True Places and
Aspects of the Planets; The Rising and Setting of the Sun; Rising,
Setting, and Southing of the Moon: the Lunations, Conjunctions,
Eclipses; and the Rising, Setting, and Southing of the Planets and
Noted Fixed Stars. Philadelphia: Printed and Sold by Joseph Crukshank, No. 87, High Street. [1792]. (Listed by Evans, but no
locations given.)

6. *Benjamin Banneker's Pennsylvania, Delaware, Maryland*
and Virginia Almanack and Ephemeris, For the Year of our Lord
1793; Being the first after Bissextile, or Leap-Year, and the Seven-
teenth Year of American Independence, which commenced July
4th, 1776: Containing the Motions of the Sun and Moon, the true
Places and Aspects of the Planets, the Rising and Setting of the Sun
and the Rising, Setting and Southing, Place and Age of the Moon,
&c.—The Lunations, Conjunctions, Eclipses, Judgment of the
Weather, Festivals, and other remarkable Days; Days for holding
the Supreme and Circuit Courts of The United States, as also the
Usual Courts in Pennsylvania, Delaware, Maryland, and Virginia.—
Also, Several useful Tables and valuable Receipts.—Various, Selec-

tions, from the Commonplace-Book of the Kentucky Philosopher, an American Sage; with interesting and Entertaining Essays, in Prose and Verse—the Whole Comprising a Greater, more Pleasing, and Useful Variety, than any Work of the Kind and Price in North-America [Four Lines of verse]. Baltimore: Printed and Sold Wholesale and Retail, by William Goddard and James Angell, at their Printing-Office, in Market-Street. [1792].

7. *Banneker's Almanack and Ephemeris for the Year of our Lord 1794; Being the Second After Bissextile or Leap Year: Containing the Motions of the Sun and Moon; The True Places and Aspects of the Planets; The Rising and Setting of the Sun; Rising, Setting, and Southing of the Moon; The Lunations, Conjunctions and Eclipses; and the Rising, Setting and Southing of the Planets and Noted Fixed Stars.* Philadelphia: Printed and sold by Joseph Crukshank, No. 87, High Street.

8. *Benjamin Banneker's Pennsylvania, Delaware, Maryland and Virginia Almanac and Ephemeris. For the Year of our Lord, 1794* . . . Baltimore: Printed and sold, wholesale and retail by James Angell, at his Printing-Office in Market-Street. [1793].

9. *Benjamin Banneker's Almanac for 1794.* Philadelphia: Printed for William Young, Bookseller, No. 52, the Corner of Chestnut and Second Streets [1793].

10. *The Virginia Almanack for 1794.* By Benjamin Banneker. Petersburg: Printed for William Prentis [1793].

11. *Bannaker's* [sic] *New-Jersey, Pennsylvania, Delaware, Maryland and Virginia Almanac, or Ephemeris, For the Year of our Lord 1795; Being the Third after Leap-Year;—the Nine-teenth Year of American Independence, and the Seventh of our Federal Government—Which may the Governor of the World prosper. Containing the Motions of the Sun and Moon; the true Places and Aspects of the Eight Planets, the Rising and Setting of the Sun; the Rising, Setting, Southing, Node, Age and Latitude of the Moon, &c.—Also, the Lunations, Conjunctions, and Eclipses; remarkable Days; judgment of the Weather; length of Days and Nights; the Time that Courts are held in New-Jersey, Pennsylvania, Delaware, Maryland and Virginia; Post-Roads, with a Variety of instructive and entertaining Matter in Prose and Verse.* Wilmington: Printed by S. & J. Adams. [1794].

12. *Bannaker's* [sic] *Wilmington Almanac, or Ephemeris,*

For the Year of Our Lord 1795; Being the Third after Leap-Year;—the Nineteenth Year of American Independence, and the Seventh of our Federal Government—Which May the Governor of the World prosper!—Containing the Motions of the Sun and Moon; the true Places and Aspects of the Eight Planets; the Rising and Setting of the Sun; the Rising, Setting, Southing, Node, Age and Latitude of the Eclipses; remarkable Days and Nights; the Time that Courts are held in New-Jersey, Pennsylvania, Delaware, Maryland and Virginia, Post-Roads, with a Variety of instructive and entertaining Matter in Prose and Verse. Wilmington: Printing by S. & J. Adams, for Frederick Craig. [1794].

13. *Banneker's Almanac, For the Year 1795: Being the Third after Leap Year. Containing, (Besides every Thing Necessary in an Almanac,) An Account of the Yellow Fever, Lately Prevalent in Philadelphia; With the Number of those who Died, from the First of August till the Ninth of November, 1793.* Philadelphia: Printed for William Young, Bookseller, No. 52, the Corner of Chestnut and Second Streets. [1794].

14. *Benjamin Bannaker's* [sic] *Pennsylvania, Delaware, Maryland and Virginia Almanac, for the Year of our Lord 1795; Being the Third after Leap-Year.* [Portrait of Banneker]. Philadelphia: Printed for William Gibbons, Cherry Street. [1794].

15. *Benjamin Bannaker's* [sic] *Pennsylvania, Delaware, Maryland, and Virginia Almanac, For the Year of our Lord 1795; Being the Third after Leap-Year.* [Portrait of Banneker]. Philadelphia: Printed for Jacob Johnson & Co. No. 147 Market-Street. [1794].

16. *Bannaker's* [sic] *Wilmington Almanac, or Ephemeris for the Year of Our Lord 1795; Being the Third After Leap-Year.* Wilmington: Printed by S. & J. Adams [1794].

17. *Bannaker's* [sic] *Wilmington Almanack for the Year of Our Lord 1795; Being the Third After Leap-Year.* Wilmington: S. & J. Adams for W. C. Smyth [1794]. (Listed by Evans as No. 1397 but no copies are known.)

18. *Benjamin Bannaker's* [sic] *Pennsylvania, Delaware, Maryland and Virginia Almanac for 1795.* Wilmington: S. & J. Adams [1794]. (Listed by Evans as No. 1398 but no copies are known.)

19. *Banneker's New-Jersey, Pennsylvania, Delaware, Mary-*

land and Virginia Almanac, or Ephemeris for 1795. Baltimore: S. & J. Adams [1794].

20. *New-Jersey & Pennsylvania Almanac, For The Year of our Lord 1795; Being the Third after Leap-Year, and the Twentieth of American Independence, after the Fourth of July. Containing, Besides the usual Requisites of an Almanac, A Variety of Entertaining Matter, in Prose and Verse. To Which is Added, An Account of the Yellow Fever, in Philadelphia. The Astronomical Calculations By Benjamin Banneker, An African.* Trenton: Printed and Sold, Wholesale and Retail by Matthias Day. [1794].

21. *Bannaker's* [sic] *New-Jersey, Pennsylvania, Delaware, Maryland and Virginia Almanac, or Ephemeris, For the Year of our Lord 1795; Being the Third after Leap-Year.* [Portrait of Bannaker]. Wilmington: Printed by S. & J. Adams. [1794].

22. *The Pennsylvania, Delaware, Maryland and Virginia Almanack, for the Year of our Lord, 1795.* Balto., Printed by James Angell for Fisher and Coale. [1794]. (Listed by Charles W. Evans but no locations given; Drake No. 2239. See Reference Notes, III, 1.)

23. *The Pennsylvania, Delaware, Maryland and Virginia Almanack for the Year of our Lord, 1795; Being the Third after Leap-Year.* Wilmington: Printed and sold by S. and J. Adams. [1794].

24. *Benjamin Bannaker's* [sic] *Pennsylvania, Delaware, Maryland and Virginia Almanac, For the Year of Our Lord 1795; Being the Third After Leap Year.* Baltimore: Printed for, and Sold by John Fisher, Stationer. [1794]. (Portrait of Banneker on title-page.)

25. *Bannaker's* [sic] *Maryland, Pennsylvania, Delaware, Virginia, Kentucky and North Carolina Almanack and Ephemeris For the Year of our Lord 1796; Being Bissextile, or Leap-Year; The Twentieth Year of American independence and Eighth Year of the Federal Government.* Baltimore: Printed for Philip Edwards, James Keddie, and Thomas, Andrews and Butler; and Sold at their respective Stores, Wholesale and Retail. [1795].

26. *Bannaker's* [sic] *Virginia and North Carolina Almanack and Ephemeris for the Year of our Lord 1797; Being First after Bissextile, or Leap-year; The Twenty-First Year of American Independence, and Ninth Year of the Federal Government.* Petersburg: Printed by William Prentis and William Y. Murray. [1796].

27. *Bannaker's* [sic] *Virginia, Pennsylvania, Delaware, Maryland and Kentucky Almanack and Ephemeris, for the Year of Our Lord 1797; Being First Year after Bissextile, or Leap-Year; The Twenty-First Year of American Independence, and Ninth Year of Federal Government.* Balto: Printed by Christopher Jackson, No. 67 Market Street for George Keatinge's bookstore [Copyright secured]. [1796].

28. *Bannaker's* [sic] *Virginia, Pennsylvania, Delaware, Maryland and Kentucky Almanack and Ephemeris, for the Year of Our Lord 1797; Being First After Bissextile, or Leap-Year; The Twenty-First Year of American Independence, and the Ninth Year of Federal Government.* Richmond: Printed by Samuel Pleasants, jun. near the Vendue Office [by privelege]. [1796].

29. *Bannaker's* [sic] *Maryland and Virginia Almanack and Ephemeris, for the Year of Our Lord 1797; Being First After Bissextile, or Leap-Year. The Twenty-First Year of American Independence, and Ninth Year of the Federal Government.* Baltimore: Printed by Christopher Jackson, for George Keatinge's Wholesale and Retail Book-Store, No. 140 Market-street. [1796].

II. WORKS RELATING TO BANNEKER

In addition to the twenty-eight editions of Banneker's almanacs issued over a period of six years, and the pamphlet containing his correspondence with Thomas Jefferson, the published literature relating to Benjamin Banneker includes numerous references and biographical sketches published in a great variety of periodicals and books from 1792 to the present time.

To assist scholars and students in further studies of Banneker's work or of related aspects of the history of science in America, such references and accounts as can presently be compiled are listed herewith. The annotations designate original material or indicate when possible the sources of other work.

Of the one hundred and two references only five are biographical sketches based on contemporary sources utilizing information from acquaintances of Banneker in his lifetime. These are the accounts published by James McHenry, Susanna Mason, and John H. B. Latrobe, and the two works by Martha Ellicott Tyson. It is on these that the numerous other accounts and references have principally relied for their information, frequently perpetuating minor errors of dates and data.

In order to show how interest in Banneker has fluctuated over the years, these references are presented chronologically by date of publication.

The list is undoubtedly incomplete, and additional references may come to light from time to time. Perhaps the present work will stimulate the discovery of additional original information and publications about Banneker.

1. "Account of Benjamin Banneker, a free Negro," *Universal Asylum,* November 1791, pp. 300–301.

Reprint of the letter from James McHenry to Goddard & Angell, written August 20, 1791, and published in Banneker's almanac for 1792. (See also Items 2 and 3).

2. "Account of a Negro Astronomer. A Letter from Mr. James McHenry to the Editors of the Pennsylvania, Delaware, Maryland and Virginia Almanack, containing particulars respecting Benjamin Banneker, a free Negro," *New York Magazine, or Literary Repository*, 1791, vol. 2, pp. 557–558.

Reprint of McHenry's letter of August 20, 1791. (See also Items 1 and 3).

3. "A letter from mr. James McHenry, to messrs. Goddard and Angel, containing particulars reflecting Benjamin Banneker, a free negro," *American Museum* (Philadelphia), vol. 12, no. 2, September 1792, pp. 185–187.

Reprint of McHenry's letter of August 20, 1791. (See also items 1 and 2.)

4. "Letter from the famous self-taught ASTRONOMER, BENJAMIN BANNEKER, a black man, to THOMAS JEFFERSON, Esq. Secretary of State," *Universal Asylum*, October 1792, pp. 222–224.

Reprint of Banneker's letter to Jefferson and the latter's reply. (See also Bibliography, Part I, item 1.)

This correspondence was also reprinted under the title "From a Virginia Newspaper To The Printer" as a front page feature in *The Providence* [R. I.] *Gazette and Country Journal*, vol. XXIX, no. 44, November 3, 1792.

5. "Account of Benjamin Banneker, A Negro Calculator, Prefixed to His Pennsylvania, Delaware, Maryland, and Virginia Almanack and Ephemers, For the Year of Our Lord 1792. Baltimore, Printed and Sold by W. Goddard and J. Angell. *For the Bee.*," *The Bee, or Literary Weekly Intelligencer,* . . . by James Anderson, LLD, Edinburgh, vol. 13, 1793, pp. 291–293.

Reprint of McHenry's letter of August 20, 1791. (See also items 1, 2 and 3.)

6. Gilbert Imlay. *A Topographical Description of the Western Territory of North America.* 2nd ed. London, 1793, pp. 212–213.

In the second edition of this work (first published in 1792), reference is made to an unnamed New England Negro who had composed an ephemeris. Imlay's statement is mentioned by Gregoire (item 11), with a speculation as to whether Imlay was referring to Banneker or to another Negro savant in the American colonies. Imlay's passage is in rebuttal to Jefferson's argument in his *Notes on Virginia* and other writings, in which the latter had asked

". . . if the world has produced more than two poets acknowledged to be such by all nations, how many mathematicians, how many great inventors in arts and sciences had Europe, north of the Alps, when the Romans crossed those mountains? and then he says, 'it was sixteen centuries before a Newton could be formed.' And after asking these questions, he [Jefferson] absurdly expects that black poets and mathematicians are to spring up like mushrooms.

"However, a black in New England has composed an ephemeris, which I have seen, and which men, conversant in the science of astronomy declare exhibits marks of acute reason and genius."

7. [George Buchanan]. *An Oration Upon the Moral and Political Evil of Slavery. Delivered at a Public Meeting of the Maryland Society for Promoting the Abolition of Slavery, and the Relief of Free Negroes, and others unlawfully held in Bondage. Baltimore, July 4th, 1791. By George Buchanan, M.D., Member of the American Philosophical Society.* Baltimore. Printed by Philip Edwards, MDCCXCIII, p. 10.

Brief mention of Banneker as an outstanding member of his race, along with Phillis Wheatley and others.

8. William Loughton Smith. *The Pretensions of Thomas*

Bibliography

Jefferson to the Presidency Examined; And the Charges Against John Adams Refuted. Addressed to the Citizens of America in General; And Particularly to the Electors of the President. United States, October 1796, pp. 7–14.

This pamphlet constitutes a vicious attack on Jefferson, particularly in his role as a philosopher. Smith dwelt at length upon the apparent inconsistencies in Jefferson's published statements on the Negro and on slavery. He made extensive use of Jefferson's remarks on skin pigmentation in his *Notes on Virginia,* cited Jefferson's reply to Banneker as further evidence of insincerity, questioned whether Jefferson did in fact forward Banneker's ephemeris to de Condorcet, and then attacked de Condorcet for the absurdities he claimed to have found in his constitution.

9. Henry W. De Sassure. *Address to the Citizens of South Carolina.* Charleston, S. C.: For W. D. Young, 1800, p. 16.

Discussion of Jefferson's position on slavery, quoting his reply to Banneker in part.

10. Thomas Green Fessenden. *Democracy Unveiled or Tyranny Stripped of the Garb of Patriotism by Christopher Caustic.* New York, 1806, vol. II, p. 52, ftn.

Refers to Jefferson's apparent reversal of attitude toward the Negroes as expressed in his reply to Banneker. Fessenden was quite as vicious in his attack on Jefferson as he was, by implication, in his comments on "Banneker, *said to be* [italics S. A. B.] the author of an almanack, &c.," and on ". . . the wonderful phenomenon of a Negro Almanack, (probably enough made by a white man). . . ."

11. Bishop Henri Gregoire. *De la littérature des Nègres, ou Recherches sur leurs facultés intellectuelles, leurs qualités morales et leur littérature; suivies de Notices sur la vie et les ouvrages des Nègres qui se sont distingués dans les Sciences, les Lettres et les Arts.* Paris, Chez Maradan, Libraire, 1808, pp. 211–212.

This work was translated into English and published in the United States two years later with the title *An Enquiry concerning the Intellectual and Moral Faculties and Literature of Negroes; Followed with an Account of the Life and Works of Fifteen Negroes and Mulattoes.* Translated by D. B. Warden. Brooklyn, Thomas Kirk, 1810.

Among the sketches of fifteen Negroes is included one of Banneker, which incorporates a number of errors. It mentions briefly the almanacs for 1794 and 1795 without reference to the earlier or later issues. The author was apparently unaware that Banneker had died two years prior to the publication of his book. He mentioned a letter to Banneker from Jefferson but not the letter which Banneker had sent to him. Footnotes mention the two almanacs as well as the works of Fessenden (item 10) and Imlay (item 6).

12. Alexander Mott. *Biographical Sketches and Interesting Anecdotes of Persons of Colour. To Which is Added a Selection of Pieces of Poetry.* New York, Mahlon Day, 1826, p. 219.

The biographical sketch of Banneker consists of a single paragraph, which appears to be merely a translated summary of the sketch published by Bishop Gregoire (item 11).

13. [Susanna Mason]. *Selections from the Letters and Manuscripts of the Late Susanna Mason; With a Brief Memoir of Her Life, By Her Daughter.* Philadelphia, Rackliff & Jones, 1836, pp. 242–246.

Included among the letters and writings of Susanna Mason are an account of her visit to Banneker's home about 1796, with a poem she composed about him after her visit (Document 26). One of the earliest first-hand accounts about Banneker.

14. Jno. H. B. Latrobe. "Memoir of Benjamin Banneker, Read Before the Historical Society of Maryland," *Maryland Colonization Journal*, New Series, vol. 2, no. 23, May 1845, pp. 353–364.

The first published account devoted exclusively to the life and work of Banneker; provides much of the authenticated data subsequently copied by later writers. Latrobe indicated that his sketch was based on memoranda collected by Benjamin H. Ellicott of Baltimore, to which he added "the materials furnished by his record book." (See also items 15 and 16.)

15. John H. B. Latrobe. "Memoir of Benjamin Banneker," *The African Repository (Colonizationist).*

No copy of this article has been found. (See also items 14 and 16.)

16. [John H. B. Latrobe]. "Memoir of Benjamin Banneker," *The New National Era.*

No copy of this article has been found. (See also items 14 and 15.)

17. "Benjamin Banneker: The Colored Astronomer of

Maryland," *Plea For the Oppressed And Enslaved.* Austinburg
(Ohio), February 2, 1847, vol. I, no. 3, pp. 1–2.

The full front page and part of a second page of this small
journal are devoted to an anonymous presentation of Banneker as
an example of intellectual achievement of a member of the Negro
race. It consists chiefly of a comprehensive sketch of his life and accomplishments, largely derived from Latrobe's "Memoir" (item 14).
The journal *Plea For the Oppressed And Enslaved* was published
by The Ladies' Anti-Slavery Society of Ashtabula County, Ohio,
and approximately 4,000 copies of each issue were distributed without charge. According to an editorial note, the present issue was
the last to be published.

18. Benjamin Kurtz. "The Learned Negro," *The Lutheran
Observer* [Lancaster, Pennsylvania], vol. 16, no. 31, August 25,
1848, pp. 134–135.

An article of one and one-third columns, preceded by a note
stating:

"For the gratification of our readers we have prepared a hasty
sketch of Banneker, the Learned Negro, which will be found in
another column, and will doubtless be read with interest. The facts
we have collected from a pamphlet, entitled: Memoir of Benjamin
Banneker, read before the Maryland Historical Society, at the
monthly meeting, May 1, 1845, by John H. Latrobe, Esq."
(See item 14).

19. Wilson Armistead. *A Tribute for the Negro: Being a
Vindication of the Moral, Intellectual, and Religious Capabilities of
the Coloured portion of Mankind; With Particular Reference to
The African Race.* Manchester, William Irwin, 1848, pp. 126, 350–
356.

This English work was widely distributed by the antislavery
movement. The title page indicated that the American agent for the
publication was "Wm. Harned, Anti-Slavery Office, 61, John Street,
New York; and may be had of H. Longstreth and G. W. Taylor,
Philadelphia." It is a compilation from other published works about
the Negro.

Banneker is mentioned in two parts of the work. In Chapter XI
in which "The African race [is] examined in an Intellectual point
of view," he is described among Negroes having made achievements

in the arts and sciences. He was identified as "Richard" Banneker, and the author noted that ". . . his calculations were so thorough and exact, as to excite the approbation of Pitt, Fox, Wilberforce, and many other eminent persons. An almanac which he composed, was produced in the British House of Commons, as an argument in favour of the mental cultivation of the Coloured people, and of their liberation from their wretched thraldom." This section was based on the biographical sketch of Banneker published by Gregoire (item 11) and so stated. In a later section a short biography of Banneker features the correspondence with Jefferson, which is quoted in full. Reference is made also to the comment by Imlay (item 6) concerning an American Negro who calculated an almanac.

20. William G. Allen. *Wheatley, Banneker, and Horton.* Boston, Daniel Laing, Jr., 1849, pp. 28–38, "Benjamin Banneker" by John H. B. Latrobe.

A condensed version of Latrobe's memoir as published in the *Maryland Colonization Journal* (item 14), of which selected paragraphs are included verbatim. In his Introduction, Allen states:

"The sketches of Wheatley, Banneker and Horton were written by white persons distinguished for character and standing. It is worthy of remark that not one of the writers is identified with the anti-slavery movement; but on the contrary two of them reside in slave States. This fact, with the letters of Washington and Jefferson, will add to the interest of these sketches and confirm their authenticity. . . .

"Banneker excelled in the department of intellect to which the colored man has usually been regarded as being but illy adapted. He was an astronomer and mathematician. He was also a mechanic of the highest order,—working not by patterns but by principles. The sketch here presented was read before the Maryland Historical Society."

The copy used for the present book has on the title page an inscription stating that it was a presentation from "Wm. H. Minton to the Banneker Institute" and that a former owner was J. B. White, Jr. It is now in the collection of the Historical Society of Pennsylvania.

21. "A Negro Almanac-Maker," *The Leisure Hour* (London), no. 56, January 20, 1853, pp. 54–58.

Bibliography

Anonymous account of Banneker based on Latrobe's "Memoir" (item 14), with errors in dates and data.

22. [Martha E. Tyson]. *A Sketch of the Life of Benjamin Banneker; From Notes Taken in 1836.* Read by J. Saurin Norris, Before the Maryland Historical Society, October 1854. Baltimore, John D. Toy [n. d.], 20 pp.

The *Sketch* was compiled by Martha E. Tyson with the encouragement of her mother, Mrs. George Ellicott, to provide material for a biography of Banneker planned by Rachel Mason, daughter of Susanna Mason (see item 13). Rachel Mason abandoned the project shortly before her death in 1849, and Mrs. Tyson then prepared the paper for the Society to serve as a correction for erroneous data previously presented by Latrobe (item 14). She interviewed various individuals who had known Banneker in his lifetime, as well as surviving relatives, in order to produce what is one of the most valuable original sources on Banneker.

J. Saurin Norris, who read the *Sketch* before the Maryland Historical Society, was Mrs. Tyson's nephew-in-law.

23. [Moncure D. Conway]. "Banneker The Black Astronomer," *The Southern Literary Messenger*, vol. XXIII, New Series vol. II, July 1856, pp. 65–66.

Brief, relatively accurate account of Banneker and his works, containing a few minor errors. (See also items 26 and 27).

24. [Daniel Alexander Payne]. "A Literary Curiosity— Letter from Benjamin Banneker to Hon. Thos. Jefferson," *Repository of Religion and Literature and of Science and Art*, vol. IV, no. 7, July 1862, pp. 168–171.

The first of a series of articles about Banneker which the Reverend Daniel Alexander Payne planned to publish in the *Repository*, of which he served as editor from 1858–1862. It consists primarily of the letters exchanged between Banneker and Jefferson, with a brief summary of Banneker's life. Payne commented:

"If our young men would but follow the noble example set by this *black son* of Maryland, they would by their intellectual culture, correct deportment, pure habits and chaste manners, prove their *manhood* and *equality*, and compel the respect of all who now hate our race unless they be so stupified by prejudice and malice towards one portion of God's creatures that no truth—no ray of light— can reach them."

Payne mentioned that Banneker's letter to Jefferson was brought to his attention by John H. Pinder, a teacher in Ebenezer Sabbath School. (See also item 39.)

25. William Wells Brown. "A Celebrated Negro American. Benjamin Banneker," *Sunday Dispatch* (Philadelphia), September 1, 1861.

Fairly extensive biographical sketch of Banneker, including several erroneous statements; quotes largely from his letter to Jefferson and the latter's reply.

26. Moncure D. Conway. "Benjamin Banneker, The Negro Astronomer," *The Atlantic Monthly*, vol. XI, no. LXIII, January 1863, pp. 79–84.

A concise account of Banneker's life and accomplishments based on the articles by Tyson (item 22) and Latrobe (item 14). Includes some clarification of Banneker's involvement in astronomical studies not provided in other accounts. There is no original material. A version was reprinted in *Sharpe's London Magazine*, vol. 37, 1863, pp. 133–134.

27. [Moncure D. Conway]. *Benjamin Banneker, The Negro Astronomer. Reprinted from "The Atlantic Monthly." By M. D. Conway. Tract No. 9.* London, Printed and Published for the Ladies' London Emancipation Society, by Emily Faithfull, Printer and Publisher in Ordinary to Her Majesty, Victoria Press, Princes Street, Hanover Square, April 1864.

This pamphlet, a reprint of Conway's article (item 26), was sold for 1d. or 5s. per hundred copies and consists of fifteen pages. The reverse of the cover bears the names of the officers and committee members of the Ladies' London Emancipation Society.

28. Lydia Maria Child. *The Freedmen's Book.* Boston, Ticknor and Fields, 1865, pp. 14–23.

Sketch of Banneker's life and work based on Latrobe (item 14) and Tyson (item 22). Well written and generally accurate, although the author makes the unsubstantiated claim that in 1803 Jefferson invited Banneker to visit him at Monticello, and there are some errors in dates picked up from the sources stated.

29. Commissioner of Education, *Report on the Condition and Improvement of the Public Schools. Submitted to the Senate and House of Representatives June 1868 and 1870.* Washington,

Bibliography

Government Printing Office, 1871, pp. 297–298, 300. "Banneker, the Astronomer."

A short survey of Banneker's career, with numerous erroneous dates and details, prepared by M. B. Goodwin and addressed to Henry Barnard, Commissioner of Education, as part of a report on "Schools of the Coloured Population." The account of a debate in the U.S. Senate in March 1864, the date of Sumner's amendment providing for no exclusion from the cars to the bill incorporating the Metropolitan railroad of Washington, which led Senator Reverdy Johnson to respond spiritedly if not quite accurately to Senator Saulsbury's disparagement of the Negro race with an erroneous reference to Banneker, although he did not mention his name:

"Many of those born free have become superior men. One of them was employed in Maryland in surveying, several of our boundary lines—Mason's and Dixon's particularly—and some of the calculations made on that occasion, astronomical as well as mathematical in the higher sense, were made by a black Maryland man who had been a slave."

30. William Frederick Poole. *Anti-Slavery Opinions Before the Year 1800.* Cincinnati, Robert Clarke & Co., 1873, pp. 10, 27–28.

The letters between Banneker and Jefferson are quoted in relation to Jefferson's published statements on the subject of slavery. The oration of Dr. George Buchanan (item 7) is reproduced in its entirety.

31. "A Learned American Negro," *The Chronotype*, vol. I, no. 1, 1873, Published by the American College of Heraldry and Genealogical Registry, pp. 24–26.

Unsigned brief résumé of Banneker's life and work based on earlier sources.

32. Mary Clemmer Ames. *Ten Years in Washington. Life and Scenes in the National Capital, As a Woman Sees Them.* Hartford, Connecticut, A. D. Worthington & Co., 1874, pp. 49–50.

Contains a short description of Banneker's career based on other sources, including Latrobe (item 14) and possibly Conway (item 26).

33. David MacRae. *Amongst the Darkies.* Glasgow, John S. Marr & Sons, 1876, pp. 28–30.

In a tour of the Southern States MacRae visited many schools

for Negro children. In his work he incorporated accounts of outstanding Negroes in all fields of endeavor, including a brief account
of Banneker's life and achievements which he used to illustrate the
fallacy of the assertion that "The negro has strong emotions and
may orate and poetise, but he is destitute of invention and contriv-
ance." Based on other published sources, the account perpetuates
erroneous dates and such apocryphal claims as that in 1803 Banneker was invited to visit Jefferson at Monticello.

34. George W. Williams. *History of the Negro Race in
America from 1619–1880.* New York, G. P. Putnam's Sons, 1883,
pp. 386–398.

Comprehensive account of the life and work of Banneker based
on Tyson (item 22) and Latrobe (item 14).

35. [John R. Slattery]. "Benjamin Banneker, The Negro
Astronomer," *The Catholic World,* vol. XXXVIII, December 1883,
pp. 342–354. Biographical sketch based on Latrobe (item 14) and
Tyson (item 22).

36. *Letters of Lydia Maria Child, With a Biographical
Introduction by John G. Whittier and an Appendix by Wendell
Phillips.* Boston, Houghton Mifflin and Company, 1883, p. 184.

In a letter to Miss Eliza Scudder written from Wayland in
1864, Lydia Child commented on Lincoln and Johnson with particular reference to antislavery demonstrations in Nashville and in
Baltimore where there was erected ". . . the triumphal arch in the
streets of Baltimore, whereon, with many honored historical names,
were inscribed the names of Benjamin Banneker and R. R. Forten,
two colored men! Glory to God! This is marvellous progress!"

37. Martha E. Tyson. *Banneker, the Afric-American Astronomer. From the Posthumous Papers of Martha E. Tyson. Edited
by Her Daughter.* Philadelphia, Friends' Book Association, 1884.
72 pp.

This account of Banneker is the most extensive and authoritative of all the published sources on the subject. It is an amplification
of item 22, to which were added data collected from surviving contemporaries who had known Banneker.

38. Rev. William J. Simmons. *Men of Mark: Eminent,
Progressive and Rising.* Cleveland, George M. Rewell & Co., 1887,
pp. 344–351.

Bibliography

The chapter on Banneker is based primarily on the work of Latrobe (item 14) as taken from Williams (item 34).

39. Daniel Alexander Payne. *Recollections of Seventy Years*. Nashville, Tenn., Publishing House of the A.M.E. Sunday School Union, 1888, pp. 77–78.

Payne, who was appointed historiographer of the A.M.E. Church and became bishop in 1850, describes a lecture he presented on Banneker and his visit on July 9, 1845, with members of his parish, to the site of Banneker's home and grave. Of particular interest is his interview with a local preacher who as a boy did errands for Banneker. (See also item 24).

40. Jeffrey R. Brackett. *The Negro in Maryland, A Study of the Institution of Slavery*. Baltimore, N. Murray, 1889, p. 187, fn. 1.

Reference is made, without identification, to the case of Greenbury Morten, a free Negro who had been in the habit of voting and was unaware of the new amendment of the Maryland Constitution of 1810 limiting the right of suffrage to whites. His vote was refused at the polls. Morten was Banneker's nephew. The source for the incident mentioned was given as Latrobe's "Memoir" (item 14).

41. Edward A. Johnson. *A School History of the Negro Race in America, From 1619 to 1890, With a Short Introduction as to the Origin of the Race; Also a Short Sketch of Liberia*. Raleigh, N.C., Edwards and Broughton, 1890, pp. 32–35.

A short chapter on "Benjamin Banneka, Astronomer and Mathematician" provides a brief description of his life and achievements, based on earlier sources, with no new information.

42. Florian Cajori. *The Teaching and History of Mathematics in the United States* (Bureau of Education Circular of Information No. 3, 1890 [Whole Number 167]). Washington, Government Printing Office, 1890, p. 43.

Banneker and his achievements are briefly described in relation to early American mathematicians. The information is credited to Williams (item 34).

43. Gabrielle Marie Jacobs. "The Black Astronomer," *The Chautauquan*, vol. XXIX, New Series Vol. XX, April–September, 1899, pp. 585–589.

A well-written and quite accurate biographical sketch of Banneker encompassing the important details of his life and work, based primarily on Latrobe (item 14).

44. F. R. Diffenderffer. "Andrew Ellicott," *Historical Papers and Addresses of the Lancaster County Historical Society*. Vol. IV, 1899–1900, p. 67.

Short statement describing Banneker's role in the survey of the city of Washington, with a brief biographical sketch of his life and achievements. The author stated that the association of Banneker in the survey was brought to his attention by a Dr. Joseph H. Dubbs.

45. Emily Emerson Lantz. "Suburban Baltimore," *The Baltimore Sunday Sun*, March 12, 1905.

Brief reference to Benjamin Banneker and his association with George Ellicott, in a history of the Ellicott family.

46. Prof. Silas X. Floyd. *The New Floyd's Flowers, Short Stories for Colored People Old and Young*. Washington, D.C., Austin Jenkins Co., 1905, pp. 220–224.

Includes a chapter on "Benjamin Banneker, the Negro Astronomer," which addresses itself to "The little colored boys and girls of America." Contains exaggerated claims, such as that Banneker produced the first clock of which every part was made in America and the earliest almanacs prepared for general use in this country. As the author indicates, his account is based in large part on Conway (item 26).

47. Catherine Van Cortlandt Mathews. *Andrew Ellicott, His Life and Letters*. New York, The Grafton Press, 1908, p. 86.

This is the only definitive biography of Andrew Ellicott to the present time: it was commissioned by the family. The author stated that during the first period of the survey of the Federal City early in 1791, "Major Ellicott was at this time hard at work upon the survey, assisted by Mr. Briggs, Mr. Fenwick, his brother Benjamin Ellicott and a unique character, Benjamin Banneker, the negro mathematician and astronomer." There is a further reference to Banneker in a footnote.

48. John W. Cromwell. *The Negro in American History*. Washington, The American Negro Academy, 1914, pp. 86–97, Chapter XIX, "Benjamin Banneker."

A fairly accurate account of Banneker's life, based on Latrobe (item 14) and incorporating the several errors in dates and data noted therein. Reference is made also to the article by Jacobs (item 43), to Bishop Payne (item 24) and to the public school named for Banneker in Washington, D.C.

49. William Tindall. *Standard History of the City of Washington, From A Study of Original Sources.* Knoxville, Tenn., H. W. Crew & Co., 1914, p. 57.

In a mention of Major Andrew Ellicott's assistants in the survey of the Federal Territory, the author included Banneker, "a protege of Major Ellicott and of his father." A brief description of Banneker's achievements follows. Banneker was not a protégé of either Andrew or Joseph Ellicott.

50. Letters to the Editor concerning Banneker, *The Washington Evening Star,* October 21 and 30, 1916.

One writer, W.A.L., stated that Jefferson invited Banneker to dine with him at the Executive Mansion and that he had also invited Banneker to Monticello. Another, B., disputed these statements on the basis that they were not included in the accounts by Latrobe (item 14) and Tyson (items 22 and 37). To this W.A.L. replied that Tyson's information was collected fifty years after Banneker's death from those who knew him and were too young to have known of the Jefferson invitations. No evidence of such invitations has been found. (See also item 28).

51. Phillip LePhillips. "The Negro, Benjamin Banneker; Astronomer and Mathematician, Plea for Universal Peace," *Records of the Columbia Historical Society,* vol. 20, 1917, pp. 114–120.

Paper read by LePhillips before the Society on April 18, 1916, based entirely on earlier published sources.

52. Fred. E. Woodward. "A Ramble Along the Boundary Stones of the District of Columbia With a Camera," *Records of the Columbia Historical Society,* vol. 20, 1917, pp. 65–66.

In an article about the original boundary stones of the Federal City, Woodward provides another account of Banneker's presence during the survey, without supporting documentation and with various inaccuracies about his life and associations.

53. "Thomas Jefferson's Thoughts on the Negro," *The Journal of Negro History,* vol. III, 1918, pp. 55–89.

General discussion of Jefferson's expressions about the inferiority of the Negro. Banneker is discussed in Section V, pp. 69–71, which includes Jefferson's letters to Marquis de Condorcet, Joel Barlow, and Henri Gregoire.

54. Henry E. Baker. "Benjamin Banneker, The Negro Mathematician and Astronomer," *The Journal of Negro History*, Volume III, No. 2, April 1918, pp. 99–118.

At the time of writing, Baker was an Assistant Examiner at the U.S. Government Patent Office, and based his account on the Tyson work on Banneker (item 37) which he obtained from one of her descendants, Mrs. Tyson Manly. Other sources included the accounts in *The Leisure Hour* (item 21) and *The Atlantic Monthly* (item 26), as well as the *Sketch* by Tyson (item 21), *The Southern Literary Messenger* (item 23), *The Catholic World* (item 35), Latrobe's "Memoir" in the *Maryland Colonization Journal* (item 14), as well as the work of LePhillips published in the *Records of the Columbia Historical Society* (item 51). Despite erroneous statements about the division of the farm and Banneker's involvement with the survey of the Federal Territory, the article is a generally accurate presentation of the data already provided by the basic sources.

55. Elizabeth Ross Haynes. *Unsung Heroes*. New York, Du Bois and Dill, 1921, pp. 153–164, Chapter VIII, "Benjamin Banneker, Astronomer and Surveyor 1732–1804."

A fictionalized account of Banneker's childhood and later life based on the work of Tyson (item 21) and the English reprint of the article by Conway (item 27). There is no new material, and the dates of birth and death are inaccurate.

56. Will W. Allen, assisted by Daniel Murray. *Banneker, the Afro-American Astronomer*. Washington, D.C., 1921, 80 pp.

This compilation is based on the later Tyson work (item 37) and on the articles by LePhillips (item 51) and Baker (item 54). It was read before the Banneker Association of Washington by Daniel Murray, Assistant Librarian of the Library of Congress, with an introduction in which Murray puts forward the fictional claim that it was by means of Banneker's memory that L'Enfant's plans for the city of Washington were preserved.

57. George F. Bragg, Jr. *Men of Maryland*. Baltimore, Church Advocate Press, 1925, pp. 38–40; 155–157.

Short sketch of Banneker's life, with numerous errors in details; copies of the correspondence with Jefferson.

58. Henry D. Hyde. "Maryland Negro Distinguished As Scientist in 1792," *The Baltimore Sun*, 1926.

A brief newspaper article recounting the highlights of Banneker's achievements, prompted by the acquisition of a copy of Banneker's almanac for 1792 by the Maryland Historical Society. In an effort to dramatize his subject, the author perpetuated some of the errors in dates and data from earlier accounts.

59. "The Learned Negro," *The Journal of Negro History*, vol. XIV, no. 2, April 1929, pp. 238–242.

Transcription of the article in *The Lutheran Observer*, vol. XVI, no. 31, August 25, 1848, pp. 134–135 (item 18).

Although the author is not identified, it is believed to have been writetn by the *Observer*'s editor, the Reverend Benjamin Kurtz. A concise biographical account with discrepancies in dates, based on Latrobe (item 14) and the two Tyson accounts (items 22 and 37).

60. Helen Alpert-Levin. "A Negro Genius of His Day," *The Baltimore Sun*, July 2, 1929.

A short account of Banneker's life and achievements, based probably on Latrobe (item 14). There are no new data, and a few errors have been incorporated from the sources consulted.

61. Thomas O. Fuller. *Pictorial History of the American Negro*, Memphis, Tenn., Pictorial History, Inc., 1933, pp. 37, 342–347.

In addition to a brief mention of Banneker among other outstanding Negro figures of his time, the volume includes a short "Biography of Benjamin Banneker" by John H. B. Latrobe, which is a condensed version of his more detailed "Memoir" (item 14).

62. Josephus R. Coan. *Daniel Alexander Payne, Christian Educator*. Philadelphia, The A.M.E. Book Concern, 1935, p. 78.

A brief comment on a lecture delivered by Bishop Payne about Banneker, and his visit to the farm and Banneker's grave in July 1845, based on Payne's *Recollections of Seventy Years* (item 39). Reference is made also to a series of articles on Banneker by Payne in the periodical, *Repository of Religion, Science and Literature* (item 24).

63. "Jefferson's Dilemma," *Letters* (Time, Inc.), vol. II, no. 7, April 1, 1935, pp. 3–4.

Letter from J. N. G. Finley and a reply by the editor, discussing Jefferson's comments on Banneker in his letters to de Condorcet and Barlow. In a supplementary biographical account of Banneker by the editor, there are numerous erroneous dates and data.

64. Benjamin Brawley. *Early Negro American Writers*.

Chapel Hill, The University of North Carolina Press, 1935, "Benjamin Banneker," pp. 75–86.

Thoughtful and careful account of Banneker's life and achievements based on the two works by Tyson (items 22 and 37) with a useful evaluation of the major published sources.

65. Michael Kraus. "Slavery Reform in the Eighteenth Century: An Aspect of Transatlantic Intellectual Cooperation," *Pennsylvania Magazine of Biography and History*, vol. LX, no. 1, January 1936, pp. 62–63.

In a description of the influence of the Society of Friends in the antislavery movement on both sides of the Atlantic, reference is made to a lengthy article about Banneker in *The Bee* published in Edinburgh (item 5).

66. Henry J. Cadbury. "Negro Membership in the Society of Friends," *The Journal of Negro History*, vol. XXI, no. 2, April 1936, pp. 208–209.

In a brief and accurate summary of his life, Banneker is described as a Negro well-known to the Society of Friends. Reference is made to the fact that although he did not join any denomination, he frequently attended the meetings of Friends at Ellicott's Mills, based on Tyson's account (item 37).

67. Benjamin Brawley. *Negro Builders and Heroes*. Chapel Hill, The University of North Carolina Press, 1937, Chapter 5, "Benjamin Banneker: Astronomer," pp. 25–29, 295.

Brief account based on Brawley's earlier work (item 64), with no new material.

68. Dorothy B. Porter. "Early American Negro Writings: A Bibliographical Study," *The Papers of the Bibliographical Society of America*. New York, The Bibliographical Society of America, 1945, vol. 39, pp. 204–205, 213, 221–225.

A brief account of Banneker's life and the publication of his almanacs, including a check list of nineteen issues of the almanacs. The author states erroneously that Banneker studied Latin, Greek, German, and French. The principal source is the article by Baker (item 54).

69. Saul K. Padover. "Benjamin Banneker: Unschooled Wizard," *The New Republic*, February 2, 1948, pp. 22–25.

Brief account of Banneker highlighting the outstanding events culled from the accounts of Latrobe (item 14) and Tyson (item 22), with some errors in dates and data.

70. Shirley Graham. *Your Most Humble Servant.* New York, Julian Messner, 1949.

This work is a full-length fictionalized biography of Benjamin Banneker for children, based primarily on the published accounts of Banneker by Latrobe (item 14) and Tyson (items 22 and 37) and supplemented by fictitious incidents to complete gaps in the story. Reviews which appeared in various journals, including the *Maryland Historical Magazine* (vol. XLV, 1950, pp. 63–64) and *The Washington Afro-American*, Afro Magazine Section (February 7, 1950, pp. 3–5), unfortunately selected for comment those incidents which are apparently fictional, thus creating new fictions.

71. William W. Harrison. "Banneker as Builder," *The Evening Sun*, Baltimore, February 24, 1950.

Communication to the editor relating to Banneker's role in the survey of Washington, based on earlier published sources.

72. H. Paul Caemmerer. *The Life of Pierre Charles L'Enfant, Planner of the City Beautiful: The City of Washington.* Washinton, D.C., National Republic Publishing Co., 1950, pp. 131, 199.

This useful source work on the history of the national capital reproduces on p. 131 a painting by Garnet W. Jex entitled "The Planning of Washington" showing President Washington on the scene with Ellicott, L'Enfant, the City Commissioners, James Hoban, Isaac Roberdeau, and Banneker. The original is in the library of George Washington University in Washington, D.C. The author several times describes Banneker as one of the assistants of L'Enfant, whereas he was in fact Ellicott's assistant. There are no other references to Banneker.

73. William B. Settle. "The Real Benjamin Banneker," *The Negro History Bulletin*, vol. XVI, 1953, January, pp. 90–91; February, pp. 105–108; March, pp. 129–135; April, pp. 153–158.

This four-part series presents the story of Banneker's life in an interesting manner and generally with accuracy. The author acknowledges the "Memoir" by Latrobe (item 14) and the two articles by Tyson (items 22 and 37) as his basis sources, supplemented by the account in the work by Bragg (item 57), Mason (item 13), and Conway (item 26).

74. E. Franklin Frazier. *The Negro in the United States.* rev. ed. New York, Macmillan, 1957, p. 494.

Includes a passing mention of Banneker's almanac among outstanding prose works produced by Negroes as a protest against slavery.

75. John C. Schmidt. "Benjamin Banneker's Unusual Career," Baltimore *Evening Sun*, April 3, 1960, p. 7.

Short account of Banneker's life and work containing erroneous statements relating to his correspondence with Jefferson and his involvement of the survey of the Federal City.

76. T. F. Mulcrone. "Benjamin Banneker, pioneer Negro mathematician," *The Mathematics Teacher*, vol. LIV, no. 1, January 1961, pp. 32–37.

A carefully researched account of Banneker's life, with particular emphasis on his interest and work in mathematics.

77. Benjamin Quarles. *The Negro in the American Revolution.* Chapel Hill, The University of North Carolina Press, for the Institute of Early American History and Culture, 1961, pp. 43, 187–188.

Brief references to Banneker's letter to Jefferson and of Jefferson's opinion of Banneker based on the former's correspondence.

78. Lerone Bennett, Jr. *Before the Mayflower: A History of the Negro in America 1619–1962.* Chicago, Johnson Publishing Company, 1962.

Contains a comparison of Banneker and Phillis Wheatley, and a short account of Banneker's life, accurate, except for the statement that "Banneker also wrote a dissertation on bees and put together what was probably the first clock made in America."

79. Russell L. Adams. *Great Negroes Past and Present.* Chicago, Afro-American Publishing Co., 1963, pp. 11, 18, 49.

A picture-book treatment, with a one-page biography of Banneker and two other references.

80. Silvio A. Bedini. *Early American Scientific Instruments and Their Makers* (United States National Museum Bulletin No. 231). Washington, Government Printing Office, 1964, pp. 22–25.

A brief account of Banneker's scientific career and his role in the survey of the Federal Territory, with illustrations of his letter of October 13, 1789, and the portrait from the Fisher edition of the almanac for 1795.

81. District of Columbia Board of Education Curriculum

Bibliography

Dept. The Negro in American History, A Curriculum Resource Bulletin for Secondary Schools. Washington, D.C. (Mimeographed), 1964, pp. 19–20.

One paragraph on Banneker, erroneously stating that he was the first American to make a clock, that he "predicted the location of stars," and that he was appointed a professional member "of the commission headed by Major Pierre Charles L'Enfant. . . ."

82. Jack L. Hodge. "He Looked and Remembered," *The News American* (Baltimore), February 7, 1965.

Brief newspaper account of Banneker's restoration of the plans for the Federal City from memory, which is fiction.

83. "Banneker's Memory Saved Capital Plans," *Catonsville* [Md.] *Herald-Argus*, April 15, 1965.

Brief account of Banneker's life, probably based on Graham (item 70), and erroneously claiming that from memory he was able to restore the plans of L'Enfant.

84. John W. Caughey, John Hope Franklin, Ernest R. May. *Land of the Free, A History of the United States.* New York, Benziger Brothers, 1966, pp. 192–193.

Includes a brief and inaccurate mention of the survey of the Federal City, claiming that the Commissioners for the survey were Pierre L'Enfant, Benjamin Banneker, and George Ellicott.

85. William Loren Katz. *Eyewitness, The Negro in American History.* New York, Pitman Publishing Corp., 1967, pp. 29–31, 61–62.

Brief account of Banneker's career and contributions, which are stated to have been in "the fields of science, mathematics, and political affairs," illustrated with the fictional portrait from Allen's work (item 56) and the title page of the almanac for 1793. Among the misstatements are the claims that Banneker produced the first clock made entirely with American parts, that Jefferson promised Banneker that he would end slavery, that George Ellicott worked with Banneker in the survey of Washington, that Banneker was appointed to the Commission at a suggestion made by Jefferson to Washington, and that Banneker selected the sites of the principal buildings. The fiction that Banneker re-created L'Enfant's plan from memory is again presented, and his almanacs are said to have been published for a period of ten years.

86. John Hope Franklin. *From Slavery to Freedom.* New York, Alfred A. Knopf, 1967, pp. 157–159, 662–663.

A short account of Banneker's role in the antislavery movement, apparently based on the works of LePhillips (item 51) and Baker (item 54).

87. "Voices from Negro History," *International Afro-American Museum*, vol. 2, no. 1, Spring 1967 (Detroit).

A short boxed column with numerous erroneous statements. Illustrated with a portrait, which has been exchanged with that of Jan Matzeliger who is the subject of the adjacent column.

88. Wilbur Pinder, Jr. "History Bypasses Early American Genius," *Catonsville Herald-Argus* and *Baltimore Evening Sun*, March 8, 1967.

Brief newspaper accounts of Banneker based on Graham's work (item 70).

89. [John Hope Franklin], "An Intellectual argued with a Founding Father," *Life* Magazine, November 22, 1968.

Brief statement of Banneker's achievements, emphasizing in particular Banneker's correspondence with Jefferson.

90. Winthrop D. Jordan. *White Over Black (American Attitudes Towards The Negro, 1550–1812)*. Chapel Hill, University of North Carolina Press, 1968, pp. 449–457.

Discussion of Jefferson's attitude on Banneker and Banneker's achievements, with thorough documentation; some details of Banneker's life, however, are erroneous.

91. Phillip T. Drotning. *Black Heroes in Our Nation's History*. New York, Cowles Co., Inc., 1968, pp. 34–35.

Brief statement concerning Banneker's participation in the survey of the city of Washington. The author identifies the surveyor as George Ellicott and claims that Banneker assisted L'Enfant in reconstructing the latter's plan from memory, and that Banneker and L'Enfant selected the sites for the Capitol and President's House.

92. Wilhelmena S. Robinson. *Historical Negro Biographies*. Inter-National Library of Negro Life and History. New York, Publishers Company, 1968, p. 9.

A short account in which Banneker is identified as an "engineer" who published almanacs until 1802; states that "He published also a treatise on bees and computed the cycle of the seventeen-year locust."

93. Maxwell Whiteman, ed. *Banneker's Almanack, and Ephemeris for the Year of Our Lord 1793; Being the First After*

Bissextile or Leap Year; and Banneker's Almanac, for the Year 1795: Being the Third after Leap Year. Philadelphia, Rhistoric Publications, Afro-American History Series No. 202, 1969.

Reprint of two of Banneker's almanacs in their entirety, with a short introduction describing Banneker's career and identifying several of the basic sources.

94. Peter M. Bergman. *Chronological History of the Negro in America.* New York, Harper & Row, 1969, pp. 31–32, 71, 146.

Brief account of Banneker and his accomplishments, perpetuating inaccuracies in dates and other details.

95. James W. Gibbs. " 'Black Genius' Benjamin Banneker," *Bulletin of the National Association of Watch and Clock Collectors,* 1969, vol. XIII, no. 12, pp. 1155–1157.

Brief résumé of Banneker's life, with misstatements relating to Banneker's association with David Rittenhouse, the claim that he made the first clock in Maryland, etc.

96. J. W. Haywood, Jr. "Banneker Monument" (Letter to the editor), *Washington Post,* April 5, 1969.

Recommends the creation of a suitable monument to Banneker for his role in the survey of the city of Washington.

97. Otto Lindenmeyer. *Black History: Lost, Stolen, or Strayed.* New York, Avon Books, 1970, pp. 37, 40–47.

Brief account of Banneker's life and achievements, containing the story that he was able to restore from memory the details of L'Enfant's map, and the statement that following L'Enfant's dismissal he was employed to continue the survey of Washington with Andrew Ellicott as his assistant. Another story, for which there is no known documentary basis, is that the Philadelphia publisher of his almanac "was so skeptical of Banneker's prediction of a solar eclipse that he challenged the astronomer to a wager *before* beginning to set type."

98. Sarah Gilbert. "He helped put Washington on the map, Benjamin Banneker," *Potomac Magazine, The Washington Post,* January 11, 1970, pp. 23–27.

An account of Banneker's role in the survey of Washington, based largely on Graham (item 70) and perpetuating the fictions originally published in that work. Illustrated with the sketch first published in Allen's work (item 56), which is also fiction.

99. Robb Sagendorph. *America and Her Almanacs, Wit,*

Wisdom & Weather 1639–1970. Boston, Little, Brown & Co., 1970, p. 123.

Brief mention of Banneker's almanacs with a reproduction of the cover of the almanac for 1796.

100. "Letters," *The New York Times Sunday Book Review*, November 1, 8, and 29, 1970.

Comments on the absence of a biographical sketch of Banneker in the *Dictionary of Scientific Biography*, vol. 2 (New York, Charles Scribner's Sons, 1970).

101. Silvio A. Bedini. "Benjamin Banneker and The Survey of the District of Columbia," *Records of the Columbia Historical Society of Washington*, 1969–70, pp. 7–30.

Detailed account of Banneker's participation in the survey as a scientific assistant of Major Andrew Ellicott during the winter and spring of 1791.

102. Margaret Goff Clark, *Benjamin Banneker Astronomer and Scientist* (Champaign, Ill.: Garrard Publishing Co., 1971.

A fictionalized biography for young children, presenting the salient events of Banneker's life based on the more accurate earlier accounts, including Latrobe (item 14), Tyson (items 22 and 37), and Graham (item 70).

ACKNOWLEDGMENTS

ACKNOWLEDGMENTS

❖❀❖❀❖❀❖❀❖❀❖❀❖❀❖❀❖❀❖

The re-creation of the life and times of such an elusive figure as Benjamin Banneker has involved extensive research and considerable historical detection pursued over a number of years. The book therefore owes its existence to the many individuals who contributed the small and large portions that have been assembled into the whole, as well as to the countless others who offered encouragement. It is not possible to identify all with whom the writer has corresponded on this project, but he takes this opportunity to extend his appreciation, while making grateful acknowledgment of those contributions which have been particularly substantial and rewarding:

First of all, to the American Philosophical Society, for the grant which it provided from the Penrose Fund.

To Dr. Robert T. Fitzhugh, a descendant of the George Ellicott family, for his generosity in making available for study, reproduction, and citation in the present work original Banneker, Ellicott, and Tyson family materials and memorabilia in his possession.

To various other descendants of the Ellicott family, who prefer to remain anonymous, for generously granting me permission to study, quote, and otherwise reproduce manuscripts, correspondence, and other original and published materials and memorabilia relating to Banneker and to the Ellicott, Tyson, and Mason families.

To the Maryland Historical Society, which has been deeply involved with this project since it was first initiated in 1955. Among those members of the staff who have contributed materially to this effort are Dr. Harold R. Manakee, Director; P. William Filby, Assistant Director and Librarian; Mrs. Robert H. McCauley, Curator of Graphics; Francis C. Haber, former Librarian; and Ellen Lee Barker, former Curator of Manuscripts.

To Warren J. Danzenbaker, for invaluable assistance in many aspects of this project in ways too numerous to mention, which deserves particular recognition and my sincere gratitude.

Finally, to the numerous scholars, librarians, archivists, curators, and private citizens who have assisted so willingly in this research and have made available materials which have been embodied in the present volume; the mention of their names here is a very inadequate recognition of their generous cooperation:

Dr. Thomas R. Adams, Librarian of the John Carter Brown Library, Brown University

Louisa R. Alger, Cambridge, Massachusetts

Dr. Whitfield J. Bell, Jr., Librarian of the American Philosophical Society

Charles H. Berger, Smithsonian Institution Libraries

M. Berton, Académie des Sciences, Institut de France

Dr. Julian P. Boyd, Editor of *The Papers of Thomas Jefferson*, Princeton University

Dr. Clarence S. Brigham, former Director of the American Antiquarian Society

Louis de Broglie, Secrétaire perpetuel of the Académie des Sciences, Institut de France

Dr. Lyman H. Butterfield, Editor of *The Adams Papers*, Massachusetts Historical Society

Dr. Henry J. Cadbury, Haverford, Pennsylvania

Dr. Josephus R. Coan, Gammon Interdenominational Seminary, Atlanta, Georgia

Winifred Collins, Massachusetts Historical Society

R. Courrier, Secrétaire perpetuel of the Académie des Sciences, Institut de France

Caleb Dorsey, Baltimore, Maryland

Acknowledgments

Charles Ellis Ellicott, Jr., Baltimore, Maryland

Dr. V. L. Ellicott, Baltimore, Maryland

Peter Farb, New York, New York

Robert Fellows, Jackson Heights, New York

Mrs. Henry M. Fitzhugh III

Dr. Bliss Forbush, President of the Trustees of the Sheppard and Enoch Pratt Hospital

Mrs. LaVerne Hill Forbush, Towson, Maryland

Dr. Owen Gingerich, Smithsonian Astrophysical Observatory

Jack Goodwin, Smithsonian Institution Libraries

Dr. Arnold E. Grummer, Curator of Museums, The Institute of Paper Chemistry, Appleton, Wisconsin

Mme. L. Hautecoeur-Milliez, Conservateur en chef of the Bibliothèque de l'Institut de France

Dr. Brooke Hindle, Professor of History, New York University

Dr. Oliver Wendell Holmes, Chairman of the National Historical Publications Commission at the U.S. National Archives

Samuel Hopkins, Baltimore, Maryland

Mrs. Bryce Jacobsen, Archivist, State of Maryland Hall of Records, Annapolis, Maryland

Mary M. Johnson, Research Division, U.S. National Archives

John D. Kilbourne, Curator, Historical Society of Pennsylvania

Jim Leggett, Hudson, New York

Mrs. Howard Lewis, Washington, D.C.

Mrs. Lilian Lewis, Trevor Arnett Library, The Atlanta University

Mrs. Nancy R. Long, College Park, Maryland

Dr. Marcus A. McCorison, Director, American Antiquarian Society

Dr. Keith E. Melder, Washington, D.C.

Dr. Uta C. Merzbach, The National Museum of History and Technology, Smithsonian Institution

Jean-Claude Nardin, Paris, France

Susan Nettles, former Archivist, State of Maryland Hall of Records, Annapolis, Maryland

Elmer J. O'Brien, Librarian of Garrett Biblical Institute, Evanston, Illinois

Roger Pierrot, Bibliothèque Nationale, Paris

C. Frank Poole, Department of Legislative Reference, City Hall, Baltimore, Maryland

Mrs. Dorothy B. Porter, Librarian, Howard University

Dr. Emmanuel Poulle, Ecole Nationale des Chartes, Paris

Dr. Derek J. de Solla Price, Avalon Professor of the History of Science, Yale University

Mrs. R. Joyce Ramey, Falls Church, Virginia

Dr. Clayton E. Rhodes, George Peabody Branch, Enoch Pratt Free Library, Baltimore, Maryland

Albert L. Rogers, Library of Congress

Charles H. Rowell, Vienna, Virginia

Dr. Edwin Schell, Baltimore Conference Methodist Historical Society, Baltimore, Maryland

Dr. Lee E. Sellers, Librarian, Wilberforce University

William A. Smith, Pineville, Pennsylvania

Mrs. Catherine Dietz Tucker, Oella, Ellicott City, Maryland

The Reverend B. J. S. Watkins, formerly Rector of Lydford Parish, Okehampton, Devon, England

Dr. Charles H. Wesley, Director of the Association for the Study of Negro Life and History, Inc., Washington, D.C.

Mrs. Charles E. Wilde III

Conrad Wilson, Historical Society of Pennsylvania

Dr. Edwin Wolf 2nd, Librarian, Library Company of Philadelphia

Dr. Laurence C. Wroth, John Carter Brown Library, Brown University

To my wife, Gale, I owe the greatest debt of all, for sharing with me the pleasures and disappointments of the research as it progressed, and for devoting countless hours to the usual chores of revising the manuscript and preparing an index.

ILLUSTRATION CREDITS

Grateful acknowledgment is made to the individuals and institutions that have given permission for the use of illustrative materials, as follows:

Nos. 1, 3, 7, 8: Maryland Historical Society

No. 2: Reproduced from Charles W. Evans, *Biographical and Historical Accounts of the Fox, Ellicott and Evans Families . . .* , Buffalo, N.Y., 1882

No. 4: Mrs. Henry M. Fitzhugh III and Mrs. Charles E. Wilde III

Nos. 5 and 6: Reproduced from plates IX and X respectively of *The Practical Millwright* by Thomas Ellicott, published as part of Oliver Evans, *The Young Mill-Wright & Miller's Guide*, Philadelphia, 1795

Nos. 9, 14, 15, 16, 18: The National Museum of History and Technology of the Smithsonian Institution

Nos. 10, 11, 13, 20: Objects are privately owned; photographs by Warren J. Danzenbaker

No. 12: Historical Society of Pennsylvania

No. 17: Library of Congress, Manuscripts Division

No. 19: Dr. Robert T. Fitzhugh; photograph by Jim Leggett, Hudson, N.Y.

No. 21: Maryland House; photograph by William A. Smith

INDEX

INDEX

About the Author

Silvio A. Bedini, a native of Ridgefield, Connecticut, was appointed Curator of the Division of Mechanical and Civil Engineering of the National Museum of History and Technology, Smithsonian Institution in Washington, D. C., in 1961. He became Assistant Director in 1965 and received the appointment of Deputy Director in 1971.

Mr. Bedini studied at Columbia University and in 1970 received an honorary L.L.D. from the University of Bridgeport. He was a recipient of the Abbott Payson Usher Award of the Society for the History of Technology in 1962. He is a Fellow of the Washington Academy of Sciences and a member of the Society of American Historians, the History of Science Society, the American Historical Association, and the Antiquarian Horological Society.

Among his published works are *Early American Scientific Instruments and Their Makers* and *Moon, Man's Greatest Adventure,* the latter co-authored with Wernher von Braun and Fred L. Whipple.